CONTENTS

Maps

ON THE ROAD WITH FODOR'S

WHEN I PLAN A VACATION, the first thing I do is cast around among my friends and colleagues to find someone who's just been where I'm going. That's because there's no substitute for a recommendation from a good friend who knows your tastes, your budget, and your circumstances, someone who's just been there. Unfortunately, such friends are few and far between. So it's nice to know that there's *Miami & the Keys '99*.

In the first place, this book won't stay home when you hit the road. It will accompany you every step of the way, steering you away from wrong turns and wrong choices and never expecting a thing in return. It includes a wonderful, full-color map from Rand McNally, the world's largest commercial mapmaker. Most important of all, it's written and assiduously updated by the kind of people you *would* hit up for travel tips if you knew them. They're as choosy as your pickiest friend, except they've probably seen a lot more of Miami and the Keys. In these pages, they don't send you chasing down every town and sight in Miami and the Keys but have instead selected the best ones, the ones that are worthy of your time and money. To make it easy for you to put it all together in the time you have, they've created short, medium, and long itineraries and, in cities, neighborhood walks that you can mix and match in a snap. Just tear out the map at the perforation, and join us on the road in Miami and the Keys.

About Our Writers

Our success in helping to make your trip the best of all possible vacations is a credit to the hard work of our extraordinary writers.

On her way to the Caribbean, former New York publishing exec **Pamela Acheson** stopped in the Sunshine State and fell in love, after discovering that there's much more to it than theme parks. She likes nothing better than to drive around to neat little towns, undiscovered beaches, and other less-traveled places as she writes about her new home.

Starting behind an old manual typewriter at his hometown newspaper, **Alan Macher** has written everything from human-interest stories to speeches. He makes his home in Boca Raton, where he can play tennis and bike along Route A1A year-round.

Intrepid traveler and intrepid shopper **Diane Marshall** was formerly editor and publisher of the newsletter "The Savvy Shopper: The Traveler's Guide to Shopping Around the World." From her home in the Keys, she has written for numerous travel guides, newspapers, magazines, and on-line services.

Florida native and Elvis fan **Gary McKechnie** has written humor and travel articles for newspapers and magazines nationwide and has produced award-winning training films and resort videos.

Formerly with *Southern Living* magazine, travel writer **Nancy Orr** has the delightful southern drawl that proves she's at home in northern Florida.

Connections

We're pleased that the American Society of Travel Agents continues to endorse Fodor's as its guidebook of choice. ASTA is the world's largest and most influential travel trade association, operating in more than 170 countries, with 27,000 members pledged to adhere to a strict code of ethics reflecting the Society's motto, "Integrity in Travel." ASTA shares Fodor's devotion to providing smart, honest travel information and advice to travelers, and we've long recommended that our readers—even those who have guidebooks and traveling friends—consult ASTA member agents for the experience and professionalism they bring to your vacation planning.

On Fodor's Web site (www.fodors.com), check out the new Resource Center, an on-line companion to the Gold Guide section of this book, complete with useful hot links to related sites. In our forums, you can also get lively advice from other travelers and more great tips from Fodor's experts worldwide.

Fodor's 99

Miami & the Keys

The complete guide, thoroughly up-to-date

Packed with details that will make your trip

The must-see sights, off and on the beaten path

What to see, what to skip

Mix-and-match vacation itineraries

City strolls, countryside adventures

Smart lodging and dining options

Essential local dos and taboos

Transportation tips, distances, and directions

Key contacts, savvy travel tips

When to go, what to pack

Clear, accurate, easy-to-use maps

Books to read

Excerpted from *Fodor's Florida '99*

Fodor's Travel Publications, Inc.
New York • Toronto • London • Sydney • Auckland
www.fodors.com

Fodor's Miami & the Keys

EDITOR: Andrea E. Lehman

Editorial Contributors: Pamela Acheson, David Brown, Marianne Camas, Catherine Fredman, Kendall Hamersly, Herb Hiller, Ann Hughes, Alan Macher, Diane Marshall, Gary McKechnie, Valerie Meyer, Peter Oliver, Nancy Orr, Helayne Schiff, M. T. Schwartzman (Gold Guide editor), Rowland Stiteler, Geoffrey Tomb
Editorial Production: Stacey Kulig
Maps: David Lindroth, *cartographer*; Robert Blake, *map editor*
Design: Fabrizio La Rocca, *creative director*; Guido Caroti, *associate art director*; Jolie Novak, *photo editor*
Production/Manufacturing: Rebecca Zeiler
Cover Photograph: Jack Hollingsworth

Copyright

Special Sales

Fodor's Travel Publications are available at special discounts for bulk purchases for sales promotions or premiums. Special editions, including personalized covers, excerpts of existing guides, and corporate imprints, can be created in large quantities for special needs. For more information, contact your local bookseller or write to Special Markets, Fodor's Travel Publications, 201 East 50th Street, New York, NY 10022. Inquiries from Canada should be directed to your local Canadian bookseller or sent to Random House of Canada, Ltd., Marketing Department, 2775 Matheson Boulevard East, Mississauga, Ontario L4W 4P7. Inquiries from the United Kingdom should be sent to Fodor's Travel Publications, 20 Vauxhall Bridge Road, London SW1V 2SA, England.

PRINTED IN THE UNITED STATES OF AMERICA

10 9 8 7 6 5 4 3 2 1

How to Use This Book

Organization

Up front is the **Gold Guide,** an easy-to-use section arranged alphabetically by topic. Under each listing you'll find tips and information that will help you accomplish what you need to in Miami and the Keys. You'll also find addresses and telephone numbers of organizations and companies that offer destination-related services and detailed information and publications.

The first chapter in the guide, **Destination: Miami & the Keys,** helps get you in the mood for your trip. New and Noteworthy cues you in on trends and happenings, What's Where gets you oriented, Pleasures and Pastimes describes the activities and sights that make Miami and the Keys unique, Fodor's Choice showcases our top picks, and Festivals and Seasonal Events alerts you to special events you'll want to seek out.

Chapters in *Miami & the Keys '99* are arranged by region. Each chapter begins with an Exploring section, which is subdivided by neighborhood; each subsection recommends a walking or driving tour and lists sights in alphabetical order. Each regional chapter is divided by geographical area; within each area towns are covered in logical geographical order and, within town sections, all restaurants and lodgings are grouped together.

To help you decide what to visit in the time you have, all chapters begin with our recommended itineraries. You can mix and match those from several chapters to create a complete vacation. The A to Z section that ends all chapters covers getting there and getting around. It also provides helpful contacts and resources.

Icons and Symbols

★   Our special recommendations
✕   Restaurant
🏨   Lodging establishment
⚠   Campground
☺   Good for kids (rubber duck)
☞   Sends you to another section of the guide for more information
⊠   Address
☎   Telephone number
🕙   Opening and closing times
🎫   Admission prices (those we give apply only to adults; substantially reduced fees are almost always available for children, students, and senior citizens)

Numbers in white and black circles ③ ❸ that appear on the maps, in the margins, and within the tours correspond to one another.

Dining and Lodging

The restaurants and lodgings we list are the cream of the crop in each price range. Price categories are as follows:

For restaurants:

CATEGORY	COST*
$$$$	over $50
$$$	$35–$50
$$	$20–$35
$	under $20

per person for a three-course meal, excluding drinks, service, and 6% sales tax (more in some counties)

For hotels:

CATEGORY	COST*
$$$$	over $200
$$$	$100–$200
$$	$60–$100
$	under $60

All prices are for a standard double room, excluding 6% sales tax (more in some counties) and 1%–4% tourist tax.

Hotel Facilities

We always list the facilities that are available—but we don't specify whether you'll be charged extra to use them: When pricing accommodations, always ask what's included. Assume that all rooms have private baths unless noted otherwise. In addition, when you book a room, be sure to mention if you have a disability or are traveling with children, if you prefer a private bath or a certain type of bed, or if you have specific dietary needs or other concerns.

Restaurant Reservations and Dress Codes

Reservations are always a good idea; we mention them only when they're essential or are not accepted. Book as far ahead as you can, and reconfirm as soon as you arrive. Unless otherwise noted, the restaurants listed are open daily for lunch and dinner. We mention dress only when men are required to wear a jacket or a jacket and tie. Look for an overview of local dining-out habits in the Gold Guide.

Credit Cards

The following abbreviations are used: **AE,** American Express; **D,** Discover; **DC,** Diners Club; **MC,** MasterCard; and **V,** Visa.

Don't Forget to Write

You can use this book in the confidence that all prices and opening times are based on information supplied to us at press time; Fodor's cannot accept responsibility for any errors. Time inevitably brings changes, so always confirm information when it matters—especially if you're making a detour to visit a specific place.

Were the restaurants we recommended as described? Did our hotel picks exceed your expectations? Did you find a museum we recommended a waste of time? Keeping a travel guide fresh and up-to-date is a big job, and we welcome your feedback, positive *and* negative. If you have complaints, we'll look into them and revise our entries when the facts warrant it.

If you've discovered a special place that we haven't included, we'll pass the information along to our correspondents and have them check it out. So send us your thoughts via E-mail at editors@fodors.com (specifying the name of the book on the subject line) or on paper in care of the Miami & the Keys editor at Fodor's, 201 East 50th Street, New York, NY 10022. In the meantime, have a wonderful trip!

Karen Cure

Editorial Director

The Florida Peninsula

SMART TRAVEL TIPS A TO Z

Basic Information on Traveling in Miami and the Keys, Savvy Tips to Make Your Trip a Breeze, and Companies and Organizations to Contact

AIR TRAVEL

AIRPORTS

Because South Florida is dotted with both major and regional airports, you can usually pick one quite close to your destination and often choose from nearby options. If you're destined for the north side of Miami-Dade County (metro Miami), **consider flying into Fort Lauderdale–Hollywood International;** it's much easier to use than Miami International.

➤ AIRPORT INFORMATION: **Fort Lauderdale–Hollywood International** (☎ 954/359–1200). **Key West International** (☎ 305/296–5439). **Miami International** (☎ 305/876–7000). **Palm Beach International** (☎ 561/471–7420).

BIKES IN FLIGHT

Most airlines will accommodate bikes as luggage, provided they are dismantled and put into a box. Call to see if your airline sells bike boxes (about $5; bike bags are at least $100) although you can often pick them up free at bike shops. International travelers can sometimes substitute a bike for a piece of checked luggage for free; otherwise, it will cost about $100. Domestic and Canadian airlines charge a $25–$50 fee.

BOOKING YOUR FLIGHT

Price is just one factor to consider when booking a flight: frequency of service and even a carrier's safety record are often just as important. Major airlines offer the greatest number of departures. Smaller airlines—including regional and no-frills airlines—usually have a limited number of flights daily. On the other hand, so-called low-cost airlines usually are cheaper, and their fares impose fewer restrictions, such as advance-purchase requirements. Safety-wise, low-cost carriers as a group have a good history—about equal to that of major carriers.

When you book, **look for nonstop flights** and **remember that "direct" flights stop at least once.** Try to **avoid connecting flights,** which require a change of plane. Two airlines may jointly operate a connecting flight, so ask if your airline operates every segment—you may find that your preferred carrier flies you only part of the way.

Ask your airline if it offers electronic ticketing, which eliminates all paperwork. There's no ticket to pick up or misplace. You go directly to the gate and give the agent your confirmation number. There's no worry about waiting on line at the airport while precious minutes tick by.

CARRIERS

➤ MAJOR AIRLINES: **American** (☎ 800/433–7300). **Continental** (☎ 800/525–0280). **Delta** (☎ 800/221–1212). **Midway** (☎ 800/446–4392). **Northwest** (☎ 800/225–2525). **Southwest** (☎ 800/435–9792). **TWA** (☎ 800/221–2000). **United** (☎ 800/241–6522). **US Airways** (☎ 800/428–4322).

➤ REGIONAL AIRLINES: **AirTran** (☎ 800/825–8538) to Fort Lauderdale, Miami, and West Palm Beach. **Midwest Express** (☎ 800/452–2022) to Fort Lauderdale.

➤ FROM THE U.K.: **American** (☎ 0345/789–789). **British Airways** (☎ 0345/222–111). **Continental** (☎ 0800/776–464) via Newark. **Delta** (☎ 0800/414–767). **Northwest** (☎ 0990/561–000) via Detroit or Minneapolis. **TWA** (☎ 0800/222–222) via St. Louis. **United** (☎ 0800/888–555). **Virgin Atlantic** (☎ 01293/747–747).

CHECK IN & BOARDING

Airlines routinely overbook planes, assuming that not everyone with a ticket will show up, but sometimes everyone does. When that happens, airlines ask for volunteers to give up their seats. In return these volunteers usually get a certificate for a free flight and are rebooked on the next flight out. If there are not enough volunteers, the airline must choose who will be denied boarding. The first to get bumped are passengers who checked in late and those flying on discounted tickets, so **get to the gate and check in as early as possible,** especially during peak periods. Heightened security at Miami International Airport has meant that it's suggested you check in 90 minutes before departure for a domestic flight, two hours for an international flight.

Although the trend on international flights is to drop reconfirmation requirements, many airlines still ask you to reconfirm each leg of your international itinerary. Failure to do so may result in your reservation being canceled.

Always **bring a government-issued photo ID to the airport.** You may be asked to show it before you are allowed to check in.

CONSOLIDATORS

Consolidators buy tickets for scheduled international flights at reduced rates from the airlines, then sell them at prices that beat the best fare available directly from the airlines, usually without restrictions. Sometimes you can even get your money back if you need to return the ticket. Carefully read the fine print detailing penalties for changes and cancellations, and **confirm your consolidator reservation with the airline.**

➤ CONSOLIDATORS: **Cheap Tickets** (☎ 800/377–1000). **Up & Away Travel** (☎ 212/889–2345). **Discount Travel Network** (☎ 800/576–1600). **Unitravel** (☎ 800/325–2222). **World Travel Network** (☎ 800/409–6753).

CUTTING COSTS

The least-expensive airfares to Florida are priced for round-trip travel and usually must be purchased in advance. It's smart to **call a number of airlines, and when you are quoted a good price, book it on the spot**—the same fare may not be available the next day. Airlines generally allow you to change your return date for a fee. If you don't use your ticket, you can apply the cost toward the purchase of a new ticket, again for a small charge. However, most low-fare tickets are nonrefundable. To get the lowest airfare, **check different routings.** Compare prices of flights to and from different airports if your destination or home city has more than one gateway. Also price off-peak flights, which may be significantly less expensive.

When flying within the U.S., **plan to stay over a Saturday night** and **travel during the middle of the week** to get the lowest fare. These low fares are usually priced for round-trip travel and are nonrefundable. You can, however, change your return date for a fee ($75 on most major airlines).

Travel agents, especially those who specialize in finding the lowest fares (☞ Discounts & Deals, *below*), can be especially helpful when booking a plane ticket. When you're quoted a price, **ask your agent if the price is likely to get any lower.** Good agents know the seasonal fluctuations of airfares and can usually anticipate a sale or fare war. However, waiting can be risky: The fare could go *up* as seats become scarce, and you may wait so long that your preferred flight sells out. A wait-and-see strategy works best if your plans are flexible.

➤ CHEAP RATES FROM THE U.K.: **Flight Express Travel** (✉ 77 New Bond St., London W1Y 9DB, ☎ 0171/409–3311). **Trailfinders** (✉ 42–50 Earls Court Rd., London W8 6FT, ☎ 0171/937–5400). **Travel Cuts** (✉ 295A Regent St., London W1R 7YA, ☎ 0171/637–3161).

HOW TO COMPLAIN

If your baggage goes astray or your flight goes awry, complain right away. Most carriers require that you **file a claim immediately.**

➤ AIRLINE COMPLAINTS: U.S. Department of Transportation **Aviation Consumer Protection Division** (✉ C-75, Room 4107, Washington, DC 20590, ☎ 202/366–2220). **Federal Aviation Administration Consumer Hotline** (☎ 800/322–7873).

THE GOLD GUIDE / SMART TRAVEL TIPS

BOOKS

If you plan to spend time at the beach, **bring along some good books about South Florida** to get you in the mood. Or, if you'll be doing a lot of driving, **pick up some audiotapes** (some of these titles are available on cassette).

Suspense novels that are rich in details about Florida include Pulitzer Prize winner Edna Buchanan's *Miami, It's Murder* and *Contents Under Pressure;* Les Standiford's *Done Deal,* about violence in the Miami construction business; former prosecuting attorney Barbara Parker's *Suspicion of Innocence;* Clifford Irving's *Final Argument;* Elmore Leonard's *La Brava;* John D. MacDonald's *The Empty Copper Sea;* Joan Higgins's *A Little Death Music;* and Charles Willeford's *Miami Blues.* James W. Hall features Florida in many of his big-sellers, such as *Mean High Tide,* the chilling *Bones of Coral,* and *Hard Aground.*

Peter Matthiessen's *Killing Mister Watson* re-creates turn-of-the-century lower southwest Florida, and *Princess of the Everglades,* by Charles Mink, is a novel about the 1926 hurricane. *The Tourist Season* is Carl Hiaasen's immensely funny declaration of war against the state's environment-despoiling hordes; he has also written *Double Whammy, Skin Tight, Native Tongue,* and *Strip Tease.*

Other recommended titles include Roxanne Pulitzer's *Facade,* set against a backdrop of Palm Beach; Peter Dexter's *The Paperboy;* Pat Booth's *Miami;* Sam Harrison's *Bones of Blue Coral* and *Birdsong Ascending;* T. D. Allman's *Miami;* Joan Didion's *Miami;* David Rieff's *Going To Miami;* Alice Hoffman's *Turtle Moon; Scavenger Reef* and *Florida Straits,* by Laurence Shames; *To Have and Have Not,* by Ernest Hemingway; *The Day of the Dolphin,* by Robert Merle; and *Their Eyes Were Watching God,* by Zora Neale Hurston.

Among recommended nonfiction books are *The Commodore's Story* by Ralph Munroe and Vincent Gilpin, a luminous reminiscence about the golden years (pre-railroad) of Coconut Grove; *Key West Writers and Their Homes,* by Lynn Kaufelt; *The Everglades: River of Grass,* by Marjory S. Douglas; *The Other Florida,* by Gloria Jahoda; and *Florida's Sandy Beaches,* University Press of Florida. Mark Derr's *Some Kind of Paradise* is an excellent review of the state's environmental follies; John Rothchild's *Up for Grabs,* equally good, is about Florida's commercial lunacy. Good anthologies include *The Florida Reader: Visions of Paradise* (Maurice O'Sullivan and Jack Lane, editors), *The Rivers of Florida* (Del and Marty Marth, editors), and *Subtropical Speculations: An Anthology of Florida Science Fiction* (Richard Mathews and Rick Wilber, editors).

BUS TRAVEL

Greyhound passes through practically every major city in Florida. For schedules and fares, **contact your local Greyhound Information Center.**

➤ BUS LINES: Greyhound (☎ 800/231–2222).

CAMERAS & COMPUTERS

EQUIPMENT PRECAUTIONS

Always **keep your film, tape, or computer disks out of the sun.** Carry an extra supply of batteries, and **be prepared to turn on your camera, camcorder, or laptop** to prove to security personnel that the device is real. Always **ask for hand inspection of film,** which becomes clouded after successive exposure to airport X-ray machines, and **keep videotapes and computer disks away from metal detectors.**

TRAVEL PHOTOGRAPHY

➤ PHOTO HELP: Kodak Information Center (☎ 800/242–2424). *Kodak Guide to Shooting Great Travel Pictures,* available in bookstores or from Fodor's Travel Publications (☎ 800/533–6478; $16.50 plus $4 shipping).

CAR RENTAL

Rates in Miami begin at $36 a day and $170 a week for an economy car with air conditioning, an automatic transmission, and unlimited mileage. Rates in Fort Lauderdale begin at $36 a day and $159 a week. This does not include tax on car rentals, which is 6%. Bear in mind that rates fluctuate tremendously depending on demand and the season. Rental cars are more expensive (and harder to find) during peak holidays and in season.

➤ MAJOR AGENCIES: **Alamo** (☎ 800/327–9633, 0800/272–2000 in the U.K.). **Avis** (☎ 800/331–1212, 800/879–2847 in Canada, 008/225–533 in Australia). **Budget** (☎ 800/527–0700, 0800/181181 in the U.K.). **Dollar** (☎ 800/800–4000; 0990/565656 in the U.K., where it is known as Eurodollar). **Hertz** (☎ 800/654–3131, 800/263–0600 in Canada, 0345/555888 in the U.K., 03/9222–2523 in Australia, 03/358–6777 in New Zealand). **National InterRent** (☎ 800/227–7368; 0345/222525 in the U.K., where it is known as Europcar InterRent).

➤ LOCAL FIRMS: **Aapex Rent A Car** (☎ 954/782–3400) in Fort Lauderdale. **Florida Auto Rental** (☎ 954/764–1008 or 800/327–3791) in Fort Lauderdale. **InterAmerican Car Rental** (☎ 305/871–3030) in Fort Lauderdale and Miami Beach. **Tropical Rent-a-Car** ☎ 305/294–8136) in Key West.

CUTTING COSTS

Florida is a bazaar of car rentals, with more discount companies offering more bargains—and more fine print—than any other state in the nation. For the best price, **look for the best combination rate for car and airfare.**

To get the best deal, **book through a travel agent who is willing to shop around.** When pricing cars, **ask about the location of the rental lot.** Some off-airport locations offer lower rates, and their lots are only minutes from the terminal via complimentary shuttle. You also may want to **price local car-rental companies,** whose rates may be lower still, although their service and maintenance may not be as good as those of a name-brand agency. Remember to ask about required deposits, cancellation penalties, and drop-off charges if you're planning to pick up the car in one city and leave it in another.

Also **ask your travel agent about a company's customer-service record.** How has the company responded to late plane arrivals and vehicle mishaps? Are there often lines at the rental counter? If you're traveling during a holiday period, does a confirmed reservation guarantee you a car?

INSURANCE

When driving a rented car you are generally responsible for any damage to or loss of the vehicle. You are also liable for any property damage or personal injury that you may cause while driving. Before you rent, **see what coverage you already have** under the terms of your personal auto-insurance policy and credit cards.

For about $15 to $20 per day, rental companies sell protection, known as a collision- or loss-damage waiver (CDW or LDW), that eliminates your liability for damage to the car; it's always optional and should never be automatically added to your bill.

In most states you don't need a CDW if you have personal auto insurance or other liability insurance. However, **make sure you have enough coverage to pay for the car.** If you do not have auto insurance or an umbrella policy that covers damage to third parties, purchasing liability insurance and a CDW or LDW is highly recommended.

REQUIREMENTS

In Florida you must be 21 to rent a car, and rates may be higher if you're under 25. You'll pay extra for child seats (about $3 per day), which are compulsory for children under five, and for additional drivers (about $2 per day). Non-U.S. residents will need a reservation voucher, a passport, a driver's license, and a travel policy that covers each driver, in order to pick up a car.

SURCHARGES

Before you pick up a car in one city and leave it in another, **ask about drop-off charges or one-way service fees,** which can be substantial. Note, too, that some rental agencies charge extra if you return the car before the time specified in your contract. To avoid a hefty refueling fee, **fill the tank just before you turn in the car,** but be aware that gas stations near the rental outlet may overcharge.

CAR TRAVEL

Two major interstates lead to South Florida. I–95 begins in Maine, runs south through the Mid-Atlantic states, and enters Florida just north of Jacksonville. It continues south past Daytona Beach, the Space Coast, Vero Beach, Palm Beach, and Fort Lauderdale, eventually ending in Miami.

I–75 begins in Michigan at the Canadian border and runs south through Ohio, Kentucky, Tennessee, and Georgia, then moves through the center of the state before veering west into Tampa. It follows the west coast south to Naples, then crosses the state, and ends in Fort Lauderdale.

SAFETY

Before setting off on any drive, **make sure you know where you're going** and carry a map. When you rent your car or at your hotel **ask if there are any areas that you should avoid.** Always **keep your doors locked,** and ask questions only at toll booths, gas stations, or other obviously safe locations. Also, **don't stop if your car is bumped from behind** or if you're asked for directions. One hesitates to foster rude behavior, but at least for now the roads are too risky to stop any place you're not familiar with (other than as traffic laws require). If you'll be renting a car, **ask the car-rental agency for a cellular phone.** Alamo, Avis, and Hertz are among the companies with in-car phones.

SPEED LIMITS

Speed limits are 55 mph on state highways, 30 mph within city limits and residential areas, and 55–70 mph on interstates and Florida's Turnpike. Be alert for signs announcing exceptions.

CHILDREN & TRAVEL

CHILDREN IN FLORIDA

Be sure to plan ahead and **involve your youngsters** as you outline your trip. When packing, include things to keep them busy en route. On sightseeing days try to schedule activities of special interest to your children. If you are renting a car don't forget to **arrange for a car seat** when you reserve.

FLYING

If your children are two or older, **ask about children's airfares.** As a general rule, infants under two not occupying a seat fly at greatly reduced fares or even for free.

In general the adult baggage allowance applies to children paying half or more of the adult fare.

Experts agree that it's a good idea to use safety seats aloft for children weighing less than 40 pounds. Airlines, however, can set their own policies: U.S. carriers allow FAA-approved models but usually require that you buy a ticket, even if your child would otherwise ride free, since the seats must be strapped into regular seats. Airline rules vary, so it's important to **check your airline's policy about using safety seats during takeoff and landing.** Safety seats cannot obstruct the movement of other passengers in the row, so get an appropriate seat assignment as early as possible.

When making your reservation, **request children's meals or a free-standing bassinet** if you need them; the latter are available only to those seated at the bulkhead, where there's enough legroom. Remember, however, that bulkhead seats may not have their own overhead bins, and there's no storage space in front of you—a major inconvenience.

HOTELS

Florida may have the highest concentration of hotels with organized children's programs in the United States. Activities range from simple fun and recreation to art shows (including edible art) at the Boca Raton Resort & Club and learning about the Keys' environment from marine-science counselors at Cheeca Lodge. Sometimes kids' programs are complimentary; sometimes there's a charge. Not all accept children in diapers, and some offer programs when their central reservations services say they don't. Some programs are only offered during peak seasons or restrict hours in less-busy times. It always pays to **confirm details with the hotel in advance.** And **reserve space as soon as possible;** programs are often full by the morning or evening you need them.

Most hotels in Florida allow children under a certain age to stay in their parents' room at no extra charge, but others charge them as extra adults; be sure to **ask about the cutoff age for children's discounts.**

➤ FORT LAUDERDALE: **Marriott's Harbor Beach Resort's Beachside Buddies** (✉ 3030 Holiday Dr., Fort Lauderdale, FL 33316, ☎ 954/525–4000 or 800/228–9290), ages 5–12.

➤ THE KEYS: **Cheeca Lodge's Camp Cheeca** (✉ MM 82, OS, Box 527, Islamorada, FL 33036, ☎ 800/327–2888), ages 6–12. **Westin Beach Resort's Westin Kids Club** (✉ MM 96.9, BS, 97000 Overseas Hwy., Key Largo, FL 33037, ☎ 305/852–5553 or 800/325–3535), ages 5–12.

➤ MIAMI AREA: **Sonesta Beach Resort's Just Us Kids** (✉ 350 Ocean Dr., Key Biscayne, FL 33149, ☎ 800/766–3782), ages 5–13.

➤ PALM BEACH AND THE TREASURE COAST: **Boca Raton Resort & Club's Boca Tots/Boca Bunch/Boca Sport** (✉ 501 E. Camino Real, Boca Raton, FL 33432, ☎ 800/327–0101), ages 3–13. **Club Med's Sandpiper** (Port St. Lucie [mailing address: ✉ 40 W. 57th St., New York, NY 10019], ☎ 800/258–2633), Baby Club ages 4–24 months, Mini Club ages 2–11. **Indian River Plantation Marriott Beach Resort's Pineapple Bunch Children's Camp** (✉ 555 N.E. Ocean Blvd., Hutchinson Island, Stuart, FL 34996, ☎ 561/225–3700), ages 4–12, plus a teen program.

CONSUMER PROTECTION

Whenever possible, **pay with a major credit card** so you can cancel payment or get reimbursed if there's a problem, provided that you can furnish documentation. This is the best way to pay, whether you're buying travel arrangements before your trip or shopping at your destination.

If you're doing business with a particular company for the first time, **contact your local Better Business Bureau and the attorney general's offices** in your state and the company's home state, as well. Have any complaints been filed?

Finally, if you're buying a package or tour, always **consider travel insurance** that includes default coverage (☞ Insurance, *below*).

➤ LOCAL BBBs: **Council of Better Business Bureaus** (✉ 4200 Wilson Blvd., Suite 800, Arlington, VA 22203, ☎ 703/276–0100, FAX 703/525–8277).

CUSTOMS & DUTIES

When shopping, **keep receipts** for all of your purchases. Upon reentering the country, **be ready to show customs officials what you've bought.** If you feel a duty is incorrect, appeal the assessment. If you object to the way your clearance was handled, get the inspector's badge number. In either case, first ask to see a supervisor, then write to the appropriate authorities, beginning with the port director at your point of entry.

IN AUSTRALIA

Australia residents who are 18 or older may bring back $A400 worth of souvenirs and gifts (including jewelry), 250 cigarettes or 250 grams of tobacco, and 1,125 ml of alcohol (including wine, beer, and spirits). Residents under 18 may bring back $A200 worth of goods.

➤ INFORMATION: **Australian Customs Service** (Regional Director, ✉ Box 8, Sydney, NSW 2001, ☎ 02/9213–2000, FAX 02/9213–4000).

IN CANADA

Canadian residents who have been out of Canada for at least 7 days may bring in C$500 worth of goods duty-free. If you've been away less than 7 days but more than 48 hours, the duty-free allowance drops to C$200; if your trip lasts 24–48 hours, the allowance is C$50. You may not pool allowances with family members. Goods claimed under the C$500 exemption may follow you by mail; those claimed under the lesser exemptions must accompany you. Alcohol and tobacco products may be included in the 7-day and 48-hour exemptions but not in the 24-hour exemption. If you meet the age requirements of the province or territory through which you reenter Canada, you may bring in, duty-free, 1.14 liters (40 imperial ounces) of wine or liquor *or* 24 12-ounce cans or bottles of beer or ale. If you are 16 or older you may bring in, duty-free, 200 cigarettes and 50 cigars.

You may send an unlimited number of gifts worth up to C$60 each duty-free to Canada. Label the package UNSOLICITED GIFT—VALUE UNDER $60. Alcohol and tobacco are excluded.

➤ INFORMATION: **Revenue Canada** (⊠ 2265 St. Laurent Blvd. S, Ottawa, Ontario K1G 4K3, ☎ 613/993–0534, 800/461–9999 in Canada).

IN NEW ZEALAND

Although greeted with a "Haere Mai" ("Welcome to New Zealand"), homeward-bound residents with goods to declare must present themselves for inspection. If you're 17 or older, you may bring back $700 worth of souvenirs and gifts. Your duty-free allowance also includes 4.5 liters of wine or beer; one 1,125-ml bottle of spirits; and either 200 cigarettes, 250 grams of tobacco, 50 cigars, or a combo of all three up to 250 grams.

➤ INFORMATION: **New Zealand Customs** (⊠ Custom House, ⊠ 50 Anzac Ave., Box 29, Auckland, New Zealand, ☎ 09/359–6655, ☎ 09/309–2978).

IN THE U.K.

From countries outside the EU, including the United States, you may import, duty-free, 200 cigarettes or 50 cigars; 1 liter of spirits or 2 liters of fortified or sparkling wine or liqueurs; 2 liters of still table wine; 60 milliliters of perfume; 250 milliliters of toilet water; plus £136 worth of other goods, including gifts and souvenirs.

➤ INFORMATION: **HM Customs and Excise** (⊠ Dorset House, ⊠ Stamford St., London SE1 9NG, ☎ 0171/202–4227).

IN THE U.S.

Non-U.S. residents ages 21 and older may import into the United States 200 cigarettes or 50 cigars or 2 kilograms of tobacco, 1 liter of alcohol, and gifts worth $100. Prohibited items include meat products, seeds, plants, and fruits.

➤ INFORMATION: **U.S. Customs Service** (Inquiries, ⊠ Box 7407, Washington, DC 20044, ☎ 202/927–6724; complaints, Office of Regulations and Rulings, ⊠ 1301 Constitution Ave. NW, Washington, DC 20229; registration of equipment, Resource Management, ⊠ 1301 Constitution Ave. NW, Washington DC 20229, ☎ 202/927–0540).

DINING

One cautionary word: Raw oysters have been identified as a problem for people with chronic illness of the liver, stomach, or blood, or who have immune disorders. Since 1993, all Florida restaurants serving raw oysters are required to post a notice in plain view of all patrons warning of the risks associated with consuming them.

DISABILITIES & ACCESSIBILITY

ACCESS IN SOUTH FLORIDA

➤ ACCESSIBLE ATTRACTIONS, RESTAURANTS, AND HOTELS: **Great American Vacations for Travelers with Disabilities** (available in bookstores or from Fodor's Travel Publications, ☎ 800/533–6478; $19.50).

MAKING RESERVATIONS

When discussing accessibility with an operator or reservations agent, **ask hard questions.** Are there any stairs, inside *or* out? Are there grab bars next to the toilet *and* in the shower/tub? How wide is the doorway to the room? To the bathroom? For the most extensive facilities meeting the latest legal specifications, **opt for newer accommodations,** which are more likely to have been designed with access in mind. Older buildings or ships may have more limited facilities. Be sure to **discuss your needs before booking.**

TRANSPORTATION

➤ COMPLAINTS: **Disability Rights Section** (⊠ U.S. Department of Justice, Civil Rights Division, ⊠ Box 66738, Washington, DC 20035–6738, ☎ 202/514–0301 or 800/514–0301, TTY 202/514–0383 or 800/514–0383, FAX 202/307–1198) for general complaints. **Aviation Consumer Protection Division** (☞ Air Travel, *above*) for airline-related problems. **Civil Rights Office** (⊠ U.S. Department of Transportation, Departmental Office of Civil Rights, S-30, ✉ 400 7th St. SW, Room 10215, Washington, DC, 20590, ☎ 202/366–4648, FAX 202/366–9371) for problems with surface transportation.

TRAVEL AGENCIES & TOUR OPERATORS

As a whole, the travel industry has become more aware of the needs of travelers with disabilities. In the U.S., the Americans with Disabilities Act requires that travel firms serve the needs of all travelers. Note, though, that some agencies and operators specialize in making travel arrangements for individuals and groups with disabilities.

➤ TRAVELERS WITH MOBILITY PROBLEMS: **Access Adventures** (✉ 206 Chestnut Ridge Rd., Rochester, NY 14624, ☎ 716/889–9096), run by a former physical-rehabilitation counselor. **Accessible Journeys** (✉ 35 W. Sellers Ave., Ridley Park, PA 19078, ☎ 610/521–0339 or 800/846–4537, FAX 610/521–6959), for escorted tours exclusively for travelers with mobility impairments. **CareVacations** (✉ 5019 49th Ave., Suite 102, Leduc, Alberta T9E 6T5, ☎ 403/986–6404, 800/648–1116 in Canada) has group tours and is especially helpful with cruise vacations. **Flying Wheels Travel** (✉ 143 W. Bridge St., Box 382, Owatonna, MN 55060, ☎ 507/451–5005 or 800/535–6790, FAX 507/451–1685), a travel agency specializing in customized tours and itineraries worldwide. **Hinsdale Travel Service** (✉ 201 E. Ogden Ave., Suite 100, Hinsdale, IL 60521, ☎ 630/325–1335), a travel agency that benefits from the advice of wheelchair traveler Janice Perkins.

➤ TRAVELERS WITH DEVELOPMENTAL DISABILITIES: **Sprout** (✉ 893 Amsterdam Ave., New York, NY 10025, ☎ 212/222–9575 or 888/222–9575, FAX 212/222–9768).

DISCOUNTS & DEALS

Be a smart shopper and **compare all your options** before making any choice. A plane ticket bought with a promotional coupon may not be cheaper than the least expensive fare from a discount ticket agency. For high-price travel purchases, such as packages or tours, keep in mind that what you get is just as important as what you save. Just because something is cheap doesn't mean it's a bargain.

CLUBS & COUPONS

Many companies sell discounts in the form of travel clubs and coupon books, but these cost money. You must use participating advertisers to get a deal, and only after you recoup the initial membership cost or book price do you begin to save. If you plan to use the club or coupons frequently, you may save considerably. Before signing up, find out what discounts you get for free.

➤ DISCOUNT CLUBS: **Entertainment Travel Editions** (✉ 2125 Butterfield Rd., Troy, MI 48084, ☎ 800/445–4137; $20–$51, depending on destination). **Great American Traveler** (✉ Box 27965, Salt Lake City, UT 84127, ☎ 801/974–3033 or 800/548–2812; $49.95 per year). **Moment's Notice Discount Travel Club** (✉ 7301 New Utrecht Ave., Brooklyn, NY 11204, ☎ 718/234–6295; $25 per year). **Privilege Card International** (✉ 237 E. Front St., Youngstown, OH 44503, ☎ 330/746–5211 or 800/236–9732; $74.95 per year). **Sears's Mature Outlook** (✉ Box 9390, Des Moines, IA 50306, ☎ 800/336–6330; $19.95 per year). **Travelers Advantage** (✉ CUC Travel Service, ✉ 3033 S. Parker Rd., Suite 1000, Aurora, CO 80014, ☎ 800/548–1116 or 800/648–4037; $59.95 per year). **Worldwide Discount Travel Club** (✉ 1674 Meridian Ave., Miami Beach, FL 33139, ☎ 305/534–2082; $50 per year family, $40 single).

CREDIT-CARD BENEFITS

When you use your credit card to make travel purchases you may get free travel-accident insurance, collision-damage insurance, and medical or legal assistance, depending on the card and the bank that issued it. American Express, MasterCard, and Visa provide one or more of these services, so **get a copy of your credit card's travel-benefits policy.** If you are a member of an auto club, always **ask hotel and car-rental reservations agents about auto-club discounts.** Some clubs offer additional discounts on tours, cruises, and admission to attractions.

THE GOLD GUIDE / SMART TRAVEL TIPS

DISCOUNT RESERVATIONS

To save money, **look into discount-reservations services** with toll-free numbers, which use their buying power to get a better price on hotels, airline tickets, even car rentals. When booking a room, always **call the hotel's local toll-free number** (if one is available) rather than the central reservations number—you'll often get a better price. Always ask about special packages or corporate rates.

➤ AIRLINE TICKETS: ☎ 800/FLY–4–LESS. ☎ 800/FLY–ASAP.

➤ HOTEL ROOMS: **Accommodations Express** (☎ 800/444–7666).**Central Reservation Service (CRS)** (☎ 800/548–3311). **Hotel Reservations Network** (☎ 800/964–6835). **Room Finders USA** (☎ 800/473–7829). **RMC Travel** (☎ 800/245–5738). **Steigenberger Reservation Service** (☎ 800/223–5652).

PACKAGE DEALS

Packages and guided tours can save you money, but don't confuse the two. When you buy a package, your travel remains independent, just as though you had planned and booked the trip yourself. Fly/drive packages, which combine airfare and car rental, are often a good deal.

ECOTOURISM

Florida's varied environment is one of its chief draws; it's also very fragile. If you're out in nature, follow the basic rules of environmental responsibility: Take nothing but pictures; leave nothing but footprints. Most important, **be careful around the tenuous dunes.** Picking the sea grasses that hold the dunes in place can carry stiff fines, and an afternoon of roughhousing can completely destroy a dune. Ecotours (listed in under Guided Tours in each chapter's A to Z section) operate throughout the state and can help you see some of what makes Florida so distinct, usually in a way that makes the least impact possible.

ETIQUETTE & BEHAVIOR

Floridians are generally very friendly and courteous, and depending on where you're from, you may be struck by the helpfulness of the service workers with whom you come in contact. In the cities, especially Miami, **exercise good driving etiquette—for your own safety.** Road rage has hit paradise, too, and cutting someone off, cursing, or gesturing might cause a reaction you're not prepared for. Relax. You're on vacation.

GAY & LESBIAN TRAVEL

Destinations that have a reputation for being especially gay and lesbian friendly include Miami's South Beach and Key West.

➤ GUIDES TO GAY- AND LESBIAN-FRIENDLY TRAVEL: **Fodor's Gay Guide to the USA** and *Fodor's Gay Guide to South Florida* (available in bookstores or from Fodor's Travel Publications, ☎ 800/533–6478; $19.50 and $11).

➤ GAY- AND LESBIAN-FRIENDLY TRAVEL AGENCIES: **Corniche Travel** (✉ 8721 Sunset Blvd., Suite 200, West Hollywood, CA 90069, ☎ 310/854–6000 or 800/429–8747, ℻ 310/659–7441). **Islanders Kennedy Travel** (✉ 183 W. 10th St., New York, NY 10014, ☎ 212/242–3222 or 800/988–1181, ℻ 212/929–8530). **Now Voyager** (✉ 4406 18th St., San Francisco, CA 94114, ☎ 415/626–1169 or 800/255–6951, ℻ 415/626–8626). **Yellowbrick Road** (✉ 1500 W. Balmoral Ave., Chicago, IL 60640, ☎ 773/561–1800 or 800/642–2488, ℻ 773/561–4497). **Skylink Travel and Tour** (✉ 3577 Moorland Ave., Santa Rosa, CA 95407, ☎ 707/585–8355 or 800/225–5759, ℻ 707/584–5637), serving lesbian travelers.

HEALTH

BEACH SAFETY

If you are unaccustomed to strong subtropical sun, you run a risk of sunburn and heat prostration, even in winter. So **hit the beach before 10 or after 3.** If you must be out at midday, **limit strenuous exercise, drink plenty of liquids, and wear a hat.** Even on overcast days, ultraviolet rays shine through the haze, so **use a sunscreen with an SPF of at least 15,** and have children wear a waterproof SPF 30 or better.

While you're frolicking on the beach, **steer clear of what looks like blue**

bubbles on the sand. These are either jellyfish or Portuguese man-of-wars, and their tentacles can cause an allergic reaction.

Before swimming, **make sure there's no undertow.** Rip currents, caused when the tide rushes out through a narrow break in a sandbar, can overpower even the strongest swimmer. If you're caught in one, resist the urge to swim straight back to shore—you'll never make it. Instead, stay calm, swim parallel to the shore until you are outside the current's pull, and then work your way in.

DIVERS' ALERT

Do not fly within 24 hours after scuba diving.

MEDICAL PLANS

No one plans to get sick while traveling, but it happens, so **consider signing up with a medical-assistance company.** Members get doctor referrals, emergency evacuation or repatriation, 24-hour telephone hot lines for medical consultation, cash for emergencies, and other personal and legal assistance. Coverage varies by plan, so **review the benefits of each carefully.**

➤ MEDICAL-ASSISTANCE COMPANIES: **International SOS Assistance** (✉ 8 Neshaminy Interplex, Suite 207, Trevose, PA 19053, ☎ 215/245–4707 or 800/523–6586, ℻ 215/244–9617; ✉ 12 Chemin Riantbosson, 1217 Meyrin 1, Geneva, Switzerland, ☎ 4122/785–6464, ℻ 4122/785–6424; ✉ 10 Anson Rd., 14-07/08 International Plaza, Singapore, 079903, ☎ 65/226–3936, ℻ 65/226–3937).

HOLIDAYS

Major national holidays include: New Year's Day; Martin Luther King Jr. Day (third Mon. in Jan.); President's Day (third Mon. in Feb.); Memorial Day (last Mon. in May); Independence Day (July 4); Labor Day (first Mon. in Sept.); Thanksgiving Day (fourth Thurs. in Nov.); Christmas Eve and Day; and New Year's Eve.

INSURANCE

Travel insurance is the best way to **protect yourself against financial loss.** The most useful plan is a comprehensive policy that includes coverage for trip cancellation and interruption, default, trip delay, and medical expenses (with a waiver for preexisting conditions).

Without insurance, you will lose all or most of your money if you cancel your trip, regardless of the reason. Default insurance covers you if your tour operator, airline, or cruise line goes out of business. Trip-delay covers unforeseen expenses that you may incur due to bad weather or mechanical delays. It's important to compare the fine print regarding trip-delay coverage when comparing policies.

For overseas travel, one of the most important components of travel insurance is its medical coverage. Supplemental health insurance will pick up the cost of your medical bills should you get sick or injured while traveling. Residents of the United Kingdom can buy an annual travel-insurance policy valid for most vacations taken during the year in which the coverage is purchased. If you are pregnant or have a pre-existing condition, make sure you're covered. British citizens should buy extra medical coverage when traveling overseas, according to the Association of British Insurers. Australian travelers should buy travel insurance, including extra medical coverage, whenever they go abroad, according to the Insurance Council of Australia.

Always **buy travel insurance directly from the insurance company**; if you buy it from a cruise line, airline, or tour operator that goes out of business you probably will not be covered for the agency or operator's default, a major risk. Before you make any purchase, **review your existing health and home-owner's policies** to find out whether they cover expenses incurred while traveling.

➤ TRAVEL INSURERS: In the U.S., **Access America** (✉ 6600 W. Broad St., Richmond, VA 23230, ☎ 804/285–3300 or 800/284–8300). **Travel Guard International** (✉ 1145 Clark St., Stevens Point, WI 54481, ☎ 715/345–0505 or 800/826–1300). In Canada, **Mutual of Omaha** (✉ Travel Division, ✉ 500 University Ave.,

SMART TRAVEL TIPS

THE GOLD GUIDE

Toronto, Ontario M5G 1V8, ☎ 416/598–4083, 800/268–8825 in Canada).

➤ INSURANCE INFORMATION: In the U.K., **Association of British Insurers** (✉ 51 Gresham St., London EC2V 7HQ, ☎ 0171/600–3333). In Australia, the **Insurance Council of Australia** (☎ 613/9614–1077, FAX 613/9614–7924).

LODGING

South Florida has every conceivable type of lodging—from tree houses to penthouses, mansions for hire to hostels, houseboats to house exchanges. Even with occupancy rates inching above 70%, there are almost always rooms available, except maybe at Christmas and other holidays. Affordable lodgings can be found in even the most glittery resort towns, typically motel rooms that may cost as little as $50–$60 a night; they may not be in the best part of town, mind you, but they won't be in the worst, either (perhaps along busy highways where you'll need the roar of the air-conditioning to drown out the traffic). Since beachfront properties tend to be more expensive, **look for properties a little off the beach.** Still, many beachfront properties are surprisingly affordable, too, as in places like Deerfield Beach, north of Fort Lauderdale, where there are still a number of small, family-owned properties.

Children are generally welcome everywhere. Pets are another matter, so **inquire ahead of time if you're bringing an animal with you.**

In the busy seasons—over Christmas, from late January through Easter, and during holiday weekends in summer—always **reserve ahead for the top properties.** Fall is the slowest season: Rates are low and availability is high, with the exception of Halloween in Key West, which is jampacked for Fantasy Fest. If you're not booking through a travel agent, call the visitors bureau or the chamber of commerce in the area where you're going to check whether any special event is scheduled for when you plan to arrive. If demand isn't especially high for the time you have in mind, you can often **save by showing up at a lodging in mid- to late afternoon**—

desk clerks are typically willing to negotiate with travelers in order to fill those rooms late in the day. In addition, **check with chambers of commerce for discount coupons for selected properties.**

APARTMENT & VILLA RENTALS

If you want a home base that's roomy enough for a family and comes with cooking facilities, **consider a furnished rental.** These can save you money, especially if you're traveling with a large group of people. Home-exchange directories list rentals (often second homes owned by prospective house swappers), and some services search for a house or apartment for you (even a castle if that's your fancy) and handle the paperwork. Some send an illustrated catalog; others send photographs only of specific properties, sometimes at a charge. Up-front registration fees may apply.

➤ RENTAL AGENTS: **Europa-Let/Tropical Inn-Let** (✉ 92 N. Main St., Ashland, OR 97520, ☎ 541/482–5806 or 800/462–4486, FAX 541/482–0660). **Hometours International** (✉ Box 11503, Knoxville, TN 37939, ☎ 423/690–8484 or 800/367–4668). **Interhome** (✉ 124 Little Falls Rd., Fairfield, NJ 07004, ☎ 973/882–6864 or 800/882–6864, FAX 973/808–1742). **Property Rentals International** (✉ 1008 Mansfield Crossing Rd., Richmond, VA 23236, ☎ 804/378–6054 or 800/220–3332, FAX 804/379–2073). **Rent-a-Home International** (✉ 7200 34th Ave. NW, Seattle, WA 98117, ☎ 206/789–9377 or 800/488–7368, FAX 206/789–9379). **Vacation Home Rentals Worldwide** (✉ 235 Kensington Ave., Norwood, NJ 07648, ☎ 201/767–9393 or 800/633–3284, FAX 201/767–5510). **Hideaways International** (✉ 767 Islington St., Portsmouth, NH 03801, ☎ 603/430–4433 or 800/843–4433, FAX 603/430–4444; membership $99) is a club for travelers who arrange rentals among themselves.

CAMPING

For information on camping facilities, **contact the national and state parks and forests you plan to visit and the Florida Department of Environmental Protection** (☞ Parks & Preserves, *below*). Camping is especially popular at state park campsites in the Keys, so it's essential that you make advance reservations.

To find a commercial campground, **pick up a copy of the free annual "Florida Camping Directory,"** which lists 220 campgrounds, with 66,000 sites. It's available at Florida welcome centers, from the Florida Tourism Industry Marketing Corporation (☞ Visitor Information, *below*), and from the Florida Association of RV Parks & Campgrounds.

➤ CAMPING ASSOCIATION: **Florida Association of RV Parks & Campgrounds** (⊠ 1340 Vickers Dr., Tallahassee, FL 32303-3041, ☎ 904/562–7151, FAX 904/562–7179).

CONDOS

➤ CONDO GUIDE: *The Condo Lux Vacationer's Guide to Condominium Rentals in the Southeast* (Vintage Books/Random House, New York; $9.95), by Jill Little.

HOME EXCHANGES

If you would like to exchange your home for someone else's, **join a home-exchange organization,** which will send you its updated listings of available exchanges for a year and will include your own listing in at least one of them. It's up to you to make specific arrangements.

➤ EXCHANGE CLUBS: **HomeLink International** (⊠ Box 650, Key West, FL 33041, ☎ 305/294–7766 or 800/638–3841, FAX 305/294–1148; $83 per year).

HOSTELS

No matter what your age, you can **save on lodging costs by staying at hostels.** In some 5,000 locations in more than 70 countries around the world, Hostelling International (HI), the umbrella group for a number of national youth hostel associations, offers single-sex, dorm-style beds and, at many hostels, "couples" rooms and family accommodations. Membership in any HI national hostel association, open to travelers of all ages, allows you to stay in HI-affiliated hostels at member rates (one-year membership is about $25 for adults; hostels run about $10–$25 per night). Members

also have priority if the hostel is full; they're eligible for discounts around the world, even on rail and bus travel in some countries.

➤ HOSTEL ORGANIZATIONS: **Hostelling International—American Youth Hostels** (⊠ 733 15th St. NW, Suite 840, Washington, DC 20005, ☎ 202/783–6161, FAX 202/783–6171). **Hostelling International—Canada** (⊠ 400-205 Catherine St., Ottawa, Ontario K2P 1C3, ☎ 613/237–7884, FAX 613/237–7868). **Youth Hostel Association of England and Wales** (⊠ Trevelyan House, ⊠ 8 St. Stephen's Hill, St. Albans, Hertfordshire AL1 2DY, ☎ 01727/855215 or 01727/845047, FAX 01727/844126); membership in the U.S. $25, in Canada C$26.75, in the U.K. £9.30).

HOTELS & MOTELS

Wherever you look in South Florida, it seems, you'll find lots of plain, inexpensive motels and luxurious resorts, independents alongside national chains, and an ever-growing number of modern properties as well as quite a few timeless classics. In fact, since South Florida has been a favored travel destination for some time, vintage hotels are everywhere, both grand edifices like the Breakers in Palm Beach, the Boca Raton Resort & Club in Boca Raton, the Biltmore in Coral Gables, and Marriott's Casa Marina in Key West as well as smaller, historic places, like the Miami River Inn in downtown Miami.

➤ HOTEL AND MOTEL ASSOCIATION: **Florida Hotel & Motel Association** (⊠ 200 W. College Ave., Box 1529, Tallahassee, FL 32301-1529, ☎ 904/224–2888).

➤ RESERVATION SERVICES: **Accommodations Express** (☎ 800/663–7666, FAX 609/525–0111). **Florida Hotel Network** (⊠ 521 Lincoln Rd. Miami Beach, FL 33139, ☎ 800/538–3616, FAX 305/538–3616). **Florida Sunbreak** (⊠ 169 Lincoln Rd., Miami Beach, FL 33139, ☎ 305/532–1516 or 888/786–2732, FAX 305/781–1312).

INNS & B&BS

Small inns and guest houses are increasingly numerous in Florida. Many in Key West offer bed-and-breakfast in a homelike setting; in fact, many are in private homes, and their owners treat you almost like family.

➤ HISTORIC INN ASSOCIATION: **Inn Route, Inc.** (✉ Box 6187, Palm Harbor, FL 34684, ☎ FAX 813/786–9792 or 800/524–1880).

➤ REFERRAL AND RESERVATION AGENCIES: **Bed & Breakfast Co., Tropical Florida** (✉ Box 262, Miami, FL 33243, ☎ FAX 305/661–3270). **Bed & Breakfast Scenic Florida** (✉ Box 3385, Tallahassee, FL 32315-3385, ☎ 904/386–8196). **Key West Information Center** (✉ 1601 N. Roosevelt. Blvd., Key West, FL 33040, ☎ 305/292–5000). **RSVP Florida & St. Augustine** (✉ Box 3603, St. Augustine, FL 32085, ☎ 904/471–0600).

VACATION OWNERSHIP RESORTS

Vacation ownership resorts sell hotel rooms, condominium apartments, and villas in weekly, monthly, or quarterly increments. The weekly arrangement is the most popular; it's often referred to as "interval ownership" or "time sharing." Of more than 3,000 vacation ownership resorts around the world, some 500 are in Florida. Though the heaviest concentration is in the Walt Disney World/Orlando area, there's a smaller but still significant number along the southeast coast and in the Keys. Nonowners can rent at many of these resorts by contacting the individual property or a real-estate broker in the area.

MONEY

CREDIT & DEBIT CARDS

Should you use a credit card or a debit card when traveling? Both have benefits. A credit card allows you to delay payment and gives you certain rights as a consumer (☞ Consumer Protection, *above*). A debit card, also known as a check card, deducts funds directly from your checking account and helps you stay within your budget. When you want to rent a car, though, you may still need an old-fashioned credit card. Although you can always *pay* for your car with a debit card, some agencies will not allow you to *reserve* a car with a debit card.

Otherwise, the two types of plastic are virtually the same. Both will get you cash advances at ATMs worldwide if your card is properly programmed with your personal identification number (PIN). Both offer excellent, wholesale exchange rates. And both protect you against unauthorized use if the card is lost or stolen. Your liability is limited to $50, as long as you report the card missing.

➤ ATM LOCATIONS: **Cirrus** (☎ 800/424–7787). **Plus** (☎ 800/843–7587) for locations in the U.S. and Canada, or visit your local bank.

EXCHANGING MONEY

For the most favorable rates, **change money through banks.** Although fees charged for ATM transactions may be higher abroad than at home, Cirrus and Plus exchange rates are excellent, because they are based on wholesale rates offered only by major banks. You won't do as well at exchange booths in airports or rail and bus stations, in hotels, in restaurants, or in stores, although you may find their hours more convenient. To avoid lines at airport exchange booths, **get a bit of local currency before you leave home.**

➤ EXCHANGE SERVICES: **Chase *Currency To Go*** (☎ 800/935–9935; 935–9935 in NY, NJ, and CT). **International Currency Express** (☎ 888/842–0880 on the East Coast, 888/278–6628 on the West Coast). **Thomas Cook Currency Services** (☎ 800/287–7362 for telephone orders and retail locations).

TRAVELER'S CHECKS

Do you need traveler's checks? It depends on where you're headed. If you're going to rural areas and small towns, go with cash; traveler's checks are best used in cities. Lost or stolen checks can usually be replaced within 24 hours. To ensure a speedy refund, buy your own traveler's checks—don't let someone else pay for them: irregularities like this can cause delays. The person who bought the checks should make the call to request a refund.

OUTDOOR ACTIVITIES & SPORTS

Recreational opportunities abound throughout Florida. The Governor's Council on Physical Fitness and Sports puts on the Sunshine State Games each July in a different part of the state.

➤ GENERAL INFORMATION: **Florida Department of Environmental Protection** (✉ Office of Greenways, MS 585, 3900 Commonwealth Blvd., Tallahassee, FL 32399-3000, ☎ 904/487–4784) for information on bicycling, canoeing, kayaking, and hiking trails. **Florida Sports Foundation** (✉ 107 W. Gaines St., Suite 466, Tallahassee, FL 32399-2000, ☎ 904/488–8347) for guides on baseball spring training, boating, fishing, golf, and scuba diving.

➤ MARINE CHARTS: **Tealls, Inc.** (✉ 111 Saguaro La., Marathon, FL 33050, ☎ 305/743–3942, ℻ 305/743–3942; $7.95 set, $3.60 each individual chart).

BIKING

For bike information, **check with Florida's Department of Transportation (DOT),** which publishes free bicycle trail guides, dispenses free touring information packets, and provides names of bike coordinators around the state.

➤ BICYCLE INFORMATION: **DOT state bicycle-pedestrian coordinator** (✉ 605 E. Suwannee St., MS 82, Tallahassee, FL 32399-0450, ☎ 904/487–1200).

CANOEING & KAYAKING

You can canoe or kayak along trails encompassing creeks, rivers, and springs. Both the DEP (☞ General Information, *above*) and outfitter associations provide information on trails and their conditions, events, and contacts for trips and equipment rental.

➤ OUTFITTERS AND OUTFITTING ASSOCIATIONS: **Canoe Outpost System** (✉ 2816 N.W. Rte. 661, Arcadia, FL 33821, ☎ 941/494–1215), comprising five outfitters. **Florida Canoeing and Kayaking Association** (✉ Box 20892, West Palm Beach, FL 33416,

☎ 561/575–4530). **Florida Professional Paddlesports Association** (✉ Box 1764, Arcadia, FL 34265, ☎ no phone).

FISHING

In Atlantic and gulf waters, fishing seasons and other regulations vary by location and species. You will need to **buy a license for both freshwater and saltwater fishing.** Nonresident fees for a saltwater license are $30. Nonresidents can purchase freshwater licenses good for seven days ($15) or for one year ($30). Typically, you'll pay a $1.50 surcharge at almost any marina, bait shop, Kmart, Wal-Mart, or other license vendor.

➤ FISHING INFORMATION: **Florida Game and Fresh Water Fish Commission** (✉ 620 S. Meridian St., Tallahassee, FL 32399-1600, ☎ 904/488–1960) for the free *Florida Fishing Handbook* with license vendors, regional fishing guides, and educational bulletins. **Florida Sea Grant Extension Program** (✉ Bldg. 803, University of Florida, Gainesville, FL 32611, ☎ 904/392–5870) for varied publications.

HORSEBACK RIDING

➤ HORSEBACK RIDING INFORMATION: **Horse & Pony** (✉ 6229 Virginia La., Seffner, FL 33584, ☎ 813/621–2510).

JOGGING, RUNNING, & WALKING

Local running clubs sponsor weekly public events.

➤ CLUBS & EVENTS: **USA Track & Field–Florida** (✉ Attn. Event Marketing & Management Intl., 1322 N. Mills Ave., Orlando, FL 32803, ☎ 407/944–0026, ℻ 407/897–3243; send SASE for listings). **Miami Runners Club** (✉ 7920 S.W. 40th St., Miami, FL 33155, ☎ 305/227–1500, ℻ 305/220–2450) for South Florida events.

PARI-MUTUEL SPORTS

➤ SCHEDULES: Department of Business & Professional Regulations **Division of Pari-Mutuel Wagering** (✉ 8405 N.W. 53rd St., Suite C-250, Miami, FL 33166, ☎ 305/470–5675, ℻ 305/470–5686).

TENNIS

➤ TOURNAMENT AND EVENT SCHEDULES: **United States Tennis Association Florida Section** (✉ 1280 S.W. 36th Ave., Suite 305, Pompano Beach, FL 33069, ☎ 954/968–3434, FAX 954/968–3986; yearbook $11).

WILDERNESS & RECREATION AREAS

South Florida is studded with trails, waterways, and parks (most notably the Everglades) that are ideal for hiking, bird-watching, canoeing, bicycling, and horseback riding.

➤ PUBLICATIONS: **"Florida Trails: A Guide to Florida's Natural Habitats"**, available from Florida Tourism Industry Marketing Corporation, (☞ Visitor Information, *below*) for bicycling, canoeing, horseback riding, and walking trails; camping; snorkeling and scuba diving; and Florida ecosystems. **Florida Wildlife Viewing Guide**, available from Falcon Press (✉ Box 1718, Helena, MT 59624, ☎ 800/582–2665); $7.95 plus $3 shipping, by Susan Cerulean and Ann Morrow, for marked wildlife-watching sites. **"Recreation Guide to District Lands"**, available from St. Johns River Water Management District (✉ Box 1429, Palatka, FL 32178-1429); free for marine, wetland, and upland recreational areas.

PACKING

LUGGAGE

How many carry-on bags you can bring with you is up to the airline. Most allow two, but the limit is often reduced to one on certain flights. Gate agents will take excess baggage—including bags they deem oversize—from you as you board and add it to checked luggage. To avoid this situation, make sure that everything you carry aboard will fit under your seat. Also, get to the gate early, and request a seat at the back of the plane; you'll probably board first, while the overhead bins are still empty. Since big, bulky baggage attracts the attention of gate agents and flight attendants on a busy flight, make sure your carry-on is really a carry-on. Finally, a carry-on that's long and narrow is more likely to remain unnoticed than one that's wide and squarish.

If you are flying internationally, note that baggage allowances may be determined not by piece but by weight—generally 88 pounds (40 kilograms) in first class, 66 pounds (30 kilograms) in business class, and 44 pounds (20 kilograms) in economy.

Airline liability for baggage is limited to $1,250 per person on flights within the United States. On international flights it amounts to $9.07 per pound or $20 per kilogram for checked baggage (roughly $640 per 70-pound bag) and $400 per passenger for unchecked baggage. You can buy additional coverage at check-in for about $10 per $1,000 of coverage, but it excludes a rather extensive list of items, shown on your airline ticket.

Before departure, **itemize your bags' contents** and their worth, and label the bags with your name, address, and phone number. (If you use your home address, cover it so that potential thieves can't see it readily.) Inside each bag, **pack a copy of your itinerary.** At check-in, **make sure that each bag is correctly tagged** with the destination airport's three-letter code. If your bags arrive damaged or fail to arrive at all, file a written report with the airline before leaving the airport.

PACKING LIST

South Florida is warm year-round (except for an occasional cold snap in winter) and often extremely humid in summer months. Be prepared for sudden summer storms, but keep in mind that plastic raincoats are uncomfortable in the high humidity.

Dress is casual throughout the state, with sundresses, jeans, or walking shorts appropriate during the day; **bring comfortable walking shoes or sneakers** for touring. A few restaurants request that men wear jackets and ties, but most do not. Be prepared for air-conditioning working in overdrive.

You can generally swim year-round in the Miami and the Keys region. Be sure to **take a sun hat and sunscreen** because the sun can be fierce, even in winter, even if it is chilly or overcast.

In your carry-on luggage **bring an extra pair of eyeglasses or contact lenses and enough of any medication** you take to last the entire trip. You may also want your doctor to write a spare prescription using the drug's generic name, since brand names may vary from country to country. **Never put prescription drugs or valuables in luggage to be checked.** To avoid customs delays, carry medications in their original packaging. And don't forget to copy down and carry addresses of offices that handle refunds of lost traveler's checks.

PARKS & PRESERVES

NATIONAL PARKS

Look into discount passes to **save money on park entrance fees.** The Golden Eagle Pass ($50) gets you and your companions free admission to all parks for one year. (Camping and parking are extra). Both the Golden Age Passport ($10), for those 62 and older, and the Golden Access Passport (free), for travelers with disabilities, entitle holders to free entry to all national parks, plus 50% off fees for the use of many park facilities and services. You must show proof of age and of U.S. citizenship or permanent residency (such as a U.S. passport, driver's license, or birth certificate) and, if requesting Golden Access, proof of disability. All three passes are available at all national park entrances where entrance fees are charged. Golden Eagle and Golden Access passes are also available by mail.

➤ PASSES BY MAIL: **National Park Service** (✉ National Capitol Area Office, ✉ 1100 Ohio Dr. SW, Washington, DC 20242).

STATE PARKS

Florida's Department of Environmental Protection (DEP) is responsible for hundreds of historic buildings, landmarks, nature preserves, and parks. When requesting a free *Florida State Park Guide,* mention which parts of the state you plan to visit. For information on camping facilities at the state parks, ask for the free "Florida State Parks, Fees and Facilities" and "Florida State Parks Camping Reservation Procedures" brochures. Responding to cutbacks in its budget, the DEP established Friends of Florida State Parks, a citizen support organization open to all.

➤ STATE PARKS INFORMATION: **Florida Department of Environmental Protection** (✉ Marjory Stoneman Douglas Bldg., MS 535, 3900 Commonwealth Blvd., Tallahassee, FL 32399-3000, ☎ 904/488–2850, FAX 904/488–3947; Friends of Florida State Parks ☎ 904/488–8243).

PRIVATE PRESERVES

➤ FLORIDA SANCTUARY INFORMATION: **National Audubon Society** (✉ Sanctuary Director, Miles Wildlife Sanctuary, R.R. 1, Box 294, W. Cornwall Rd., Sharon, CT 06069, ☎ 203/364–0048). **Nature Conservancy** (✉ 222 S. Westmonte Dr., Suite 300, Altamonte Springs, FL 32714, ☎ 407/682–3554; offices at ✉ 250 Tequesta Dr., Suite 301, Tequesta, FL 33469, ☎ 561/744–6668; ✉ 201 Front St., Suite 222, Key West, FL 33040, ☎ 305/296–3880; ✉ Comeau Bldg., 319 Clematis St., Suite 611, West Palm Beach, FL 33401, ☎ 561/833–4226).

PASSPORTS & VISAS

When traveling internationally, **carry a passport even if you don't need one** (it's always the best form of ID), and make **two photocopies of the data page** (one for someone at home and another for you, carried separately from your passport). If you lose your passport, promptly call the nearest embassy or consulate and the local police.

➤ U.K. CITIZENS: **U.S. Embassy Visa Information Line** (☎ 01891/200290; calls cost 49p per minute, 39p per minute cheap rate), for U.S. visa information. **U.S. Embassy Visa Branch** (✉ 5 Upper Grosvenor St., London W1A 2JB), for U.S. visa information; send a self-addressed, stamped envelope. Write the **U.S. Consulate General** (✉ Queen's House, Queen St., Belfast BTI 6EO) if you live in Northern Ireland.

PASSPORT OFFICES

The best time to apply for a passport or to renew is during the fall and winter. Before any trip, be sure to check your passport's expiration date and, if necessary, renew it as soon as possible. (Some countries won't allow you to enter on a passport that's due to expire in six months or less.)

➤ AUSTRALIAN CITIZENS: **Australian Passport Office** (☎ 13/1232).

➤ NEW ZEALAND CITIZENS: **New Zealand Passport Office** (☎ 04/494–0700 for information on how to apply, 0800/727–776 for information on applications already submitted).

➤ U.K. CITIZENS: **London Passport Office** (☎ 0990/21010), for fees and documentation requirements and to request an emergency passport.

SENIOR-CITIZEN TRAVEL

Since South Florida has a significant retired population, senior-citizen discounts are ubiquitous. To qualify for age-related discounts, **mention your senior-citizen status up front** when booking hotel reservations (not when checking out) and before you're seated in restaurants (not when paying the bill). Note that discounts may be limited to certain menus, days, or hours. (For example, in South Florida, seniors flock to restaurants with early bird specials.) When renting a car, **ask about promotional car-rental discounts,** which can be cheaper than senior-citizen rates.

➤ EDUCATIONAL PROGRAMS: **Elderhostel** (⊠ 75 Federal St., 3rd floor, Boston, MA 02110, ☎ 617/426–8056).

STUDENT TRAVEL

➤ STUDENT IDs & SERVICES: **Council on International Educational Exchange** (⊠ CIEE, 205 E. 42nd St., 14th floor, New York, NY 10017, ☎ 212/822–2600 or 888/268–6245, FAX 212/822–2699), for mail orders only, in the United States. **Travel Cuts** (⊠ 187 College St., Toronto, Ontario M5T 1P7, ☎ 416/979–2406 or 800/667–2887) in Canada.

➤ STUDENT TOURS: **Contiki Holidays** (⊠ 300 Plaza Alicante, Suite 900, Garden Grove, CA 92840, ☎ 714/740–0808 or 800/266–8454, FAX 714/740–2034).

TAXES

Florida's sales tax is currently 6%, but local sales and tourist taxes can raise that number considerably, especially for certain items, such as lodging. Miami hoteliers, for example, collect roughly 12.5% for city and resort taxes. It's best to **ask about additional costs up front,** to avoid a rude awakening.

TELEPHONES

COUNTRY CODES

The country code for the United States is 1.

DIRECTORY & OPERATOR INFORMATION

To reach directory assistance, dial the area code followed by 555–1212.

INTERNATIONAL CALLS

With the exception of Canada and certain Caribbean islands you must dial 011 followed by the appropriate country code to place an international call from the United States.

➤ ACCESS CODES: **AT&T Direct** (☎ 800/435–0812). **MCI WorldPhone** (☎ 800/444–4141). **Sprint International Access** (☎ 800/877–4646).

LONG-DISTANCE CALLS

Competitive long-distance carriers make calling within the United States relatively convenient and let you avoid hotel surcharges. By dialing an 800 number, you can get connected to the long-distance company of your choice.

➤ LONG-DISTANCE CARRIERS: **AT&T** (☎ 800/225–5288). **MCI** (☎ 800/888–8000). **Sprint** (☎ 800/366–2255).

TIPPING

Whether they carry bags, open doors, deliver food, or clean rooms, hospitality employees work to receive a portion of your travel budget. In deciding how much to give, **base your tip on what the service is and how well it's performed.**

In transit, tip an airport valet $1–$3 per bag, a taxi driver 15%–20% of the fare.

For hotel staff, recommended amounts are $1–$3 per bag for a bellhop, $1–$2 per night per guest for chambermaids, $5–$10 for special concierge service, $1–$3 for a doorman who hails a cab or parks a car, 15% of the greens fee for a caddy, 15%–20% of the bill for a massage, and 15% of a room service bill.

In a restaurant, give 15%–20% of your bill before tax to the server, 5%–10% to the maître d', 15% to a bartender, and 15% of the wine bill for a wine steward who makes a special effort in selecting and serving wine.

TOUR OPERATORS

Buying a prepackaged tour or independent vacation can make your trip to Florida less expensive and more hassle-free. Because everything is prearranged, you'll spend less time planning.

Operators that handle several hundred thousand travelers per year can use their purchasing power to give you a good price. Their high volume may also indicate financial stability. But some small companies provide more personalized service; because they tend to specialize, they may also be more knowledgeable about a given area.

BOOKING WITH AN AGENT

Travel agents are excellent resources. In fact, large operators accept bookings made only through travel agents. But it's a good idea to **collect brochures from several agencies,** because some agents' suggestions may be influenced by relationships with tour and package firms that reward them for volume sales. If you have a special interest, **find an agent with expertise in that area**; ASTA (☞ Travel Agencies, *below*) has a database of specialists worldwide.

Make sure your travel agent knows the accommodations and other services. Ask about the hotel's location, room size, beds, and whether it has a pool, room service, or programs for children, if you care about these. Has your agent been there in person or sent others you can contact?

Do some homework on your own, too: Local tourism boards can provide information about lesser-known and small-niche operators, some of which may sell only direct.

BUYER BEWARE

Each year consumers are stranded or lose their money when tour operators—even very large ones with excellent reputations—go out of business. So **check out the operator.** Find out how long the company has been in business, and ask several travel agents about its reputation. If the package or tour you are considering is priced lower than in your wildest dreams, **be skeptical.** Try to **book with a company that has a consumer-protection program.** If the operator has such a program, you'll find information about it in the company's brochure. If the operator you are considering does not offer some kind of consumer protection, then ask for references from satisfied customers.

In the U.S., members of the National Tour Association and United States Tour Operators Association are required to set aside funds to cover your payments and travel arrangements in case the company defaults. It's also a good idea to choose a company that participates in the American Society of Travel Agent's Tour Operator Program (TOP). This gives you a forum if there are any disputes between you and your tour operator; ASTA will act as mediator.

➤ TOUR-OPERATOR RECOMMENDATIONS: **American Society of Travel Agents** (☞ Travel Agencies, *below*). **National Tour Association** (✉ NTA, 546 E. Main St., Lexington, KY 40508, ☎ 606/226–4444 or 800/755–8687). **United States Tour Operators Association** (✉ USTOA, 342 Madison Ave., Suite 1522, New York, NY 10173, ☎ 212/599–6599 or 800/468–7862, ℻ 212/599–6744).

COSTS

The more your package or tour includes, the better you can predict the ultimate cost of your vacation. Make sure you know exactly what is covered, and **beware of hidden costs.** Are taxes, tips, and service charges included? Transfers and baggage handling? Entertainment and excursions? These can add up.

Prices for packages and tours are usually quoted per person, based on two sharing a room. If traveling solo, you may be required to pay the full double-occupancy rate. Some operators eliminate this surcharge if you agree to be matched with a roommate

SMART TRAVEL TIPS / THE GOLD GUIDE

of the same sex, even if one is not found by departure time.

TRAIN TRAVEL

Amtrak provides north–south service to the cities of West Palm Beach, Fort Lauderdale, and Miami.

➤ RAIL LINE: **Amtrak** (☎ 800/872–7245).

TRAVEL AGENCIES

A good travel agent puts your needs first. Look for an agency that has been in business at least five years, emphasizes customer service, and has someone on staff who specializes in your destination. In addition, **make sure the agency belongs to a professional trade organization,** such as ASTA in the United States. If your travel agency is also acting as your tour operator, *see* Buyer Beware in Tour Operators, *above*).

➤ LOCAL AGENT REFERRALS: **American Society of Travel Agents** (ASTA, ☎ 800/965–2782 24-hr hot line, FAX 703/684–8319). **Association of Canadian Travel Agents** (⊠ Suite 201, 1729 Bank St., Ottawa, Ontario K1V 7Z5, ☎ 613/521–0474, FAX 613/521–0805). **Association of British Travel Agents** (⊠ 55–57 Newman St., London W1P 4AH, ☎ 0171/637–2444, FAX 0171/637–0713). **Australian Federation of Travel Agents** (☎ 02/9264–3299). **Travel Agents' Association of New Zealand** (☎ 04/499–0104).

TRAVEL GEAR

Travel catalogs specialize in useful items, such as compact alarm clocks and travel irons, that can **save space when packing.**

➤ CATALOGS: **Magellan's** (☎ 800/962–4943, FAX 805/568–5406). **Orvis Travel** (☎ 800/541–3541, FAX 540/343–7053). **TravelSmith** (☎ 800/950–1600, FAX 800/950–1656).

VISITOR INFORMATION

TOURIST INFORMATION

For general information about attractions, contact the office below. For regional tourist bureaus and chambers of commerce see individual chapters.

➤ STATE: **Florida Tourism Industry**

Marketing Corporation (⊠ Box 1100, 661 E. Jefferson St., Suite 300, Tallahassee, FL 32302, ☎ 904/487–1462, FAX 904/224–2938).

➤ IN THE U.K.: **ABC Florida** (⊠ Box 35, Abingdon, Oxon. OX14 4TB, ☎ 0891/600555, 50p per minute; send £2 for vacation pack).

U.S. GOVERNMENT

Government agencies can be an excellent source of inexpensive travel information. When planning your trip, **find out what government materials are available.**

➤ PAMPHLETS: **Consumer Information Center** (⊠ Consumer Information Catalogue, Pueblo, CO 81009, ☎ 719/948–3334 or 888/878–3256) for a free catalog that includes travel titles.

WHEN TO GO

South Florida is a region for all seasons, although most visitors prefer October–April. Winter remains the height of the tourist season, when South Florida is crowded with "snowbirds" fleeing cold weather in the North. (It did snow in Miami once in the 1970s, but since then the average snowfall has been exactly 00.00 inches.) Hotels, bars, discos, restaurants, shops, and attractions are all crowded. Hollywood and Broadway celebrities appear in sophisticated supper clubs, and other performing artists hold the stage at ballets, operas, concerts, and theaters.

For the college crowd, spring vacation is still the time to congregate in Florida. However, Fort Lauderdale, where city officials have refashioned the beachfront more as a family resort, no longer indulges young revelers, so it's much less popular with college students than it once was.

Summer in South Florida, as smart budget-minded visitors have discovered, is often hot and very humid, but along the coast, ocean breezes make the season quite bearable and most hotels lower their prices considerably. In addition, many attractions and golf courses have lower summer rates, and even some restaurants have special, lower-priced summer menus.

CLIMATE

The following chart lists average daily maximum and minimum temperatures in South Florida.

➤ FORECASTS: **Weather Channel Connection** (☎ 900/932–8437), 95¢ per minute from a Touch-Tone phone.

KEY WEST (THE KEYS)

Jan.	76F	24C	May	85F	29C	Sept.	90F	32C
	65	18		74	23		77	25
Feb.	76F	24C	June	88F	31C	Oct.	83F	28C
	67	19		77	25		76	24
Mar.	79F	26C	July	90F	32C	Nov.	79F	26C
	68	20		79	26		70	21
Apr.	81F	27C	Aug.	90F	32C	Dec.	76F	24C
	72	22		79	26		67	19

MIAMI

Jan.	74F	23C	May	83F	28C	Sept.	86F	30C
	63	17		72	22		76	24
Feb.	76F	24C	June	85F	29C	Oct.	83F	28C
	63	17		76	24		72	22
Mar.	77F	25C	July	88F	31C	Nov.	79F	26C
	65	18		76	24		67	19
Apr.	79F	26C	Aug.	88F	31C	Dec.	76F	26C
	68	20		77	25		63	17

THE GOLD GUIDE / SMART TRAVEL TIPS

1 Destination: Miami & the Keys

THE OTHER SIDE OF PARADISE

PERHAPS NO AREA in the United States is more misunderstood than South Florida. To the visitor, it may appear to be a seamless metropolis. From South Dade to North Palm Beach, communities bump into one another in a long strip wedged between the ocean and the Everglades. It's often hard to tell towns apart, unless you're in Boca Raton, where most of the buildings are pink. (My daughter once thought it was the corporate headquarters for Pepto-Bismol.) But behind this homogenous facade lie striking dichotomies. There are rich and poor, natural and overdeveloped, and amid it all, South Florida is at once paradise and paradox.

Renowned for its sandy beaches and sunny climate, South Florida is also criticized for its unbridled growth, which threatens the fragile environment that is one of its greatest attractions. Business leaders and top names in entertainment and sports have homes (or second homes) here, drawn by world-class dining, nightlife, and golf and other recreation opportunities. But this very chicness also draws scam artists, who give the region a reputation as the "boiler room capital of the nation."

South Florida seems to have more than its share of waterside mansions, fast cars and boats, and designer drugs—often verging on wretched excess. But the region also attracts plenty of newcomers with some of the most affordable housing in the nation (and no state income tax). The quality of life is outstanding, and yet residents complain that it's hard to call South Florida home; recent development has yielded mostly cookie-cutter subdivisions and very few real neighborhoods.

Despite its shortcomings (and we haven't even mentioned hurricanes), the area continues to grow and prosper, attracting a United Nations of immigrants from Latin America and elsewhere, moneyed investors from Europe, high-tech entrepreneurs from across the United States, and retirees from everywhere. The area hums with the positives and negatives that result from this vibrant melting pot, and it works hard to polish its image and fix its problems. After several high-profile crimes against travelers many years ago, both the police and the tourism industry stepped up programs to ensure visitor safety, and they seem to be paying off. Developers no longer get their plans rubber-stamped, and regional planners are now taking a hard look at the environmental impact of new development.

There will always be plenty to criticize. Two new professional sports arenas are being built, complete with skyboxes and luxury suites, while many children attend school in portable classrooms. The Miami political scene is as zoolike as any Central Florida animal theme park. But there's also plenty to praise. Despite the vastly different characters of many South Florida communities, they do come together in time of need, as when Hurricane Andrew devastated much of South Dade in 1992, and in time of joy, as when the Marlins won the 1997 World Series.

And so Miami and the Keys remain one of the most popular U.S. vacation destinations, largely because there's always something going on. A friend who moved from Fort Lauderdale to North Carolina complained: "It's boring here. Mike Wallace never comes to Raleigh to do an investigative story. But it seems he's always in South Florida." Paradise may have its flaws, but most are the result of the change, growth, and interplay of cultures that make South Florida such a vibrant place.

–Alan Macher

NEW AND NOTEWORTHY

Over the last decade Miami has seen the opening of many hot new celebrity restaurants and renovated Deco hotels that each add volume to SoBe's considerable buzz. The buzz becomes a roar with the opening in late 1998 of the **Loews Miami Beach Hotel,** the area's first major new beachfront luxury hotel in 30 years. Built at a cost of $135 million, the 17-story gem boasts a 1:1 correspondence of rooms to beach: 800 rooms and 800 ft of oceanfront.

Inland, shopping areas continue to grow. In South Miami, the **Shoppes at Sunset Place,** opening in late 1998, is slated to be larger than any competition for Coconut Grove's CocoWalk. Also to the west, the 374-acre **Dolphin Mall,** due in 1999, should be one of the largest outlet centers in Florida. Go west, young mall.

The trend in Fort Lauderdale, as elsewhere, is to combine retail, dining, and movies in one location, as at the long-awaited **Las Olas Riverfront** complex downtown and at that suburban shopping mecca known as the **Sawgrass Mills Mall,** which now boasts an entertainment center. Las Olas Riverfront gives Fort Lauderdale its first downtown cineplex, a 23-screen giant, plus a host of upscale shops and trendy restaurants. Farther north, West Palm Beach is planning its own new downtown entertainment, retail, and dining complex—**CityPlace**—scheduled to open by 2000.

Islamorada, especially around Mile Marker 81, is the hot new place to see and be seen in the Keys, with new galleries and restaurants spicing things up. The owners of the tony Moorings resort opened a splashy new bayfront restaurant, **Morada Bay,** with food as imaginative as the decor. In keeping with Islamorada's billing as the "sportfishing capital of the world," Missouri-based Bass Pro reopened **World Wide Sportsman** as a new two-level retail center and attraction; it includes the Zane Grey Lounge, adorned with books and photos of the author/angler, and the *Pilar,* a fishing boat once owned by Ernest Hemingway. In Florida City a new **aquarium** and National Geographic–sponsored IMAX theater should be presenting films on Everglades and Biscayne national parks by the end of the century.

With high profile names like Jimmy Johnson, Pat Riley, and Jim Leyland pacing the sidelines, South Florida sports fans expect big things from their hometown teams. And sometimes they are even rewarded. Though the **Florida Marlins** won the 1997 World Series, today there's little joy in Mudville. The team was promptly dismantled amid ownership changes and a call for a new all-weather stadium. Meanwhile, other teams play musical beach chairs. Hockey's **Florida Panthers** move from Miami to the new $200 million Broward Arena in 1999. The 18,000-seat center is located in Sunrise, west of Fort Lauderdale. Basketball's **Miami Heat** plan to move to a new 20,000-seat arena by 2000. Located on the waterfront adjacent to Bayside Marketplace, the facility is expected to help revitalize Miami's downtown. The new $28 million **Roger Dean Stadium,** a spring-training facility for the St. Louis Cardinals and Montreal Expos in Jupiter, is small potatoes by Florida standards.

Miami is set to host pro football's biggest 1999 extravaganza—**Super Bowl XXXIII**—on January 31 at Pro Player Stadium. That autumn, Gulfstream Park in Hallandale will counter with Thoroughbred racing's biggest one-day program, the **Breeders Cup,** which attracts the world's top horses.

WHAT'S WHERE

The Everglades

"There are no other Everglades in the world," said Marjory Stoneman Douglas in her book *The Everglades: River of Grass.* The noted environmentalist who championed the cause of the Everglades, the 50-mi-wide stream that flows slowly through South Florida grasslands, died in 1998 at the age of 108, with much of her effort yet to be completed. As urban growth continues inland, the Everglades' future will be determined in coming decades. Meanwhile, hundreds of thousands of people visit Everglades National Park each year to see its spectacular beauty. Among its amazing flora and fauna are the manatee, the endangered Florida panther, more than 300 species of birds, and 1,000 kinds of flowering plants. Biscayne National Park, nearby, is the largest national park in the continental United States with living coral reefs.

The Florida Keys

This slender necklace of islands off the southern tip of Florida is strung together by 42 bridges along a 110-mi-long highway. From the underwater splendor of John Pennekamp Coral Reef State Park in the Upper Keys—called one of the world's most traveled-to dive and snorkel destinations—to the spectacular fireball sunsets at Mallory Square docks in Key West, visitors can be at one with nature in the Keys. The pace is slower, the style more casual, and the weather balmy and sub-tropical. Somehow, Key West manages to maintain its Old Florida charm, despite a wave of new upscale shops, franchise restaurants, and a steady stream of cruise ship passengers. Jimmy Buffet has moved to Palm Beach, but Margaritaville is still in Key West.

Fort Lauderdale and Broward County

Fort Lauderdale's 10-year effort to shed its image as a college spring break party town is finally paying off. Today, fol-lowing a multimillion dollar construction program, this city north of Miami has been transformed into an upscale desti-nation with trendy shops and restaurants and a pedestrian-friendly beachfront. The hub of activity is along the 2-mi Las Olas corridor, anchored on the west by an arts district and on the east by a beach prom-enade. Instead of shutting down at 5, Las Olas Boulevard now has so many new side-walk cafés, coffee shops, jazz clubs, movies, and bookstores that evening parking has become a problem.

Miami and Miami Beach

In the 1980s a stylized television cop show called *Miami Vice* brought notoriety to this southernmost of big Florida cities; South Beach put it on the map again in the 1990s with its revamping of the Art Deco District. At night, the trendy nightclub/restaurant strip along Ocean Drive bus-tles with a young crowd on the street, bumper-to-bumper cars, and jammed side-walk cafés. The stomping ground for celebrities such as Madonna and Sylvester Stallone, the city has gone from an enclave of retired northeasterners to an interna-tional crossroads with a Latin beat. Miami's spice is in its neighborhoods. Don't miss Coconut Grove, South Florida mainland's oldest settlement. It's chic and casual, full of bistros, cafés, and galleries. The crowded, noisy streets of Little Havana pulsate to the sounds of salsa, in contrast to the quiet, tree- and mansion-lined streets of stately Coral Gables.

Palm Beach and the Treasure Coast

For 100 years high society has made head-lines in Palm Beach. Once a playground for the rich and famous (and infamous), Palm Beach County now has attractions for everyone. To keep up with the grow-ing number of residents and visitors, the region is expanding its park system, re-nourishing its beaches, and improving roadways. From Boca Raton's Mizner Park north to Delray Beach's Atlantic Av-enue and West Palm Beach's CityPlace (now on the drawing boards), the focus is on bringing people back to downtown. As for roads less traveled, the coast north of Palm Beach County, called the Treasure Coast, is also worth exploring. Compris-ing Martin, St. Lucie, and Indian River counties, it's dotted with nature preserves, fishing villages, and towns with active cultural scenes.

PLEASURES AND PASTIMES

Beaches

Warm weather and lots of sand make beaching a major South Florida activity. But if life's a beach, how do you find the one that suits you? Beaches in South Florida, from the Keys north to Jupiter, seem to have a personality all their own. At South Beach in Miami, young, in-shape model types often arrive on their in-line skates. Farther north along Miami Beach, you'll find families and foreign visitors. Bill Baggs Cape Florida State Recreation Area, on Key Biscayne, was rated one of the na-tion's top 20 beaches in 1998 by Univer-sity of Maryland Professor Stephen Leatherman, also known as Dr. Beach. The wonderfully breezy park is also the site of the historic Cape Florida Lighthouse.

Since shedding its rowdy spring break image, Fort Lauderdale Beach has been re-claimed by families and many foreign vis-itors. With volleyball and basketball courts and a wide promenade for in-line skaters, it's also known as Workout Beach. Fam-ilies from as far south as Miami-Dade County visit Boca Raton's Red Reef Park beach for snorkeling. It's an ideal place to introduce children to snorkeling because the reef is so close to shore; the deepest water around the reef is 8 to 10 ft. If it's location you want, Palm Beach Munici-pal Beach is but a short walk from the swank shops of Worth Avenue. Still farther north in Jupiter, Blowing Rocks Preserve attracts nature lovers. At high tide, you can watch the water rush through blowholes in the rock formations.

Returning south to the Florida Keys, coral reefs and prevailing currents prevent sand from building up. The few Keys beaches are small, narrow, and generally have little or no sandy bottom. An exception is the beach at Bahia Honda State Park, the largest natural sand beach in the Keys. It's a favorite spot for campers.

Although the state owns all beaches below the high-tide line, even in front of hotels and private resorts, gaining access to them can be a problem along much of Florida's coastline. You must pay to enter and/or park at most state, county, and local beachfront parks. Where hotels dominate the beach frontage, public parking may be limited or nonexistent.

Canoeing

The Everglades has areas suitable for flatwater wilderness canoeing that are comparable to spots in the Boundary Waters region of Minnesota. Another popular canoeing river is the Loxahatchee in north Palm Beach County. The river flows through Jonathan Dickinson State Park, where canoe rentals are available. The Florida Department of Environmental Protection provides maps and brochures on 1,550 mi of canoe trails in various parts of the state. Also contact individual city and county park and recreation departments or local chambers of commerce for information on canoe trails. The best time to canoe in Florida is winter—the dry season—when you're less likely to get caught in a torrential downpour or become a snack for mosquitoes.

Dining

South Florida has launched some bigleague culinary stars. Restaurateurs like Fort Lauderdale's Mark Militello are nationally acclaimed, while others who got their start here—such as Douglas Rodriguez, formerly of Yuca when it was in Coral Gables—have gone on to glory in Manhattan.

South Florida serves up a diverse assortment of ethnic food. Latin American restaurants offer the distinctive national fare of Argentina, Brazil, Colombia, Cuba, El Salvador, Mexico, Nicaragua, and Puerto Rico, and it's also easy to find island specialties born of the Bahamas, Haiti, and Jamaica. A new fusion of tropical, Continental, and nouvelle cuisine—some call it Floribbean—has gained widespread popularity. It draws on exotic fruits, spices, and fresh seafood. Also in abundance, Asian cuisine no longer means just Chinese. Indian, Japanese, Pakistani, Thai, and Vietnamese specialties are now available. Continental cuisine (French, German, Italian, Spanish, and Swiss) is also well represented.

The region also has a high concentration of good waterfront restaurants—popular with both locals and visitors. Most menus are built around fresh seafood from local waters. They range from elegant, very pricy dining spots to casual, moderate-priced digs anchored next to fishing docks.

Every South Florida restaurant claims to make the best key lime pie. Pastry chefs and restaurant managers take the matter very seriously—they discuss the problems of getting good lime juice and maintaining top quality every day. Joe's Stone Crab in Miami Beach, for example, bakes nearly 30,000 pies annually, and key lime pie has been a staple on its menu for nearly all of the restaurant's 85 years. Traditional key lime pie is yellow, not green, with an old-fashioned graham cracker crust and meringue top. The filling should be tart and chilled but not frozen. Some restaurants make their pie with a pastry crust; most substitute whipped cream for the more temperamental meringue. Each pie will be a little different. Try several. It is, after all, a vacation.

Fishing

Opportunities for saltwater fishing abound from the Keys all the way up the southeast Florida coast. Many seaside communities have municipal fishing piers that charge a modest admission to anglers (and usually a lower rate to spectators). These piers generally have a bait-and-tackle shop. It's also easy to find a boat-charter service that will take you out into deep water. Some of the best are in Islamorada, Marathon, and Key West in the Florida Keys, but popular charter fleets are also located at Fort Lauderdale's Bahia Mar docks and at the Hillsboro Inlet in north Broward County. Depending on your taste, budget, and needs, you can charter anything from an old wooden craft to a luxurious waterborne palace with state-of-the-art amenities.

For freshwater anglers, there's 448,000-acre Lake Okeechobee, the third-largest natural lake in the United States—home to bass, bluegill, speckled perch, and succulent catfish (which the locals call "sharpies"). In addition, parts of the Everglades in Palm Beach, Broward, and Miami-Dade counties are famed as the "river of bass." The best fishing here is found in the "flats," where canals turn into shallow, vegetation-filled marshes, a haven for bass. Many fishing camps on the fringes of the Everglades have guides for hire.

Golf

Except in the heart of the Everglades, you'll never be far from one of South Florida's golf courses. Palm Beach County, the state's leading golf locale, has 150 courses. Many of the best courses allow visitors to play without being members or hotel guests.

During the winter season, you should reserve tee times in advance. Ask about golf reservations when you make your lodging reservations.

Natural Areas

Although Florida is the fourth-most-populous state in the nation, more than 10 million acres of public and private recreation facilities are set aside in national forests, parks, monuments, reserves, and seashores; state forests and parks; county parks; and nature preserves owned and managed by private conservation groups. An active greenways development plan seeks to protect wildlife habitat as much as foster recreation.

On holidays and weekends crowds flock to the most popular parks—some on islands that are accessible only by boat. Come early or risk being turned away. Winter brings flocks of northern migratory birds along with migrating humans. Many resident species breed in the warm summer months, but others (such as the wood stork) time their breeding cycle to the winter dry season. Although mosquitoes are voracious and daily afternoon thundershowers add to the humidity in summer, it's during the early part of this season

that sea turtles come ashore to lay their eggs and you're most likely to see frigate birds and other tropical species.

Pari-Mutuel Sports

South Florida has a variety of venues for sports on which you can lawfully bet. These include greyhound tracks, tracks for harness and Thoroughbred racing, and jai alai frontons.

Scuba Diving and Snorkeling

South Florida, and especially the Keys, attracts most of the state's divers and snorkelers. A multitude of dive shops schedule drift-, reef-, and wreck-diving trips all along the coast. The low-tech pleasures of snorkeling can be enjoyed throughout the Keys and elsewhere where shallow reefs hug the shore.

Shopping

ANTIQUES➤ Antiques lovers should explore U.S. 1 north of Dania Beach Boulevard in Dania, with its more than 150 shops; Southwest 28th Lane and Unity Boulevard in Miami, near the Coconut Grove Metrorail station; and the cluster of stores on South Dixie Highway in West Palm Beach.

CITRUS FRUIT➤ Fresh citrus is available most of the year, except in summer. Two kinds of citrus grow in Florida: the sweeter and more expensive Indian River fruit, from a thin ribbon of groves along the east coast, and the less costly fruit from the interior, south and west of Lake Okeechobee. A visit to a local grove can be a pleasant experience; many in western Broward and Palm Beach counties offer tours and educational programs.

Citrus is sold in ¼, ½, ¾, and full bushels. Many shippers offer special gift packages with several varieties of fruit, jellies, and other food items. Some prices include U.S. postage; others may not. Shipping may exceed the cost of the fruit. If you have a choice of citrus packaged in boxes or bags, take the boxes. They are easier to label and harder to squash.

NATIVE AMERICAN CRAFTS➤ Native American crafts are abundant in South Florida, where you'll find billowing dresses and shirts hand-sewn in striking colors and designs, handcrafted dolls, and beaded belts.

SEASHELLS➤ Shell shops, selling mostly kitschy items, abound throughout South

Florida. The coral and other shells sold in the Florida Keys have been imported for sale because of restrictions on harvesting these materials.

FODOR'S CHOICE

Beaches

★ **Bahia Honda State Park, Bahia Honda Key.** Bahia Honda translates from Spanish as "deep bay," a good description of the waters surrounding this park with a natural sandy beach, unusual in the Keys. The beach extends on both gulf and ocean sides, and activities in the park abound, from hawk-watching to hiking. It's also a popular spot for weddings.

★ **Bill Baggs Cape Florida State Recreation Area, Key Biscayne.** Consistently voted one of South Florida's best beaches, this 414-acre park is constantly buffeted by warm breezes and boasts a plethora of facilities, a historic lighthouse, and great views of sunsets and the Miami skyline.

★ **Fort Lauderdale Beach.** The area along Route A1A between Las Olas and Sunrise boulevards is a hot spot again, thanks to a pedestrian-friendly promenade and the absence of spring breakers. It's mostly frequented by families and foreign visitors.

★ **Spanish River Park, Boca Raton.** The newly renourished beach is connected to a large park by pedestrian tunnels under Route A1A. Filled with native vegetation, the park has nature trails and plenty of picnic tables and grills.

Lodging

★ **The Breakers, Palm Beach.** The building, originally built over a century ago to resemble an opulent Italian Renaissance palace, is remarkable, as is the resort's ability to balance old-world luxury with modern conveniences. $$$$

★ **Delano Hotel, Miami Beach.** An air of surrealism hangs about this much talked-about SoBe hotel, *the* hot spot for celebrities and other well-to-do visitors. $$$$

★ **Little Palm Island.** On its own palm-fringed island 3 mi off the shores of Little Torch Key, this dazzling resort of thatch-roof villas on stilts provides a se-cluded, one-of-a-kind experience you could only have in the Keys. $$$-$$$$

★ **La Casa Del Mar, Fort Lauderdale.** Bed-and-breakfasts are rare in Broward County, but this one located near the beach is a gem. $$$

Dining

★ **Cafe des Artistes, Key West.** Chef Andrew Berman's brilliant tropical version of French cuisine is served in a series of intimate dining rooms filled with art and an upstairs outdoor patio. $$$-$$$$

★ **Norman's, Coral Gables.** Chef Norman Van Aken turns out artful masterpieces of New World cuisine, combining bold tastes from Latin, American, Caribbean, and Asian traditions. $$-$$$$

★ **Mark's Las Olas, Fort Lauderdale.** Chef/owner Mark Militello offers dazzling Florida-style creations, adding flavors from the Mediterranean, Caribbean, and Southwest. $$-$$$

★ **Armadillo Cafe, Davie.** The atmosphere is as creative and fun as the award-winning southwestern-style South Florida seafood. $$

★ **Tom's Place, Boca Raton.** Tom Wright serves up legendary barbecue ribs, friendly service, and moderate prices at this local landmark. $

Views

★ **Everglades National Park from the tower on Shark Valley Loop.** This 50-ft observation tower yields a splendid panorama of the wide River of Grass as it sweeps southward toward the Gulf of Mexico.

★ **Ocean Drive in the Art Deco District, Miami Beach.** Feast your eyes on brilliantly restored vintage Art Deco hotels at every turn. Since their restoration, this palm-lined beachfront has been hopping 24 hours a day.

★ **Seven Mile Bridge, Marathon.** One of the world's longest, this Middle Keys bridge lifts you above the shimmering waters of ocean and bay, providing a spectacular blend of color and light. The only time it's closed to vehicles and open to pedestrians is during the Seven Mile Bridge Run in April.

★ **Sunset scene at Mallory Square, Key West.** Here sunset draws street performers, vendors, and thousands of onlookers to Mallory Dock and the eponymous square nearby.

Historic Sites and Museums

★ **Hemingway House, Key West.** The home where Ernest Hemingway wrote several of his famous novels remains Key West's most popular attraction.

★ **Morikami Museum and Japanese Gardens, Delray Beach.** The leading U.S. center for Japanese and American cultural exchange is housed in a model of a Japanese imperial villa. On display is a permanent exhibition on the area's Yamato Colony, a turn-of-the-century settlement of immigrant Japanese farmers.

★ **Museum of Discovery and Science, Fort Lauderdale.** Providing hands-on experiences, this playground for kids (and adults) contains fun, interactive exhibits on ecology, health, and other sciences.

★ **Vizcaya Museum and Gardens, Coconut Grove.** The estate of industrialist James Deering, overlooking Biscayne Bay, has an Italian Renaissance–style villa containing Renaissance, Baroque, Rococo, and Neoclassical art and furniture.

FESTIVALS AND SEASONAL EVENTS

WINTER

DEC.➤ Lighted boat parades are common throughout South Florida during the holiday season. The biggest is the **Winterfest Boat Parade** on the Intracoastal Waterway, Fort Lauderdale (☎ 954/767–0686). In Key West, the Heritage House Museum holds a free **Christmas House Tour** late in the month (☎ 305/296–3573).

JAN.➤ Early in the month, **Polo Season** opens at the Palm Beach Polo and Country Club (☎ 561/793–1440). Mid-month, **Art Deco Weekend** spotlights Miami Beach's historic district with an Art Deco street fair, a 1930s-style Moon Over Miami Ball, live entertainment, and tours of the district (☎ 305/672–2014). **Martin Luther King Jr. Festivals** are celebrated throughout South Florida, including Hollywood (☎ 954/921–3404). **Taste of the Grove Food and Music Festival** is a popular fundraiser put on in Coconut Grove's Peacock Park by area restaurants (☎ 305/444–7270). The **South Florida Folk Festival** features national acts at Easterlin Park in Fort Lauderdale (☎ 954/384–2197). In late January, **Miami Rivers Blues Festival** takes place on the south bank of the river next to Tobacco Road (☎ 305/374–1198).

FEB.➤ The **Coconut Grove Art Festival,** mid-month, is the state's largest, drawing nearly a million folks to the four-day event (☎ 305/447–0401). The **Miami Film Festival,** sponsored by the Film Society of America, is 10 days of international, domestic, and local films (☎ 305/377–3456). **Seminole Tribal Festival** draws participants from many tribes to Hollywood for a weekend of competitions and traditional dance and music (☎ 954/966–6300).

FEB.–MAR.➤ The **Winter Equestrian Festival,** at the Palm Beach Polo and Country Club in West Palm Beach, includes more than 1,000 horses and three grand-prix equestrian events (☎ 561/798–7000).

SPRING

MAR.➤ **Calle Ocho's street festival**—a celebration of Cuban life and culture—has become Miami's biggest (☎ 305/644–8888). The **Las Olas Art Festival** has been a fixture in downtown Fort Lauderdale for more than 25 years (☎ 954/525–5500). Taste some of the best food from Upper Keys restaurants at the **Taste of the Keys Bird Bash,** a fund-raiser for the Florida Keys Wild Bird Rehabilitation Center, in Key Largo (☎ 305/453–9643).

APR.➤ The **Delray Affair,** in early April, is the biggest event in the area and features arts, crafts, and food (☎ 561/278–0424). Near the end of the month, the **River Cities Festival,** a three-day event in Miami Springs and Hialeah, focuses attention on the Miami River and the need to keep it clean (☎ 305/887–1515).

LATE APR.–EARLY MAY➤ The 10-day **Conch Republic Celebration** honors the founding fathers of the Conch Republic, "the small island nation of Key West" (☎ 305/296–8803).

MAY➤ The **Shell Air & Sea Show** draws more than 2 million to the Fort Lauderdale beachfront for a weekend of performances by big names in aviation, such as the navy's Blue Angels and the air force's Thunderbirds (☎ 954/467–3555). **Sunfest,** in West Palm Beach, includes a wide variety of cultural and sporting events the first weekend in May (☎ 561/659–5980 or 800/833–5733). In mid-May, the **Arabian Nights Festival,** in Opa-locka, is a mix of contemporary and fantasy-inspired entertainment (☎ 305/758–4166).

SUMMER

JUNE➤ The **Miami-Bahamas Goombay Festival,** in Miami's Coconut Grove, celebrates the city's Bahamian heritage the first weekend of the month (☎ 305/443–7928 or 305/372–9966).

JULY➤ The **Fourth of July Festival,** on the Florida Atlantic University grounds in Boca Raton, features a concert by the

Boca Pops, lots of tailgate parties, and, of course, fireworks (☎ 561/393–7806). For more than 20 years, the **Roots Cultural Festival,** at Pompey Park in Delray Beach, has celebrated black pride and heritage (☎ 561/276–2099).

AUTUMN

OCT.➤ The **Fort Lauderdale International Boat Show,** the world's largest show based on exhibit size, displays boats of every size, price, and description at the Bahia Mar marina and four other venues (☎ 954/764–7642). The **Fort Lauderdale International Film Festival** showcases independent cinema from around the world (☎ 954/563–0500). **Fantasy Fest,** in Key West, is a no-holds-barred Halloween costume party, parade, and town fair (☎ 305/296–1817).

NOV.➤ The **Miami Book Fair International,** the largest book fair in the United States, is held on the Wolfson campus of Miami-Dade Community College (☎ 305/237–3258).

EARLY NOV.–LATE FEB.➤ The **Orange Bowl** and **Junior Orange Bowl Festival,** in the Miami area, are best known for the King Orange Jamboree Parade and the Orange Bowl Football Classic but also include more than 20 youth-oriented events (☎ 305/371–3351).

2 Miami and Miami Beach

Miami is arguably the most exotic city that Americans can visit without a passport. On a typical evening in South Beach, you'll witness the energy and passion of Rio, Monte Carlo, Havana, and Hemingway's Paris. Other neighborhoods also bring the world into clearer focus through diverse architecture, dining, and customs, sparking a renaissance for Miami and its sultry sister, Miami Beach, that's reminiscent of the cities' glory days in the 1920s.

WHAT MAKES MIAMI DIFFERENT from the rest of the United States is quickly apparent from the air. With the vast Everglades at the west-

By Herb Hiller

Updated by
Gary
McKechnie

ern edge and the Atlantic to the east, Miami clings to a ribbon of drained land near the southeastern tip of the country. Still vulnerable to mosquitoes, periodic flooding, and potential devastation by hurricanes, Miami 100 years after its founding is still the wrong place for a city, but it's the right place for an international crossroads. And that's exactly what this hot, humid melting pot has become.

Long before Spain's gold-laden treasure ships passed through the Gulf Stream offshore, the Tequesta Indians who lived here had begun to trade with mainland neighbors to the north and island brethren to the south. Repeating this pattern, more than 150 U.S. and multinational companies now locate their Latin American headquarters in Greater Miami, and more than 40% of all U.S. exports to South America, Central America, and the Caribbean travel through the Miami Customs District. The city has unparalleled airline connections to the western hemisphere, and its port welcomes more than 3 million cruise passengers a year while serving double duty as Florida's largest cargo port. Greater Miami gets down to business with more than 40 foreign bank agencies, 11 Edge Act banks, 23 foreign trade offices, 31 binational chambers of commerce, and 53 foreign consulates. No western hemisphere city is so universally simpatico.

First-time visitors are always struck by the billboards in Spanish. Initially these seem an affectation, an attempt to promote Miami's exotic international image. But the language and the Latin influence are everywhere. Only after you hear Spanish spoken all around you, or after a computerized elevator announces the floor stops as *primer piso* and *segundo piso,* do you realize that the city *Newsweek* called "America's Casablanca" is really the capital of Latin America. Though Cubans make up most of this Spanish-speaking population, there are also significant communities from Colombia, El Salvador, Nicaragua, Panama, Puerto Rico, and Venezuela. The Spanish place-names George Merrick affixed to the streets in Coral Gables in the 1920s—Alhambra, Alcazar, Salzedo—may have been romantic pretense, but today's renamed Avenida Gen. Maximo Gomez and Carlos Arboleya Way are earnest celebrations of a contemporary city's heroes—as is Little Havana's Ronald Reagan Boulevard (renamed after the Gipper had lunch there in 1983). Likewise, balladeers Sinatra and Streisand have given way in the hearts of Miamians to Iglesias and Estefan.

In addition to the dominant Spanish-speaking population, 6.5% of metropolitan Miami's 2 million residents represent other nationalities, including Haitians, Brazilians, Chinese, Germans, Greeks, Iranians, Israelis, Italians, Jamaicans, Lebanese, Malaysians, Russians, and Swedes—all speaking a veritable babel of tongues. Most either know or are trying to learn English, and communication is eased by speaking slowly and distinctly.

Established Miami has warmed up to its newcomers—a big step forward. Not too long ago metropolitan government enacted an ordinance forbidding essential public information from appearing in Spanish, but in 1993 that restrictive affront was rescinded, and resisters have adjusted or moved north. Yesterday's immigrants have become today's citizens, and the nation's most international city now offers a style expressed in its many languages, its world-beat music, and its wealth of exotic restaurants.

Miami has changed fast. Old Miami Beach has been transformed from a run-down geriatric center to South Beach, the Deco darling of the world. Since 1980 the average age of Miami Beach residents has dropped from 66 to 44, and summer brings an influx of young visitors. Two of every three are male, and three of every four are single. Lincoln Road, once the 5th Avenue of the South and only recently an embarrassing derelict row, has been stunningly brought back to life. On weekends it rivals the pedestrian malls of Cambridge, Lyons, and Munich for its crowds and festivity. Now that the revival is in full swing, it's hard to imagine that this area ever was—or ever will be again—depressed. Next on the revitalization calendar are North Beach and the southern neighborhoods of South Beach, whose derelict buildings are a flashback to the prerenaissance days of the 1980s. Miami Beach is now largely a real-world Magic Kingdom, proving it's possible and relatively inexpensive to build community by preserving distinctive architecture rather than by "imagineering" pseudo worlds.

More changes are in store in this city that seems fueled by caffeine (stop by the window serving station of any Cuban café for a *tinto*, the city's high-test coffee). Not surprisingly, much of the change is taking place in areas hardest hit by Hurricane Andrew in 1992, although nature and contractors have largely restored, and in many cases improved, the natural and man-made beauty of the area. In the Redlands district, the Redlands Conservancy is introducing bicycle trails and B&Bs as a way of preserving South Dade County's agricultural heritage. Coral-rock walls and avocado groves may prove as distinctive in their own way as Art Deco hotels. Additional bike-friendly projects include a planned 200-mi network of trails linking Biscayne and Everglades national parks. For those wanting a quicker pace, Homestead has become a state-of-the-art hub for car racing (☞ Chapter 4).

Miami also has a dark side, evidenced by a high level of poverty, traffic, significant violent and property crimes, and an inability to keep criminals behind bars. Yet some widely publicized crimes against tourists led to stepped-up visitor-safety programs. Highway direction signs with red sunburst logos are installed at ¼-mi intervals on major roads and lead directly to such tourist hot spots as Coconut Grove, Coral Gables, South Beach, and the Port of Miami. Patrol cars bearing the sunburst logo are driven by TOP Cops (Tourist Oriented Police), who cruise heavily touristed areas and add a sense of safety. Identification making rental cars conspicuous to would-be criminals has been removed, and multilingual pamphlets on avoiding crime are widely distributed. The precautions have had a positive impact: From 1992 to 1996 the number of tourist robberies in Greater Miami decreased 80.3%. Despite all the high-crime hype, Miami still has heated allure with a climate, beaches, and international sophistication that few places can match.

Though winter *is* the best time to visit, if money is an issue, come in the off-season—after Easter and before October. You'll find plenty to do, and room rates are lowered considerably. Summer brings many European and Latin American vacationers, who find Miami congenial despite the heat, humidity, and intense afternoon thunderstorms.

Contrary to Orlando's claim to be Hollywood East, it's Miami that's set the stage for the Florida film industry. In recent years Arnold Schwarzenegger and Jamie Lee Curtis filmed *True Lies* here, Al Pacino and Johnny Depp dropped by to shoot scenes for *Donnie Brasco,* Jim Carrey rose to stardom through the Miami-based *Ace Ventura: Pet Detective,* and Robin Williams and Nathan Lane used two Deco buildings on Ocean Drive as their nightclub in *The Birdcage.* All in all, it's a far cry from when Esther Williams used to perform water ballet in Coral Gables's Venetian Pool. Add to this mix daily fashion-magazine and TV shoots, and you'll see that Miami is made for the media.

It may be this synergy that prompted a slew of international celebrities to move or purchase homes here: Madonna, Whitney Houston, and Michael Caine, for instance. Three major-league sports franchises call Miami home, along with the Doral-Ryder Open Tournament, the Lipton Championships, and the culture-contributing Miami City Ballet and Florida Grand Opera. On the verge of its centennial year and barely two years after Hurricane Andrew roared through, Miami played host to both the Summit of the Americas and the Super Bowl and welcomes Super Bowl competitors again in 1999. Nearly 10 million tourists arrive annually to see what's shaking in the newly renamed Miami-Dade County, discovering a multicultural metropolis that works and plays with vigor and that invites the world to celebrate its diversity.

Pleasures and Pastimes

Beaches

Greater Miami has numerous free beaches to fit every style. A sandy, 300-ft-wide beach with several distinct sections extends for 10 mi from the foot of Miami Beach north to Haulover Beach Park. Amazingly, it's all man-made. Seriously eroded during the mid-1970s, the beach was restored in a $51.5 million project between 1977 and 1981 and remains an ongoing project for environmental engineers, who spiff up the sands every few years. Between 23rd and 44th streets, Miami Beach built boardwalks and protective walkways atop a dune landscaped with sea oats, sea grape, and other native plants whose roots keep the sand from blowing away. Key Biscayne adds more great strands to Miami's collection. Even if the Deco District didn't exist, the area's beaches would be enough to satisfy tourists.

Boating

It's not uncommon for traffic to jam at boat ramps, especially on weekend mornings, but the waters are worth the wait. If you have the opportunity to sail, do so. Blue skies, calm seas, and a view of the city skyline make for a pleasurable outing—especially at twilight, when the fabled "moon over Miami" casts a soft glow on the water. Key Biscayne's calm waves and strong breezes are perfect for sailing and windsurfing, and though Dinner Key and the Coconut Grove waterfront remain the center of sailing in Greater Miami, sailboat moorings and rentals are located along other parts of the bay and up the Miami River.

Miami's idle rich prefer attacking the water in sleek and fast cigarette boats, but there's plenty of less powerful powerboating to enjoy as well. Greater Miami has numerous marinas, and dockmasters can provide information on any marine services you may need. Ask for *Teall's Tides and Guides, Miami-Dade County,* and other nautical publications.

Dining

Miami cuisine is what mouths were made for. The city serves up a veritable United Nations of dining experiences, including dishes native to Spain, Cuba, and Nicaragua as well as China, India, Thailand, Vietnam, and other Asian cultures. Chefs from the tropics combine fresh, natural foods—especially seafood—with classic island-style dishes, creating a new American cuisine that is sometimes called *Floribbean.*

Nightlife

Greater Miami's heaviest concentration of nightspots is on South Beach along Ocean Drive, Washington Avenue, and Lincoln Road

Mall. Other nightlife centers on Little Havana, Coconut Grove, and on the fringes of downtown Miami.

Individual clubs offer jazz, reggae, salsa, various forms of rock, techno-pop, and Top 40 sounds on different nights of the week—most played at a body-thumping, ear-throbbing volume. Some clubs refuse entrance to anyone under 21, others to those under 25, so if that is a concern, call ahead. On South Beach, where the sounds of jazz and reggae spill into the streets, photographers and wafer-thin models frequent the lobby bars of small Art Deco hotels. Throughout Greater Miami bars and cocktail lounges in larger hotels operate nightly discos with live weekend entertainment. Many hotels extend their bars into open-air courtyards, where patrons dine and dance under the stars throughout the year. It's a good idea to ask in advance about cover charges; policies change frequently. And be warned: Even the most popular club can fall out of favor quickly. Ask your hotel's concierge, check Friday's *Miami Herald,* or grab a copy of *New Times,* an entertainment tabloid that includes listings of alternative clubs and live bands. With this and some insider info from locals, you should be able to tell what's hot and what's just a dying ember.

Spectator Sports

Greater Miami has franchises in basketball, football, and baseball. Despite an unfortunate string of Super Bowl losses, fans still turn out en masse for the Dolphins, as they do for basketball's Heat and the 1997 World Series champion Marlins. Miami also hosts top-rated events in boat racing, jai alai, and tennis. Generally you can find daily listings of local events in the sports section of the *Miami Herald,* whereas Friday's "Weekend" section carries more detailed schedules and coverage.

Activities of the annual Orange Bowl and Junior Orange Bowl Festival take place from early November well into the new year. Best known for its King Orange Jamboree Parade and the Federal Express/Orange Bowl Football Classic, the festival also includes two tennis tournaments. The Junior Orange Bowl Festival is the world's largest youth festival, with more than 20 events between November and January, including sports, cultural, and performing arts activities held throughout Miami-Dade County.

EXPLORING MIAMI AND MIAMI BEACH

Disney captured Miami's family trade, *Miami Vice* smacked the city upside the head with notoriety, the winds of Hurricane Andrew literally shook its foundation, and South Beach made it a global resort for the turn of the 21st century. Through this, the city went from an enclave of retired northeasterners to the ultimate joyride with a Latin beat. There's hardly a part of the city not caught up in change. Meanwhile, sightseeing—which used to be pretty much limited to picking fruit off citrus trees and watching alligator wrestling—has become a fun way to glimpse the city at work and at play.

Most visitors to the Greater Miami area don't realize that Miami and Miami Beach are separate cities. Miami, on the mainland, is South Florida's commercial hub. Miami Beach, on 17 islands in Biscayne Bay, is sometimes considered America's Riviera, luring refugees from winter with its warm sunshine; sandy beaches; graceful, shady palms; and ever-rocking nightlife. These same visitors might also fail to realize that there's more to Miami Beach than the bustle of South Beach and its Deco District. Indeed there are quieter areas to the north, with names like Sunny Isles, Surfside, Bal Harbour, and—you guessed it—North Beach.

Downtown has become the lively hub of the mainland city, now more accessible thanks to the Metromover extension (☞ Getting Around by Train *in* Miami and Miami Beach A to Z, *below*). Other major attractions include Coconut Grove, Little Havana, and the South Beach/Art Deco District, but since these areas are spread out beyond the reach of public transportation, you'll have to drive. Rent a convertible if you can. There's nothing quite like wearing cool shades and feeling the wind in your hair as you drive across one of the causeways en route to Miami Beach.

You're in luck: Finding your way around Greater Miami is easy if you know how the numbering system works—just as quantum mechanics is easy for physicists. Miami is laid out on a grid with four quadrants—northeast, northwest, southeast, and southwest—which meet at Miami Avenue and Flagler Street. Miami Avenue separates east from west, and Flagler Street separates north from south. Avenues and courts run north–south; streets, terraces, and ways run east–west. Roads run diagonally, northwest–southeast. But other districts—Miami Beach, Coral Gables, and Hialeah—may or may not follow this system, and along the curve of Biscayne Bay, the symmetrical grid may shift diagonally. It's best to buy a detailed map, stick to the major roads, and ask directions early and often. However, make sure you're in a safe neighborhood or public place when you seek guidance; cabbies and cops are good resources.

Numbers in the text correspond to numbers in the margin and on the Miami Beach; Downtown Miami; Miami, Coral Gables, Coconut Grove, and Key Biscayne; and South Dade maps.

Great Itineraries

IF YOU HAVE 3 DAYS

To recuperate from your journey, grab a beach towel and a bottle of suntan lotion, and head for Ocean Drive on South Beach to catch some rays while relaxing on the white sands. Afterward, take a guided or self-guided tour of the Art Deco District to see what all the fuss is about. Keep the evening free to socialize with the oh-so-trendy people who gather at Ocean Drive cafés. The following day cruise up Collins Avenue to some of the monolithic hotels, such as the Fontainebleau Hilton and Eden Roc; continue north to the swank shops of Bal Harbour; and head back for an evening of shopping, drinking, and outdoor dining at Lincoln Road Mall. On the third day wander around Calle Ocho in Little Havana, visit Vizcaya Museum and Gardens, and wrap up the evening a few blocks away in Coconut Grove, enjoying its partylike atmosphere and many nightspots.

IF YOU HAVE 5 DAYS

Follow the suggested three-day itinerary, and add a visit to the beaches of Virginia Key and Key Biscayne. From here you can depart on a diving trip or fishing excursion or learn to windsurf. On the final day head over to Coral Gables to take in the eye-popping display of 1920s Mediterranean Revival architecture in the city center and the majestic Biltmore Hotel; then take a dip in the fantastic, thematic Venetian Pool. That night indulge in an evening of fine dining at your choice of gourmet restaurants in Coral Gables.

IF YOU HAVE 7 DAYS

A week gives you just enough time to experience fully the multicultural, cosmopolitan, tropical mélange that is Greater Miami and its beaches. With two extra days see where it all began: Use the Miami

Metromover to zip around downtown Miami (if possible, on a tour with historian Dr. Paul George), take the afternoon to shop in the Miami International Arts and Design District, and in the evening check out the shops and clubs at Bayside Marketplace. The final day can be used to visit South Dade, site of Miami's Metrozoo and Monkey Jungle. Keep the evening free to revisit your favorite nightspots and have a drink with your new pals, Whitney and Madonna.

South Beach/Miami Beach

The hub of South Beach (SoBe, to the truly hip) is the 1-square-mi Art Deco District, fronted on the east by Ocean Drive and on the west by Alton Road. The story of South Beach has become the story of Miami. In the early 1980s South Beach's vintage hotels were badly run down, catering mostly to infirm retirees. But a group of visionaries led by Barbara Baer Capitman, a spirited New York transplant, saw this collection of buildings as an architectural treasure to be salvaged from a sea of mindless urban renewal. It was, and is, a peerless grouping of Art Deco architecture from the 1920s to 1950s, whose forms and decorative details are drawn from nature, the streamlined shapes of modern transportation and industrial machinery, and human extravagance.

Investors started fixing up the interiors of these hotels and repainting their exteriors with a vibrant pastel palette—a look made famous by *Miami Vice*. International bistro operators sensed the potential for a new café society. Fashion photographers and the media took note, and celebrities like singer Gloria Estefan; the late designer Gianni Versace, whose fashions captured the feel of the awakening city; and record executive Chris Blackwell bought a piece of the action.

As a result, South Beach now holds the distinction of being the nation's first 20th-century district on the National Register of Historic Places, with 800 significant buildings making the roll. But it hasn't all been smooth. Miami officials seem to lack the gene enabling them to appreciate residents who help the city. Barbara Capitman was well into her sixties when she stepped in front of bulldozers ready to tear down the Senator, a Deco hotel. Her reward for helping to save the Deco District and laying the groundwork for a multibillion-dollar tourist trade is a side street named in her honor.

More recently, SoBe hoteliers were similarly rewarded for successfully renovating old or abandoned buildings by having their taxes quadrupled—an attempt by the local government to make up for the lack of tax revenues generated in other areas of Dade (now Miami-Dade) County. Nevertheless, SoBe continues to roll 24 hours a day. Photographers pose beautiful models for shoots, tanned skaters zip past palm trees, and tourists flock to see the action. Yet Miami Beach is also still a collection of quiet neighborhoods where Little Leaguers play ball, senior citizens stand at bus stops, and locals do their shopping away from the prying eyes of visitors.

Several things are plentiful in SoBe: pierced body parts, cell phones, and meter maids. Tickets are given freely when meters expire, and towing charges are high. Check the meter to see when parking fees are required; times vary by district. From mid-morning on, parking is scarce along Ocean Drive. You'll do better on Collins or Washington avenues, the next two streets to the west. Fortunately, there are several surface parking lots south and west of the Jackie Gleason Theatre, on 17th Street, and parking garages on Collins Avenue at 7th and 13th streets, on Washington Avenue at 12th Street, and west of Washington at 17th Street.

A Good Walk

The stretch of Ocean Drive from 1st to 23rd streets—primarily the 10-block stretch from 5th to 15th streets—has become the most talked-about beachfront in America. A bevy of Art Deco jewels hug the drive, while across the street lies palm-fringed **Lummus Park** ①, whose south end is a good starting point for a walk. Beginning early (8 AM) gives you the pleasure of watching the awakening city without distraction. Sanitation men hose down dirty streets, merchants prepare window displays, bakers bake, and construction workers change the skyline one brick at a time. Cross to the west side of Ocean Drive, where there are many sidewalk cafés, and walk north, taking note of the Park Central Hotel, built in 1937 by Deco architect Henry Hohauser.

At 10th Street recross Ocean Drive to the beach side and visit the **Art Deco District Welcome Center** ② in the 1950s-era Oceanfront Auditorium. Here you can rent tapes or hire a guide for a Deco District tour.

Look back across Ocean Drive and take a peek at the wonderful flying-saucer architecture of the Clevelander, at Number 1020. On the next block you'll see the late Gianni Versace's Spanish Mediterranean **Amsterdam Palace** ③. Graceful fluted columns stand guard at the Leslie (Number 1244) and the **Carlyle** ④.

Walk two blocks west (away from the ocean) on 13th Street to Washington Avenue, where a mix of chic restaurants, avant-garde shops, delicatessens, produce markets, and nightclubs have spiced up a once-derelict neighborhood. Turn left on Washington and walk 2½ blocks south to the **Wolfsonian–FIU Foundation Gallery** ⑤, which showcases artistic movements from 1885 to 1945.

Provided you haven't spent too long in the museum, return north on Washington Avenue past 14th Street, and turn left on **Espanola Way** ⑥, a narrow street of Mediterranean Revival buildings, eclectic shops, and a weekend market. Continue west to Meridian Avenue and turn right. Three blocks north of Espanola Way is the redesigned **Lincoln Road Mall** ⑦, which is often paired with Ocean Drive as part of must-see South Beach.

The next main street north of Lincoln Road is 17th Street, and to the east is the Miami Beach Convention Center. Walk behind the massive building to the corner of Meridian Avenue and 19th Street to see the chilling **Holocaust Memorial** ⑧, a monumental record honoring the 6 million Jewish victims of the Holocaust.

Head east and return to Ocean Drive in time to pull up a chair at an outdoor café, order an espresso, and settle down for an evening of people-watching, SoBe's most popular pastime. Or grab some late rays at one of the area's beaches, offering different sands for different tans. You can go back to Lummus Park or head north, where there's a boardwalk, but skating and bicycling are not allowed.

TIMING

To see only the Art Deco buildings on Ocean Drive, allow one hour minimum. Depending on your interests, schedule at least five hours and include a drink or meal at a café and browsing time in the shops on Ocean Drive, along Espanola Way, and at Lincoln Road Mall.

Start your walking tour as early in the day as possible. In winter the street becomes crowded as the day wears on, and in summer afternoon heat and humidity can be unbearable, wilting even the hardiest soul. Finishing by mid-afternoon also enables you to hit the beach and cool your heels in the warm sand.

Sights to See

❸ Amsterdam Palace. In the early 1980s, before South Beach became the hotbed of chicness, the late Italian designer Gianni Versace purchased this run-down Spanish Mediterranean residence, built before the arrival of Deco. Today the home is an ornate three-story palazzo with a guest house and a copper-dome rooftop observatory and pool that were added at the expense of a 1950s hotel, the Revere. Its loss and the razing of the fabled Deco Senator became a rallying point for preservationists, who like to point out that although they lost a few, they saved 40. In July 1997 Versace was tragically shot and killed in front of his home—still an eerie spot that, strangely, attracts picture-taking tourists. ✉ *1114 Ocean Dr.*

❷ Art Deco District Welcome Center. Run by the Miami Design Preservation League, this clearinghouse in the Oceanfront Auditorium provides information about the buildings in the Art Deco District. A well-stocked gift shop sells 1930s–1950s Art Deco memorabilia, posters, and books on Miami's history. Several tours—covering Lincoln Road, Espanola Way, North Beach, the entire Art Deco District, and more—start here. You can choose to rent audiotapes for a self-guided tour, join the regular Saturday-morning or Thursday-evening walking tour, or take bicycle tour, all providing detailed histories of the Deco hotels. ✉ *1001 Ocean Dr., at Barbara Capitman Way,* ☎ *305/531–3484.* 🖃 *Free.* ☉ *Daily 11–6, open later Thurs.–Mon. in season.*

Bal Harbour. This tony community, known for its upscale shops, has a stretch of prime beach real estate, where wealthy condominium owners cluster during the winter. Look close, and you may spy Bob Dole sunning himself outside his condo. ✉ *Collins Ave. between 96th and 103rd Sts.*

Bass Museum of Art. A diverse collection of European art is the focus of this fortresslike museum made of keystone, a short drive north of SoBe's key sights. Works on display include *The Holy Family,* a painting by Peter Paul Rubens; *The Tournament,* one of several 16th-century Flemish tapestries; and works by Albrecht Dürer and Henri de Toulouse-Lautrec. An $8 million, three-phase expansion, to be completed shortly after 2000, will add a new wing, cafeteria, and theater, doubling the museum's size. ✉ *2121 Park Ave.,* ☎ *305/673–7530.* 🖃 *$5.* ☉ *Tues.–Sat. 10–5, except 1–9 the 2nd and 4th Wed. of each month; Sun. 1–5.*

❹ The Carlyle. Built in 1941, this empty Deco building no longer functions as a hotel, but it's still popular as a movie location. Fans will recognize it and its neighbor, the Leslie, as the nightclub from *The Birdcage,* starring Robin Williams and Nathan Lane. ✉ *1250 Ocean Dr.*

★ ❻ Espanola Way. The Mediterranean Revival buildings along this road were constructed in 1925 and frequented through the years by artists and writers. In the 1930s future bandleader Desi Arnaz strapped on a conga drum and started beating out a rumba rhythm at a nightclub that is now the Clay Hotel, a youth hostel. Visit this quaint avenue on a Sunday afternoon, when itinerant dealers and craftspeople set up shop to sell everything from garage-sale items to handcrafted bongo drums. Between Washington and Drexel avenues, the road has been narrowed to a single lane, and Miami Beach's trademark pink sidewalks have been widened to accommodate sidewalk cafés and shops selling imaginative clothing, jewelry, and art.

★ Fontainebleau Hilton Resort and Towers. For a sense of what Miami was like during the Fabulous '50s, take a drive north to see the finest example of SoBe's grandiose architecture. By the 1950s smaller Deco-

20

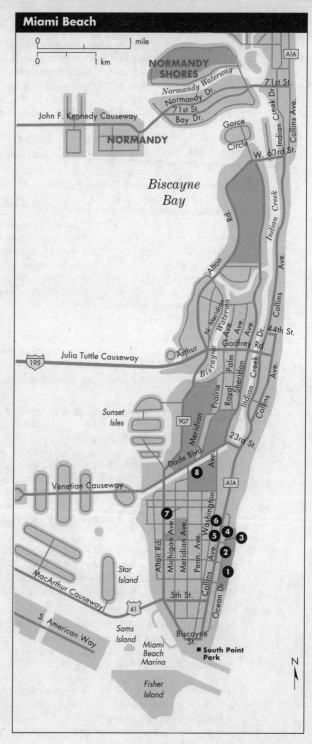

era hotels were passé, and architects like Morris Lapidus got busy designing free-flowing hotels that affirmed the American attitude of "bigger is better." Even if you're not a guest, wander through the lobby and pool area just to feel the energy generated by an army of bellhops, clerks, concierges, and travelers. ⊠ *4441 Collins Ave.,* ☎ *305/538–2000.*

Haulover Beach Park. At this park, far from the action of SoBe, you can see the Miami of 30 years ago. Pack a picnic, use the barbecue grills, or grab a snack at the concession stand. If you're into fitness, you may like the tennis and volleyball courts or paths designed for exercise, walking, and bicycling. When you work up a sweat, take advantage of the shower facilities. The beach is nice for those who want the water close to the upland. Eroded sand was never replaced, and the strand is mercifully narrow, a plus for older visitors who don't like long marches across hot sand. ⊠ *10800 Collins Ave., Sunny Isles,* ☎ *305/947–3525.* ☞ *$3.50 per vehicle.* ☉ *Daily sunrise–sunset.*

❽ Holocaust Memorial. The focus of the memorial is a 42-ft-high bronze arm rising from the ground, with sculptured people climbing the arm seeking escape. Don't stare from the street. Enter the courtyard to see the chilling memorial wall and hear the eerie songs that seem to give voice to the victims. ⊠ *1933–1945 Meridian Ave.,* ☎ *305/538–1663.* ☞ *Donations welcome.* ☉ *Daily 9–9.*

NEED A BREAK?	If your feet are still holding up, head to the **Delano Hotel** (⊠ 1685 Collins Ave., ☎ 305/674–6400) for a drink. This surrealistic hotel, like a Calvin Klein ad come to life, continues to generate a buzz among SoBe's fashion models and hepcats.

★ ❼ Lincoln Road Mall. A playful redesign of this grande dame of Miami Beach overran its original $16 million budget, but the results were worth the extra bucks. The renovation spruced up the futuristic 1950s vision of Fontainebleau designer Morris Lapidus and added a grove of 20 towering date palms and five linear pools. Indicative of the road's resurgence is the restoration of dozens of buildings, including a former Jehovah's Witness hall that actor Michael Caine transformed into a restaurant. The best times to hit the road are during Sunday-morning farmers' markets and on weekend evenings, when cafés are bustling; art galleries, like Romero Britto's Britto Central, schedule openings; street performers take the stage; and bookstores, import shops, and clothing stores are open for late-night purchases.

In the classical four-story Deco gem with friezes at 541–545 Lincoln Road, the **New World Symphony,** a national advanced-training orchestra led by Michael Tilson Thomas, rehearses and performs. To the west toward Biscayne Bay, the street is lined with chic food markets, cafés, and boutiques. Farther west is the **South Florida Art Center,** home to one of the first arts groups to help resurrect the area, and farther still is a black-and-white Deco movie house with a Mediterranean barrel-tile roof, which is now the **Colony Theater.** ⊠ *Lincoln Rd. between Collins Ave. and Alton Rd.*

☾ ❶ Lummus Park. Once part of a turn-of-the-century plantation owned by brothers John and James Lummus, this palm-shaded oasis on the beach side of Ocean Drive attracts beach-going families with its children's play area. Senior citizens predominate early in the day. Volleyball, in-line skating along the wide and winding sidewalk, and a lot of posing go on here, and officials don't enforce the law against topless female bathers, as long as everyone behaves with decorum. Gays like the beach between 11th and 13th streets. The lush foliage is a pleasing, natural counterpoint to the ultrachic atmosphere just across the street, where endless sidewalk cafés make it easy to come ashore for everything from burgers to quiche. Like New York's Central Park, this is a natural venue for big-name public concerts by such performers as Luciano Pavarotti and past Art Deco Weekend stars Cab Calloway and Lionel Hampton. ⊠ *East of Ocean Dr. between 5th and 15th Sts.*

North Beach. Families and those who like things quiet prefer this section of beach. Metered parking is ample right behind the dune and a block behind Collins Avenue along a pleasant, old shopping street. With high prices discouraging developers from SoBe, this area will no doubt see some redevelopment in years to come. However, without the cafés or 300-ft-wide beach to lure tourists, it may never match SoBe's appeal. ⊠ *Ocean Terr. between 73rd and 75th Sts.*

OFF THE
BEATEN PATH
OLETA RIVER STATE RECREATION AREA – At more than 1,000 acres, this is the largest urban park in Florida. It's backed by lush tropical growth rather than hotels and offers interpretive talks, group and youth camping, 14 log cabins, kayak and canoe rentals, bicycle trails, and a fishing pier. Popular with outdoors enthusiasts, it also attracts dolphins, ospreys, and manatees, who arrive for the winter. ⊠ *3400 N.E. 163rd St., North Miami.* 🎫 *$3.25 per vehicle with up to 8 people, $1 for pedestrians.* ☉ *Daily 8–sunset.*

South Pointe Park. From the 50-yard Sunshine Pier, which adjoins the 1-mi-long jetty at the mouth of Government Cut, you can fish while watching huge ships pass. No bait or tackle is available in the park. Facilities include two observation towers, rest rooms, and volleyball courts. ⊠ *1 Washington Ave.*

Surfside. *Parlez-vous français?* If you do, you'll feel quite comfortable in and around this community, a French Canadian enclave. Many folks have spent their winters along this stretch of beach (and elsewhere down to 72nd Street) for years. ⊠ *Collins Ave. between 88th and 96th Sts.*

❺ **Wolfsonian–FIU Foundation Gallery.** An elegantly renovated 1927 storage facility is now both a research center and home to the 70,000-plus-item collection of modern design and "propaganda arts" amassed by Miami native Mitchell Wolfson Jr., a world traveler and connoisseur. Included in the museum's eclectic holdings, representing Art Moderne, Art Nouveau, Arts and Crafts, and other artistic movements, are 8,000 matchbooks collected by King Farouk. (The name Wolfsonian, by the way, is intended to echo Smithsonian.) ⊠ *1001 Washington Ave.,* ☎ *305/531–1001.* 🎫 *$5.* ☉ *Tues.–Wed. and Fri.–Sat. 11–6, Thurs. 11–9, Sun. noon–5.*

Downtown Miami

From a distance you see downtown Miami's future—a 21st-century skyline stroking the clouds with sleek fingers of steel and glass. By day this icon of commerce and technology sparkles in the subtropical sun; at night it basks in the man-made glow of neon and floodlights. But although Miami has become one of the great international cities of the Americas, it perpetually teeters on the verge of bankruptcy. At times it has seemed as though political corruption, cronyism, nepotism, shortsightedness, and insensitivity would dissolve Miami as it nearly did in 1997. A proposal to disband the city actually reached voters, but they voted overwhelmingly to keep it, flaws and all.

Nevertheless, by day there's plenty of activity downtown, as office workers and motorists crowd the area. Staid, suited lawyers and bankers share the sidewalks with Latino merchants wearing open-neck, intricately embroidered shirts called guayaberas. Fruit merchants sell their wares from pushcarts, young European travelers with backpacks stroll the streets, and foreign businesspeople haggle over prices in import-export shops. You hear Arabic, Chinese, Creole, French, German, Hebrew, Hindi, Japanese, Portuguese, Spanish, Swedish, Yiddish, and even a little English now and then. But what's best in the heart of downtown Miami is its Latinization and the sheer energy of Latino shoppers.

At night, however, downtown is sorely neglected. Except for Bayside Marketplace and the Miami Arena, the area is deserted, and arena patrons rarely linger. Visitors spend little time here since most tourist attractions are in other neighborhoods, but there is a movement afoot to bring a renaissance to downtown. Though nothing has yet been built, a new waterfront arena for the Miami Heat has been approved, and a new performing arts center and a CocoWalk-style pedestrian mall are expected in 2000.

Thanks to the Metromover (☞ Getting Around by Train *in* Miami and Miami Beach A to Z, *below*), which has inner and outer loops through downtown plus north and south extensions, this is an excellent tour to take by rail. Attractions are conveniently located within about two blocks of the nearest station. Parking downtown is no less convenient or more expensive than in any other city, but the best idea is to leave your car at an outlying Metrorail station and take the train downtown.

A Good Tour

Get off the Metrorail train at Government Center, where the 21-mi elevated Metrorail commuter system connects with the Metromover. As you leave the station, notice the **Dade County Courthouse** ⑨, to the east. West on Flagler Street is the **Metro-Dade Cultural Center** ⑩, which contains the city's main art museum, historical museum, and library.

Take some time to wander a bit on Flagler Street, downtown Miami's commercial spine. As you look at the steel-and-glass structures, keep in mind that this was one of the first areas of Miami to be carved out of the pine woods and palmetto scrub when Flagler's railroad arrived in 1896. Reboard the Metromover where convenient, and, if you want to see more architecturally interesting skyscrapers, take the spur to the Brickell District. It runs across the Miami River along **Brickell Avenue** ⑪, a southward extension of Southeast 2nd Avenue.

Return to Metromover's outer loop, and get off at the Bayfront Park stop, opposite **Mildred and Claude Pepper Bayfront Park** ⑫. South of the park, the lobby of the Hotel Inter-Continental Miami contains *The Spindle,* a huge sculpture by Henry Moore. West of Bayfront Park Station stands the tallest building in Florida, the **First Union Financial Center** ⑬.

As you continue north on the Metromover, take in the fine view of Bayfront Park's greenery, the bay beyond, the Port of Miami in the bay, and Miami Beach across the water. The next Metromover stop, 1st Street, places you a block north of Flagler Street and the landmark **Gusman Center for the Performing Arts** ⑭, a stunningly beautiful movie palace that now serves as downtown Miami's concert hall.

The College/Bayside Metromover stop serves the downtown campus of **Miami-Dade Community College** ⑮, which has two fine galleries.

As the Metromover rounds the curve after College/Bayside Station, look northeast for a view of the vacant **Freedom Tower** ⑯, an important milepost in the history of Cuban immigration. (To see the tower up close, walk north from Edcom Station to Northeast 6th Street, then two blocks east to Biscayne Boulevard.) At this point in the loop, a spur curves north to the Omni District.

A two-block walk south from Edcom Station brings you to the **U.S. Courthouse** ⑰, a building with a depression-era mural. As you round the northwest corner of the loop, at State Plaza/Arena Station, look two blocks north to see the round, windowless, pink **Miami Arena** ⑱.

TIMING

To walk and ride to the various points of interest, allow two hours. If you want to spend additional time eating and shopping at Bayside, allow at least four hours. To include museum visits, allow six hours.

Sights to See

🦢 **American Police Hall of Fame and Museum.** This museum exhibits more than 11,000 law enforcement–related items, including weapons, a jail cell, and an electric chair, as well as a 400-ton marble memorial listing the names of police officers killed in the line of duty since 1960. ⊠ *3801 Biscayne Blvd.,* ☎ *305/573–0070.* ☞ *$6.* ☼ *Daily 10–5:30.*

⑪ **Brickell Avenue.** A canyon rimmed by tall buildings, this street has the largest concentration of international banking offices in the United States. From the end of the Metromover line you can look south to where several architecturally interesting condominiums rise between Brickell Avenue and Biscayne Bay. Arquitectonica, an internationally prominent architectural firm based in Miami, designed three of these buildings: the **Palace** (⊠ 1541 Brickell Ave.), the **Imperial** (⊠ 1627 Brickell Ave.), and the **Atlantis** (⊠ 2025 Brickell Ave.). Israeli artist Yacov Agam painted the rainbow exterior of **Villa Regina** (⊠ 1581 Brickell Ave.).

⑨ **Dade County Courthouse.** Built in 1928, this was once the tallest building south of Washington, D.C. Unlike Capistrano, turkey vultures— not swallows—return to roost here in winter. ⊠ *73 W. Flagler St.*

⑬ **First Union Financial Center.** The tallest building in Florida is this 55-story structure. Towering royal palms grace the 1-acre Palm Court plaza beneath the steel-and-glass frame. ⊠ *200 S. Biscayne Blvd.*

⑯ **Freedom Tower.** In the 1960s this imposing Spanish baroque structure was used by the Cuban Refugee Center to process more than 500,000 Cubans who entered the United States after fleeing Fidel Castro's regime. Built in 1925 for the *Miami Daily News,* it was inspired by the Giralda, an 800-year-old bell tower in Seville, Spain. Preservationists were pleased to see the tower restored to its original grandeur in 1988, but the building remains vacant awaiting the arrival of a proposed Cuban museum. ⊠ *600 Biscayne Blvd.*

★ ⑭ **Gusman Center for the Performing Arts.** This former movie palace has been restored as a concert hall. Resembling a Moorish courtyard with twinkling stars in the sky, it hosts performances by the Miami City Ballet and the New World Symphony. ⊠ *174 E. Flagler St.,* ☎ *305/372–0925.*

★ 🦢 ⑩ **Metro-Dade Cultural Center.** Containing three important cultural resources, this 3-acre complex is one of the focal points of downtown. The **Miami Art Museum** (☎ 305/375–1700) puts on major touring exhibitions of work by international artists, focusing on work completed since 1945. Open Tuesday–Friday 10–5 and weekends noon–5, the museum charges $5 admission. At the **Historical Museum of Southern**

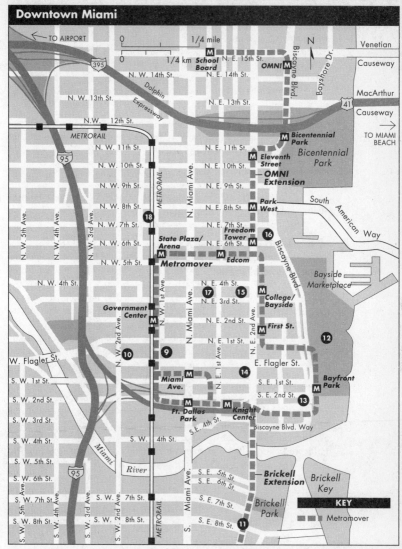

Downtown Miami

TO AIRPORT

0   1/4 mile

0   1/4 km

N

395

Dolphin Expressway

METRORAIL

95

N.W. 14th St.
N.W. 13th St.
N.W. 12th St.
N.W. 11th St.
N.W. 10th St.
N.W. 9th St.
N.W. 8th St.
N.W. 7th St.
N.W. 6th St.
N.W. 5th St.
N.W. 4th St.

N. E. 15th St.
School Board
N. E. 14th St.
N. E. 13th St.

N. E. 11th St.
N. E. 10th St.
N. E. 9th St.
N. E. 8th St.
N. E. 7th St.
N. E. 6th St.

OMNI
Biscayne Blvd.
Bayshare Dr.

Venetian
Causeway
MacArthur
Causeway
41
TO MIAMI BEACH

Bicentennial Park
Bicentennial Park
Eleventh Street
OMNI Extension
Park West
South American Way

Freedom Tower

State Plaza/Arena
Metromover
Edcom

16

N. E. 4th St.
N. E. 3rd St.
N. E. 2nd St.
N. E. 1st St.

17   15

College/Bayside
First St.

Bayside Marketplace

Government Center

10   9

W. Flagler St.
S.W. 1st St.
S.W. 2nd St.
S.W. 3rd St.
S.W. 4th St.
S.W. 5th St.
S.W. 6th St.
S.W. 7th St.
S.W. 8th St.

Miami Ave.

Ft. Dallas Park

Knight Center

E. Flagler St.
S.E. 1st St.
S.E. 2nd St.

14

13

12

Bayfront Park

Biscayne Blvd. Way

Brickell Extension

Brickell Key

Miami River

Biscayne Blvd.

S.E. 4th St.
S.W. 4th St.
S.E. 5th St.
S.E. 6th St.
S.E. 7th St.
S.E. 8th St.

Brickell Park

11

18

KEY
Metromover

N. 5th Ave.
N. 4th Ave.
N. 3rd Ave.
N.W. 2nd Ave.
N. Miami Ave.
N.W. 1st Ave.
N. Miami Ave.
N. E. 1st Ave.
N. E. 2nd Ave.

Brickell Avenue, **11**

Dade County Courthouse, **9**

First Union Financial Center, **13**

Freedom Tower, **16**

Gusman Center for the Performing Arts, **14**

Metro-Dade Cultural Center, **10**

Miami Arena, **18**

Miami-Dade Community College, **15**

Mildred and Claude Pepper Bayfront Park, **12**

U.S. Courthouse, **17**

Florida (☎ 305/375–1492), visitors are treated to pure Floridiana, including an old Miami streetcar, cigar labels, and a railroad exhibit as well as a display on prehistoric Miami. Admission is $4, and hours are Monday–Wednesday and Friday–Saturday 10–5, Thursday 10–9, and Sunday noon–5. The **Main Public Library** (☎ 305/375–2665), open Monday–Wednesday and Friday–Saturday 9–6, Thursday 9–9, and Sunday 1–5, contains nearly 4 million holdings and offers art exhibits in the auditorium and second-floor lobby. ⊠ *101 W. Flagler St.*

⑱ Miami Arena. Currently the home of the NBA's Miami Heat, the arena also hosts a variety of other sports and entertainment events. ⊠ *701 Arena Blvd.,* ☎ *305/530–4444.*

⑮ Miami-Dade Community College. The campus houses two fine galleries: The larger, third-floor **Centre Gallery** hosts various photography, painting, and sculpture exhibitions, and the fifth-floor **Frances Wolfson Art Gallery** houses smaller photo exhibits. ⊠ *300 N.E. 2nd Ave.,* ☎ *305/237–3278.* ▣ *Free.* ☉ *Mon.–Thurs. 9–5.*

⑫ Mildred and Claude Pepper Bayfront Park. An oasis among the skyscrapers, this park extends east from busy, palm-lined Biscayne Boulevard to the bay. An urban landfill in the 1920s, it became the site of a World War II memorial in 1943, which was revised in 1980 to include the names of later victims. Japanese sculptor Isamu Noguchi redesigned the park before his death in 1989 to include two amphitheaters, a memorial to the *Challenger* astronauts, and a fountain honoring the late Florida congressman Claude Pepper and his wife. At the park's north end, the Friendship Torch was erected to honor JFK during his presidency, and dedicated in 1964. ⊠ *Biscayne Blvd. between 2nd and 3rd Sts.*

⑰ U.S. Courthouse. Made of keystone, the courthouse was erected in 1931 as Miami's main post office. In what was once the second-floor central courtroom is *Law Guides Florida Progress,* a huge depression-era mural by Denman Fink. Surrounding the central figure of a robed judge are several images that define the Florida of the 1930s: fish vendors, palm trees, and a Pan Am airplane winging off to Latin America. No cameras or tape recorders are allowed. ⊠ *300 N.E. 1st Ave.* ☉ *Building weekdays 8:30–5, security guards open courtroom on request.*

Little Havana

Nearly 40 years ago the tidal wave of Cubans fleeing the Castro regime flooded into an older neighborhood west of downtown Miami. This area became known as Little Havana, today a somewhat dirty but still intriguing enclave. With a million Cubans and other Latinos—more than half the metropolitan population—dispersed throughout Greater Miami, Little Havana and neighboring East Little Havana remain magnets for Hispanics and Anglos alike, who come to experience the flavor of traditional Cuban culture. That culture, of course, functions in Spanish. Many Little Havana residents and shopkeepers speak little or no English. If parking is a problem, head west of Ronald Reagan Avenue (Southwest 12th Avenue).

A Good Tour

From downtown go west on Flagler Street across the Miami River to Teddy Roosevelt Avenue (Southwest 17th Avenue) and pause at **Plaza de la Cubanidad** ⑲, on the southwest corner. The plaza's monument is indicative of the prominent role of Cuban history and culture here.

Turn left at Douglas Road (Southwest 37th Avenue), drive south to **Calle Ocho** ⑳ (Southwest 8th Street), and turn left again. You are now on the main commercial thoroughfare of Little Havana. After you cross

Unity Boulevard (Southwest 27th Avenue), Calle Ocho becomes a one-way street eastbound through the heart of Little Havana.

At Avenida Luis Muñoz Marín (Southwest 15th Avenue), stop at **Domino Park** ㉑, where elderly Cuban men pass the day with their black-and-white play tiles. The **Brigade 2506 Memorial** ㉒, commemorating the victims of the unsuccessful 1961 Bay of Pigs invasion, stands at Memorial Boulevard (Southwest 13th Avenue). A block south are several other monuments relevant to Cuban history, including a bas-relief of and quotations by José Martí. Finish the tour by driving five blocks south of Calle Ocho on Ronald Reagan Avenue to the **Cuban Museum of the Americas** ㉓.

TIMING

If the history hidden in the monuments is your only interest, set aside two hours. Allow more time for a strong cup of Cuban coffee on Calle Ocho or a Honduran cigar hand-rolled in America by Cubans.

Sights to See

㉒ **Brigade 2506 Memorial.** To honor those who died in the Bay of Pigs invasion, an eternal flame burns atop a simple stone monument with the inscription: CUBA—A LOS MARTIRES DE LA BRIGADA DE ASALTO ABRIL 17 DE 1961. The monument also bears a shield with the Brigade 2506 emblem, a Cuban flag superimposed on a cross. ⊠ *S.W. 8th St. and S.W. 13th Ave.*

㉒ **Calle Ocho.** In Little Havana's commercial heart, experience such Cuban customs as hand-rolled cigars or sandwiches piled with meats and cheeses. Though it all deserves exploring, if time is limited, try the stretch from Southwest 14th to 11th avenues. ⊠ *S.W. 8th St.*

㉓ **Cuban Museum of the Americas.** Created by Cuban exiles to preserve and interpret the heritage of their homeland, the museum is inside a small house and has a staff of one, so call first. ⊠ *1300 S.W. 12th Ave.,* ☏ *305/858–8006.* 🎫 *$3.* ☉ *Tues.–Fri. 10–3, weekends by appointment.*

㉑ **Domino Park.** Officially known as Maximo Gomez Park, this is a major gathering place for elderly, guayabera-clad Cuban males, who, after 40 years, still pass the day playing dominoes while arguing anti-Castro politics. ⊠ *S.W. 8th St. and S.W. 15th Ave.* ☉ *Daily 9–6.*

⑲ **Plaza de la Cubanidad.** Redbrick sidewalks surround a fountain and monument with the words of José Martí, a leader in Cuba's struggle for independence from Spain and a hero to Cuban refugees and immigrants in Miami. The quotation, LAS PALMAS SON NOVIAS QUE ESPERAN (The palm trees are girlfriends who will wait), counsels hope and fortitude to the Cubans. ⊠ *W. Flagler St. and S.W. 17th Ave.*

Coral Gables

This planned community of broad boulevards and Spanish Mediterranean architecture justifiably calls itself the City Beautiful—a moniker it acquired by following the Garden City method of urban planning in the 1920s. George E. Merrick began selling Coral Gables lots in 1921 and incorporated the city in 1925. He named most of the streets for Spanish explorers, cities, and provinces and even contracted architects trained abroad to create themed neighborhood villages, such as Florida pioneer, Chinese, French city, Dutch South African, and French Normandy. Like much of Miami, Coral Gables has realized the aesthetic and economic importance of historic preservation and has passed a Mediterranean design ordinance, rewarding businesses for maintaining their building's architectural style. Street signs are holdovers from the '40s. Though quite awkward to read (especially at night), the

Miami, Coral Gables, Coconut Grove and Key Biscayne

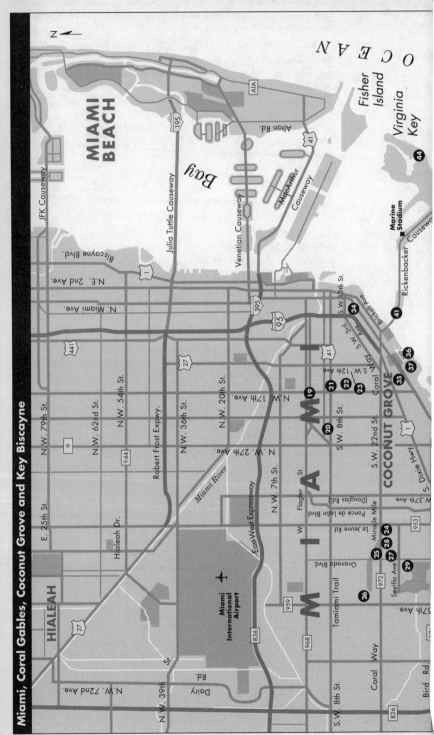

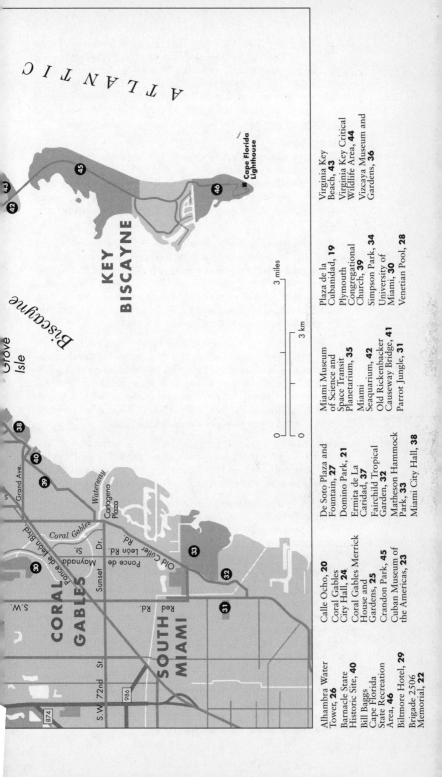

ATLANTIC

KEY
BISCAYNE

Cape Florida
Lighthouse

Biscayne

Grove
Isle

3 miles

3 km

Alhambra Water
Tower, **26**
Barnacle State
Historic Site, **40**
Bill Baggs
Cape Florida
State Recreation
Area, **46**
Biltmore Hotel, **29**
Brigade 2506
Memorial, **22**

Calle Ocho, **20**
Coral Gables
City Hall, **24**
Coral Gables Merrick
House and
Gardens, **25**
Crandon Park, **45**
Cuban Museum of
the Americas, **23**

De Soto Plaza and
Fountain, **27**
Domino Park, **21**
Ermita de La
Caridad, **37**
Fairchild Tropical
Garden, **32**
Matheson Hammock
Park, **33**
Miami City Hall, **38**

Miami Museum
of Science and
Space Transit
Planetarium, **35**
Miami
Seaquarium, **42**
Old Rickenbacker
Causeway Bridge, **41**
Parrot Jungle, **31**

Plaza de la
Cubanidad, **19**
Plymouth
Congregational
Church, **39**
Simpson Park, **34**
University of
Miami, **30**
Venetian Pool, **28**

Virginia Key
Beach, **43**
Virginia Key Critical
Wildlife Area, **44**
Vizcaya Museum and
Gardens, **36**

ground-level markers on whitewashed concrete cornerstones are nevertheless of historical value.

Unfortunately for Merrick, the devastating no-name hurricane of 1926 and the Great Depression prevented him from fulfilling many of his plans. The city languished until after World War II but then grew rapidly. Today Coral Gables has a population of about 41,000. In its bustling downtown, more than 140 multinational companies maintain headquarters or regional offices, and the University of Miami campus in the southern part of Coral Gables brings a youthful vibrancy.

A Good Tour

Coming from downtown, take Southwest 3rd Avenue, which turns into Coral Way (Southwest 24th Street). An arch of banyan trees prepares you for the grand entrance onto Miracle Mile. Actually only ½ mi long, this retailing stretch of Coral Way, from Douglas Road (37th Avenue) to LeJeune Road (42nd Avenue), is the heart of downtown Coral Gables.

Upscale yet neighborly, this is how all downtown commercial districts should look. Cafeterias mingle with high-tone jewelers, and independent bookstores share customers with major book chains. Heading west past the plentiful shops, you'll pass the 1930s Colony Theater, which now serves as home of the Actors Playhouse. Keep heading west, cross LeJeune Road, bear left onto Biltmore Way, and catch an eyeful of the ornate Spanish Renaissance **Coral Gables City Hall** ㉔.

The going gets tricky, but it's worth the effort. Continue west on Biltmore Way to Toledo Street, turn right, and park behind **Coral Gables Merrick House and Gardens** ㉕, Merrick's boyhood home. If you love planned development, stop in to pay your respects. As you leave the parking lot, turn left on Toledo Street and continue to South Greenway Drive. You'll see the Granada Golf Course, a gorgeously green 9-hole course amid Coral Gables's largest historic district.

Turn left on South Greenway Drive, follow it to Alhambra Circle, and turn right. One block ahead on your left, at the intersection of Alhambra Circle, Greenway Court, and Ferdinand Street, is the restored **Alhambra Water Tower** ㉖, a city landmark dating from 1925.

Now drive south on Alhambra Circle four short blocks to Coral Way. Turn left and after six blocks turn right on Granada Boulevard. You are now approaching **De Soto Plaza and Fountain** ㉗. Follow the traffic circle almost completely around the fountain to northeast-bound De Soto Boulevard. On your right in the next block is the **Venetian Pool** ㉘, an exotic and unusual public swimming pool.

Return to the De Soto Fountain and follow De Soto Boulevard southwest to the reborn **Biltmore Hotel** ㉙. From the hotel turn right on Anastasia Avenue, go east to Granada Boulevard, and turn right. Continue south on Granada Boulevard over a bridge across the Coral Gables Waterway, which empties into Biscayne Bay. In the hotel's heyday, Venetian gondolas plied the waterway, bringing guests to a bay-side beach.

At Ponce de León Boulevard turn right. On your left is Metrorail's Stonehenge-like concrete structure, and on your right is the main campus of the **University of Miami** ㉚. Turn right at the first stoplight (Stanford Drive) to enter the campus, and park in the lot on your right designated for visitors to the Lowe Art Museum.

TIMING

Strolling Miracle Mile will only take an hour, unless you plan to shop—and you should—in which case allow four hours. Save time for a refreshing dip at the Venetian Pool, and plan to spend at least an hour getting acquainted with the Biltmore—longer if you'd like to order a drink and linger poolside. If you can pull yourself away from the lap of luxury, allow an hour to visit the University of Miami campus.

Sights to See

26 Alhambra Water Tower. In 1925 this city landmark stored water and was clad in a decorative moresque, lighthouselike exterior. After more than 50 years of disuse and neglect, the windmill-like tower was completely restored in 1993 with a copper-rib dome and multicolor frescoes. ⊠ *Alhambra Circle, Greenway Ct., and Ferdinand St.*

29 Biltmore Hotel. Bouncing back from dark days as an army hospital, this hotel has become the jewel of Coral Gables. After extensive renovations it reopened in 1992 and hosted the Summit of the Americas in 1994. Its 16-story tower, like the Freedom Tower in downtown Miami, is a replica of Seville's Giralda Tower. To the west is the Biltmore Country Club, a richly ornamented Beaux Arts–style structure with a superb colonnade and courtyard; it was reincorporated into the hotel in 1989. ⊠ *1200 Anastasia Ave.,* ☎ *305/445–1926.*

24 Coral Gables City Hall. This 1928 building has a three-tier tower topped with a clock and a 500-pound bell. A mural by Denman Fink (George Merrick's uncle and artistic adviser for Coral Gables), inside the dome ceiling on the second floor, depicts the four seasons. ⊠ *405 Biltmore Way,* ☎ *305/446–6800.* ☉ *Weekdays 8–5.*

NEED A BREAK?

Whether you want to relax or grab an on-the-go snack, you can't miss with **Wrapido** (⊠ 2334 Ponce de León Blvd., ☎ 305/443–1884), Florida's first wrapper restaurant. The funky, upbeat atmosphere shows signs of SoHo, and the healthy sandwiches, soups, and smoothies are made from scratch. Strawberry Fields, the best-selling smoothie, is prepared with fresh bananas, strawberries, apple juice, and low-fat yogurt.

25 Coral Gables Merrick House and Gardens. In 1976 the city of Coral Gables acquired George Merrick's boyhood home. Restored to its 1920s appearance, it contains Merrick family furnishings and artifacts. The lush and lazy tropical atmosphere of the home suggests the inspiration for George's masterpiece: Coral Gables. ⊠ *907 Coral Way,* ☎ *305/460–5361.* ⊡ *House $2, grounds free.* ☉ *House, Wed.–Sun. 1–4; grounds, daily 8–sunset.*

27 De Soto Plaza and Fountain. Water flows from the mouths of four sculpted faces on a classical column on a pedestal in this Denman Fink–designed fountain from the early 1920s. The closed eyes of the face looking west symbolize the day's end. ⊠ *Intersection of Granada Blvd. and Sevilla Ave.*

30 University of Miami. With almost 14,000 full-time, part-time, and noncredit students, UM is the largest private research university in the southeast. Walk around campus and visit the **Lowe Art Museum,** which has a permanent collection of 8,000 works that include Renaissance and Baroque art, American paintings, Latin American art, and Navajo and Pueblo Indian textiles and baskets. The museum also hosts traveling exhibitions. ⊠ *1301 Stanford Dr.,* ☎ *305/284–3535 or 305/284–3536.* ⊡ *$5.* ☉ *Tues.–Wed. and Fri.–Sat. 10–5, Thurs. noon–7, Sun. noon–5.*

★ ☁ **28 Venetian Pool.** Sculpted from a rock quarry in 1923 and fed by artesian wells, this municipal pool remains quite popular due to its themed architecture—a fantasized version of a waterfront Italian village—created by Denman Fink. The pool has earned a place on the National

Register of Historic Places and showcases a nice collection of vintage photos depicting 1920s beauty pageants and swank soirees held long ago. Paul Whiteman played here, Johnny Weissmuller and Esther Williams swam here, and you should, too. A snack bar, lockers, and showers make this must-see user-friendly as well. ✉ *2701 De Soto Blvd.,* ☎ *305/460–5356.* 🎫 *$5, free parking across De Soto Blvd.* ☉ *Weekends 10–4:30; plus June–Aug., weekdays 11–7:30; Sept.–Oct. and Apr.–May, Tues.–Fri. 11–5:30; and Nov.–Mar., Tues.–Fri. 10–4:30.*

South Miami

South of Miami and Coral Gables is a city called South Miami, which is not to be confused with the region known as South Dade. A pioneer farm community, it grew into a suburb but retains its small-town charm. Fine old homes and stately trees line Sunset Drive, a city-designated Historic and Scenic Road to and through the town. A local chamber of commerce provides a free map listing u-pick farms where your fresh fruit can be blended in with a creamy milk shake. All this could change slightly, however, with the coming of the Shoppes at Sunset Place, a complex expected to be larger than Coconut Grove's CocoWalk.

A Good Tour

Drive south from Sunset Drive on Red Road and turn right just before Killian Drive (Southwest 112th Street) into the 13-acre grounds of **Parrot Jungle** ㉛, one of Greater Miami's oldest and most popular commercial tourist attractions.

From Parrot Jungle follow Red Road ⅓ mi south and turn left on scenic Old Cutler Road, which curves north along the uplands of southern Florida's coastal ridge toward the 83-acre **Fairchild Tropical Garden** ㉜. Just north of the gardens, Old Cutler Road traverses Dade County's lovely **Matheson Hammock Park** ㉝.

TIMING

Most people should allow at least half a day to see these three natural attractions, but dedicated ornithologists and botanists will want to leave a full day. Driving from SoBe should take only 25 minutes—longer during afternoon rush hour.

Sights to See

🖐 ㉜ **Fairchild Tropical Garden.** Comprising 83 acres, this is the largest tropical botanical garden in the continental United States. Eleven lakes, a rain forest, and lots of flowers, including orchids, mountain roses, bellflowers, coral trees, bougainvillea, and fire trees, make it a garden for the senses. Spicing up the social calendar are garden sales, theatrical performances, moonlight strolls, and symphony concerts. A combination bookstore–gift shop is a popular source for books on gardening and horticulture, ordered by botanists the world over. ✉ *10901 Old Cutler Rd.,* ☎ *305/667–1651.* 🎫 *$8.* ☉ *Daily 9:30–4:30.*

🖐 ㉝ **Matheson Hammock Park.** In the 1930s the Civilian Conservation Corps developed this 100-acre tract of upland and mangrove swamp on land donated by a local pioneer, Commodore J. W. Matheson. The park, Miami-Dade County's oldest and most scenic, features a bathing beach where the tide flushes a saltwater "atoll" pool through four gates. In 1997 the marina was expanded to include 243 slips, 71 dry-storage spaces, a bait-and-tackle shop, and a restaurant. ✉ *9610 Old Cutler Rd.,* ☎ *305/665–5475.* 🎫 *Parking for beach and marina $3.50 per car, $8 per car with trailer, $6 per RV; limited free upland parking.* ☉ *Daily 6–sunset; pool lifeguards winter, daily 8:30–5; summer, weekends 8:30–6.*

🐾 ㉛ **Parrot Jungle.** One of South Florida's original tourist attractions, Parrot Jungle opened in 1936 and is now home to more than 1,100 exotic birds, who look for handouts from visitors. After watching a trained-bird show, stroll among orchids and other flowering plants nestled in ferns, bald cypress, and massive live oaks. Peaceful and exotic, the "jungle" is home to 75 Caribbean flamingos (costars on *Miami Vice*). Plans are in the works to relocate the attraction to Watson Island by late 1999. ✉ *11000 S.W. 57th Ave.,* ☎ *305/666–7834.* ☞ *$12.95.* ☉ *Daily 9:30–6, last admission 5; café daily 8–4.*

Coconut Grove

South Florida's oldest settlement, the Grove was inhabited as early as 1834 and established by 1873, two decades before Miami. Its early settlers included Bahamian blacks, "Conchs" (white Key Westers, many originally from the Bahamas), and New England intellectuals. They built a community that attracted artists, writers, and scientists to establish winter homes. By the end of World War I more people listed in *Who's Who* gave addresses in Coconut Grove than any other place in the country.

To this day Coconut Grove reflects its pioneers' eclectic origins. Posh estates mingle with rustic cottages, modest frame homes, and stark modern dwellings, often on the same block. To keep Coconut Grove a village in a jungle, residents lavish affection on exotic plantings while battling to protect remaining native vegetation.

The historic center of the Village of Coconut Grove went through a hippie period in the 1960s, a laid-back funkiness in the 1970s, and a teenybopper invasion in the early 1980s. Today the tone is upscale and urban, with a mix of galleries, boutiques, restaurants, bars, and sidewalk cafés. On weekends the Grove is jam-packed with both locals and tourists shopping at the Streets of Mayfair, CocoWalk, and small boutiques. Parking can be a problem, especially on weekend evenings, when police direct traffic and prohibit turns at some intersections to prevent gridlock. Be prepared to walk several blocks from the periphery into the heart of the Grove.

A Good Tour

From downtown Miami take Brickell Avenue south and follow the signs pointing to Vizcaya and Coconut Grove. Soon you'll be on South Bayshore Drive, the easiest route into the village. If you want to saunter through a jungle of tropical flora and fauna first, however, you'll have to travel one block west of Brickell to South Miami Avenue, where at 17th Road you'll see **Simpson Park** ㉞.

Continuing south, you'll see on your right the **Miami Museum of Science and Space Transit Planetarium** ㉟, a participatory museum with animated displays for all ages. Farther down the block on the left is the entrance to the don't-miss **Vizcaya Museum and Gardens** ㊱, an estate with an Italian Renaissance–style villa. Just past Vizcaya, through the entrance to LaSalle High School, is **Ermita de La Caridad** ㊲, a religious site sacred to Cubans.

As you approach the village, South Miami Avenue becomes South Bayshore Drive. Take a quick detour down Pan American Boulevard to see **Miami City Hall** ㊳, in the 1930s Art Deco Pan Am terminal. Nearby are the Coconut Grove Convention Center, where antiques, boat, and home shows are held, and Dinner Key Marina, where seabirds soar and sailboats ride at anchor.

Now it's time to hit the village. South Bayshore Drive heads directly into McFarlane Road, which takes a sharp right into the center of the action. If you can forsake instant gratification, turn left on Main Highway and drive less than ½ mi to Devon Road and the interesting **Plymouth Congregational Church** ㊴ and its gardens.

Return to Main Highway and travel northeast toward the historic Village of Coconut Grove. As you reenter the village center, note on your left the Coconut Grove Playhouse. On your right, beyond the benches and shelter, is the entrance to the **Barnacle State Historic Site** ㊵, a pioneer residence built by Commodore Ralph Munroe in 1891. After getting your fill of history, relax and spend the evening mingling with Coconut Grove's artists and intellectuals.

TIMING

Plan on devoting from six to eight hours to enjoy Vizcaya, other bayfront sights, and the village's shops, restaurants, and nightlife.

Sights to See

㊵ **Barnacle State Historic Site.** The oldest Miami home still on its original foundation rests in the middle of 5 acres of native hardwood and landscaped lawns surrounded by flashy Coconut Grove. Built by Florida's first snowbird—New Yorker Commodore Ralph Munroe—the home features many original furnishings, a broad sloping roof, and deeply recessed verandas that channel sea breezes into the house. If your timing is right, you may catch one of the monthly Moonlight Concerts. ✉ *3485 Main Hwy.,* ☎ *305/448–9445.* 🎟 *$1.* ⏲ *Fri.–Sun. 9–4; tours 10, 11:30, 1, and 2:30, but call ahead; group tours (10 or more) Mon.–Thurs. by reservation; concerts on day near full moon 6–9 PM, but call ahead.*

NEED A BREAK? Although **Joffrey's Coffee Co.** (✉ 3434A Main Hwy., ☎ 305/448–0848) is a chain, it's still a nice place to drop by for a cappuccino, espresso, tea, or chilled coffee. Tables at the sidewalk café enable you to critique the trendies that inhabit the neighborhood. Muffins and cakes bring the bill to about $5.

㊲ **Ermita de La Caridad (Our Lady of Charity Shrine).** This conical building 90 ft high and 80 ft wide overlooks Biscayne Bay, so worshipers face Cuba. A mural above the shrine's altar depicts Cuba's history. ✉ *3609 S. Miami Ave.,* ☎ *305/854–2404.* ⏲ *Daily 9–9.*

㊳ **Miami City Hall.** Built in 1934 as the terminal for the Pan American Airways seaplane base at Dinner Key, the building retains its nautical-style Art Deco trim. ✉ *3500 Pan American Dr.,* ☎ *305/250–5400.* ⏲ *Weekdays 8–5.*

㉟ **Miami Museum of Science and Space Transit Planetarium.** This museum is chock-full of hands-on sound, gravity, and electricity displays for children and adults alike. A wildlife center houses native Florida snakes, turtles, tortoises, and birds of prey. Outstanding traveling exhibits appear throughout the year, and virtual reality, life-science demonstrations, and Internet technology are on hand every day. ✉ *3280 S. Miami Ave.,* ☎ *305/854–4247; 305/854–2222 planetarium information.* 🎟 *Museum, planetarium, and wildlife center $10, laser-light rock-and-roll concert $6.* ⏲ *Daily 10–6.*

㊴ **Plymouth Congregational Church.** Opened in 1917, this handsome coral-rock structure resembles a Mexican mission church. The front door, made of hand-carved walnut and oak with original wrought-iron fittings, came from an early 17th-century monastery in the Pyrenees. Also on the 11-acre grounds are natural sunken gardens; the first schoolhouse in Miami-Dade County (one room), which was moved to this property; and the site of the original Coconut Grove waterworks and electric works. ⊠ *3400 Devon Rd.,* ☎ *305/444–6521.* ☉ *Weekdays 9–4:30, Sun. service 10 AM.*

③④ **Simpson Park.** Enjoy a fragment of the dense tropical jungle that once covered the 5 mi from downtown Miami to the Grove. Large gumbo-limbo trees, marlberry, banyans, and black calabash provide a glimpse of how things were before the high-rises towered. In summer mosquitoes are unrelenting. ⊠ *55 S.W. 17th Rd.,* ☎ *305/856–6801.* ☉ *Tues.–Fri. 8–3:30, Sat. 10–5.*

★ ③⑥ **Vizcaya Museum and Gardens.** Built between 1912 and 1916 by a quarter of Miami's existing labor force, this palace was the winter residence of Chicago industrialist James Deering. Once comprising 180 acres, the grounds now cover a still-substantial 30-acre tract, including a native hammock and more than 10 acres of formal gardens and fountains overlooking Biscayne Bay. The house, open to the public, contains 70 rooms, 34 of which are filled with paintings, sculpture, antique furniture, and other decorative arts dating from the 15th through the 19th centuries and representing the Renaissance, Baroque, rococo, and neoclassical styles. So unusual and impressive is Vizcaya, its guest list has included Ronald Reagan, Pope John Paul II, and Queen Elizabeth II. Guided 45-minute tours are available, and group tours are given by appointment. ⊠ *3251 S. Miami Ave.,* ☎ *305/250–9133.* ☜ *$10.* ☉ *House and ticket booth daily 9:30–4:30, garden daily 9:30–5:30.*

Virginia Key and Key Biscayne

Government Cut and the Port of Miami separate the city's dense urban fabric from two of its playground islands, Virginia Key and Key Biscayne. Parks occupy much of both keys, providing facilities for golf, tennis, softball, picnicking, and sunbathing, plus uninviting but ecologically valuable stretches of dense mangrove swamp. Key Biscayne's long and winding roads are great for rollerblading and bicycling, and its lush, lazy setting provides a respite from the buzz-saw tempo of SoBe.

A Good Tour

To reach Virginia Key and Key Biscayne take the Rickenbacker Causeway ($1 per car) across Biscayne Bay from the mainland at Brickell Avenue and Southwest 26th Road, about 2 mi south of downtown Miami. The causeway links several islands in the bay.

The William M. Powell Bridge rises 75 ft above the water to eliminate the need for a draw span. The panoramic view from the top encompasses the bay, keys, port, and downtown skyscrapers, with Miami Beach and the Atlantic Ocean in the distance. Just south of the Powell Bridge, a stub of the **Old Rickenbacker Causeway Bridge** ㊶, built in 1947, is now a fishing pier with a nice view.

Immediately after crossing the Rickenbacker Causeway onto Virginia Key, you'll see a long strip of bay front popular with windsurfers and jet skiers. Look for the gold dome of the **Miami Seaquarium** ㊷, one of the country's first marine attractions. Opposite the causeway from the Seaquarium, a road leads north to **Virginia Key Beach** ㊸ and the adjacent **Virginia Key Critical Wildlife Area** ㊹, which is often closed to the public to protect nesting birds.

From Virginia Key the causeway crosses Bear Cut to the north end of Key Biscayne and becomes Crandon Boulevard. The boulevard bisects 1,211-acre **Crandon Park** ㊺, which has a popular Atlantic Ocean beach and nature center. On your right are entrances to the Crandon

Park Golf Course and the Tennis Center at Crandon Park, home of the Lipton Championships.

From the traffic circle at the south end of Crandon Park, Crandon Boulevard continues to the **Bill Baggs Cape Florida State Recreation Area** ㊻, a 460-acre park containing, among other things, the brick Cape Florida Lighthouse and light-keeper's cottage.

Follow Crandon Boulevard back to Crandon Park through Key Biscayne's downtown village, where shops and a 10-acre village green cater mainly to local residents. On your way back to the mainland, pause as you approach the Powell Bridge to admire the Miami skyline. At night the brightly lighted NationsBank Tower looks like a clipper ship running under full sail before the breeze.

TIMING

Set aside the better part of a day for this tour, saving a few late-afternoon hours for Crandon Park and the Cape Florida Lighthouse. Birdwatching at the Virginia Key Critical Wildlife Area can only be done in its three-month season, if even then.

Sights to See

★ ㊻ **Bill Baggs Cape Florida State Recreation Area.** Thanks to great beaches, amenities, sunsets, and a lighthouse, this park at Key Biscayne's southern tip is worth the drive. Since Hurricane Andrew, it has returned better than ever, with new boardwalks, 18 picnic shelters, and a café that serves light lunches. An additional 54 acres of wetlands were acquired in 1997, and a marina is on the drawing board. A stroll or ride along walking and bicycle paths and boardwalks provides wonderful views of Miami's dramatic skyline. Also on site are bicycle and skate rentals, a playground, fishing piers, kayak rentals, and, on request, guided tours of the cultural complex and the **Cape Florida Lighthouse,** South Florida's oldest structure. The lighthouse was erected in 1845 to replace an earlier one destroyed in an 1836 Seminole attack, in which the keeper's helper was killed. Climb 118 steps to visit a replica of the keeper's house. ⊠ *1200 S. Crandon Blvd.,* ☎ *305/361–5811 or 305/361–8779.* ☐ *$4 per vehicle with up to 8 people; $1 per person on bicycle, bus, motorcycle, or foot.* ☉ *Daily 8–sunset.*

㊺ **Crandon Park.** This laid-back park in northern Key Biscayne is popular with families, and many educated beach enthusiasts rate the 3½-mi county beach here among the top 10 beaches in North America. The sand is soft, there's a great view of the Atlantic, and parking is both inexpensive and plentiful. At the north end of the beach is the free **Marjory Stoneman Douglas Biscayne Nature Center** (☎ 305/642–9600). Explore a variety of natural habitats by taking a tour. Nature center hours vary, so call ahead. ⊠ *4000 Crandon Blvd.,* ☎ *305/361–5421.* ☐ *$3.50 per vehicle.* ☉ *Daily 8–sunset.*

㊷ **Miami Seaquarium.** This popular attraction has six daily shows featuring sea lions, dolphins, and Lolita, a killer whale. (Lolita's tank is small for seaquariums—just three times her length—and some wildlife advocates are trying to get her back to sea.) Exhibits include a shark pool, a 235,000-gallon tropical-reef aquarium, and manatees. Glass-bottom boats take tours of Biscayne Bay. ⊠ *4400 Rickenbacker Causeway,* ☎ *305/361–5705.* ☐ *$19.95, parking $3.* ☉ *Daily 9:30–6, last admission 4:30.*

㊶ **Old Rickenbacker Causeway Bridge.** Here you can watch boat traffic pass through the channel, pelicans and other seabirds soar and dive, and dolphins cavort in the bay. Park at its entrance, about a mile from the tollgate, and walk past anglers tending their lines to the gap where the center draw span across the Intracoastal Waterway was removed. ⊠ *South of Powell Bridge.*

43 **Virginia Key Beach.** This City of Miami park with a 2-mi stretch of oceanfront offers shelters, barbecue grills, ball fields, nature trails, and a fishing area. It may be closed to protect wildlife. ⊠ *Rickenbacker Causeway,* ☎ *305/361–2749.* ☒ *Parking $2.* ☉ *Daily 9–sunset.*

44 **Virginia Key Critical Wildlife Area.** Plans are in the works to safeguard this 400-acre portion of mangrove-edged island. Residents include reddish egrets, black-bellied plovers, black skimmers, and roseate spoonbills—but you can only see them in May, June, and July. The area is left undisturbed during the other nine months in order to make it attractive to migratory shorebirds. Enter at Virginia Key Beach.

DINING

The success stories of Miami's better restaurants inspire hopefuls to pour millions into designing their masterpiece, only to realize three months later they'd need to sell 6 million bowls of pasta a day to pay their banknote. Restaurants come and go, but most listed below have passed the test of time (although a few experimental eateries may be gone by the time you arrive).

American

Miami Beach

$ ✕ **11th Street Diner.** Wow. The sights, sounds, and smells of the '50s
★ are captured here without the artificial ambience of James Dean cutouts and poodle skirts. Since serving its first plate of meat loaf in 1992, the diner has become a low-priced, unpretentious hangout for locals. This busy, bustling eatery (inside a 1948 Deco dining car) is where you can grab a corner booth and order a cherry cola, blue plate special, and milk shake and pretend you're your parents. Ten to one the waitress will call you "honey." ⊠ *11th St. and Washington Ave.,* ☎ *305/534–6373. AE, MC, V.*

American/Casual

Coconut Grove

$–$$ ✕ **Planet Hollywood.** Miami has become a second home for members of Hollywood's A-list, which may explain why Willis, Stallone, and Schwarzenegger chose it for one of their themed eateries. Not surprisingly, the decor is as if a movie studio warehouse exploded inside the restaurant. Although you're more likely to see fellow tourists than real celebs, you should walk away satisfied with the service and attention lavished on you and your food. The fare may seem standard (pizza, pasta, burgers, salads), but the creative preparation places it a few notches above that of other chains. ⊠ *3390 Mary St.,* ☎ *305/445–7277. AE, D, DC, MC, V.*

Downtown Miami

$–$$ ✕ **Hard Rock Cafe.** Here you'll find cool stuff on the walls, hot stuff on the plates. The location (a few miles from SoBe) is a drawback for those who want their nightlife concentrated on Ocean Drive. Nevertheless, you can find the requisite T-shirts, key chains, and ball caps for which the Hard Rock is famous. Oh yeah, they also sell food: hamburgers, cheeseburgers, fajitas, steak, fried chicken, etc. ⊠ *401 Biscayne Blvd.,* ☎ *305/377–3110. AE, DC, MC, V.*

Miami Area Dining

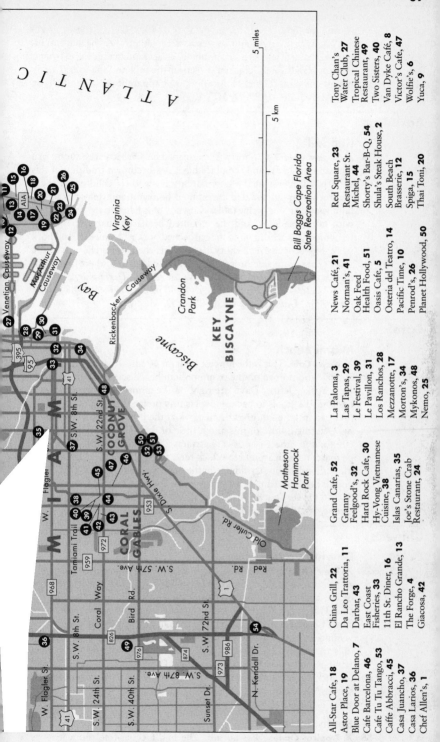

39

ATLANTIC

Venetian Causeway

MacArthur Causeway

Biscayne Bay

Rickenbacker Causeway

Virginia Key

Crandon Park

KEY BISCAYNE

Biscayne

Bill Baggs Cape Florida
State Recreation Area

Matheson Hammock Park

MIAMI

CORAL GABLES

COCONUT GROVE

W. Flagler St.
W. Flagler St.
Tamiami Trail
S.W. 8th St.
S.W. 22nd St.
S.W. 8th St.
Coral Way
Bird Rd.
S.W. 24th St.
S.W. 40th St.
Sunset Dr.
Coral Way
S. Dixie Hwy.
Old Cutler Rd.
Red Rd.
S.W. 57th Ave.
S.W. 72nd St.
S.W. 87th Ave.
N. Kendall Dr.

5 miles
5 km
0

Miami Beach

\$\$–\$\$\$ ✕ **All-Star Cafe.** Sports heroes (Woods, Griffey, Gretzky, Seles, et al.) have lent their names and suggestions to yet another themed restaurant in Miami. The sports decor should attract fans, but the menu (wings, burgers, salads, fried chicken) is run-of-the-mill and the energy of its parent company, Planet Hollywood, isn't apparent yet. ⊠ *960 Ocean Dr.,* ☎ *305/604–1999. D, MC, V.*

Barbecue

Kendall

\$ ✕ **Shorty's Bar-B-Q.** Shorty Allen opened his barbecue restaurant in a log cabin in 1951, and the place has since become a tradition in this suburb southwest of the city. Parents bring their children to show them where mom and dad ate on their honeymoon. Meals are served family style at long picnic tables. Cowboy hats hang on the walls, along with horns, saddles, and the mounted heads of boar and caribou. Longtime fans are drawn to the barbecued pork ribs, chicken, and pork steak slow-cooked over hickory logs and drenched in Shorty's own warm, spicy sauce, with side orders of tangy baked beans and big chunks of pork, corn on the cob, and coleslaw. ⊠ *9200 S. Dixie Hwy.,* ☎ *305/ 670–7732;* ⊠ *11575 S.W. 40th St.,* ☎ *305/227–3196;* ⊠ *5989 S. University Dr., Davie,* ☎ *954/680–9900. D, MC, V.*

Café

Miami Beach

\$ ✕ **News Café.** This is the hippest joint on Ocean Drive. Owners Marc
★   Soyka, who trained on the cosmopolitan beach scene in Tel Aviv, and New Yorker Jeffrey Davis are right on the money. Although there's a bar with 12 stools in back, most visitors prefer sitting outside, where they can feel the salt breeze and gawk at the beautiful people walking by. Offering a little of this and a little of that—bagels, pâtés, chocolate fondue—the 24-hour café attracts a big crowd all the time, with people coming in around the clock for a snack, a light meal, or an aperitif and, invariably, to indulge in the people parade. In 1997 the café's popularity led to a new location—twice as large—in Coconut Grove. ⊠ *800 Ocean Dr.,* ☎ *305/538–6397;* ⊠ *2901 Florida Ave., Coconut Grove,* ☎ *305/774–6397. AE, DC, MC, V.*

Chinese

Downtown Miami

\$–\$\$\$\$ ✕ **Tony Chan's Water Club.** One of a pair of outstanding Chinese
★   restaurants on the mainland, this beautiful dining room just off the lobby of the high-rise DoubleTree Grand Hotel looks onto a bay-side marina. Filled with art and chrome, the long room is modern rather than stock Chinese. On the menu of more than 200 appetizers and entrées is minced quail tossed with bamboo shoots and mushrooms wrapped in lettuce leaves. Indulge in a seafood spectacular with shrimp, conch, scallops, fish cakes, and crabmeat tossed with broccoli in a bird's nest or pork chops sprinkled with green pepper in a black bean–garlic sauce. A low-cal favorite is steamed sea bass with ginger and garlic. ⊠ *1717 N. Bayshore Dr.,* ☎ *305/374–8888. AE, D, DC, MC, V.*

South Dade

\$–\$\$ ✕ **Tropical Chinese Restaurant.** The big, lacquer-free room feels as
★   open and busy as a railway station. You'll find unfamiliar items on the menu—early spring leaves of snow pea pods, for example, which are sublimely tender and flavorful. The extensive menu is filled with tofu

combinations, poultry, beef, and pork, as well as tender seafood. A dim sum lunch is served from great carts. In the big open kitchen, 10 chefs prepare everything as if for dignitaries. ⊠ *7991 S.W. 40th St.,* ☎ *305/ 262–7576 or 305/262–1552. AE, DC, MC, V.*

Contemporary

Coconut Grove

$$$ ✕ **Grand Cafe.** Understated elegance is the hallmark of the Grand Bay
★ Hotel's (☞ Lodging, *below*) bilevel dining room, which has fanlight windows, brass details, pink tablecloths, and floral bouquets. French chef Pascal Oudin's starter specialties include pan-seared Florida crab cake and cherrywood-smoked Chilean salmon. Among entrées, favorites are the baked macadamia-and-ginger-crusted salmon and seared rare yellowfin tuna. For dessert try the dark-chocolate and praline *crousilliant* (crispy chocolate topped with chocolate mousse and coated with chocolate shavings and sauce). ⊠ *2669 S. Bayshore Dr.,* ☎ *305/858– 9600. AE, DC, MC, V.*

$ ✕ **Cafe Tu Tu Tango.** Local artists set up their easels in the rococo-modern arcades of this eclectic café-lounge on the second story of Coconut Grove's highly popular CocoWalk. The artistic concept follows through to the menu, which allows you to pick appetizers as if you were selecting paints from a palette. Outside offers some of the best people-watching in the South. Inside, guests graze on chips, dips, breads, and spreads. House specials include frittatas, crab cakes, *picadillo* empanadas (spicy ground beef served with cilantro sour cream), and chicken and shrimp orzo paella, all to be enjoyed with some of the best sangria in the city. ⊠ *3015 Grand Ave. (CocoWalk),* ☎ *305/529–2222. AE, MC, V.*

Coral Gables

$$–$$$$ ✕ **Norman's.** This elegantly casual restaurant, which has won as many
★ awards as it has customers, turns out gourmet cuisine with an edge. Chef Norman Van Aken has created a buzz by perfecting the art of New World cuisine—a combination rooted in Latin, American, Caribbean, and Asian influences. Bold tastes are delivered in every dish, whether it's a simple black-and-white bean soup with sour cream, chorizo, and tortillas or a rum-and-pepper-painted grouper on a mango-*habanero mojo* sauce. From the comfortable decor to the staff that never seems harried, even when all seats are filled (usually every minute between opening and closing), Norman's has captured the essence of Miami dining. ⊠ *21 Almeria Ave.,* ☎ *305/446–6767. AE, DC, MC, V. Closed Sun. No lunch Sat.*

$$$ ✕ **Restaurant St. Michel.** The setting is utterly French, the little hotel
★ it's in (☞ Lodging, *below*) is Mediterranean, the town is very Spanish, but the cuisine is American. Stuart Bornstein's window on Coral Gables is a lace-curtained café with sidewalk tables that could be across from a railroad station in Avignon or Bordeaux. A sculpted bust here, a circus poster there, deco chandeliers, and a mirrored, palm frond–shape mosaic all create a whimsical, foreign feel. Lighter dishes include moist couscous chicken and pasta primavera. Among the heartier entrées are a plum, soy, and lemon-glazed fillet of salmon; sesame-coated loin of tuna; and local yellowtail snapper. ⊠ *162 Alcazar Ave.,* ☎ *305/ 444–1666. AE, DC, MC, V.*

$$ ✕ **Two Sisters.** Competition among Coral Gables restaurants means
★ that food has to be better than fantastic. This restaurant, on the ground floor of the Hyatt Regency (☞ Lodging, *below*), approaches nirvana. Though the mood is understated, the Pacific Rim–inspired dishes add definite pizzazz. Entrées such as wokked tangled shrimp with jungle curry, rice ribbons, and coconut glaze or jerk marinated snapper with

red onion confit and ginger butter might make you consider a vacation in Polynesia. Servers are attentive, and desserts are so delicious you may end up spending the night with Two Sisters. ⊠ *50 Alhambra Plaza,* ☎ *305/441–1234. AE, MC, V.*

Downtown Miami

$$$–$$$$ ✕ **Le Pavillon.** The mahogany, jade marble, and leather appointments
  ★ of the dining room in the Hotel Inter-Continental (☞ Lodging, *below*)
evoke the conservative air of an English private club. Beautiful floral displays enhance the mood as the attentive staff serves regional American fare from a limited but frequently changing menu, including items low in calories, cholesterol, and sodium. Specialties are char-grilled bluefin tuna fillet, poached yellowtail snapper, panfried corn-fed squab, roasted free-range chicken, spring lamb, and roasted fillet of milk-fed veal. For a light dessert try red berry soup with vanilla ice cream. The wine list is extensive. ⊠ *100 Chopin Plaza,* ☎ *305/577–1000, ext. 4494 or 4462. AE, DC, MC, V. Closed Sun.*

  $ ✕ **Granny Feelgood's.** "Granny" is a nice gentleman named Irving Fields, who has been catering to health-conscious downtowners for 25 years. Specialties include chicken salad with raisins, apples, and cinnamon; spinach fettuccine with pine nuts; grilled tofu; apple crumb cake; and carrot cake. ⊠ *111 N.W. 1st St.,* ☎ *305/579–2104. No credit cards. No breakfast or lunch weekends.*

Miami Beach

$$$–$$$$ ✕ **Blue Door at Delano.** In a hotel where style seems favored over substance, service and meals here are surprisingly satisfying. Perhaps this is due to the arrival of acclaimed chef Claude Troisgros, who combined the decor and dishes of classic French cuisine with South American influences to create dishes like the Big Raviole, filled with taro-root mousseline and white-truffle oil, and *boeuf au Manioc* (a beef tenderloin in a Cabernet sauce and yuca biscuit). The dessert menu showcases such selections as a Brazilian coffee and sweet chocolate mousse as well as banana puff pastry with strawberries and cinnamon. Equally pleasing is dining with the crème de la crème of Miami (and New York and Paris) society. Bon appétit! ⊠ *1685 Collins Ave.,* ☎ *305/674–6400. Reservations essential. AE, D, DC, MC, V.*

$$$–$$$$ ✕ **China Grill.** This crowded, noisy place has no view, but that doesn't detract from its popularity or that of the original China Grill in New York. Jack Nicholson, Joe Pesci, and other celebs are regulars—perhaps hoping to live the dream of finishing the Grill's 38-ounce porterhouse steak. Contrary to what you might think, chef Ephraim Kadish turns out not Chinese food but rather "world cuisine," and portions are large and intended for sharing. Crispy duck with caramelized black vinegar sauce and scallion pancakes is a nice surprise, as is pork and beans with green apple and balsamic *mojo.* Don't miss the broccoli rabe dumpling starter, the wild mushroom pasta entrée, or the flash-fried crispy spinach that shatters when eaten. ⊠ *404 Washington Ave.,* ☎ *305/534–2211. AE, DC, MC, V. No lunch Sat.*

$$–$$$$ ✕ **Astor Place.** The hotel has already earned a reputation for service, so it's only natural that this basement turned bright and airy restaurant would follow suit. Diners are wowed by creative spins on appetizers like yellowtail snapper soft tacos and entrées that include ancho-cinnamon pork tenderloin and skillet-steamed sea bass. Service is fast and friendly, the setting is spacious, and the lunch menu is just as creative as the one at dinner. The festive Sunday-morning gospel brunch is another reason to give thanks for Astor Place. ⊠ *956 Washington Ave.,* ☎ *305/672–7217. AE, DC, MC, V.*

$$–$$$$ ✕ **Pacific Time.** This cool restaurant is packed nearly every night. The
★ superb eatery, co-owned by chef Jonathan Eismann, has a high blue
ceiling and banquettes, accents of mahogany and brass, plank floors,
and an open-window kitchen. The American-Asian cuisine includes such
entrées as cedar-roasted salmon, rosemary-roasted chicken, and dry-
aged Colorado beef grilled with shiitake mushrooms. Rices, potatoes,
and vegetables are à la carte; however, a pretheater prix-fixe dinner
($20), served 6–7, comes with a noodle dish, Szechuan mixed grill, and
grilled ginger chicken. Desserts (around $7) include a fresh pear-pecan
spring roll. There's an extensive California wine list. ⊠ *915 Lincoln
Rd.,* ☎ *305/534–5979. AE, DC, MC, V.*

$$–$$$ ✕ **Nemo.** Back in 1994, chef Michael Schwartz took a chance open-
ing this restaurant in the struggling south end of SoBe. Today, how-
ever, Nemo is receiving raves from gourmands, and the neighborhood
is on the verge of a comeback as impressive as the revival of bustling
Ocean Drive. So get here while you can still find a table. The open atmo-
sphere, bright colors, copper fixtures, and tree-shaded courtyard lend
casual comfort, and a menu that blends Caribbean, Japanese, and
Southeast Asian influences promises an explosion of cultures in each
bite. Popular appetizers include garlic-cured salmon rolls with *tabiko*
caviar and wasabi mayo and crispy prawns with spicy salsa *cruda*. Fa-
vorite entrées? Try the wokked, charred salmon or the grilled Indian-
spiced pork chop—and there's more where those came from. ⊠ *100
Collins Ave.,* ☎ *305/532–4550. AE, MC, V.*

$$–$$$ ✕ **South Beach Brasserie.** How does owner Michael Caine manage to
appear in a movie a month and still run a successful Miami Beach restau-
rant? He's managing quite well, thank you. Appetizers that include spring
rolls and lobster salads and entrées showcasing sea bass, ahi tuna, and
prime meat combine classic American and international cuisines. In ad-
dition to the food, Caine's celebrity has been instrumental in making
this one of Miami Beach's most popular eateries. A nice walk on the
Lincoln Road Mall is a great after-dinner treat. ⊠ *910 Lincoln Rd.,*
☎ *305/534–5511. AE, D, DC, MC, V.*

$–$$ ✕ **Van Dyke Café.** Marc Soyka's second restaurant quickly attracted
the artsy crowd, just as his News Café draws the fashion crowd. Of
course, tourists like it, too. In the restored 1924 Van Dyke Hotel, this
place seems livelier than its café cousin, with pedestrians passing by
on the Lincoln Road Mall and live jazz upstairs every evening. Three
meals are served—from soups and grilled dolphinfish sandwiches to
basil-grilled lamb and pasta dishes—and a 15% gratuity is included.
⊠ *846 Lincoln Rd.,* ☎ *305/534–3600. AE, DC, MC, V.*

North Miami Beach

$$$–$$$$ ✕ **Chef Allen's.** In this Art Deco world of glass block, art, neon trim,
★ and fresh flowers, your gaze remains riveted on the kitchen. Chef
Allen Susser designed it with a picture window 25 ft wide, so you can
watch him create contemporary American masterpieces from a menu
that changes nightly. After a salad of baby greens and warm wild
mushrooms or rock-shrimp hash with roasted corn, consider *orecchi-
ette* pasta with sun-dried tomatoes, goat cheese, spinach, and toasted
pine nuts; swordfish with conch-citrus couscous, macadamia nuts,
and lemon; or grilled lamb chops with eggplant timbale and a three-
nut salsa. Take home a bottle of chef Allen's mango ketchup as a tasty
souvenir. A favorite dessert is the double-chocolate soufflé with lots
of nuts. ⊠ *19088 N.E. 29th Ave.,* ☎ *305/935–2900. AE, DC, MC,
V.*

Continental

Miami Beach

$$$ ✗ **The Forge.** Often compared to a museum, this landmark restaurant, which bills itself as "the Versailles of steak," stands behind a facade of 19th-century Parisian mansions, where a forge once stood. Each intimate dining salon has its own historical artifacts, including a chandelier that hung in James Madison's White House. The wine cellar contains 380,000 bottles—including more than 500 dating from 1822 (and costing as much as $35,000) and recorked in 1989 by experts from Domaines Barons de Rothschild. In addition to steak, specialties include Norwegian salmon served over fresh garden vegetables with spinach vinaigrette and free-range Wisconsin duck roasted with black currants. For dessert try the blacksmith pie. This place is a hot party spot on Wednesday night, and a private cigar club, the Cuba Club, is very popular with the rich and famous. ✉ *432 Arthur Godfrey Rd.,* ☎ *305/538–8533. AE, DC, MC, V. No lunch.*

North Miami

$$–$$$ ✗ **La Paloma.** This Swiss Continental restaurant offers a total sensory experience: fine food, impeccable service, and the ambience of an art museum. Since 1977 owners Werner and Maria Staub have displayed the ornate European antiques they've been collecting for decades: Baccarat crystal, Limoges china, Meissen porcelain, and Sèvres clocks. The staff speaks Spanish, French, German, Portuguese, and Arabic. Specialties include fresh local fish and shellfish; Wiener schnitzel; lamb chops coated with bread crumbs, mustard, garlic, and herbs; veal chop with morel sauce; and for dessert, lemon sherbet with fresh kiwifruit and vodka. ✉ *10999 Biscayne Blvd.,* ☎ *305/891–0505. AE, MC, V. No lunch weekends.*

Cuban

Little Havana

$$–$$$ ✗ **Victor's Cafe.** This popular restaurant was inspired by the *casona,* the great house of colonial Cuba. The mood is old Havana, with Cuban art and antiques and a glass-covered fountain courtyard. Owner Victor del Corral, who emigrated from Cuba in 1957, first made his mark in Manhattan. Now he works with his daughter Sonia Zaldivar and her son Luis. Come on Friday afternoon, when the tapas bar is packed and lunch often lasts until dusk, in Cuban fashion. Entrées come with rice and black beans. Hot appetizers, such as a puff pastry filled with aromatically herbed lump crabmeat or a savory cassava turnover filled with Florida lobster, are enough for a meal. Truly jumbo shrimp are served with yam quenelles in a creamy champagne sauce sprinkled with salmon roe. Romantic music plays nightly. ✉ *2340 S.W. 32nd Ave.,* ☎ *305/445–1313. AE, MC, V.*

$ ✗ **Islas Canarias.** Since 1976 this has been a gathering place for Cuban poets, pop-music stars, and media personalities. Murals depict a Canary Islands street scene (owner Santiago Garcia's grandfather came from Tenerife). The low-priced menu, which includes breakfast, carries such Canary Islands dishes as baked lamb, ham hocks with boiled potatoes, and tortilla *Española* (Spanish omelet with onions and chorizo), as well as Cuban standards like *palomilla* steak and fried kingfish. Don't miss the three superb varieties of homemade chips—potato, *malanga,* and plantain. ✉ *285 N.W. 27th Ave.,* ☎ *305/649–0440. D, MC, V.* ✉ *Coral Way and S.W. 137th Ave., Westchester,* ☎ *305/559–6666. AE, D, MC, V.*

Miami Beach

$$–$$$$ ✕ **Yuca.** Top-flight Cuban dining can be had at this bistro-chic restaurant on renovated Lincoln Road. The name stands for the potatolike staple of Cuban kitchens and is also used to refer to young urban Cuban-Americans. High standards are first evident in the setting and carry over to the food: traditional corn tamale filled with conch and a spicy jalapeño and creole cheese pesto, the namesake yuca stuffed with *mamacita's* picadillo and dressed in wild mushrooms on a bed of sautéed spinach, and plantain-coated dolphinfish with a tamarind tartar sauce. Featured desserts include classic Cuban rice pudding in an almond basket and coconut pudding in its coconut. A Sunday gospel brunch is served from noon to 4, and Friday- and Saturday-evening entertainment is provided by Albita, a popular Cuban chanteuse. ⊠ *501 Lincoln Rd.,* ☎ *305/532–9822. AE, DC, MC, V.*

West Dade

$ ✕ **Casa Larios.** Yes, South Florida has 1,000 Cuban restaurants, but this one stands out for its consistently excellent food. Chicken soup is golden yellow, pearly, salty—the perfect elixir. Look for specials like roast pork loin, roasted lamb, *caldo gallego* (white-bean soup with ham and greens), and the Argentine-inspired *churrasco,* a boneless strip steak with *chimichurri* (a cooling sauce of parsley, garlic, onion, and oil). The restaurant is a favorite of the Estefans, who took the concept and helped open Larios on the Beach, on Ocean Drive. ⊠ *7929 N.W. 2nd St.,* ☎ *305/266–5494. AE, MC, V.*

Delicatessen

Miami Beach

$ ✕ **Wolfie's.** If there's one place in Miami that screams New York, this is it. A bakery featuring giga-caloric desserts, bowls filled with matzo ball soup, and sandwiches stacked high with pastrami make this seem as if you're dining on Broadway. If you want to see what Miami looked like 40 years ago, sidle up to the counter or share a rounded booth in Celebrity Corner. Open 24 hours, this is a perfect place to soak up some local color or satisfy a late-night craving for corned beef. ⊠ *2038 Collins Ave.,* ☎ *305/538–6626. D, DC, MC, V.*

French

Coral Gables

$$–$$$$ ✕ **Le Festival.** The canopied entrance to this classical French restaurant belies the elegance within, where decor celebrates Parisian *moderne* with etched-glass filigree posh burgundy, mahogany, and rose-tinted details. A second room, for smokers, is more gilded. Main courses include fillet of grouper in bouillabaisse sauce; stuffed quail with grape and red-wine sauce; milk-fed veal sautéed with mushrooms, grapes, and brandy cream sauce; and chateaubriand for two. Desserts comprise various pastries, mousses, and soufflées. The wine list includes 100 selections, many priced less than $30. ⊠ *2120 Salzedo St.,* ☎ *305/ 442–8545. Reservations essential for dinner and for lunch parties of 5 or more. AE, D, DC, MC, V. Closed Sun. No lunch Sat.*

Greek

Five Points, Miami

$–$$ ✕ **Mykonos.** Since 1973 this busy and active Miami fixture has brightened the intersection at Five Points (in the Roads section of town) with a beautiful mural of the Aegean. Inside, a sparkling blue-and-white setting is dressed up with Greek travel posters. Specialties include gyros, moussaka, marinated lamb and chicken, calamari and octopus sautéed in wine and onions, and sumptuous Greek salads thick with feta cheese and briny olives. Vegetarian moussaka, eggplant roll, lasagna, and a Greek-style omelet are also on the menu. ⊠ *1201 Coral Way,* ☎ *305/ 856–3140. AE, DC, MC, V. No lunch Sun.*

Indian

Coral Gables

$–$$ ✕ **Darbar.** Owner Bobby Nangia's impeccably arranged Darbar (In-
★ dian for "Royal Court") is the glory of Miami's Indian restaurants. It's authentic, right down to the portraits of turbaned maharajas. Flavors rise as if in a dance from the *bangan bharta* (eggplant mashed with onions, tomatoes, herbs, and spices and baked in a tandoor). The menu's focus is on northern Indian or frontier cuisine—various kebabs, tandoori platters, and *tikkas* (chicken or lamb marinated in yogurt and spices and cooked tandoori style)—although there are also curries from different regions and *biryani* specialties prepared with basmati rice and garnished with boiled egg, tomato, nuts, and raisins. Everything, including the unusual Indian breads, is cooked to order. ⊠ *276 Alhambra Circle,* ☎ *305/448–9691. AE, DC, MC, V. No lunch Sun.*

Italian

Coral Gables

$$$–$$$$ ✕ **Giacosa.** Named for one of Puccini's librettists, this is another of
★ the superbly evocative—and just plain superb—restaurants in Coral Gables. The ambience is wonderfully informed—a thickly carpeted room like a smart Venetian salon, fresh flowers, chair cushions inspired by tapestry. From putting your napkin in your lap to whisking a tower of airy pita bread with olive oil in a carafe to the table, the smooth staff is the standard of competence. Parmesan is freshly grated to the plate. A salad *tricolore* imparts the bitter kiss of arugula; pastas, veal, and fresh seafood are all prepared for peak taste. ⊠ *394 Giralda Ave.,* ☎ *305/445–5858. AE, DC, MC, V. No lunch weekends.*

$$–$$$ ✕ **Caffe Abbracci.** Although the kitchen closes at midnight, the last wave
★ of customers—usually Brazilians—is still partying to flamenco or salsa music on weekends at 2. The setting is graciously deco, with huge bursts of flowers, frosted glass, and fresh roses on white linens; lights above each table operate with individual dimmers. After the cold and hot antipasti—various carpaccios, porcini mushrooms, calamari, grilled goat cheese, shrimps, mussels—come festive entrées. Most pasta is made fresh, so consider sampling two or three, maybe with pesto sauce, Gorgonzola, and fresh tomatoes. Room for dessert? Napoleons and tiramisu are made here daily, and there's always a choice of fresh fruit tarts. ⊠ *318 Aragon Ave.,* ☎ *305/441–0700. Reservations essential. AE, DC, MC, V. No lunch weekends.*

Miami Beach

$$–$$$ ✕ **Mezzanotte.** Sometime between 6 PM and 10 PM, the big square room with the square bar transforms from an empty catering hall to a New Year's Eve party. Trendoids call for their capellini with fresh tomato and basil; calamari in clam juice, garlic, and red wine; or scallopini with mushroom, pepper, and white wine, and then top it off with their *dolci*: fresh napoleon, chocolate mousse, or tiramisu. Chic and intimate, Mezzanotte is known for fine food at moderate prices, but watch out for the coffee at $2.25 a pop! ⊠ *1200 Washington Ave.,* ☎ *305/673– 4343;* ⊠ *3390 Mary St., Coconut Grove,* ☎ *305/448–7677. AE, D, DC, MC, V. No lunch in Miami Beach.*

$$–$$$ ✕ **Osteria del Teatro.** Thanks to word of mouth, this northern Italian
★ restaurant is constantly full. Orchids grace the tables in the intimate
gray, gray, and gray room with a low, laced canvas ceiling, deco lamps,
and the most refined clink and clatter along Washington Avenue's remarkable restaurant row. You'll start with large, unevenly sliced hunks
of homemade bread lightly toasted. Then try an appetizer of grilled
Portobello mushrooms topped with fontina cheese and served over a
bed of arugula with a green peppercorn–brandy sauce, and for the main
course, linguine sautéed with chunks of jumbo shrimp, roasted peppers, capers, black olives, fresh diced tomato, and herbs in a tangy garlic olive oil sauce. ⊠ *1443 Washington Ave.,* ☎ *305/538–7850. AE,
DC, MC, V. Closed Tues. No lunch.*

$$ ✕ **Da Leo Trattoria.** Tables from this little restaurant spill across the
Lincoln Road Mall, staying full thanks to consistently good food at
prices less than half of what trendier places charge. The volume keeps
the mood festive and the standards high. You'll be amazed by the art,
which covers the walls so completely you might think the canvasses
provide structural support. The look is ancient Roman town house
(though owner Leonardo Marchini hails from Lucca), with banquettes
along one wall and wainscoting along the other. Pastas, fish, veal, and
fowl make up most of the entrées, and homemade desserts are a plus.
Simpler appetites are satisfied at Da Leo Pizza é Via, directly across
the mall. ⊠ *819 Lincoln Rd. Mall,* ☎ *305/674–0350. AE, DC, MC,
V. No lunch weekends.*

$–$$ ✕ **Spiga.** Miami offers so much exotic fare, it's nice that this place gets
back to the basics with modestly priced Italian standards served with
flair. Carpaccio *di salmone* (thinly sliced salmon with mixed greens)
is a typical appetizer, and ravioli *di vitello ai funghi shitaki* is, as the
name implies, homemade ravioli stuffed with veal and sautéed with
shiitake mushrooms. Homemade is the key here: Pastas and breads are
made daily. The cozy restaurant has become a neighborhood favorite
where customers can—and do—bring in CDs for their personal en-
joyment. ⊠ *1228 Collins Ave.,* ☎ *305/534–0079. AE, D, DC, MC,
V.*

Mediterranean

Miami Beach

$–$$ ✕ **Oasis Cafe.** Fresh flavors and innovative food at budget prices de-
fine this quasi–Middle Eastern, quasi-vegetarian spot north of South
Beach. As you'd expect, hummus, grape leaves, feta cheese, and *kala-
mata* olives figure on the starter menu, but grilled sesame tofu and sautéed
garlic spinach are surprising. For entrées, ask for pan-seared turkey chop;
roasted vegetable lasagna; penne with turkey, tomato, saffron, and pine
nuts; or grilled fresh fish on focaccia. Homemade desserts are luscious.
⊠ *976 41st St.,* ☎ *305/674–7676. AE, D, DC, MC, V.*

Mexican

Miami Beach

$–$$ ✕ **El Rancho Grande.** The location (just off Lincoln Road) and the menu
(mainstream Mexican) have made this neighborhood restaurant popular with locals and have earned it a slew of "best" awards in area dining polls. Prices are reasonable, and service is casual and laid-back. Beef
falutas, chicken enchiladas, *taquitas,* and more are served in a cantina-
style setting. This is a good option for a quick and inexpensive meal.
⊠ *1626 Pennsylvania Ave.,* ☎ *305/673–0480. AE, MC, V.*

Nicaraguan

Downtown Miami

$–$$$
★
✕ **Los Ranchos.** Owner Carlos Somoza, nephew of Nicaragua's late president Anastasio Somoza, sustains the tradition of Managua's original Los Ranchos by serving Argentine-style beef—lean, grass-fed tenderloin with chimichurri. Nicaragua's own sauces are a tomato-based marinara and the fiery *cebollitas encurtidas*, with jalapeño and pickled onion. Specialties include chorizo and *cuajada con maduro* (skim cheese with fried bananas). Don't look for veggies or brewed decaf, but there is live entertainment. ⊠ *Bayside Marketplace, 401 Biscayne Blvd.,* ☎ *305/375–8188 or 305/375–0666;* ⊠ *125 S.W. 107th Ave., Little Managua,* ☎ *305/221–9367;* ⊠ *Kendall Town & Country, 8505 Mills Dr., Kendall,* ☎ *305/596–5353;* ⊠ *The Falls, 8888 S.W. 136th St., Suite 303, South Miami,* ☎ *305/238–6867;* ⊠ *2728 Ponce de León Blvd., Coral Gables,* ☎ *305/446–0050. AE, DC, MC, V.*

Russian

Miami Beach

$$–$$$
✕ **Red Square.** It may have taken the Soviet Union 70 years to self-destruct, but it took the China Grill capitalists only a few years to determine that Americans want to dine at a Communist-themed restaurant. Delicacies include iced oysters, smoked fish, and chilled Russian borscht, and the place may end up succeeding on the strength of its selection of 100 frozen vodkas. If you're looking for a hot meal, this isn't the place, but if you want to witness the possible birth of a trend, head to the Russian front. ⊠ *411 Washington Ave.,* ☎ *305/672–0200. AE, MC, V.*

Seafood

Downtown Miami

$$–$$$$
★
✕ **East Coast Fisheries.** This friendly family-owned restaurant and retail fish market on the Miami River offers fresh Florida seafood from its own 38-boat fleet in the Keys. From tables along the second-floor balcony, watch the cooks prepare your dinner in the open kitchen below. Specialties include a complimentary fish-pâté appetizer, blackened pompano with owner Peter Swartz's personal herb-and-spice recipe, lightly breaded fried grouper, and a homemade key lime pie. ⊠ *360 W. Flagler St.,* ☎ *305/372–1300. AE, MC, V. Beer and wine only.*

Miami Beach

$–$$
★
✕ **Joe's Stone Crab Restaurant.** "Before SoBe, Joe Be," touts this fourth-generation family restaurant, which reopened in 1996 with a chest-puffing facade and elegant interior on Washington Avenue. You go to wait, people-watch, and finally settle down to an ample à la carte menu. About a ton of stone-crab claws is served daily (except in summer), with drawn butter, lemon wedges, and piquant mustard sauce (recipe available). Popular side orders include salad with a brisk vinaigrette, creamed garlic spinach, french-fried onions, fried green tomatoes, and hash browns. Save room for dessert—key lime pie or apple pie with a crumb-pecan topping. ⊠ *227 Biscayne St.,* ☎ *305/673–0365, 305/673–4611 for takeout, 800/780–2722 for overnight shipping. AE, D, DC, MC, V. Closed Sept. 1–Oct. 15. No lunch Sun.–Mon.*

$–$$
✕ **Penrod's.** This started out like other Penrod's—with drinking contests, wet T-shirt contests, bikini contests, and the like—but corporate business is more lucrative. Now fine meals, such as stone crabs (in season), Maine lobster, steak, salads, and the house specialty, a grouper sandwich, are served. Up to 5,000 guests can be accommodated with

a 20,000-square-ft beach, 12 full-service bars, eight volleyball courts, a Caribbean village, sports bars, and nightclubs. Even if you aren't a "suit," on vacation or otherwise, this is a happening place. ⊠ *1 Ocean Dr.,* ☎ *305/538–1111. AE, MC, V.*

Spanish

Coral Gables

$$ ✕ **Cafe Barcelona.** This room with high ceilings and coral walls is highlighted by gilt-framed art and beautiful, slender ceiling lamps with tiny fluted green shades. The dim glow illuminates the food but little else, yielding an ambience that's part art gallery and part private home. Exceptional food matches the exceptional mood, and in a city where fresh fish has gotten priced off the deep end, entrées here range a good $5 below comparable dishes at first-class restaurants. They do a sea bass in sea salt for two, a traditional codfish with garlic confit, and a grouper in a clay pot with seafood sauce as well as lamb, duck, and several affordable rice dishes, including three types of paella. The *crema Catalana,* a version of flan, is not to be missed. ⊠ *160 Giralda Ave.,* ☎ *305/448–0912. AE, D, DC, MC, V.*

Downtown Miami

$–$$ ✕ **Las Tapas.** Overhung with dried meats and enormous show breads, this popular spot with terra-cotta floors and an open kitchen offers a lot of imaginative creations. Tapas ("little dishes") give you a variety of tastes during a single meal. Specialties include *la tostada* (smoked salmon on melba toast, topped with a dollop of sour cream, baby eels, black caviar, capers, and chopped onion) and *pincho de pollo a la plancha* (grilled chicken brochette marinated in brandy and onions). Also available are soups, salads, sandwiches, and standard-size dinners. ⊠ *Bayside Marketplace, 401 Biscayne Blvd.,* ☎ *305/372–2737. Reservations essential for large parties. AE, D, DC, MC, V.*

Little Havana

$$ ✕ **Casa Juancho.** This meeting place for the movers and shakers of the Cuban community is also a haven for lovers of fine Spanish regional cuisine. The exterior is marked by *tinajones,* the huge earthen urns of eastern Cuba, but the interior recalls old Castile. Strolling balladeers (university students from Spain) serenade you among brown brick, roughhewn dark timbers, and walls adorned with hooks of smoked meats and colorful Talavera platters. Try the hake prepared in a fish stock with garlic, onions, and white wine flown in from Spain or the *carabineros a la plancha* (jumbo red shrimp with head and shell on, split and grilled). For dessert the crema Catalana has a delectable crust of burnt caramel atop a rich pastry custard. The house features the largest list of reserved Spanish wines in the States. ⊠ *2436 S.W. 8th St.,* ☎ *305/642–2452. AE, D, DC, MC, V.*

Steak

Downtown Miami

$$–$$$ ✕ **Morton's.** The famed Chicago steak house has had franchises for years, but it wasn't until late 1997 that one opened in downtown Miami, followed by another, in North Miami, in mid-1998. As at the original, the atmosphere here is like that of a private club, courtesy of dark-mahogany-paneled rooms, spacious leather booths, subdued lighting, and casual white tablecloths. The open kitchen shows diners how a real steak restaurant prepares double filet mignon, New York strip sirloin, and broiled Block Island swordfish steak. The downtown location is on the first floor of an office building—not a bad move, since Morton's caters to a business clientele. ⊠ *1200 Brickell Ave.,* ☎

305/400–9990; ⊠ *17355 Biscayne Blvd., North Miami,* ☎ *305/945–3131. AE, MC, V.*

West Dade

$$–$$$$ ✕ **Shula's Steak House.** Prime rib, fish (including dolphin), and award-winning steaks are almost an afterthought to the icons in this shrine for the NFL-obsessed. Dine in a woody setting with a fireplace, surrounded by memorabilia of retired coach Don Shula's perfect 1972 season with the Miami Dolphins, including game footballs, assistant coach Howard Schnellenberger's pipe, and a playbook autographed by President Richard Nixon. Polish off the 48-ounce porterhouse steak and achieve a sort of immortality—your name on a plaque and an autographed picture of Shula. Also for fans, there's shula's steak 2 (lowercase borrowed from espn2), a sports celebrity hangout in Don Shula's Hotel (☞ *Lodging, below*). ⊠ *7601 N.W. 154th St., Miami Lakes,* ☎ *305/820–8102. AE, DC, MC, V.*

Thai

Miami Beach

$–$$ ✕ **Thai Toni.** An Indochinese setting with bamboo floors and teakwood tables brings to mind Laos, Vietnam, and other Southeast Asian countries, but there is no conflict here—just upscale dining in an exceptional restaurant. The mellow Thai Singha beer complements the spicy jumping squid appetizer with chili paste and hot pepper or the hot, hot pork. Choose from a large variety of inexpensive noodle, fried-rice, and vegetarian dishes or such traditional entrées as beef and broccoli, basil duck, or hot-and-spicy deep-fried whole snapper with basil leaves and mixed vegetables. Fresh whole fish fillets are specialties. The homemade lemonade is distinctly tart. ⊠ *890 Washington Ave.,* ☎ *305/538–8424. AE, MC, V. No lunch.*

Vegetarian

Coconut Grove

$ ✕ **Oak Feed Health Food.** If Oak Feed hadn't existed since 1970, someone would build it. The bohemian atmosphere of Coconut Grove is a perfect backdrop for this natural foods grocery store and lunch counter. In addition to a deli and bakery serving baked tofu and homemade soups, Oak Feed offers other healthy standards, such as organic produce, vitamins, macrobiotic foods, a juice bar, and cruelty-free cosmetics. ⊠ *2911 Grand Ave.,* ☎ *305/448–7595. AE, MC, V.*

Vietnamese

Little Havana

$–$$ ✕ **Hy-Vong Vietnamese Cuisine.** Beer-savvy Kathy Manning has in-
★   troduced a half-dozen top brews (Double Grimbergen, Moretti, and Spaten, among them), and magic continues to pour forth from the tiny kitchen of this plain little restaurant. Come before 7 to avoid a wait. Favorites include spring rolls (a Vietnamese version of an egg roll, with ground pork, cellophane noodles, and black mushrooms wrapped in homemade rice paper), whole fish panfried with *nuoc man* (a garlic-lime fish sauce), and thinly sliced pork, barbecued with sesame seeds and fish sauce and served with bean sprouts, rice noodles, and slivers of carrots, almonds, and peanuts. ⊠ *3458 S.W. 8th St.,* ☎ *305/446–3674. No credit cards. Closed Mon. and 2 weeks in Aug. No lunch.*

LODGING

Few urban areas can match Greater Miami's diversity of accommodations. South Beach had more than 2,000 rooms until the arrival of the Loews Miami Beach Hotel in late 1998 boosted that number by 800. Miami offers hundreds more hotels, motels, resorts, spas, and B&Bs, with prices ranging from $12 a night in a dormitory-style hostel to $2,000 a night in a luxurious presidential suite. Although some hotels (especially on the mainland) have adopted steady year-round rates, many still adjust their rates to reflect seasonal demand. The peak occurs in winter, with a dip in summer (prices are often more negotiable than rate cards let on). You'll find the best values between Easter and Memorial Day (a delightful time in Miami but a difficult time for many people to travel) and in September and October (the height of hurricane season). Keep in mind that Miami hoteliers collect roughly 12.5%—ouch—for city and resort taxes, and many hotels in the South Beach area tack on parking fees of up to $16 per evening, so if money is an issue, ask for all charges in advance.

Coconut Grove

$$$$ 🏨 **Grand Bay Hotel.** Combining the classical elegance of Greece, a
★ stepped facade that feels vaguely Aztec, a hint of the South, and a brush of the tropical, this hotel is like no other in South Florida. Guest rooms are filled with superb touches, such as antique sideboards that hold house phones, and matched woods, variously inlaid and fluted. Whoopi, Schwarzenegger, and Willis have all stayed here, perhaps enjoying the easterly views that look over the bay. Afternoon tea is served. ✉ *2669 S. Bayshore Dr., 33133,* ☎ *305/858–9600 or 800/327–2788,* 🖷 *305/ 858–1532. 132 rooms, 49 suites. Restaurant, bar, lounge, pool, beauty salon, hot tub, massage, saunas, health club. AE, DC, MC, V.*

$$$$ 🏨 **Mayfair House.** This European-style luxury hotel sits within the Streets of Mayfair, an exclusive open-air shopping mall. Public areas have Tiffany windows, polished mahogany, marble, imported ceramics and crystal, and an impressive glassed-in elevator. The individually furnished suites have outdoor terraces facing the street, screened by vegetation and wood latticework. Each has a relatively small Japanese hot tub on the balcony or a Roman tub inside, and 10 have antique pianos. One bonus is a rooftop recreation area, but the miniature lap pool is odd for such a large hotel. Because of the nightclub, Ensign Bitters, ask for a quiet suite. ✉ *3000 Florida Ave., 33133,* ☎ *305/441–0000 or 800/433–4555,* 🖷 *305/447–9173. 177 suites. Snack bar, pool, hot tubs, sauna, nightclub. AE, D, DC, MC, V.*

Coral Gables

$$$$ 🏨 **Biltmore Hotel.** Miami's grand boom-time hotel has undergone two
★ renovations since 1986 but still recaptures a bygone era. Now owned by Coral Gables and operated by Westin, the 1926 Biltmore was the centerpiece of Merrick's City Beautiful. It rises like a sienna-color wedding cake in the heart of a residential district. The vaulted lobby has hand-painted rafters on a twinkling sky blue background. Large guest rooms are done in a restrained Moorish style. For $1,800 you can book the Everglades (a.k.a. Al Capone) Suite—President Clinton's room when he's in town. Each month a visiting French chef drops by to surprise diners and teach Biltmore chefs something new. Historical tours are given Sunday at 1:30, 2:30, and 3:30. ✉ *1200 Anastasia Ave., 33134,* ☎ *305/445–1926 or 800/727–1926,* 🖷 *305/913– 3159. 237 rooms, 38 suites. Restaurant, café, lounge, pool, sauna, spa,*

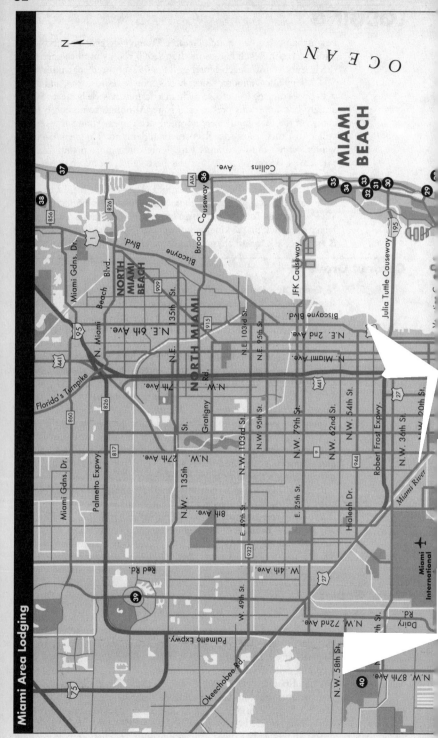

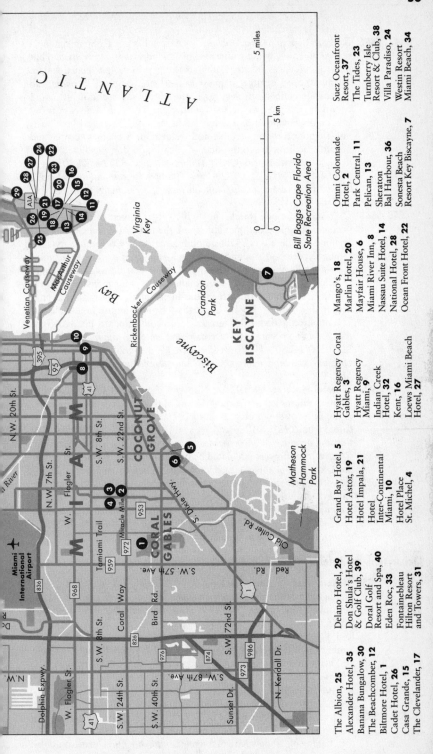

ATLANTIC

5 miles

5 km

Bill Baggs Cape Florida
State Recreation Area

KEY
BISCAYNE

Virginia
Key

Crandon
Park

Biscayne
Bay

Rickenbacker Causeway

Venetian Causeway

MacArthur Causeway

N.W. 20th St.

N.W. 7th St.

W. Flagler St.

S.W. 8th St.

S.W. 22nd St.

COCONUT
GROVE

Matheson
Hammock
Park

S. Dixie Hwy.

Old Cutler Rd.

Tamiami Trail

Miracle Mile

CORAL
GABLES

Miami
International
Airport

Dolphin Expwy.

W. Flagler St.

S.W. 24th St.

S.W. 40th St.

S.W. 8th St.

Coral Way

Bird Rd.

Sunset Dr.

S.W. 57th Ave.

S.W. 72nd St.

S.W. 87th Ave.

N. Kendall Dr.

Red Rd.

Coral Way

The Albion, **25**
Alexander Hotel, **35**
Banana Bungalow, **30**
The Beachcomber, **12**
Biltmore Hotel, **1**
Cadet Hotel, **26**
Casa Grande, **15**
The Clevelander, **17**

Delano Hotel, **29**
Don Shula's Hotel
& Golf Club, **39**
Doral Golf
Resort and Spa, **40**
Eden Roc, **33**
Fontainebleau
Hilton Resort
and Towers, **31**

Grand Bay Hotel, **5**
Hotel Astor, **19**
Hotel Impala, **21**
Hotel
Inter-Continental
Miami, **10**
Hotel Place
St. Michel, **4**

Hyatt Regency Coral
Gables, **3**
Hyatt Regency
Miami, **9**
Indian Creek
Hotel, **32**
Kent, **16**
Loews Miami Beach
Hotel, **27**

Mango's, **18**
Marlin Hotel, **20**
Mayfair House, **6**
Miami River Inn, **8**
Nassau Suite Hotel, **14**
National Hotel, **28**
Ocean Front Hotel, **22**

Omni Colonnade
Hotel, **2**
Park Central, **11**
Pelican, **13**
Sheraton
Bal Harbour, **36**
Sonesta Beach
Resort Key Biscayne, **7**

Suez Oceanfront
Resort, **37**
The Tides, **23**
Turnberry Isle
Resort & Club, **38**
Villa Paradiso, **24**
Westin Resort
Miami Beach, **34**

18-hole golf course, 10 lighted tennis courts, health club, meeting rooms. AE, DC, MC, V.

$$$$ ⊞ **Hyatt Regency Coral Gables.** The exterior is overtly Spanish, courtesy of tile roofs, white-frame casement windows, and pink stucco, but interior influences are more subliminal: traces in the headboard design, a stair-stepped outline at guest information, and fall browns and blonds. As befits a business hotel, the staff is savvy and helpful, and rooms are designed as alternative offices. An extra $15 buys in-room fax, computer hookup, free local calls, and a Continental breakfast. Still the mood is comfortable and residential. A business center and meeting facilities are to the side, so vacationers don't feel they're still in the corporate world. ⊠ *50 Alhambra Plaza, 33134, ☎ 305/441–1234, FAX 305/441–0520. 192 rooms, 50 suites. Restaurant, lounge, pool, sauna, steam rooms, health club, business services, meeting rooms. AE, D, DC, MC, V.*

$$$–$$$$ ⊞ **Omni Colonnade Hotel.** The twin 13-story towers of this hotel, office, and shopping complex dominate the heart of Coral Gables, and architectural details echo the adjoining two-story Corinthian-style rotunda. On display throughout the hotel—only four stories of the building—are old photos, paintings, and other heirlooms from George Merrick's family. Oversize rooms come in 26 floor plans and several styles, each with a sitting area, built-in armoires, and traditional mahogany furnishings. Rooms are ready for modems and fax machines. The pool, on a 10th-floor terrace, looks south toward Biscayne Bay. Ask for a room with a private balcony. ⊠ *180 Aragon Ave., 33134, ☎ 305/441–2600, FAX 305/445–3929. 157 rooms, 17 suites. Restaurant, in-room modem lines, pool, 2 saunas, exercise room. AE, D, DC, MC, V.*

$$$ ⊞ **Hotel Place St. Michel.** Art Nouveau chandeliers suspended from
★   vaulted ceilings grace the public areas of this intimate boutique hotel in the heart of downtown. Built in 1926, the historic low-rise was restored from 1981 to 1986 and yet again after a 1995 fire. Within easy walking distance of Miracle Mile, the charming inn is filled with the scent of fresh flowers circulated by paddle fans, and its fine restaurant (☞ *Dining, above*) is an undeniable asset. Each room has its own dimensions, personality, and antiques imported from England, Scotland, and France, although plusher beds would be a more welcome accent. A complimentary Continental breakfast is served. ⊠ *162 Alcazar Ave., 33134, ☎ 305/444–1666 or 800/848–4683, FAX 305/529–0074. 24 rooms, 3 suites. Restaurant, bar. AE, DC, MC, V.*

Downtown Miami

$$$$ ⊞ **Hotel Inter-Continental Miami.** From the pool deck you don't see the ragtag street, only the clean view Miami likes best of itself: the Disneyesque Metromover, Brickell Avenue, the booming port, the beautiful bay, and Key Biscayne. With all the lobby's marble, it could easily look like a mausoleum, but palms and oversize wicker add softness. Sunlight streams through the atrium from a skylight. Rooms, in grays and beiges and dark chintz, are traditional with a Latin flavor. ⊠ *100 Chopin Plaza, 33131, ☎ 305/577–1000 or 800/327–3005, FAX 305/577–0384. 644 rooms, 34 suites. 3 restaurants, lounge, pool, spa, jogging. AE, DC, MC, V.*

$$$–$$$$ ⊞ **Hyatt Regency Miami.** The blend of leisure and business should position the Hyatt well for the downtown renaissance that began with the opening of the new Miami Avenue Bridge in 1996. Distinctive public spaces are more colorful than businesslike, and guest rooms are done in an unusual combination of avocado, beige, and blond. Rooms yield views of the river or port, and not surprisingly the best ones are from the upper floors. The James L. Knight International Center is accessible without stepping outside, as is the downtown Metromover and its Metrorail connection. ✉ *400 S.E. 2nd Ave., 33131,* ☎ *305/358–1234,* ℻ *305/358–0529. 615 rooms, 25 suites. Restaurant, lounge, pool. AE, D, DC, MC, V.*

$$–$$$ 🏨 **Miami River Inn.** Preservationist Sallye Jude has restored these five 1904 clapboard buildings, the only group of Miami houses left from that period. The inn is an oasis of country hospitality in a working-class neighborhood—one of Miami's safest even if it doesn't look it. Rooms (some with tub only) are filled with antiques. Guests, including many Europeans, receive a free Continental breakfast and can use a refrigerator. The most popular rooms look over the river from the second and third floors. Avoid the tiny rooms in Building D with a view of a condo. The city's heart is a 10-minute stroll across the 1st Street Bridge, and José Martí Park, frequented by kids during the day and by bums at night, is a few hundred feet away. Though this may sound unappealing, the inn is a true sanctuary. ✉ *118 S.W. South River Dr., 33130,* ☎ *305/325–0045 or 800/468–3589,* ℻ *305/325–9227. 40 rooms (2 with shared bath). Pool. AE, D, DC, MC, V.*

Key Biscayne

$$$$ 🏨 **Sonesta Beach Resort Key Biscayne.** Always one of Miami's best,
★ this resort with a great seaside setting is now more tropical than ever. Sea views are stunning, at least from those units facing east. Rooms are done in a sand tone with fabrics in emerald, purple, gold, and ruby. Villas are actually three-bedroom homes with full kitchen and screened pool. Don't miss the museum-quality modern art by prominent painters and sculptors, especially Andy Warhol's drawings of rock star Mick Jagger in the hotel's disco bar, Desires. The 750-ft beach, one of Florida's best, has a big variety of recreational opportunities, including catamarans and sailing lessons. ✉ *350 Ocean Dr., 33149,* ☎ *305/361–2021 or 800/766–3782,* ℻ *305/361–3096. 284 rooms, 14 suites, 2 villas. 3 restaurants, bar, snack bar, pool, massage, steam rooms, 9 tennis courts (3 lighted), aerobics, health club, beach, windsurfing, parasailing, children's program. AE, D, DC, MC, V.*

Miami Beach

$$$$ 🏨 **The Albion.** With the revival of Lincoln Road, it was only a matter of time before someone reopened a hotel here. The Albion did it in style, its 1939 nautical Art Deco theme by Igor Polevitzky updated 60 years later by Ecuadoran Carlos Zapata. The focal point is a two-story lobby, which sweeps into a secluded courtyard and is framed by a flowing indoor waterfall. A mezzanine-level pool is unusual for its depth (9 ft) and its artificial beach, Florida's first. The blond-wood Fallabella Bar recalls the styling of Heywood-Wakefield, and guest rooms are minimalist in design though filled with what travelers expect: data ports, two-line phones, minibars, and stereos. ✉ *1650 James Ave., 33139,* ☎ *305/913–1000 or 888/665–0008,* ℻ *305/674–0507. 93 rooms, 17 suites. Bar, minibars, pool. AE, D, DC, MC, V.*

$$$$ 🏨 **Alexander Hotel.** Amid the high-rises of the mid-Beach district, this
★ 16-story hotel represents the elegance for which the Beach was once famous. It has immense suites furnished with antiques and reproductions, each with a terrace affording ocean or bay views and each with a living and dining room, kitchen, and two baths. Everything is understated, from the marquetry-paneled and landscaped lobby to the oceanfront dining rooms, featuring contemporary cuisine. Service is of the highest standard and includes twice-daily maid service (on request). ✉ *5225 Collins Ave., 33140,* ☎ *305/865–6500 or 800/327–*

6121, ⚏ 305/864–8525. 150 1- and 2-bedroom suites. Restaurant, coffee shop, 2 pools, spa, beach, boating. AE, D, DC, MC, V.

$$$$ 🏨 **Casa Grande.** The first of SoBe's new top-flight hotels, this is still
★   one of the best, with the level of quality characteristic of Chris Blackwell's other five Miami hotels: the Marlin, Tides, Kent , Cavalier, and Leslie. The lobby's teak, tile, and recessed lighting create a warm and relaxing look. Luxurious suites capture the fashionable air of Ocean Drive yet are in fine taste and without the invasion of its hectic sounds. Done in teak and mahogany, units have dhurrie rugs, beautiful Indonesian fabrics and artifacts, two-poster beds with ziggurat turns, full electric kitchens with fine European utensils, and large baths—unheard of in the Deco District—adorned with green decorator tiles. Goodies range from a daily newspaper and in-room coffee to fresh flowers, TV/VCR/CD/radio entertainment stations, and evening turndown with Italian chocolates. Book well in advance for peak periods. ⊠ *834 Ocean Dr., 33139,* ☎ *305/672–7003 or 800/688–7678,* ⚏ *305/673–3669. 33 suites. Café, kitchenettes, in-room VCRs, laundry service and dry cleaning, concierge. AE, DC, MC, V.*

$$$$ 🏨 **Delano Hotel.** If Calvin Klein had teamed with Salvador Dalí to build
★   a hotel, this weird, wonderful, and a bit snooty property would be it. Tourists marvel at the lobby decorated in massive white, billowing drapes and try to act casual while watching for U2, Elvis Costello, George Clooney, Michael Keaton, and Spike Lee (an actual week's roster of celebrity guests.) Female fashion models and men of independent means gather beneath cabanas, pose by the pool, and sniff fragrances wafting in from the orchard. Business travelers are offered comprehensive executive services, guests can access 1,500 videos, and women have the run of a rooftop bathhouse and solarium. Although the standard rooms are of average size, their stark whiteness makes them appear larger. The gift shop carries magazines you wouldn't want your parents to see. The real appeal here is the Alice in Wonderland–inspired surrealism. ⊠ *1685 Collins Ave., 33139,* ☎ *305/672–2000 or 800/555–5001,* ⚏ *305/532–0099. 184 rooms, 24 suites. Restaurant, bar, pool, spa, health club, business services. AE, D, DC, MC, V.*

$$$$ 🏨 **Eden Roc.** Who knows why this grand 1950s hotel designed by Mor-
★   ris Lapidus is overshadowed by the larger, more prominent Fontainebleau (☞ *below*)? From the moment you enter, the free-flowing lines of its steamship-style architecture make it casual and comfortable. A $30 million renovation added three new ballrooms and meeting facilities, as well as an indoor basketball court and rock-climbing wall for fitness and motivation. A resort yacht is available for oceangoing meetings. The 55,000-square-ft Spa of Eden usually runs full tilt, while Dolphins coach Jimmy Johnson's beachside sports bar caters to those who prefer lifting weights 16 ounces at a time. Rooms blend a touch of the '50s with informal '90s elegance. ⊠ *4525 Collins Ave., 33140,* ☎ *305/ 531–0000 or 800/327–8337,* ⚏ *305/674–5555. 346 rooms. 2 restaurants, sports bar, pool, massage, spa, basketball, exercise room, racquetball, meeting rooms. AE, MC, V.*

$$$$ 🏨 **Fontainebleau Hilton Resort and Towers.** This is the Grand Central of area hotels—the busiest, the biggest, and the most ornate. Convention facilities rank second only to the city-owned convention center, and a 30,000-square-ft beachside spa is ideal for self-indulgence. Tower rooms are country in spirit, light and flowery, yet come with traditional amenities and the security of special elevator keys. Other themes vary from the 1950s to contemporary. Even the smallest room is large by most standards. The Continental breakfast is banquetlike, and views seem to extend halfway to the Azores. Guests enjoy complimentary admission to *Club Tropigala,* a Vegas-style floor show with a Latin twist.

Babalu-I-Ay! ✉ *4441 Collins Ave., 33140,* ☎ *305/538–2000 or 800/ 548–8886,* 🆉 *305/531–9274. 1,146 rooms, 60 suites. 12 restaurants, 4 lounges, 2 pools, saunas, spa, 7 lighted tennis courts, health club, volleyball, beach, windsurfing, boating, parasailing, children's programs, convention center. AE, D, DC, MC, V.*

$$$$ 🏨 **Loews Miami Beach Hotel** Miami has been waiting for a major new beachfront luxury hotel for 30 years. Although others have been renovated, this $135 million, 17-story, 700-room gem was built from the blueprints up. Not only did Loews manage to snag 800 ft of oceanfront, it took over the vacant St. Moritz next door and restored it to its original 1939 Deco splendor, adding another 100 rooms to the complex. The resort features kids' programs (Camp SoBe), a health spa, and 85,000 square ft of meeting space with a 28,000-square-ft, ocean-view grand ballroom. Dining, too, is a pleasure, courtesy of the Gaucho Room Argentinian Steakhouse, SoBe Coffee Bar, and Hemispheres Lounge. ✉ *1601 Collins Ave., 33139,* ☎ *305/604–1601,* 🆉 *305/531–8677. 743 rooms, 57 suites. 4 restaurants, 2 bars, lobby lounge, pool, spa, beach, children's programs, meeting rooms. AE, D, DC, MC, V.*

$$$$ 🏨 **National Hotel.** Reopened in May 1997, this resurrected 1939 shorefront hotel has all the elements to succeed and is now waiting for them to gel. Miami Beach's longest (205 ft) tropical pool sparkles at night with illuminated messages and logos, but with curtains closed, the rooms could be generic Holiday Inn, displaying little of the creativity of other recent arrivals. Perhaps the National is trying to reach a more conservative business clientele who wants access to SoBe's action but isn't ready to participate fully. Applause is in order, however, for preserved pieces, such as the original dining-room chandelier and furniture, as well as such modern in-room amenities as ironing boards, safes, data ports, and robes. Another notable is the intimate '30s-style Press Room cigar bar and meeting room. Unfair, however, is the $16 per day parking fee. ✉ *1677 Collins Ave., 33139,* ☎ *305/532–2311 or 800/327–8370,* 🆉 *305/534–1426. 115 rooms, 39 suites. Restaurant, bar, in-room safes, pool, beach, concierge, meeting rooms, parking (fee). AE, DC, M, V.*

$$$$ 🏨 **Sheraton Bal Harbour.** Want to get away from the traffic of SoBe? Go to NoBe. Sensing Miami's renaissance would head north, the owners of this Lapidus-designed hotel gave it a $52 million face-lift in 1996, including a new lush oceanfront garden with waterfalls, a funky neon-laced bistro and bar, upgraded units, and 73,000 square ft of improved meeting space. Rooms offer full or partial views of the city, ocean, or Bal Harbour, and the ritzy Bal Harbour Shops are across the street. Elegant without being pretentious, the hotel's design is complemented by a staff that has service down to a science. ✉ *9701 Collins Ave., Bal Harbour 33154,* ☎ *305/865–7511,* 🆉 *305/864–2601. 755 rooms, 53 suites. 3 restaurants, piano bar, pool, wading pool, hot tub, massage, sauna, health club, windsurfing, video games, baby-sitting, meeting rooms. AE, D, DC, MC, V.*

$$$$ 🏨 **The Tides.** Miami hotels like white decor, and this is no exception. However, the nice twist here is the added features that arrived with a $9.6 million renovation. Some touches are small—spyglasses in each room (fitting since they all face the ocean), a blackboard for messages to maids. Others are large—large beds, large closets, large post-Moderne baths, the result of turning 115 rooms into 45 suites. Elvis would have liked the blackout curtains and private VIP entrance. The downstairs lobby is large and austere (and white), and facilities include a reading room, terrace dining, and a mezzanine pool where women can go topless (total nudity is "undesirable"). The beach is 20 steps away. This is the newest hotel to generate a buzz, so check it out, hipsters. ✉ *1220 Ocean Dr.,*

33139, ☎ 305/604–5000 or 800/688–7678, FAX 305/604–5180. 45 suites. Restaurant, café, pool, exercise room. AE, D, DC, MC, V.

$$$$ 🏨 **Westin Resort Miami Beach.** Of the great Miami Beach hotels, this 18-story glass tower remains a standout. A six-month, $30 million renovation, completed in early 1998, upgraded the lobby, pool, facade, sleeping rooms, meeting rooms, and landscaping. Warm-tone guest rooms are filled with nice details: mini-refrigerators; three sets of drapes, including blackout curtains; big closets; and bathrooms with high-quality toiletries and a magnifying mirror. Two presidential suites were designed in consultation with the Secret Service, and a rooftop meeting room offers views of bay and ocean. Free transportation to Doral Golf Resort and Spa (☞ Chapter 2) is provided. ⊠ *4833 Collins Ave., 33140, ☎ 305/532–3600 or 800/203–8368, FAX 305/534–7409. 383 rooms, 40 suites. 3 restaurants, 3 lounges, pool, tennis court, exercise room, beach, helipad, meeting rooms. AE, D, DC, MC, V.*

$$$–$$$$ 🏨 **Hotel Astor.** How does yet another Deco hotel stand out from the crowd? This hotel does it by double-insulating walls against noise and offering such subtle luxuries as ambient low-voltage lighting, thick towels, paddle fans, and a seductive pool. The renovation also included expansion of guest rooms and baths and the addition of custom-milled French furniture, Roman shades, muted colors, and sleek sound and video systems. The Astor Place restaurant (☞ Dining, *above*) is noteworthy. ⊠ *956 Washington Ave., 33139, ☎ 305/531–8081 or 800/270–4981, FAX 305/531–3193. 42 rooms. Restaurant, bar, pool, massage. AE, MC, V.*

$$$–$$$$ 🏨 **Hotel Impala.** One of the nicest inns in the area, the former La Flora
★   is tropical Mediterranean Revival, not Deco. Iron, mahogany, and stone on the inside are in synch with the sporty white-trim ocher exterior. Rooms, among the cleanest in SoBe, are elegant, comfortable, and complete, with a TV/VCR/stereo and a stock of CDs and videos. It's all very European, from mineral water and orchids to the Mediterranean-style armoires, wrought-iron furniture, Italian fixtures, heavy ornamental drapery rods, and Spanish surrealist art above white-on-white, triple-sheeted modified Eastlake sleigh beds. (Not surprisingly, Continental breakfast is included.) Everything from wastebaskets to towels to toilet paper is of exceptional quality. ⊠ *1228 Collins Ave., 33139, ☎ 305/673–2021 or 800/646–7252, FAX 305/673–5984. 17 rooms, 3 suites. Restaurant, lounge, in-room VCRs. AE, DC, MC, V.*

$$$–$$$$ 🏨 **Indian Creek Hotel.** Not as grand as the North Beach behemoths or as hectic as the Ocean Drive offerings, this 1936 Pueblo Deco jewel may just be Miami's most charming and sincere lodge. Owner Marc Levin rescued the inn by adding a cozy dining room with an eclectic and appetizing menu, relandscaping a lush pool and garden, and restoring rooms with Deco furniture, much of it discovered in the basement. Items were cleaned, reupholstered, and put on display, helping the hotel win the Miami Design Preservation League's award for outstanding restoration. Suites have refrigerators, and safe deposit boxes are available. Stay a while, and manager Zammy Migdal and his staff will have you feeling like family. ⊠ *2727 Indian Creek Dr., 33140, ☎ 305/531–2727, FAX 305/531–5651. 61 rooms. Restaurant, pool, concierge. AE, D, DC, MC, V.*

$$$–$$$$ 🏨 **Marlin Hotel.** The Marlin is so Jamaican that it could be the island's cultural showcase—a fitting theme considering that owner Chris Blackwell runs Island Records. Fun and funky art complements striking handpainted furniture, woven grass rugs, batiklike shades, and rattan and mahogany furniture. Every room is different, some with sharp accents of ocher and plum; some with pale sky blue, and some with kitchenettes, but all are completely detailed with VCRs, minibars, and orchid decorations. Even studio suites, with rattan sitting areas, are sizable; larger suites are like villas. For sunbathing, check out the rooftop deck. ⊠ *1200 Collins Ave., 33139,* ☎ *305/673–8770,* ℻ *305/673–9609. 11 suites. Bar, minibars, in-room VCRs. AE, D, DC, MC, V.*

\$\$\$–\$\$\$\$ 🏨 **Ocean Front Hotel.** If the street signs didn't read Ocean Drive, you might suspect you were whiling away the day on the Riviera. The tropical French feel is evident when you enter the shaded, bougainvillea-draped courtyard and see diners enjoying a complimentary casual breakfast in the hotel's brasserie. Pleasant surprises continue inside rooms, where pleasing decor is highlighted by soft beds, authentic 1930s Deco pieces, large foldout couches, and clean, spacious baths. The occasional kitchenette makes this a smart option for families, and if you spring for the penthouse suite, be sure to settle on the balcony and grab an eyeful of ocean. ⊠ *1230–38 Ocean Dr., 33139,* ☎ *305/672–2579,* ℻ *305/672–7665. 4 rooms, 23 suites. Restaurant, bar, concierge. AE, DC, MC, V.*

\$\$\$–\$\$\$\$ 🏨 **Park Central.** Across from the glorious beach, this seven-story Deco hotel—painted blue, with wraparound corner windows—makes all the right moves to stay in the forefront of the Art Deco revival. Many fashion models visiting town come to this property, which dates from 1937. Black-and-white photos of old beach scenes, hurricanes, and familiar faces attest to its longevity, and board games in the lobby add to its charm. Rooms are decorated with Philippine mahogany furnishings—originals that have been restored. Incorporated in the property, the Imperial Hotel next door has an additional 36 rooms. ⊠ *640 Ocean Dr., 33139,* ☎ *305/538–1611 or 800/727–5236,* ℻ *305/534–7520. 121 rooms. Bar, pool, exercise room. AE, DC, MC, V.*

\$\$\$ 🏨 **The Clevelander.** In a row of high-tone hotels, this place prefers to party. A giant pool-bar area attracts revelers for happy-hour drink specials and live music seven nights a week. The drinking flows into the lobby, which is 40% hospitality and 90% sports bar. Bar food (naturally) is served, as are more upscale entrées. Thankfully, the staff seems to be having a blast. ("We take all major credit cards—we just don't give 'em back," says one.) Rooms have generous-size baths. If you need to work out, the South Beach Gym, within the hotel, extends reduced rates to guests. ⊠ *1020 Ocean Dr., 33139,* ☎ *305/531–3485,* ℻ *305/534–4707. 53 rooms. Restaurant, 2 bars, pool, exercise room. AE, DC, MC, V.*

\$\$\$ 🏨 **Kent.** Chris Blackwell has done it again, this time with a moderately priced island outpost that may be one of SoBe's best bargains. Functional and basic, the hotel is clean and cheerful with a bright and airy Jamaican feel. Rooms are equipped with minibars and CD players, and if you get a suite in back, you'll have a view of the ocean—at least until someone builds a hotel on the lot behind. ⊠ *1131 Collins Ave., 33139,* ☎ *305/604–5000,* ℻ *305/604–5180. 52 rooms, 2 suites. Minibars, meeting room. AE, D, DC, MC, V.*

\$\$\$ 🏨 **Nassau Suite Hotel.** The sister property of the Beachcomber (☞ *below*), this relative bargain offers huge studio suites at a third of the price demanded by Ocean Drive properties. The original 1937 floor plan of 50 rooms gave way to 22 spacious and smart-looking suites. King beds, fully equipped kitchens, hardwood floors, white wood blinds, voice mail, data ports, plush sofas, free local calls, mini-refrigerators, Beachcomber bistro privileges . . . why they don't charge more is a mystery. The hotel is in the heart of the action yet quiet enough to give travelers the rest they need. ⊠ *1414 Collins Ave., 33139,* ☎ *305/531–3755 or 888/305–4683,* ℻ *305/673–8609. 22 suites. Kitchenettes, concierge. AE, D, DC, MC, V.*

$$$ 🏨 **Pelican.** Dazzling, brilliant spaces with Deco-inspired frivolity have turned another tired Ocean Drive home for the elderly into pop-eyed digs for the gay, hip, and adventurous. Rooms, with names like Leaf-forest, Best Whorehouse, People from the 1950s, and Cubarrean, are all different, but all have small sleeping chambers and triple-size bathrooms with outrageous industrial piping. Best Whorehouse envelops you in black silk and thoroughly red-flocked wallpaper flecked with gold. Ornaments are bordello extravagant: a heart-shape red-velvet chair, hideously aqua night tables, whorish art, and griffins with voluptuous mammaries. Each room comes with its own cylindrical entertainment center. Guests have included JFK Jr. and Yoko Ono. ⊠ *826 Ocean Dr., 33139,* ☎ *305/673–3373 or 800/773–5422,* FAX *305/673–3255. 25 units, penthouse. Restaurant, café, concierge. AE, MC, V.*

$$$ 🏨 **Villa Paradiso.** A tropical courtyard ushers guests into this hotel just half a block from the beach. Large studio apartments with full-size kitchens and living rooms have polished hardwood floors and French doors, and the personal touch of the new owners is present inside and out. Free local calls and the prospect of enjoying conversation with fellow guests on the tropical patio make this a safe and relatively affordable bet. ⊠ *1415 Collins Ave., 33139,* ☎ *305/532–0616,* FAX *305/673–5874. 17 studios. Kitchenettes, coin laundry. AE, DC. MC, V.*

$$–$$$ 🏨 **Mango's.** If you'd rather party than sleep, this two-story hotel in the heart of Ocean Drive may be the place to crash. You can stay up until the bands downstairs blow a fuse and then stumble upstairs for some shut-eye. Any earlier and you'll want to crank up the air-conditioning to drown out the sound of the bands and party people downstairs in Mango's bar. If you're a light sleeper, ask for a back room by the palm garden waterfall. Though units have kitchenettes with usable refrigerators, no cooking is allowed. Furnishings are basic—a bed, table, and two chairs—and some rooms may have a sofa or easy chair. ⊠ *900 Ocean Dr., 33139,* ☎ *305/673–4422,* FAX *305/674–0311. 15 rooms. Restaurant, bar, kitchenettes, refrigerators. AE, D, DC, MC, V.*

$$–$$$ 🏨 **Suez Oceanfront Resort.** Several miles north of Miami Beach in what's known as Motel Row, the carousel-striped, family-run Suez stands out from the area's fancy but nondescript motels. Look beyond the tacky sphinx icons to the quiet, gardenlike lounge and the landscaped palm courtyard. Rooms have chinois furniture and dazzling color, offsetting generally small spaces. Those in the north wing, with parking-lot views, are the smallest and least expensive. Modified American Plan, refrigerators in all rooms, kitchens in some, free laundry service, and special kids' rates make this an especially good value, popular with Europeans. ⊠ *18215 Collins Ave., Sunny Isles 33160,* ☎ *305/932–0661 or 800/327–5278, 800/432–3661 in FL;* FAX *305/937–0058. 196 rooms. Restaurant, bar, refrigerators, freshwater and saltwater pools, wading pool, lighted tennis court, shuffleboard, volleyball, beach, playground, laundry service. AE, DC, MC, V.*

$$ 🏨 **The Beachcomber.** One of the best finds in SoBe, this small hotel
★   could easily get lost in the shuffle though it should stand out from the crowd. Relaxed, tropical rooms offer ample space, hardwood floors, clean bathrooms, and amenities such as circulating fans, alarm clocks, data ports, and voice mail. The restaurant, open nearly all the time, serves breakfast, brunch, lunch, tea, and dinner. If this hotel were one block east on the ocean, you'd shell out twice as much. Save your money and take a walk. The Beachcomber's sister hotels, Bayliss and Nassau (☞ *above*), are equally nice. ⊠ *1340 Collins Ave., 33139,* ☎ *305/531–3755 or 888/305–4683,* FAX *305/673–8609. 28 rooms. Restaurant, bar. AE, D, DC, MC, V.*

$$ ⛨ **Cadet Hotel.** Clark Gable stayed in Room 225 when he came for army air corps training in the 1940s. Although this Lincoln Road district lodging doesn't have the glamour to attract stars today, it's still a clean, friendly, and perfectly placed little hotel. Just a few minutes' walk from the Theater of the Performing Arts and the convention center and five minutes from the ocean, it's about half the cost of an Ocean Drive hotel. The other big difference is that the staff doesn't act like it's doing you a favor to let you stay here. Bright without glitz, the Cadet features soft pastels in the lobby, blues and creams in rooms. Ordinary furniture is mixed but not necessarily matched—nor is it crummy. Tiled baths have tubs. A complimentary breakfast is served in the lobby or on the terrace. ⊠ *1701 James Ave., 33139,* ☎ *305/672–6688 or 800/432–2338,* 𝔽𝔸𝕏 *305/532–1676. 44 rooms. AE, D, DC, MC, V.*

$–$$ ⛨ **Banana Bungalow.** This may seem like a university dormitory—indeed, some rooms have dorm-style bunk beds for about $14 a night—but the cleanliness, friendliness, and number of activities make this lodge worth checking into, especially for student travelers. A large pool, the bungalow's social center, is surrounded by a patio bar, Ping-Pong table, game room, outdoor grills, a café, and an activity board announcing Wave Runner rentals, scenic flights, and beach volleyball games held across the street. Some may be put off by the smell of the brackish canal nearby, but it's a small price to pay for a small price to stay. ⊠ *2360 Collins Ave., 33139,* ☎ *305/538–1951 or 800/746–7835,* 𝔽𝔸𝕏 *305/531–3217. 40 private rooms, 20 dorm-style rooms, all with bath. Bar, café, pool, Ping-Pong, billiards, recreation room, video games. MC, V.*

North Dade

$$$$ ⛨ **Turnberry Isle Resort & Club.** Finest of the grand resorts, Turnberry
★ sits on 300 superbly landscaped acres by the bay. Choose from the Yacht Club, on the Intracoastal Waterway; the intimate Marina Hotel; a beautiful three-wing Mediterranean-style annex; and the Mizner-style Country Club Hotel. Oversize rooms have light woods and earth tones, large curving terraces, Jacuzzis, honor bars, and safes. The marina has moorings for 117 boats up to 150 ft, and there's a free shuttle to the beach club and the Aventura Mall. A new seven-story building, adding 128 rooms, offices, and a terrace restaurant, will open by 1999. ⊠ *19999 W. Country Club Dr., Aventura 33180,* ☎ *305/932–6200 or 800/ 327–7028,* 𝔽𝔸𝕏 *305/933–6560. 300 rooms, 40 suites. 7 restaurants, 5 lounges, 4 pools, saunas, spa, steam rooms, 2 golf courses, 24 tennis courts (18 lighted), health club, jogging, racquetball, beach, dive shop, docks, windsurfing, boating, helipad. AE, D, DC, MC, V.*

West Dade

$$$$ ⛨ **Doral Golf Resort and Spa.** This 650-acre golf-and-tennis resort has put $30 million into renovations, adding a lighter tone to the eight separate three- and four-story lodges nestled beside golf courses. At the world-renowned spa, a 148,000-square-ft paradise, massages from head to foot, European facials, aroma scrubs and wraps, stress reduction, hypnotherapy, and several dozen other indulgences rejuvenate the mind, body, and soul. Dining ranges from a sports bar to an informal trattoria to an elegant seafood restaurant. The famed Blue Monster course has been redesigned, and the other four courses were increased in size and difficulty. The resort hosts the annual $2 million Doral-Ryder Open Tournament. Beach transportation is provided. ⊠ *4400 N.W. 87th Ave., 33178-2192,* ☎ *305/592–2000,* 𝔽𝔸𝕏 *305/594–4682. 592 rooms, 102 suites. 4 restaurants, 3 lounges, 4 pools, spa, 5 golf courses, 15 tennis* *courts (7 lighted), health club, jogging, fishing, bicycles, pro shop. AE, D, DC, MC, V.*

$$$–$$$$ 🏨 **Don Shula's Hotel & Golf Club.** This low-rise resort is part of Miami Lakes, a planned town about 14 mi northwest of downtown. Opened in 1962, the golf resort includes a championship course, a lighted executive course, and a golf school. All rooms have balconies, and the decor is English traditional, rich in leather and wood. The hotel, on the other hand, has a typical Florida-tropics look—light pastels and furniture of wicker and light wood. In both locations the best rooms are near the lobby for convenient access; ask for a room away from the elevators. ⊠ *6840 Main St., Miami Lakes 33014,* ☎ *305/821–1150 or 800/247–4852,* FAX *305/879–8298. 269 rooms, 32 suites. 5 restaurants, 2 lounges, 2 pools, saunas, steam rooms, 2 golf courses, 9 lighted tennis courts, aerobics, basketball, health club, racquetball, volleyball. AE, DC, MC, V.*

NIGHTLIFE AND THE ARTS

For information on what's happening around town, Greater Miami's English-language daily newspaper, the *Miami Herald,* publishes reliable reviews and comprehensive listings in its "Weekend" section on Friday and in the "Lively Arts" section on Sunday. Call ahead to confirm details. *El Nuevo Herald* is the paper's Spanish version.

If you read Spanish, check *Diario Las Américas,* the area's largest independent Spanish-language paper, for information on the Spanish theater and a smattering of general performing arts news.

A good source of information on the performing arts and nightspots is the calendar in *Miami Today,* a free weekly newspaper available each Thursday in downtown Miami, Coconut Grove, and Coral Gables. The best, most complete source is the *New Times,* a free weekly distributed throughout Miami-Dade County each Thursday. Various tabloids reporting on Deco District entertainment and society come and go on Miami Beach. *Ocean Drive* outglosses everything else. *Wire* reports on the gay community.

The free *Greater Miami Calendar of Events* is published twice a year by the Dade County Cultural Affairs Council (⊠ 111 N.W. 1st St., Suite 625, 33128, ☎ 305/375–4634).

Real Talk/WTMI (93.1 FM, ☎ 305/856–9393) provides classical concert information in on-air reports three times daily at 7:30, 12:50, and 6:30. Call the station if you miss the report.

The Arts

Miami's performing arts aficionados will tell you they survive quite nicely, despite the area's historic inability to support a county-based professional symphony orchestra. In recent years this community has begun to write a new chapter in its performing arts history.

In addition to established music groups, several churches and synagogues run classical-music series with international performers. In theater, Miami offers English-speaking audiences an assortment of professional, collegiate, and amateur productions of musicals, comedy, and drama. Spanish theater also is active.

The not-for-profit **Concert Association of Florida** (⊠ 555 17th St., Miami Beach 33139, ☎ 305/532–3491), directed by Judith Drucker, is the South's largest presenter of classical arts, music, and dance.

To order tickets for performing arts events by telephone, call **Ticketmaster** (☎ 305/358–5885).

Arts Venues

What was once a movie theater has become the 465-seat **Colony Theater** (✉ 1040 Lincoln Rd., Miami Beach 33139, ☎ 305/674–1026). The city-owned performing arts center features dance, drama, music, and experimental cinema.

If you have the opportunity to attend a concert, ballet, or touring stage production at the **Gusman Center for the Performing Arts** (✉ 174 E. Flagler St., Miami 33131, ☎ 305/372–0925), do so. The 1,739-seat downtown landmark, originally a movie palace, is as far from a mall multiplex as you can get. The stunningly beautiful hall resembles a Moorish courtyard, with twinkling stars and rolling clouds skirting across the ceiling and Roman statues guarding the wings.

Not to be confused with the ornate Gusman theater, **Gusman Concert Hall** (✉ 1314 Miller Dr., Coral Gables 33146, ☎ 305/284–2438) is a 600-seat facility on the University of Miami campus. It has good acoustics and plenty of room, but parking is a problem when school is in session.

Acoustics and visibility are perfect for all 2,700 seats in the **Jackie Gleason Theater of the Performing Arts** (✉ TOPA, 1700 Washington Ave., Miami Beach 33139, ☎ 305/673–7300). Renamed for Gleason after his death, it hosts the Broadway Series, with five or six major productions annually; guest artists, such as David Copperfield, Stomp, and Liza Minnelli; and classical-music concerts.

Miami-Dade County Auditorium (✉ 2901 W. Flagler St., Miami 33135, ☎ 305/545–3395) satisfies patrons with 2,498 comfortable seats, good sight lines, and acceptable acoustics. Opera, concerts, and touring musicals are usually on the schedule.

Dance

The **Miami City Ballet** (✉ 905 Lincoln Rd., Miami Beach 33139, ☎ 305/532–7713 or 305/532–4880) has risen rapidly to international prominence in its relatively short existence. Under the direction of Edward Villella (a principal dancer with the New York City Ballet under George Balanchine), Florida's first major, fully professional resident ballet company has become a world-class ensemble. The company re-creates the Balanchine repertoire and introduces works of its own during its September–March season. Performances are held at the Jackie Gleason Theater of the Performing Arts; the Broward Center for the Performing Arts; Bailey Concert Hall, also in Broward County; the Raymond F. Kravis Center for the Performing Arts; and the Naples Philharmonic Center for the Arts. Villella narrates children's and works-in-progress programs.

Film

Alliance Film/Video Project (✉ Sterling Building, Suite 119, 927 Lincoln Rd. Mall, Miami Beach 33139, ☎ 305/531–8504) presents cutting-edge international cinema and art films, with special midnight shows.

Screenings of new films from all over the world—including some made here—are held as part of the **Miami Film Festival** (✉ 444 Brickell Ave., Suite 229, Miami 33131, ☎ 305/377–3456). Each year more than 45,000 people descend on the Gusman Center for the Performing Arts for 10 days in late January and early February.

Music

Friends of Chamber Music (⊠ 44 W. Flagler St., Suite 1725, Miami 33130, ☎ 305/372–2975) presents an annual series of chamber concerts by internationally known guest ensembles, such as the Emerson and Guarneri quartets.

Since Greater Miami has no resident symphony orchestra, the **New World Symphony** (⊠ 541 Lincoln Rd., Miami Beach 33139, ☎ 305/673–3331 or 305/673–3330), a unique advanced-training orchestra conducted by Michael Tilson Thomas, helps fill the void. Musicians ages 22–30 who have finished their academic studies perform here before moving on to other orchestras. The orchestra began its 11th season, running from October to May, in 1998.

Opera

South Florida's leading company, the **Florida Grand Opera** (⊠ 1200 Coral Way, Miami 33145, ☎ 305/854–1643) presents five operas each year in the Dade County Auditorium, featuring the Florida Philharmonic Orchestra (James Judd, artistic director). The series brings such luminaries as Placido Domingo and Luciano Pavarotti. (Pavarotti made his American debut with the company in 1965 in *Lucia di Lammermoor.*) Operas are sung in the original language, with English subtitles projected above the stage.

Theater

Actors' Playhouse (⊠ 280 Miracle Mile, Coral Gables 33134, ☎ 305/ 444–9293), a professional Equity company, presents musicals, comedies, and dramas year-round in the very cool renovated 600-seat Miracle Theater. Productions of musical theater for younger audiences began in the Children's Balcony Theatre in 1997.

Built in 1926 as a movie theater, the **Coconut Grove Playhouse** (⊠ 3500 Main Hwy., Coconut Grove 33133, ☎ 305/442–4000 or 305/442–2662) became a legitimate theater in 1956 and is now owned by the state of Florida. The apricot-hue Spanish rococo Grove fixture stages tried-and-true Broadway plays and musicals as well as experimental productions in its main theater and cabaret-style Encore Room. It held its most popular event in 1996, when David Letterman hosted an on-the-road *Late Show* here. Parking is $4 during the day, $5 in the evening.

The **Florida Shakespeare Theatre** (⊠ 1200 Anastasia Ave., Coral Gables 33134, ☎ 305/446–1116) presents classic and contemporary theater in a 154-seat hall at the Biltmore Hotel. Two Shakespeare productions are given a year.

The **Gold Coast Theatre Company** (⊠ 345 W. 37th St., Miami Beach 33140, ☎ 305/538–5500), in Miami since 1989, performs a combination of physical theater, mime, and vaudeville comedy. The touring company performs year-round; call to find its current venue.

The **New Theatre** (⊠ 65 Almeria Ave., Coral Gables 33134, ☎ 305/ 443–5909) is a showcase for contemporary and classical plays.

On the campus of the University of Miami, **Ring Theater** (⊠ 1380 Miller Dr., Coral Gables 33124, ☎ 305/284–3355) is the 311-seat hall of UM's Department of Theatre Arts. Six plays a year are performed.

SPANISH THEATER

Spanish theater prospers, although many companies have short lives. About 20 Spanish companies perform light comedy, puppetry, vaudeville, and political satire. To locate them, read the Spanish newspapers. When you call, be prepared for a conversation in Spanish—few box-office personnel speak English.

The 255-seat **Teatro de Bellas Artes** (✉ 2173 S.W. 8th St., Miami 33135, ☎ 305/325–0515), on Calle Ocho, presents eight Spanish plays and musicals year-round. Midnight musical follies and female impersonators round out the showbiz lineup.

Nightlife

Bars and Lounges

COCONUT GROVE

The **Hungry Sailor** (✉ 3064½ Grand Ave., ☎ 305/444–9359), with two bars, serves up Jamaican-English food, British beer, and live music from Wednesday to Saturday. The **Taurus Steak House** (✉ 3540 Main Hwy., ☎ 305/448–0633) is an unchanging oasis in the trendy Grove. The bar, built of native cypress in 1919, draws an over-30 singles crowd nightly that drifts outside to a patio. A band plays from Tuesday through Saturday.

CORAL GABLES

In a building that dates from 1926, **Stuart's Bar-Lounge** (✉ 162 Alcazar Ave., ☎ 305/444–1666), inside the charming Hotel Place St. Michel, was named one of the best new bars of 1987 by *Esquire,* and it's still favored by locals. The style is fostered by beveled mirrors, mahogany paneling, French posters, pictures of old Coral Gables, and art-nouveau lighting. Stuart's is closed Sunday.

MIAMI

Tobacco Road (✉ 626 S. Miami Ave., ☎ 305/374–1198), opened in 1912, holds Miami's oldest liquor license: 0001! Upstairs, in space occupied by a speakeasy during Prohibition, local and national blues bands perform nightly. There's excellent bar food, a dinner menu, single-malt Scotch, bourbon, and cigars.

MIAMI BEACH

Blue Steel (✉ 2895 Collins Ave., ☎ 305/672–1227) is a cool but unpretentious hangout with pool tables, darts, live music, comfy old sofas, and beer paraphernalia. Open-mike night is Friday, and there's a jam on Monday. German *Vogue* liked it so much they named it the "hippest and hottest" club in SoBe. *Ach du lieber!* **Mac's Club Deuce** (✉ 222 14th St., ☎ 305/673–9537) is a South Beach gem where top international models pop in to have a drink and shoot some pool (surprising, considering the working-class atmosphere). All you get late at night are minipizzas, but the pizzazz lasts long. In a nondescript motel row with nudie bars, baby stores, and bait-and-tackle shops, **Molly Malone's** (✉ 166 Sunny Isles Blvd., ☎ 305/948–9143) is the only cool, down-to-earth spot that thrives in this neighborhood. The Irish pub, a big local fave, has a traditional European look, with oak paneling, live Irish music on Friday, and acoustic sounds Saturday. **Rose's Music Bar & Lounge** (✉ 754 Washington Ave., ☎ 305/532–0228) has the best in local bands from Hendrix-style rock and rap/funk to jazz jams and Afro-Cuban/world beat, with the occasional national act. Though it doesn't take credit cards, there is an ATM. It's open seven nights, but it's packed from Wednesday through Saturday.

Dance Clubs

KEY BISCAYNE

Stefano's of Key Biscayne (✉ 24 Crandon Blvd., ☎ 305/361–7007) is a northern Italian restaurant with disco. The music is live from Tuesday through Sunday, and there's a cover charge Friday and Saturday.

MIAMI BEACH

Amnesia (✉ 136 Collins Ave., ☎ 305/531–5535), open Thursday–Sunday, feels like a luxurious amphitheater in the tropics, complete with rain forest, what used to be called go-go dancers, and frenzied dancing in the rain when showers pass over the open-air ground-level club. Themes (e.g., Latin, gay, Gothic) change nightly. At **Bash** (✉ 655 Washington Ave., ☎ 305/538–2274), two DJs spin dance music— sometimes reggae, sometimes Latin, plenty of loud disco, and world-beat sounds in the garden, where there are artsy benches. There are bars inside, where it's grottolike, and out, where you can check out the "magical patio." You can also try to join the chic crowd in either of three VIP rooms. The **Bermuda Bar & Grille** (✉ 3509 N.E. 163rd St., ☎ 305/945–0196) plays *loud* music for disco dancing. Male bartenders wear knee-length kilts, while female bartenders are in matching minis. The atmosphere and crowd, though, are stylish island casual, and there's a big tropical-forest scene, booths you can hide in, and six bars and pool tables. Draft beer is served in yard glasses and frosted mugs. The place is closed Monday and Tuesday.

The still hot, still happenin' **Groove Jet** (✉ 323 23rd St., ☎ 305/532–2002) doesn't break new ground, but it will break your eardrums with hypnotic dance music played by guest DJs during street parties, gay nights, and other evenings when you can revisit the "days of sex and sleaze." I'll be home late, Mom! **Liquid** (✉ 1439–37 Washington Ave., ☎ 305/532–9154) is a high-energy dance club with themed evenings. Thursday's NFA (No Fu____ Around) is hip-hop, Fridays bring the Kingdom, Saturdays welcome top New York DJs, Sundays are Manwich nights (for gays), and Mondays throb to funk and soul during Fat Black Pussycat. The 10 PM–5 AM hours should give you enough time to embarrass yourself. With 10 years to its credit, **Warsaw Ballroom** (✉ 1450 Collins Ave., ☎ 305/531–4555) has outlasted most other clubs and earned a reputation as a SoBe institution, with a guest list that's included Madonna, Sean Penn, Jack Nicholson, and George Clooney. Despite an occasional straight night, most nights (Wednesday to Saturday only) are turning gay. Beware of cover charges ranging from $7 on up to $40 to cover the occasional $12,000-a-night DJ.

Jazz

MIAMI BEACH

Normandy Fountain Café & Jazz Bar (✉ 928 71st St., ☎ 305/865–2636), formerly the MoJazz Cafe, has changed formats but still presents jazz by guest artists as well as its owner, Mo Morgen. In the revamped neighborhood of Normandy Isle, the club opens at 7 Tuesday–Sunday, with music from 9 to 1 (until 2 on Friday and Saturday). More restaurant than jazz club, **Van Dyke Café** (✉ 846 Lincoln Rd., ☎ 305/534–3600) serves music on the second floor seven nights a week. Its location on the Lincoln Road Mall makes it a great spot to take a break during an evening shopping excursion.

Nightclub

MIAMI BEACH

The Fontainebleau Hilton's **Club Tropigala** (✉ 4441 Collins Ave., ☎ 305/672–7469), popular with such stars as Sylvester Stallone, Madonna, and Elton John, is a four-tier round room. Decorated with orchids, banana leaves, philodendrons, and cascading waterfalls, it feels like a tropical jungle. A 10-piece band plays standards as well as Latin music for dancing on the wooden floor. Hotel guests are comped, but others pay a $15 cover. Reservations are suggested, and men should wear jackets.

OUTDOOR ACTIVITIES AND SPORTS

In addition to contacting the addresses below directly, you can get tickets to major events from **Ticketmaster** (☎ 305/358–5885).

Auto Racing

Hialeah Speedway, the area's only independent raceway, holds stock-car races on a ⅓-mi asphalt oval in a 5,000-seat stadium. Five divisions of cars run weekly. The Marion Edwards, Jr., Memorial Race, for late-model cars, is held in November. The speedway is on U.S. 27, ¼ mi east of the Palmetto Expressway (Route 826). ⊠ *3300 W. Okeechobee Rd., Hialeah,* ☎ *305/821–6644.* ⊡ *$10, special events $12.* ☉ *Late Jan.–early Dec., Sat.; gates open at 5, racing 7–11.*

Baseball

The Eastern Division **Florida Marlins** (⊠ 2267 N.W. 199th St., Miami 33056, ☎ 305/626–7400) began their sixth season in 1998, after winning the 1997 World Series. Home games are played at Pro Player Stadium, which is 16 mi northwest of downtown. On game days the Metro-Dade Transit Agency runs buses to the stadium.

Basketball

The **Miami Heat** (⊠ 1 S.E. 3rd Ave., Miami 33131, ☎ 305/577–4328), Miami's NBA franchise, plays home games November–April at the Miami Arena, a block east of Overtown Metrorail Station. They plan to move to the 20,000-seat, waterfront American Airlines Arena, adjacent to Bayside Marketplace, by the end of 1999.

Biking

Perfect weather and flat terrain make Miami-Dade County a popular place for cyclists. A color-coded map outlining roads suitable for bike travel is available for $3.50 from area bike shops and from the **Miami-Dade County Bicycle Coordinator** (⊠ Metropolitan Planning Organization, 111 N.W. 1st St., Suite 910, Miami 33128, ☎ 305/375–4507, ext. 1735), whose purpose in life is to share with you the glories of Miami's bicycle-friendly roads, featuring wide shoulders and mile markers. For information on dozens of monthly group rides, contact the **Everglades Bicycle Club** (⊠ Box 430282, South Miami 33243-0282, ☎ 305/598–3998). For bike rentals, check out the **Miami Beach Bicycle Center** (⊠ 601 5th St., Miami Beach, ☎ 305/674–0150), in business since 1975. MBBC's proximity to Ocean Drive and the ocean itself make it worth the $14 per day (or $5 per hour), which includes a helmet, lock, and basket on a mountain bike or cruiser. Tours of the Deco District are offered twice a month.

Boating

At the popular full-service **Crandon Park Marina,** you can rent sail- and powerboats, embark on deep-sea fishing excursions, or dine at a marina restaurant. ⊠ *4000 Crandon Blvd., Key Biscayne,* ☎ *305/361–1281.* ☉ *Office 7 AM–11 PM.*

Named for an island where early settlers had picnics, **Dinner Key Marina** is Greater Miami's largest, with 581 moorings at nine piers. There is space for transients and a boat ramp. Castle Harbor (☎ 305/858–3212), in operation since 1949, offers sailboat rentals, lessons, racing, and charters. ⊠ *3400 Pan American Dr., Coconut Grove,* ☎ *305/579–6980.* ☉ *Daily 7 AM–11 PM.*

Haulover Marine Center is low on glamour but high on service. It offers a bait-and-tackle shop, marine gas station, and boat launch. ⊠

15000 Collins Ave., Miami Beach, ☎ *305/945–3934.* ☉ *Bait shop and gas station open 24 hours.*

A happening waterfront mecca, **Miami Beach Marina** is the nearest marina to the Deco District, about a 15-minute walk away. It has restaurants, charters, boat and vehicle rentals, a complete marine hardware store, dive shop and excursions, large grocery store, fuel dock, concierge services, and 400 slips accommodating vessels up to 190 ft. Facilities include air-conditioned rest rooms, washers and dryers, U.S. Customs clearing, and a heated pool. One charter outfit here is family-owned Florida Yacht Charters (☎ 305/532–8600 or 800/537–0050). After completing a checkout cruise and paperwork, slap down a deposit and take off for the Caribbean on a catamaran, sailboat, or motor yacht. Charts, lessons, and captains are available if needed. Call for a comprehensive info kit. ⊠ *300 Alton Rd., Miami Beach,* ☎ *305/673–6000.* ☉ *Daily 7–6.*

Dog Racing
In the middle of Little Havana, **Flagler Greyhound Track** has dog racing during its June–November season. Closed-circuit TV brings harness-racing action here as well. The track is five minutes east of Miami International Airport, off Dolphin Expressway (Route 836) and Douglas Road (Northwest 37th Avenue). ⊠ *401 N.W. 38th Ct., Miami,* ☎ *305/649–3000.* ☞ *$1, clubhouse $3, parking 50¢–$2.* ☉ *Racing daily 7:30, plus Tues.–Wed. and Sat. 12:30.*

Fishing
Before there was fashion, there was fishing. Deep-sea fishing is still a major draw, and anglers drop a line for sailfish, kingfish, dolphin, snapper, grouper, and tuna. Smaller charter boats can cost $350–$400 for a half day, so you might be better off paying around $25 for passage on a larger fishing boat. Rarely are they filled to capacity. Nearby general stores sell essentials such as fuel, tackle, sunglasses, and beer. Don't let them sell you a fishing license, however; a blanket license should cover all passengers.

Many ocean-fishing charters sail out of **Haulover Park** (⊠ 10800 Collins Ave., Miami Beach), including Blue Waters Sportfishing Charters (☎ 305/944–4531), Kelley Fleet (☎ 305/945–3801), and *Therapy IV* (☎ 305/945–1578). Among the charter services at the **Miami Beach Marina** (⊠ 300 Alton Rd., MacArthur Causeway, Miami Beach) is Reward Fleet (☎ 305/372–9470). It operates two boats at moderate prices: $28 per person including bait, rod, reel, and tackle, less for kids.

Football
Despite the resignation of legendary coach Don Shula in 1995, fans keep coming to watch the NFL's **Miami Dolphins**—probably still waiting for a repeat of the 17–0 record of 1972 (a record that still stands). The team plays at the former Joe Robbie Stadium, renamed Pro Player Stadium in honor of a sports apparel company and a $20 million check. The state-of-the-art stadium, which has 75,000 seats and a grass playing surface, is on a 160-acre site 16 mi northwest of downtown Miami, 1 mi south of the Miami-Dade–Broward County line and accessible from I–95 and Florida's Turnpike. On game days the Metro-Dade Transit Agency runs buses to the stadium. ⊠ *2269 N.W. 199th St., Miami 33056,* ☎ *305/620–2578.* ☉ *Box office weekdays 10–6, also Sat. during season.*

After calling the venerable Orange Bowl home for many years, the **University of Miami Hurricanes** (⊠ 1 Hurricane Dr., Coral Gables 33146,

In case you want to be welcomed there.

We're here to see that you're always welcomed at establishments everywhere. That's why millions of people carry the American Express® Card – for peace of mind, confidence, and security, around the world or just around the corner.

do more

Cards

In case you're running low.

We're here to help with more than 118,000 Express Cash locations around the world. In order to enroll, just call American Express before you start your vacation.

do more

Express Cash

And just in case.

We're here with American Express® Travelers Cheques and Cheques *for Two*.® They're the safest way to carry money on your vacation and the surest way to get a refund, practically anywhere, anytime.
Another way we help you...

do more ®

Travelers Cheques

☎ 305/284–2263), once contenders for the top collegiate ranking, are playing their 1999 home games at Pro Player Stadium (☞ *above*) from September to November.

Golf

Greater Miami has more than 30 private and public courses. To get a "Golfer's Guide for South Florida," which includes information on most courses in Miami and surrounding areas, call 800/864–6101. The cost is $3.

The 18-hole **Biltmore Golf Course** (⊠ 1210 Anastasia Ave., Coral Gables, ☎ 305/460–5364), known for its scenic layout, has been restored to its original Donald Ross design, circa 1925. The gorgeous hotel makes a scenic backdrop. The **California Club** (⊠ 20898 San Simeon Way, North Miami Beach, ☎ 305/651–3590) has an 18-hole course made challenging by a tight front 9 and 3 of the area's toughest finishing holes. Overlooking the bay, the **Crandon Park Golf Course** (⊠ 6700 Crandon Blvd., Key Biscayne, ☎ 305/361–9129), formerly the Links at Key Biscayne, is a top-rated public course. **Don Shula's Hotel & Golf Club** (⊠ 7601 Miami Lakes Dr., Miami Lakes, ☎ 305/820–8106) has one of the longest championship courses in Miami (7,055 yards), a lighted par-3 course, a golf school, and more than 100 tournaments a year. With four championship and one executive courses, the **Doral Golf Resort and Spa** (⊠ 4400 N.W. 87th Ave., Doral, ☎ 305/592–2000 or 800/713–6725) is known for the Blue Monster course and the annual Doral-Ryder Open Tournament, with $2 million in prize money. **Normandy Shores Golf Course** (⊠ 2401 Biarritz Dr., Miami Beach, ☎ 305/868–6502) is good for seniors, with some modest slopes and average distances. The **Turnberry Isle Resort & Club** (⊠ 19999 W. Country Club Dr., Aventura, ☎ 305/933–6929) has 36 holes designed by Robert Trent Jones.

Horse Racing

The **Calder Race Course,** opened in 1971, is Florida's largest glass-enclosed, air-conditioned sports facility. It often has an unusually extended season, from late May to early January, though it's a good idea to call the track for specific starting and wrap-up dates. Calder and Hialeah Park rotate their race dates, so be sure to check with each park to see where the horses are running. Each year between November and early January, Calder holds the Tropical Park Derby for three-year-olds. The track is on the Miami-Dade–Broward County line near I–95 and the Hallandale Beach Boulevard exit, ¾ mi from Pro Player Stadium. ⊠ *21001 N.W. 27th Ave., Miami,* ☎ *305/625–1311.* 🎫 *$2, clubhouse $4, parking $1–$3.* ☉ *Gates open at 11, racing 1–5:30.*

A superb setting for Thoroughbred racing, **Hialeah Park** has 228 acres of meticulously landscaped grounds surrounding paddocks and a clubhouse built in a classic French-Mediterranean style. Since it opened in 1925, Hialeah Park has survived hurricanes and now seems likely to survive even changing demographics, as the racetrack crowd has steadily moved north and east. Although Hialeah tends to get the less prestigious racing dates from March to May, it still draws crowds. The park is open year-round for free sightseeing, during which you can explore the gardens and admire the park's breeding flock of 800 Cuban flamingos. Metrorail's Hialeah Station is on the grounds. ⊠ *2200 E. 4th Ave., Hialeah,* ☎ *305/885–8000.* 🎫 *Weekdays, grandstand $1, clubhouse $2; weekends, grandstand $4, clubhouse $4; parking $1–$4.* ☉ *Gates open at 10:30, racing 1–5:30.*

Jai Alai

Built in 1926, the **Miami Jai-Alai Fronton,** a mile east of the airport, is America's oldest fronton. It presents 13 games—14 on Friday and Saturday—some singles, some doubles. This game, invented in the Basque region of northern Spain, is the world's fastest. Jai-alai balls, called pelotas, have been clocked at speeds exceeding 170 mph. The game is played in a 176-ft-long court, and players literally climb the walls to catch the ball in a cesta—a woven basket—with an attached glove. You can bet on a team to win or on the order in which teams will finish. Dinner is available. ⊠ *3500 N.W. 37th Ave., Miami,* ☎ *305/633–6400.* ☒ *$1, reserved seats $2, Courtview Club $5.* ۞ *Mon., Wed., and Fri.– Sat. noon–5 and 7–midnight; Thurs. 7–midnight; Sun. 1–7.*

Jogging

Try these recommended jogging routes: in Coconut Grove, along the pedestrian-bicycle path on South Bayshore Drive, cutting over the causeway to Key Biscayne for a longer run; from the south shore of the Miami River, downtown, south along the sidewalks of Brickell Avenue to Bayshore Drive, where you can run alongside the bay; in Miami Beach, along Bay Road (parallel to Alton Road) or on the sidewalk skirting the Atlantic Ocean, opposite the cafés of Ocean Drive; and in Coral Gables, around the Riviera Country Club golf course, just south of the Biltmore Country Club. A good source of running information is the **Miami Runners Club** (⊠ 7920 S.W. 40th St., Miami, ☎ 305/227–1500). **Foot Works** (⊠ 5724 Sunset Dr., South Miami, ☎ 305/ 667–9322), a running-shoe store, is a good resource as well.

Scuba Diving and Snorkeling

Though winter storms can cause dive boats to vary their schedules, summer diving conditions in Greater Miami have been compared to those in the Caribbean. Chances are excellent you'll come face to face with a flood of tropical fish. One option is to find real reefs, such as Fowey, Triumph, Long, and Emerald, in 10- to 15-ft dives that are perfect for snorkelers and beginning divers. On the edge of the continental shelf, these reefs are ¼ mi from depths greater than 100 ft. Another option is to paddle around the tangled prop roots of the mangrove trees that line the coast, peering at the fish, crabs, and other creatures hiding there.

Perhaps the most unusual option, however, is to dive on one of the local artificial reefs. In 1981 Dade County's Department of Environmental Resources Management (DERM) started sinking tons of limestone boulders and more than 65 tankers, trawlers, tugs, a water tower, two M-60 tanks, and a 727 jet to create a "wreckreational" habitat where divers can swim with yellow tang, barracudas, nurse sharks, snapper, eels, and grouper. Most dive shops sell a book listing the location of these wrecks.

Information on wreck diving can be obtained from the Miami Beach Chamber of Commerce's **WaterSports Marketing Council** (⊠ 1920 Meridian Ave., Miami Beach, ☎ 305/672–1270 or 888/728–2262), composed of hotels and dive shops involved in finding big stuff to sink.

Bubbles Dive Center (⊠ 2671 S.W. 27th Ave., Miami, ☎ 305/856–0565) is an all-purpose dive shop with PADI affiliation. Its boat, *Divers Dream,* is kept on Watson Island on MacArthur Causeway. **Divers Paradise of Key Biscayne** (⊠ 4000 Crandon Blvd., Key Biscayne, ☎ 305/ 361–3483) has a complete dive shop and diving-charter service, including equipment rental and scuba instruction, with PADI affiliation. The PADI-affiliated **Diving Locker** (⊠ 223 Sunny Isles Blvd., North Miami Beach, ☎ 305/947–6025) offers full sales, service, and repairs, plus three-day and three-week international certification courses as well as more advanced certifications. Wreck and reef sites are reached aboard fast and comfortable six-passenger dive boats.

Tennis

Greater Miami has more than a dozen tennis centers open to the public. Countywide nearly 500 public courts are open to visitors; nonresidents are charged an hourly fee.

Biltmore Tennis Center has 10 hard courts and the added bonus of being located at the beautiful Biltmore Hotel (☞ Lodging, *above*). ☒ *1150 Anastasia Ave., Coral Gables,* ☎ *305/460–5360.* ▨ *Day rate $4.30, night rate $5 per person per hour.* ⊘ *Weekdays 8 AM–9 PM, weekends 8–8.*

Very popular with locals, **Flamingo Tennis Center** has 19 clay courts. ☒ *1000 12th St., Miami Beach,* ☎ *305/673–7761.* ▨ *Day rate $2.67, night rate $3.20 per person per hr.* ⊘ *Weekdays 8 AM–9 PM, weekends 8–8.*

North Shore Tennis Center has six clay and five hard courts. ☒ *350 73rd St., Miami Beach,* ☎ *305/993–2022.* ▨ *Day rate $2.66, night rate $3.20 per person per hr.* ⊘ *Weekdays 8 AM–9 PM, weekends 8–7.*

The $18 million, 30-acre **Tennis Center at Crandon Park** is one of America's best. Included are 2 grass, 8 clay, and 17 hard courts. Reservations are required for night play. The only time courts are closed to the public is during the Lipton Championships (☎ 305/442–3367), held for 11 days each spring. The tournament is one of the largest in the world in terms of attendance, and with $4.6 million in prize money in 1998, had the fifth-largest purse—enough to attract players like Michael Chang, Pete Sampras, Venus Williams, and Martina Hingis. It's played in a 14,000-seat stadium. ☒ *7300 Crandon Blvd., Key Biscayne,* ☎ *305/365–2300.* ▨ *Laykold courts day rate $3, night rate $5 per person per hr; clay courts $6 per person per hour.* ⊘ *Daily 8 AM–9 PM.*

Windsurfing

New lightweight boards and smaller sails make learning windsurfing easy. The safest and most popular windsurfing area in city waters is south of town at Windsurfer Beach, around Virginia Key and Key Biscayne. Miami Beach's best windsurfing is at 1st Street just north of the Government Cut jetty and at 21st Street. You can also windsurf from Lummus Park at 10th Street and around 3rd, 14th, and 21st streets.

Sailboards Miami, just past the tollbooth for the Rickenbacker Causeway, rents equipment and is the largest windsurfing school in the United States. It offers year-round lessons and claims to be able to teach anyone within two hours. ☒ *Key Biscayne,* ☎ *305/361–7245.* ▨ *1 hr $20, 10 hrs $150, 2-hr lesson $49.* ⊘ *Daily 10–5:30.*

SHOPPING

Visitors to Greater Miami are never more than 15 minutes from a major shopping area and the familiar *ca-ching* of a cash register. Miami-Dade County has more than a dozen major malls, an international free-trade zone, and hundreds of miles of commercial streets lined with stores and small shopping centers. Latin neighborhoods contain a wealth of Latin merchants and merchandise, including children's *vestidos de fiesta* (party dresses) and men's guayaberas (a pleated, embroidered tropical shirt), conveying the feel of a South American *mercado* (market).

Malls

Aventura Mall (☒ 19501 Biscayne Blvd., Aventura) has more than 200 shops anchored by Macy's, Lord & Taylor, JCPenney, Sears, and a

Bloomingdale's that opened in late 1997. A new Burdines and multiplex theater should be in place by 1999. In a tropical garden setting, **Bal Harbour Shops** (⊠ 9700 Collins Ave., Bal Harbour) is a swank collection of 100 shops, boutiques, and department stores, such as Chanel, Gucci, Cartier, Fendi, Bruno Magli, Neiman Marcus, and Florida's largest Saks Fifth Avenue. It was named by fashionable *Elle* magazine as one of the top five shopping collections in the United States. **Bayside Marketplace** (⊠ 401 Biscayne Blvd., Miami), the 16-acre shopping complex on Biscayne Bay, has 150 specialty shops, entertainment, tour-boat docks, and a food court. It's open late (10 during the week, 11 on Friday and Saturday), but its restaurants stay open even later.

A complex of clapboard, coral-rock, and stucco buildings, **Cauley Square** (⊠ 22400 Old Dixie Hwy., Goulds) was erected in 1907–20 as housing for railroad workers who built and maintained the line to Key West. Crafts, clothing, and antiques shops are well represented. **CocoWalk** (⊠ 3015 Grand Ave., Coconut Grove) has three floors of nearly 40 specialty shops (Victoria's Secret, the Gap, Banana Republic, among others) that stay open almost as late as the popular restaurants and clubs. A 16-screen theater is also here. If you're ready for an evening of people-watching, this is the place.

The oldest retail mall in the county, **Dadeland** (⊠ 7535 N. Kendall Dr., Miami) is always upgrading. It sits at the south side of town close to the Dadeland North and Dadeland South Metrorail stations. Retailers include Saks Fifth Avenue, JCPenney, Lord & Taylor, more than 175 specialty stores, 17 restaurants, and the largest Burdines, Limited, and Limited Express in Florida. When it opens in 1999, the $220 million **Dolphin Mall** (west of Miami) will contain plenty of shopping, plus theaters, hotels, and an entertainment center. The **Falls** (⊠ 8888 S.W. 136th St., at U.S. 1, Miami), which derives its name from the several waterfalls inside, is the most upscale mall on the south side of the city. It contains a Macy's and Bloomingdale's as well as another 50 specialty stores, restaurants, and a 12-theater multiplex.

Omni International Mall (⊠ 1601 Biscayne Blvd., Miami) rises vertically alongside the atrium of the Crowne Plaza Miami, whose eye-popping feature is an old-fashioned carousel. Among the 85 shops are a JCPenney, many restaurants, and 10 movie screens. To compete with trendy Coconut Grove, the **Shoppes at Sunset Place** (⊠ U.S. 1 and Red Rd. [S.W. 57th Ave.], South Miami), scheduled to open in late 1998, is expected to be larger than CocoWalk. The family-oriented complex will contain a Spielberg-movie-inspired virtual-reality attraction wrapped into a restaurant. **Streets of Mayfair** (⊠ 2911 Grand Ave., Coconut Grove) is an active, bustling group of shops both day and night. Thanks to its Grove setting, along with the new News Café, Planet Hollywood, the Limited, Borders, and a few dozen other shops and restaurants, this is a safe bet. Entertainment is provided by an improv comedy club, a 10-screen theater, and the Iguana Cantina, a nightclub, martini bar, and pool room.

Outdoor Markets

Coconut Grove Farmers Market (⊠ Grand Ave., 1 block west of MacDonald Ave. [S.W. 32nd Ave.], Coconut Grove), open Saturday 8–2, originated in 1977 and was the first in the Miami area. The **Espanola Way Market** (⊠ Espanola Way, Miami Beach), Sunday noon–9, has been a city favorite since its debut in 1995. Scattered among the handcrafted items and flea market merchandise, musicians beat out Latin rhythms on bongos, conga drums, steel drums, and guitars. Food vendors sell inexpensive Latin snacks and drinks. Each Saturday morning from mid-January to late March, some 25 produce and plant vendors sell herbs, fruits, fresh-squeezed juices, chutneys, cakes, and muffins at the **Farmers Market at Merrick Park** (⊠ LeJeune Rd. [S.W. 42nd Ave.] and Biltmore Way, Coral Gables). Regular features include gardening workshops, children's activities, and cooking demonstrations offered by Coral Gables's master chefs. More than 500 vendors sell a variety of goods at the **Flagler Dog Track** (⊠ 401 N.W. 38th Ct., Miami), every weekend 9–4. **Lincoln Road Farmers Market** (⊠ Lincoln Rd. between Meridian and Euclid Aves., Miami Beach), open Sunday November–March, brings about 15 local produce vendors coupled with plant workshops and children's activities. With 1,200 dealers, **Opa-Locka/Hialeah Flea Market** (⊠ 12705 N.W. 47th Ave., Miami) is one of the largest in South Florida. Though it's open seven days, weekends are best.

Shopping Districts

The shopping is great on a two-block stretch of **Collins Avenue** (⊠ Between 6th and 8th Aves., Miami Beach). Vidal Sassoon, Nicole Miller, Nike, Kenneth Cole, Guess, and Banana Republic are among the high-profile tenants, and a parking garage is just a block away. There are 500 garment manufacturers in Miami and Hialeah, and many sell their clothing locally in the **Miami Fashion District** (⊠ 5th Ave. east of I–95, between 25th and 29th Sts., Miami), making Greater Miami the fashion marketplace for the southeastern United States, the Caribbean, and Latin America. Most of the more than 30 factory outlets and discount fashion stores are open Monday–Saturday 9–5. The **Miami International Arts and Design District** (⊠ Between N.E. 38th and N.E. 42nd Sts. and between Federal Hwy. and N. Miami Ave., Miami), also known as 40th Street, contains some 225 wholesale stores, showrooms, and galleries specializing in interior furnishings, decorative arts, and a rich mix of exclusive and unusual merchandise. Since 1993 the district has undergone a revival, and there are several new art studios and showrooms. **Miracle Mile** (⊠ Coral Way between 37th and 42nd Aves., Coral Gables) consists of some 160 shops along a wide, tree-lined boulevard. Shops range from posh boutiques to bargain basements, from beauty salons to chain restaurants. As you go west, the quality increases.

Specialty Stores

ANTIQUES

Alhambra Antiques Center (⊠ 3640 Coral Way, Miami, ☎ 305/446–1688) is a collection of four antiques dealers that sell high-quality decorative pieces from Europe. **Architectural Antiques** (⊠ 2500 S.W. 28th La., Coconut Grove, ☎ 305/285–1330) carries large and eclectic items—railroad crossing signs, statues, English roadsters—in a setting so cluttered that shopping here becomes an adventure promising hidden treasures for the determined. **A&J Unique Deco** (⊠ 2000 Biscayne Blvd., Miami, ☎ 305/576–5170) is constantly rotating its inventory of Deco furniture, collected from Europe and the United States. In a world of reproductions, this is the real thing: Cool armoires, dressers, beds, and bars are here in abundance.

BOOKS

Like others in the superstore chain, **Barnes & Noble** (⊠ 152 Miracle Mile, Coral Gables, ☎ 305/446–4152) manages to preserve the essence of a neighborhood bookstore by encouraging customers to pick a book off the shelf and lounge on a couch without being hassled. A well-stocked magazine and national/international news rack and an espresso bar–café complete the effect. Greater Miami's best English-language bookstore, **Books & Books, Inc** (⊠ 296 Aragon Ave., Coral Gables, ☎ 305/442–4408; ⊠ Sterling Bldg., 933 Lincoln Rd., Miami Beach, ☎ 305/532–3222) specializes in books on the arts, architecture, Florida, and contemporary and classical literature. At the Coral Gables location, collectors enjoy browsing through the rare-book room upstairs, which doubles as a photography gallery. There are frequent poetry readings and book signings. If being in the Grove prompts you to don a beret, grow a goatee, and sift through a volume of Kerouac, head to **Borders** (⊠ Grand Ave. and Mary St., Coconut Grove, ☎ 305/447–1655). Its 100,000 book titles, 70,000 CDs, 10,000 video titles, and more than 2,000 periodicals and newspapers in 10 languages from 15 countries make it seem like the southern branch of the Library of Congress.

CHILDREN'S BOOKS AND TOYS

A Kid's Book & Toy Shoppe (⊠ 1895 N.E. Miami Gardens Dr., Skylake Center, North Miami Beach, ☎ 305/937–2665) is an excellent resource on children's books and educational toys. **A Likely Story** (⊠ 5740 Sunset Dr., South Miami, ☎ 305/667–3730) has been helping Miamians choose books and educational toys appropriate to children's interests and stages of development since 1978.

CIGARS

Although Tampa is Florida's true cigar capital, Miami's Latin population is giving it a run for its money. Smoking anything even remotely affiliated with a legendary Cuban has boosted the popularity of Miami cigar stores and the small shops where you can buy cigars straight from the press.

A celebration of Cuban culture, **Babalu** (⊠ 500 Espanola Way, Miami Beach, ☎ 305/538–0679) sells postcards, books, and crafts. To complete the effect, owner Heriberto Sosa has dedicated part of his shop to producing hand-rolled cigars from the petite $3 Palm Gold to the $7 Churchill and $9 Imperial Gold. Although you can also buy a Babalu at Bloomingdale's, it's more fun here. The **Cigar Connection** (⊠ 534 Lincoln Road Mall, Miami Beach, ☎ 305/531–7373) is hoping to capture the trendy tastes of pedestrians strolling on Lincoln Road. Carrying such premium cigars as the Arturo Fuente Opus X and Paul Garmirians, the shop also serves coffees and cappuccino. In the heart of Little Havana, **El Credito** (⊠ 1106 S.W. 8th St., Miami, ☎ 305/858–4162 or 800/726–9481) seems to have been transported from the Cuban capital lock, stock, and stogie. Rows of workers at wooden benches rip through giant tobacco leaves, cut them with rounded blades, wrap them tightly, and press them in vises. Dedicated smokers like Robert De Niro, Gregory Hines, and George Hamilton have found their way here to pick up a $90 bundle or peruse the *gigantes, supremos,* panatelas, and Churchills available in natural or maduro wrappers.

Havana Ray's (⊠ 3399 Virginia St., Coconut Grove, ☎ 305/446–4003 or 800/732–4427) continues a cigar-making dynasty that began in 1920s Cuba. The Quirantes family's devotion to cigars has resulted in this cozy shop where you can buy cigars and related accouterments. **Smokers' Notch** (⊠ 425 Washington Ave., Miami Beach, ☎ 305/534–4090 or 888/537–6653) has a terrific location (across from the China Grill), which means celebs (Nicholson) and regular folks (you) can drop in for an after-dinner smoke or stock up on pipe tobacco, cutters, humidors, cigar mags, and more than 100 cigar brands, including Sweet Millionaires (flavored cigars). **South Beach News and Tobacco** (⊠ 710 Washington Ave., No. 9, Miami Beach, ☎ 305/673–3002) has expanded beyond simple cigars to carry imported wines and beers, gourmet espresso and coffee, and international newspapers and magazines. But the real draw is cigars made on the premises or imported from the Dominican Republic, Nicaragua, and Honduras.

COLLECTIBLES

Gotta Have It! Collectibles (⊠ 504 Biltmore Way, Coral Gables, ☎ 305/
446–5757) will make fans of any kind break out in a cold sweat. Autographed sports jerseys, canceled checks from the estate of Marilyn
Monroe, fabulously framed album jackets signed by all four Beatles,
and an elaborate autographed montage of all the *Wizard of Oz* stars
are among this intriguing shop's museum-quality collectibles. Looking for an Einstein autograph? A Jack Nicklaus–signed scorecard?
Look no further. And if they don't have the autograph you desire, fear
not—they'll track one down.

DECORATIVE AND GIFT ITEMS

American Details (⊠ 3107 Grand Ave., Coconut Grove, ☎ 305/448–
6163) sells colorful, trendy arts and crafts handmade by American artists.
Jewelry and handblown glass are popular sellers. The **Indies Company**
(⊠ 101 W. Flagler St., Miami, ☎ 305/375–1492), the Historical Museum of Southern Florida's gift shop, offers interesting artifacts reflecting
Miami's history, including some inexpensive reproductions. The collection of books on Miami and South Florida is impressive.

ESSENTIALS

Wall-to-wall merchandise is found at the **Compass Market** (⊠ 860 Ocean
Dr., Miami Beach, ☎ 305/673–2906), a cute and cozy basement shop
that carries all the staples you'll need, especially if you're staying in an
efficiency. The market stocks sandals, souvenirs, cigars, deli items,
umbrellas, newspapers, and produce.

JEWELRY

Stones of Venice (⊠ 550 Biltmore Way, Coral Gables, ☎ 305/444–4474),
operated by a three-time winner of the DeBeers Diamond Award for
jewelry, sells affordable creations. Customers have included Elliott
Gould, Pope John Paul II, and film director Barbet Schroeder.

LIGHTING

Lunatika (⊠ 1019 Lincoln Rd., Miami Beach, ☎ 305/534–8585) lights
up SoBe with funky, creative lighting from chandeliers to wall sconces
to floor lamps. One look and you'll say "yowsa!"

SIDE TRIP

South Dade

Although the population of these suburbs southwest of Dade County's
urban core was largely dislocated by Hurricane Andrew in 1992, little damage is evident today. Indeed, FEMA grants and major replant-
ing have made the area better than ever. All attractions—which are
especially interesting for kids—have reopened, and a complete exploration of them would probably take two days. Keep an eye open for
hand-painted signs announcing agricultural attractions, such as orchid
farms, fruit stands, u-pick farms, and horseback riding.

🐾 ④⑦ Aviation enthusiasts touch down at **Weeks Air Museum** to view some
25 planes of WWII vintage. Sadly, Hurricane Andrew destroyed the
WWI aircraft, and WWII suffered damage as well. By late 1998 the B-
17 Flying Fortress bomber and P-51 Mustang should be back on display. The museum is inside Tamiami Airport. ⊠ *14710 S.W. 128th St.,*
☎ *305/233–5197.* ᵀ *$5.95.* ⊙ *Daily 10–5.*

One of the only zoos in the United States in a subtropical environment,
🐾 ④⑧ the first-class, 290-acre **Metrozoo** is state-of-the-art. Inside the cageless zoo, some 1,000 animals roam on islands surrounded by moats.
Major attractions include the Tiger Temple, where white tigers roam,

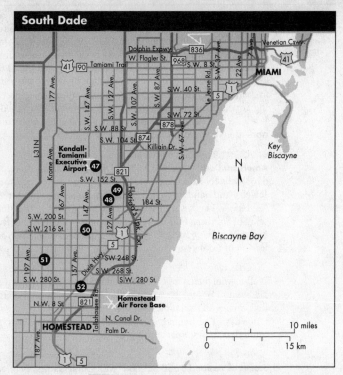

and the African Plains exhibit, where giraffes, ostriches, and zebras graze in a simulated habitat. There are also koalas, Komodo dragons, and other animals whose names begin with a *K*. Paws, a petting zoo for children, features three shows daily; during the Wildlife Show, trained animals demonstrate natural behavior on cue. Kids can touch Florida animals such as alligators and possums at the Ecology Theater. ⊠ *12400 Coral Reef Dr. (S.W. 152nd St.),* ☎ *305/251–0401.* ☞ *$8, 45-min tram tour $2.* ⊙ *Daily 9:30–5:30, last admission 4.*

Historic railroad cars on display at the **Gold Coast Railroad Museum** include a 1949 *Silver Crescent* dome car and the *Ferdinand Magellan,* the only Pullman car constructed specifically for U.S. presidents. It has been used by Franklin Delano Roosevelt, Harry Truman, Dwight Eisenhower, and Ronald Reagan. A train ride is included in the price of admission to the museum, which is next to the zoo. ⊠ *12450 Coral Reef Dr. (S.W. 152nd St.),* ☎ *305/253–0063.* ☞ *$5.* ⊙ *Weekdays 11–3, weekends 11–4.*

Home to more than 300 monkeys representing 25 species—including orangutans from Borneo and Sumatra and golden lion tamarins from Brazil—**Monkey Jungle** is high on kids' lists of things to do and remains a kitschy attraction for adults. Four different performing-monkey shows begin at 10 and run continuously at 30-minute intervals. The walkways of this 30-acre attraction are caged; the monkeys roam free. ⊠ *14805 Hainlin Mill Dr. (S.W. 216th St.),* ☎ *305/235–1611.* ☞ *$11.50.* ⊙ *Daily 9:30–5, last admission 4.*

The 30-acre **Redland Fruit & Spice Park** has been a Dade County treasure since 1944, when it was opened as a 20-acre showcase of tropical fruits and vegetables. Two of the park's three historic buildings were ruined by the hurricane, as well as about half of its trees and plants, but it's now back in full swing. Plants are now grouped by country of origin and include more than 500 economically important varieties of exotic fruits, herbs, spices, nuts, and poisonous plants from around the world. A sampling reveals 65 types of bananas, 40 varieties of grapes, and 100 kinds of citrus fruits. A gourmet food and fruit shop offers many varieties of tropical-fruit products, jellies, seeds, aromatic teas, and reference books. ⊠ *24801 Redland Rd. (S.W. 187th Ave.),* ☎ *305/ 247–5727.* ☜ *$2, guided tour $1.50.* ☉ *Daily 10–5, tours weekends 1 and 3.*

☾ ⑤ **Coral Castle of Florida** was born when 26-year-old Edward Leed-skalnin, a Latvian immigrant, was left at the altar by his 16-year-old fiancée. She went on with her life, while he went off the deep end and began carving a castle out of coral rock. Built between 1920 and 1940, the 3-acre castle is one of South Florida's original tourist attractions. There is a 9-ton gate a child can open, an accurate working sundial, and a telescope of coral rock aimed at the North Star. The place is weird and wonderful. ⊠ *28655 S. Dixie Hwy.,* ☎ *305/248–6344 or 305/238– 6345.* ☜ *$7.75.* ☉ *Daily 9–6.*

MIAMI AND MIAMI BEACH A TO Z

Arriving and Departing

By Boat

If you enter the United States in a private vessel along the Atlantic Coast south of Sebastian Inlet, you must call the **U.S. Customs Service** (☎ 800/432–1216 near Miami or ☎ 305/536–5263 otherwise). Customs clears most boats of less than 5 tons by phone, but you may be directed to a marina for inspection.

The **Port of Miami** (⊠ 1015 North American Way, Miami, ☎ 305/347–4860) bills itself as the "cruise capital of the world," appropriate since its 15 cruise ships and seven cruise lines accommodate 3 million passengers a year. Almost like an airport, the port has car rental agencies and a limousine service, and it's a great hopping-off point to the Bahamas, Mexico, Jamaica, and other island getaways. Cruise lines operating out of the port are Carnival Cruise Lines (☎ 305/599–2600), Discovery Cruise Lines (☎ 800/937–4477), Dolphin Cruise Line (☎ 800/358–2111), Majesty Cruise Lines (☎ 800/645–8111), Norwegian Cruise Lines (☎ 800/327–7030), Royal Caribbean Cruise Lines (☎ 800/255–4373), and Tropicana Cruises (☎ 800/965–3999).

By Bus

Greyhound (☎ 800/231–2222) buses stop at four terminals in Greater Miami (⊠ 700 Biscayne Blvd., Miami; ⊠ 4111 N.W. 27th St., Miami; ⊠ 16560 N.E. 6th Ave., North Miami; ⊠ 20505 S. Dixie Highway, South Miami) and at Miami International Airport.

By Car

The main highways into Greater Miami from the north are Florida's Turnpike (a toll road) and I–95. From the northwest take I–75 or U.S. 27 into town. From the Everglades, to the west, use the Tamiami Trail (U.S. 41), and from the south use U.S. 1 and the Homestead Extension of Florida's Turnpike.

By Plane

Miami International Airport (MIA, ☎ 305/876–7000), 6 mi west of downtown Miami, is the only airport in Greater Miami that provides scheduled service. With a daily average of 1,400 flights, it handled 35 million passengers in 1996, more than half of them international travelers. MIA is also the nation's busiest airport for international freight.

Altogether more than 130 airlines serve 200 cities and five continents with nonstop or one-stop service. MIA has 102 aircraft gates and eight concourses.

Anticipating continued growth, the airport has begun a more than $4 billion expansion program that is expected to be completed by 2005. Passengers will mainly notice rebuilt and expanded gate and public areas, which should reduce congestion.

A greatly underused convenience for passengers who have to get from one concourse to another in this long, horseshoe-shape terminal is the Moving Walkway, on the skywalk level, with access points at every concourse. Also available on site is the 259-room Miami International Airport Hotel (⊠ Concourse E, upper level, ☎ 305/871–4100), which has the Top of the Port restaurant on the seventh floor and the Port Lounge on the eighth. MIA, the first to offer duty-free shops, now boasts 18, carrying liquors, perfumes, electronics, and various designer goods.

Heightened security at MIA has meant that it's suggested you check in 90 minutes before departure for a domestic flight, two hours for an international flight. Services for international travelers include 24-hour multilingual information and paging phones and currency conversion booths throughout the terminal. There is an information booth with a multilingual staff across from the 24-hour currency exchange at the entrance of Concourse E on the upper level. Other tourist information centers are at the customs exit, Concourse E, lower level (daily 5 AM–11 PM); customs exit, Concourse B, second level (daily 11–11); Concourse G, lower level (daily 11–7); Concourse D, lower level (daily 11–11); and Satellite Terminal (daily 11–7).

Airlines that fly into MIA include Aeroflot (☎ 888/340–6400), Aerolineas Argentinas (☎ 800/333–0276), Aeromexico (☎ 800/237–6639), AeroPeru (☎ 800/777–7717), Air Aruba (☎ 800/882–7822), Air Canada (☎ 800/776–3000), Air France (☎ 800/237–2747), Air Jamaica (☎ 800/523–5585), Alitalia (☎ 800/223–5730), American and American Eagle (☎ 800/433–7300), American TransAir (☎ 800/225–2995), Avensa (☎ 800/428–3672), Avianca (☎ 800/284–2622), Aviateca (☎ 800/327–9832), Bahamasair (☎ 800/222–4262), British Airways (☎ 800/247–9297), BWIA (☎ 305/371–2942), Cayman Airways (☎ 800/422–9626), Comair (☎ 800/354–9822), Continental (☎ 800/525–0280), Delta (☎ 800/221–1212), El Al (☎ 800/223–6700), Finnair (☎ 800/950–5000), Gulfstream International (☎ 800/992–8532), Guyana Airways (☎ 800/242–4210), Iberia (☎ 800/772–4642), LAB (☎ 800/327–7407), Lacsa (☎ 800/225–2272), Lan Chile (☎ 800/735–5526), Lauda Air (☎ 800/645–3880), LTU (☎ 800/888–0200), Lufthansa (☎ 800/645–3880), Martinair Holland (☎ 800/366–4655), Mexicana (☎ 800/531–7921), Northwest (☎ 800/225–2525), Paradise Island (☎ 800/786–7202), Saeta (☎ 800/827–2382), Servivensa (☎ 800/428–3672), South African Airways (☎ 800/722–9675), Taca (☎ 800/535–8780), Tower Air (☎ 800/348–6937), Transbrasil (☎ 800/872–3153), TWA (☎ 800/221–2000), United (☎ 800/241–6522), US Airways and US Airways Express (☎ 800/428–4322), Varig (☎ 800/468–2744), and Virgin Atlantic (☎ 800/862–8621).

Pan Am Air Bridge (⊠ 1000 MacArthur Causeway, Miami, ☎ 305/373–1120 or 800/424–2557) is starting over where the original Pan Am began—with seaplane flights. Departing from Watson Island, the 30- to 60-minute rides to Bimini, Paradise Island, and Walkers Cay in the Bahamas are exciting, anachronistic, and somewhat cramped.

By Bus: The county's **Metrobus** (☎ 305/638–6700) still costs $1.25, though equipment has improved. From the airport you can take Bus 7 to downtown (weekdays 5:30 AM–9 PM every 40 minutes; weekends 6:30 AM–7:30 PM every 40 minutes), Bus 37 south to Coral Gables and South Miami (6 AM–11:30 PM every 30 minutes) or north to Hialeah (5:30 AM–11:30 PM every 30 minutes), Bus J south to Coral Gables (6 AM–12:30 AM every 30 minutes) or east to Miami Beach (4:30 AM–11:30 PM every 30 minutes), and Bus 42 to Coconut Grove (5:30 AM–7:20 PM hourly). Some routes change to 60-minute schedules after 7 PM, so be prepared to wait.

By Limousine: Miami has more than 100 limousine services, though they're frequently in and out of business. If you rely on the Yellow Pages, look for a company with a street address, not just a phone. Offering 24-hour service, **Club Limousine Service** (✉ 12050 N.E. 14th Ave., Miami 33161, ☎ 305/893–9850 or 800/824–4820, 800/325–9834 in FL) has shuttle vans and minibuses as well as limos. One of the oldest companies in town is **Vintage Rolls Royce Limousines of Coral Gables** (✉ 4501 Monserrate St., Coral Gables 33146, ☎ 305/444–7657 or 800/888–7657), which operates a 24-hour reservation service and provides chauffeurs for privately owned, collectible Rolls-Royces from the 1940s.

By Taxi: Except for the flat-fare trips described below, cabs cost $1.75 per mile plus a $1 toll for trips originating at MIA or the Port of Miami. Approximate fares from MIA include $19 to Coral Gables, $22–$29 to downtown Miami, and $32–$37 to Key Biscayne. Fares to the beaches are $42–$47 to Golden Beach and Sunny Isles, north of Haulover Beach Park; $34 from Surfside through Haulover Beach Park; $29 between 63rd and 87th streets; and $24 from 63rd Street south to the foot of Miami Beach. These fares are per trip, not per passenger, and include tolls and $1 airport surcharge but not tip. The approximate fare between MIA and the Port of Miami is $18.

For taxi service to destinations in the immediate vicinity, ask a uniformed county taxi dispatcher to call an **ARTS** (Airport Region Taxi Service) cab for you. These special blue cabs offer a short-haul flat fare in two zones. An inner-zone ride is $7; the outer-zone fare is $10. The area of service is north to 36th Street, west to the Palmetto Expressway (77th Avenue), south to Northwest 7th Street, and east to Douglas Road (37th Avenue). Maps are posted in cab windows on both sides.

By Van: SuperShuttle (from MIA, ☎ 305/871–2000; ☎ 954/764–1700 from Broward [Fort Lauderdale] ; ☎ 800/874–8885 from elsewhere) vans transport passengers between MIA and local hotels, the Port of Miami, and even individual residences on a 24-hour basis. The company's service area extends from Palm Beach to Monroe County (including the Lower Keys). Drivers provide narration en route. Service from MIA is available around the clock on demand; for the return it's best to make reservations 24 hours in advance, although the firm will try to arrange pickups within Miami-Dade County on as little as four hours' notice. The cost from MIA to downtown hotels runs $8–$11. Additional members of a party pay a lower rate for many destinations, and children under four ride free with their parents. There's a pet transport fee of $5 for animals in kennels.

By Train

Amtrak (☎ 800/872–7245) runs three trains daily between New York City and Miami (✉ 8303 N.W. 37th Ave., ☎ 305/835–1223 for recorded arrival and departure information, 800/368–8725 for shipping); the trains make several stops along the way.

Tri-Rail (✉ 1 River Plaza, 305 S. Andrews Ave., Suite 200, Fort Lauderdale, ☎ 800/874–7245) is Florida's only commuter train system. Daily runs connect Miami with Broward and Palm Beach, stopping at 18 stations along the 70-mi route. Fares are established by zones, with prices ranging from $2 to a high of $9.25 round-trip. Tri-Rail connects with Miami's Metrorail, so you may not have to drive at all.

Getting Around

Greater Miami resembles Los Angeles in its urban sprawl and traffic. You'll need a car to visit many attractions and points of interest. Some are accessible via the public transportation system, run by a department of the county government—the **Metro-Dade Transit Agency,** which consists of 650 Metrobuses on 70 routes, the 21-mi Metrorail elevated rapid-transit system, and the Metromover, an elevated light-rail system. Free maps, schedules, and a "First-Time Rider's Kit" are available. ✉ *Government Center Station, 111 N.W. 1st St., Miami 33128; ☎ 305/654–6586 for Maps by Mail, 305/638–6700 for route information weekdays 6 AM–10 PM, weekends 9–5.*

By Bus

Metrobus stops are marked by blue-and-green signs with a bus logo and route information. The frequency of service varies widely, so call in advance to obtain specific schedules. The fare is $1.25 (exact change), transfers 25¢; 60¢ with 10¢ transfers for people with disabilities, senior citizens (65 and older), and students. Some express routes carry surcharges of $1.50. Reduced-fare tokens, sold 10 for $10, are available from Metropass outlets. Lift-equipped buses for people with disabilities are available on 16 routes, including one from the airport that links up with many routes in Miami Beach as well as Coconut Grove, Coral Gables, Hialeah, and Kendall. All but four of these routes connect with Metrorail (☎ 305/638–6700). Those unable to use regular transit service should call **Special Transportation Services** (☎ 305/ 263–5400) for information on such services as curb-to-curb van pickup.

By Car

In general, Miami traffic is the same as in any other big city, with the same rush hours and the same likelihood that parking garages will be full at peak times. Many drivers who aren't locals and don't know their way around might turn and stop suddenly, or drop off passengers where they shouldn't. Some drivers are short-tempered and will assault those who cut them off or honk their horn.

Motorists need to be careful, even when their driving behavior is beyond censure, however, especially in rental cars. Despite the removal of identifying marks, cars piled with luggage or otherwise showing signs that a tourist is at the wheel remain prime targets for thieves. Long-time residents know that Miami is more or less as safe for a visitor as any American city its size. The city has also initiated a TOP (Tourist Oriented Police) Cops program to assist tourists with directions and safety. For more safety advice on driving in Miami, *see* Driving *in* the Gold Guide.

By Taxi

One cab "company" stands out immeasurably above the rest. It's actually a consortium of drivers who have banded together to provide good service, in marked contrast to some Miami cabbies, who are rude, unhelpful, unfamiliar with the city, or dishonest, taking advantage of visitors who don't know the area. To plug into this consortium—they don't have a name, simply a number—call the dispatch service (☎ 305/888–4444)—although they can be hard to understand over the phone. If you have to use another company, try to be familiar with your route and destination. For information call the **Metro-Dade Passenger Transportation Regulatory Service** (☎ 305/375–2460), also known as the Hack Bureau. It takes complaints and monitors all for-hire vehicles.

Starting in 1998, fares were set at $1.50 for the first ¼ mi, and 25¢ every ⅛ mi after that, which balances out to $3 per first mile and $2 every mile after, with no additional charge for up to five passengers, luggage, and tolls. Taxis can be hailed on the street, although you may not always find one when you need one—it's better to call for a dispatch taxi or have a hotel doorman hail one for you. Some companies with dispatch service are **Central Taxicab Service** (☎ 305/532–5555), **Diamond Cab Company** (☎ 305/545–5555), **Metro Taxicab Company** (☎ 305/888–8888), **Miami-Dade Yellow Cab** (☎ 305/633–0503), **Society Cab Company** (☎ 305/757–5523), **Super Yellow Cab Company** (☎ 305/888–7777), **Tropical Taxicab Company** (☎ 305/945–1025), and **Yellow Cab Company** (☎ 305/444–4444). Many now accept credit cards; inquire when you call.

By Train

Elevated **Metrorail** trains run from downtown Miami north to Hialeah and south along U.S. 1 to Dadeland, daily 5:30 AM–midnight. Trains run every five minutes in peak hours, every 15 minutes at other times. The fare is $1.25. Transfers, which cost 25¢, must be bought at the first station entered. Parking at train stations costs $2.

Metromover has two loops that circle downtown Miami, linking major hotels, office buildings, and shopping areas. The system spans 4½ mi, including the 1½-mi Omni extension, with six stations to the north, and the 1-mi Brickell extension, with six stations to the south. Service runs daily every 90 seconds, 6 AM–midnight. The fare is 25¢. Transfers to Metrorail are $1.

By Trolley

The latest step-saver in Miami Beach is the **Electro-Wave** (☎ 305/535–9160), a fleet of free electric trolleys that run every few minutes to shuttle tourists and locals up and down Washington Avenue between 5th and 17th streets. Trolleys operate Monday–Wednesday 8 AM–2 AM, Thursday–Saturday 8 AM–4 AM, and Sunday and holidays 10 AM–2 AM.

By Water Taxi

A **water taxi service** (☎ 954/467–6677), inaugurated in 1988 in Fort Lauderdale, began Miami area operations in 1993. Canopied boats, 28 ft and longer, run between Miami Beach and the Bayside Marketplace. Routes cover downtown restaurants and the Watson Island airboat station. Taxi hours vary by season, with average fares from Bayside Marketplace of $3.50 one-way and $6 round-trip to waterfront stops in Miami and $7 one-way and $13 round-trip to Miami Beach.

Contacts and Resources

Emergencies

Dial **911** for police or ambulance. You can dial free from pay phones.

AMBULANCE

Randle Eastern Ambulance Service Inc. (✉ 7255 N.W. 19th St., Suite C, Miami 33126, ☎ 305/718–6400) operates at all hours, although in an emergency they'll direct you to call 911.

DENTISTS
East Coast District Dental Society (✉ 420 S. Dixie Hwy., Suite 2E, Coral Gables, ☎ 305/667–3647) is open weekdays 9–4:30 for dental referral. After hours stay on the line and a recording will direct you to a dentist. Services include general dentistry, endodontics, periodontics, and oral surgery.

DOCTORS
Dade County Medical Association (✉ 1501 N.W. North River Dr., Miami, ☎ 305/324–8717) is open weekdays 9–5 for medical referral.

HOSPITALS
Miami has 32 hospitals and more than 34,000 health-care professionals. The following hospitals have 24-hour emergency rooms:

In Miami Beach: **Miami Heart Institute** (✉ 4701 N. Meridian Ave., Miami Beach, ☎ 305/672–1111; 888/432–7848 physician referral), **Mt. Sinai Medical Center** (✉ Off Julia Tuttle Causeway, I–195 at 4300 Alton Rd., Miami Beach, ☎ 305/674–2121; 305/674–2200 emergency; 305/674–2273 physician referral), and **South Shore Hospital & Medical Center** (✉ 630 Alton Rd., Miami Beach, ☎ 305/672–2100).

In the north: **Parkway East** (✉ 160 N.W. 170th St., North Miami Beach, ☎ 305/651–1100; physician referral 800/833–8005).

In central Miami: **Coral Gables Hospital** (✉ 3100 Douglas Rd., Coral Gables, ☎ 305/445–8461; physician referral 305/444–2100), **Jackson Memorial Medical Center** (✉ 1611 N.W. 12th Ave., near Dolphin Expressway, Miami, ☎ 305/585–1111; emergency 305/585–6901; physician referral 305/547–5757), **Mercy Hospital** (✉ 3663 S. Miami Ave., Coconut Grove, ☎ 305/854–4400; emergency 305/285–2171; physician referral 305/285–2929), and **Pan American Hospital** (✉ 5959 N.W. 7th St., Miami, ☎ 305/264–1000; emergency 305/264–6125; physician referral 305/264–5118).

In the south: **Baptist Hospital of Miami** (✉ 8900 N. Kendall Dr., Miami, ☎ 305/596–1960; emergency 305/596–6556; physician referral 305/596–6557) and **South Miami Hospital** (✉ 6200 S.W. 73rd St., South Miami, ☎ 305/661–4611; emergency 305/662–8181; physician referral 305/596–6557).

LATE-NIGHT PHARMACIES
Eckerd Drug (✉ 1825 Miami Gardens Dr. NE, at 185th St., North Miami Beach, ☎ 305/932–5740) is open until midnight. **Eckerd Drug** (✉ 200 Lincoln Rd., ☎ 305/532–6978) has a pharmacy open until 8 PM. The following are open 24 hours: **Eckerd Drug** (✉ 9031 S.W. 107th Ave., Miami, ☎ 305/274–6776) and **Walgreens** (✉ 500-B W. 49th St., Palm Springs Mall, Hialeah, ☎ 305/557–5468; ✉ 2750 W. 68th St., Hialeah, ☎ 305/828–0268; ✉ 12295 Biscayne Blvd., North Miami, ☎ 305/893–6860; ✉ 5731 Bird Rd., Miami, ☎ 305/666–0757; ✉ 1845 Alton Rd., Miami Beach, ☎ 305/531–8868; ✉ 791 N.E. 167th St., North Miami Beach, ☎ 305/652–7332).

Car Rentals
The following agencies have booths near the baggage-claim area on MIA's lower level: **Alamo** (☎ 800/468–2583), **Avis** (☎ 800/331–1212), **Budget** (☎ 800/527–0700), **Dollar** (☎ 800/800–4000), **Hertz** (☎ 800/654–3131), and **National** (☎ 800/227–7368). Avis and Budget have offices at the Port of Miami.

RAC (☎ 305/608–6326) rents BMWs, Porsches, Ferraris, and Mercedes—just right for a family outing.

Guided Tours

BOAT TOURS

Heritage of Miami II offers sightseeing cruises on board a two-masted, 85-ft topsail schooner. Tours start and end at Bayside Marketplace (✉ 401 Biscayne Blvd., ☎ 305/442–9697). One-hour sails cost $7 per person, and two-hour sails are $12. Tours loop through lower Biscayne Bay, with views of the Vizcaya Museum and Gardens, the homes of movie stars, the Cape Florida Lighthouse, the Port of Miami, and several residential islands. It's a little money for a lot of fun.

Island Queen, Island Lady, and *Pink Lady* are 150-passenger double-decker tour boats docked at Bayside Marketplace (✉ 401 Biscayne Blvd., ☎ 305/379–5119). They go on daily 90-minute narrated tours of the Port of Miami and Millionaires' Row, costing $12.

Casino gambling is illegal in Florida, which explains the popularity of *SeaKruz* (✉ 300 Alton Rd., Miami Beach, ☎ 305/538–8300). For $15 you can travel into international waters and drop cash into craps, roulette, blackjack, and even pai gow—whatever floats your boat! Cruises depart from the Miami Beach Marina on weekdays at 1:30 and 5:30, Saturday 12:30 and 5:30, and Sunday at 1:30 AM.

HISTORICAL TOURS

Art Deco District Tour (✉ 1001 Ocean Dr., Bin L, Miami Beach 33139, ☎ 305/672–2014), operated by the Miami Design Preservation League, is a 90-minute guided walking tour ($6) departing from the league's welcome center at the Oceanfront Auditorium at 10:30 AM Saturday and 6:30 PM Thursday. Private group tours can be arranged with advance notice. A two-hour bike tour leaves from the Miami Beach Bicycle Center (✉ 601 5th St., Miami Beach, ☎ 305/674–0150) at 10:30 on the first and third Sundays of the month. This tour costs $10 with a rental bike, $5 with your own bike. You can go at your own pace with a self-guided $5 audio tour, which takes roughly an hour. The league also sells the *Art Deco District Guide,* a book of six detailed walking or driving tours of the Art Deco District, for $10.

Deco Tours Miami Beach (✉ 420 Lincoln Rd., Suite 412, Miami Beach, ☎ 305/531–4465) offers walking tours of the Art Deco District, with 24-hour notice for reservations preferred. These 90-minute tours, which cost $15, depart from various locations and take in Lincoln Road, Washington Avenue, Espanola Way, Ocean Drive, Lummus Park, and the Art Deco Welcome Center. Tours of the city are conducted in vans and buses.

Professor Paul George (✉ 1345 S.W. 14th St., Miami, ☎ 305/858–6021), a history professor at Miami-Dade Community College and past president of the Florida Historical Society, leads a variety of walking tours as well as boat tours and tours that make use of the Metrorail and Metromover. Pick from tours covering downtown, historic neighborhoods, cemeteries, Coconut Grove, and the Miami River. They start Saturday at 10 and Sunday at 11 at various locations, depending on the tour, and generally last about 2½ hours. Call for each weekend's schedule and for additional tours by appointment. The fee is $15.

RICKSHAW TOURS

Majestic Rickshaw (✉ 75 N.E. 156th St., Biscayne Gardens) has two-person rickshaws along Main Highway in Coconut Grove's Village Center, nightly 8 PM–2 AM. You can take a 10-minute ride through Coconut Grove or a 20-minute lovers' moonlight ride to Biscayne Bay.

Motorcycle Rentals

Budget Rentals (⊠ 3901 N.W. 28th St., Miami, ☎ 305/871–1040 or 800/736–8433) rents new Harleys for half days, full days, or longer. **Rolling Thunder Tours** (⊠ 4537 Ponce de León Blvd., Coral Gables, ☎ 305/668–4600 or 800/851–7420) rents nothing but hogs.

Services for People with Hearing Impairments

Fire, police, medical, rescue (☎ 305/595–4749 TDD, 305/595–6263 or 911 voice).

Operator and directory assistance (☎ 800/855–1155 TDD).

Deaf Services of Miami (⊠ 9100 S. Dadeland Blvd., Suite 104, Miami 33156; ☎ 305/668–3323 TDD, 305/668–4407 voice; 305/668–4693 24-hour hot line; 305/806–6090 24-hour emergency numerical pager for interpreters).

Florida Relay Service (☎ 800/955–8771 TDD; 800/955–8770 voice).

Visitor Information

Greater Miami Convention & Visitors Bureau (⊠ 701 Brickell Ave., Suite 2700, Miami 33131, ☎ 305/539–3063 or 800/283–2707). Satellite tourist information centers are at Bayside Marketplace (⊠ 401 Biscayne Blvd., Miami 33132, ☎ 305/539–2980) and South Dade Visitor Information Center (⊠ 160 U.S. 1, Florida City 33034, ☎ 305/245–9180 or 800/388–9669, ℻ 305/247–4335).

Coconut Grove Chamber of Commerce (⊠ 2820 McFarlane Rd., Coconut Grove 33133, ☎ 305/444–7270, ℻ 305/444–2498). **Coral Gables Chamber of Commerce** (⊠ 50 Aragon Ave., Coral Gables 33134, ☎ 305/446–1657, ℻ 305/446–9900). **Florida Gold Coast Chamber of Commerce** (⊠ 1100 Kane Concourse, Suite 210, Bay Harbor Islands 33154, ☎ 305/866–6020) serves the beach communities of Bal Harbour, Bay Harbor Islands, Golden Beach, North Bay Village, Sunny Isles, and Surfside. **Greater Miami Chamber of Commerce** (⊠ 1601 Biscayne Blvd., Miami 33132, ☎ 305/350–7700, ℻ 305/374–6902). **Greater North Miami Chamber of Commerce** (⊠ 13100 W. Dixie Hwy., North Miami 33181, ☎ 305/891–7811, ℻ 305/893–8522). **Greater South Dade/South Miami Chamber of Commerce** (⊠ 6410 S.W. 80th St., South Miami 33143-4602, ☎ 305/661–1621, ℻ 305/666–0508). **Key Biscayne Chamber of Commerce** (⊠ Key Biscayne Bank Bldg., 95 W. McIntyre St., Key Biscayne 33149, ☎ 305/361–5207). **Miami Beach Chamber of Commerce** (⊠ 1920 Meridian Ave., Miami Beach 33139, ☎ 305/672–1270, ℻ 305/538–4336). **Surfside Tourist Board** (⊠ 9301 Collins Ave., Surfside 33154, ☎ 305/864–0722 or 800/327–4557, ℻ 305/861–1302).

3 The Everglades

South Florida's wide, slow-moving "River of Grass"—the largest roadless expanse in the United States—is home to Everglades National Park and spectacular plant and animal life found no place else in the country. Nearby Biscayne National Park protects living coral reefs, mangroves, undeveloped islands, a shallow bay, and all the wild things that come with them. Both areas, within minutes of Miami's metropolis, maintain a fragile balance between humans and nature.

Updated by
Diane P.
Marshall

THE ONLY METROPOLITAN AREA in the United States
with two national parks in its backyard is Miami. Everglades National Park, created in 1947, was meant
to preserve the slow-moving "River of Grass"—a freshwater river 50
mi wide but only 6 inches deep, flowing from Lake Okeechobee
through marshy grassland into Florida Bay. Along the Tamiami Trail
(U.S. 41), marshes of cattails extend as far as the eye can see, inter-
spersed only with hammocks or tree islands of bald cypress and mahogany, while overhead southern bald eagles make circles in the sky.
A wide variety of trees and flowers, including ferns, orchids, and
bromeliads, share the brackish waters with otters, turtles, marsh rabbits, and occasionally that gentle giant, the West Indian manatee. Not
so gentle, though, is the saw grass. Deceptively graceful, these tall, wil-
lowy sedges have small sharp teeth on the edges of their leaves.

Biscayne National Park, established as a national monument in 1968
and 12 years later expanded and designated a national park, is the nation's largest marine park and the largest national park within the continental United States with living coral reefs. A small portion of the
park's almost 274 square mi consists of mainland coast and outlying
islands, but 96% is under water, much of it in Biscayne Bay. The islands contain lush, heavily wooded forests with an abundance of ferns
and native palm trees. Of particular interest are the mangroves and their
tangled masses of stiltlike roots and stems that thicken the shorelines.
These "walking trees," as locals sometimes call them, have striking curved
prop roots, which arch down from the trunk, while aerial roots drop
from branches. These trees draw freshwater from saltwater and create a coastal nursery capable of sustaining all types of marine life.

Unfortunately, Miami's backyard is threatened by suburban sprawl and
agriculture. What results is competition among environmental, agricultural, and developmental interests. The biggest issue is water. Originally, alternating floods and dry periods maintained wildlife habitat
and regulated the water flowing into Florida Bay. The brackish seasonal flux sustained a remarkably vigorous bay, including the most pro-
ductive shrimp beds in American waters, with thriving mangrove
thickets and coral reefs at its Atlantic edge. The system nurtured sea
life and attracted anglers and divers. Starting in the 1930s, however,
a giant flood-control system began diverting water to canals running
to the gulf and the ocean. As you travel Florida's north–south routes,
you cross this network of canals symbolized by a smiling alligator representing the South Florida Water Management District, ironically
known as "Protector of the Everglades."

The unfortunate side effect of flood control has been devastation of
the wilderness. Park visitors decry diminished bird counts (a 90% re-
duction over 50 years); the black bear has been eliminated, and the
Florida panther is nearing extinction. In 1997 the nonprofit group American Rivers again ranked the Everglades among the most threatened
rivers of North America. Meanwhile, the loss of freshwater has made
Florida Bay more salty, devastating breeding grounds and creating
dead zones where pea green algae has replaced sea grasses and sponges.

Even as the ecosystem fades, new policies, still largely on paper, hold
promise. Some 40% of what is commonly called Big Cypress Swamp
was established as Big Cypress National Preserve in 1974 to protect
the watershed of Everglades National Park. Some 22 government agencies and a host of conservation groups and industries are working on
restoration plans. Some of the 40,000 acres of filtration marshes that

will remove harmful agricultural nutrients before they enter the protected wetlands have been constructed as part of the Everglades Forever Act. Within the next decade farming must sharply reduce its phosphorus runoff, and the U.S. Army Corps of Engineers, which maintains Florida's flood-control system, proposes restoring a more natural flow of water into the Everglades and its related systems. Although the future of the natural system hangs uncertainly as engineers and ecologists battle over what to do and when to do it, there are promising signs.

Pleasures and Pastimes

Biking and Hiking

In the Everglades there are several nice places to ride and hike. The Shark Valley Loop Road (15 mi round-trip) makes a good bike trip. "Foot and Canoe Trails of the Flamingo Area," a leaflet, lists others. Inquire about insect conditions before you go and plan accordingly, stocking up on insect repellent, sunscreen, and water, as necessary.

Boating and Canoeing

One of the best ways to experience the Everglades is by boat, and almost all of Biscayne National Park is accessible only by water. Boat rentals are available in both parks. Rentals are generally for half day (four hours) and full day (eight hours).

In the Everglades the 99-mi inland Wilderness Trail between Flamingo and Everglades City is open to motorboats as well as canoes, although powerboats may have trouble navigating the route above Whitewater Bay. Flat-water canoeing is best in winter, when temperatures are moderate, rainfall is minimal, and mosquitoes are tolerable. You don't need a permit for day trips, but tell someone where you're going and when you expect to return. Getting lost is easy, and spending the night without proper gear can be unpleasant, if not dangerous.

On the Gulf Coast you can explore the nooks, crannies, and mangrove islands of Chokoloskee Bay, as well as many rivers near Everglades City. The Turner River Trail, a good day trip, passes through mangrove, dwarf cypress, coastal prairie, and freshwater slough ecosystems of Everglades National Park and Big Cypress National Preserve.

Dining

With a few exceptions, dining centers on low-key mom-and-pop places that serve hearty home-style food and small eateries specializing in local fare: seafood, conch, alligator, turtle, and frogs' legs. Native American restaurants add another dimension, serving local favorites as well as catfish, Indian fry bread (a flour-and-water dough), pumpkin bread, Indian burgers (ground beef browned, rolled in fry-bread dough, and deep-fried), and tacos (fry bread with chili, lettuce, tomato, and shredded cheddar cheese on top). Restaurants in Everglades City appear to operate with a "captive audience" philosophy: Prices run high, service is mediocre, and food preparation is uninspired. The closest good restaurants are in Naples, 35 mi northwest.

Although both Everglades and Biscayne national parks are wilderness areas, there are restaurants within a short drive. Most are between Miami and Shark Valley along the Tamiami Trail (U.S. 41), in the Homestead–Florida City area, in Everglades City, and in the Florida Keys along the Overseas Highway (U.S. 1). The only food service in either park is at Flamingo, in the Everglades, but many independent restaurants will pack picnics. (You can also find fast-food establishments on the Tamiami Trail east of Krome Avenue and along U.S. 1 in Homestead–Florida City.)

Fishing

Largemouth bass are plentiful in freshwater ponds, while snapper, redfish, and sea trout are caught in Florida Bay. The mangrove shallows of the Ten Thousand Islands, along the gulf, yield tarpon and snook. Whitewater Bay is also a favorite spot. Note: The state has issued health advisories for sea bass, largemouth bass, and other freshwater fish, especially those caught in the canals along the Tamiami Trail, due to their high mercury content. Signs are posted throughout the park, and consumption should be limited.

Exploring the Everglades

The southern tip of the Florida peninsula is largely taken up by Everglades National Park, but land access to it is primarily by two roads. The main park road traverses the southern Everglades from the gateway towns of Homestead and Florida City to the outpost of Flamingo, on Florida Bay. In the northern Everglades you can take the Tamiami Trail (U.S. 41) from the Greater Miami area in the east to the western park entrance in Everglades City. In far southeastern Florida, Biscayne National Park lies almost completely offshore. As a result, most sports and recreational opportunities in both national parks are based on water, the study of nature, or both, so even on land, be prepared to get a bit damp on the region's marshy trails.

Though relatively compact, as compared with the national parks of the West, these parks still require a bit of time to see. The narrow, two-lane roads through the Everglades make for long travel, whereas it's the necessity of sightseeing by boat that takes time at Biscayne.

Numbers in the text correspond to numbers in the margin and on the Everglades and Biscayne National Parks map.

Great Itineraries

IF YOU HAVE 1 DAY

You'll have to make a choice—the Everglades or Biscayne. If you want quiet and nature, go with the Everglades. If you're interested in boating or underwater flora and fauna, Biscayne is your best bet. Either way, you'll experience a little of what's left of the "real" Florida.

For a day in Everglades National Park, begin in **Florida City** ⑬, gateway to the park and site of a museum on Florida pioneer life. Head to the **Ernest F. Coe Visitor Center** ① for an overview of the park and its ecosystems and continue to the **Royal Palm Visitor Center** ② for a look at several unique plant systems. Then go to **Flamingo** ③, where you can rent a boat or take a tour of Florida Bay.

If Biscayne is your preference, begin at **Convoy Point** ⑭ for an orientation before forsaking dry land. Sign up for a snorkel or dive trip or an outing on a glass-bottom boat, or explore an island.

IF YOU HAVE 3 DAYS

With three days you can explore both the northern and southern Everglades as well as Biscayne National Park. Start in the north by driving west along the Tamiami Trail, stopping at **Everglades Safari Park** ④ for an airboat ride; at **Shark Valley** ⑥ for a tram tour, walk, or bicycle trip; at the **Miccosukee Indian Village** ⑦ for lunch; at the Big Cypress Gallery to see Clyde Butcher's photographs; and then at the **Ochopee post office** ⑨, before ending in ⊞ **Everglades City** ⑪, home of the Gulf Coast Visitor Center. From here you can visit historic Smallwood's Store on Chokoloskee Island and watch the sunset. Day two is for exploring the south. Return east on the Tamiami Trail to **Homestead** ⑫, pausing at Everglades Air Tours to take a sightseeing trip before following the one-day Everglades itinerary above and overnighting in ⛺ **Florida City** ⑬. Biscayne National Park is the subject of day three. If you plan to scuba or take the glass-bottom boat, get an early start. You can explore the visitor center at **Convoy Point** ⑭ when you return and finish your day checking out sights in Florida City and Homestead. Snorkel trips leave later, giving you time to see Florida City and Homestead, have lunch, and learn about the park's ecosystem at the visitor center first. Be warned that though you can fly and then scuba dive, you can't dive and then fly within 24 hours. So if you're flying out, reverse the days' sequence accordingly.

IF YOU HAVE 5 DAYS

Follow day one above, spending the night in ⛺ **Everglades City** ⑪. Begin the second day with a canoe, kayak, or boat tour of the Ten Thousand Islands. In the late afternoon take a walk on the boardwalk at **Faka-hatchee Strand State Preserve** ⑩ to see rare epiphytic orchids or on a 2½-mi trail at the Big Cypress National Preserve. Drive east to Coop-ertown and take a nighttime airboat tour with Ray Cramer. Spend the night in ⛺ **Florida City** ⑬. Day three is spent at Biscayne National Park, then sightseeing in **Homestead** ⑫ and **Florida City** ⑬ as suggested above. Begin day four at Everglades Air Tours in Homestead; then browse the antiques shops along Krome Avenue before picking up a picnic lunch and seeing some of South Dade's other nearby attractions. On day five, augment your picnic lunch with goodies from the remarkable fruit stand Robert is Here, before heading to the southern portion of Everglades National Park, as described above.

When to Tour the Everglades

Winter is the best time to visit Everglades National Park. Temperatures and mosquito activity are low to moderate, low water levels concentrate the resident wildlife around sloughs that retain water all year, and migratory birds swell the avian population. Winter is also the busiest time in the park. Make reservations and expect crowds at Flamingo, the main visitor center (known officially as the Ernest F. Coe Visitor Center), and Royal Palm.

In spring the weather turns hot and rainy, and tours and facilities are less crowded. Migratory birds depart, and you must look harder to see wildlife. Be careful with campfires and matches; this is when the wild-fire-prone saw grass prairies and pinelands are most vulnerable.

Summer brings intense sun and billowing clouds unleashing torrents of rain almost every afternoon. Start your outdoor activities early to avoid the rain and the sun's strongest rays, and use sunscreen. Water levels rise and wildlife disperses. Mosquitoes hatch, swarm, and descend on you in voracious clouds. (Carrying mosquito repellent is a good idea at any time of year, but it's a necessity in summer.) Europeans constitute 80% of the summer visitors.

Even if you're not lodging in Everglades National Park, try to stay until dusk, when dozens of bird species feed around the ponds and trails. While shining a flashlight over the water in marshy areas, look for two yellowish-red reflections above the surface—telltale alligator signs.

EVERGLADES NATIONAL PARK

11 mi southwest of Homestead, 45 mi southwest of Miami International Airport.

The best way to experience the real Everglades is to get your feet wet, like paddling a canoe into the River of Grass to stay in a backcountry campsite. Most visitors won't do that, however. Luckily, there are several ways to see the wonders of the park with dry feet. Take a boat tour in Everglades City or Flamingo, ride the tram at Shark Valley, or walk the boardwalks along the main park road. And there's more to see than natural beauty. Miccosukee Indians operate a range of attractions and restaurants worthy of a stop.

Admission to Everglades National Park is valid at all entrances for seven days. Coverage below begins in the southern Everglades, followed by the northern Everglades, starting in the east and ending in Everglades City.

The Main Park Road

The main park road (Route 9336) travels from the main visitor center to Flamingo, across a section of the park's eight distinct ecosystems: hardwood hammock, freshwater prairie, pineland, freshwater slough, cypress, coastal prairie, mangrove, and marine-estuarine. Highlights of the trip include a dwarf cypress forest, the ecotone (transition zone) between saw grass and mangrove forest, and a wealth of wading birds at Mrazek and Coot Bay ponds. Boardwalks, looped trails, several short spurs, and observation platforms allow you to stay dry.

❶ The **Ernest F. Coe Visitor Center,** at park headquarters, houses numerous interactive exhibits and films. Stand in a simulated blind and peer through a spyglass to watch birds in the wild; though it's actually a film, the quality is so good you'll think you're outside. Move on to a bank of telephones to hear differing viewpoints on the Great Water Debate. There's a 15-minute film on the park, two movies on hurricanes, and a 45-minute wildlife film for children. Computer monitors present a schedule of daily ranger-led activities park-wide as well as information on canoe rentals and boat tours. In the Everglades Discovery Shop you can browse through lots of neat nature, science, and kids' stuff and pick up the insect repellent you forgot. The center provides information on the entire park. ⊠ *11 mi southwest of Homestead on Rte. 9336,* ☎ *305/242–7700.* ◫ *Park $10 per car, $5 per pedestrian or bicyclist, $5 per motorcycle.* ⊙ *Daily 8–5.*

❷ The **Royal Palm Visitor Center** is a must for anyone who wants to experience the real Everglades. You can stroll along the Anhinga Trail boardwalk or follow the Gumbo Limbo Trail through a hardwood hammock. The visitor center has an interpretive display, a bookstore, and vending machines. ⊠ *4 mi west of Ernest F. Coe Visitor Center on Rte. 9336,* ☎ *305/242–7700.* ⊙ *Daily 8–5.*

Flamingo

❸ *38 mi southwest of Ernest F. Coe Visitor Center.*

Here at the far end of the main road you'll find a cluster of buildings containing a visitor center, lodge, restaurant and lounge, gift shop, marina, and bicycle rentals, plus an adjacent campground. Tour boats narrated by interpretive guides, fishing expeditions of Florida Bay, and canoe and kayak trips all leave from here. Nearby is Eco Pond, one of the most popular wildlife observation areas.

The **Flamingo Visitor Center** provides an interactive display and has natural history exhibits in the Florida Bay Museum. Check the schedule for ranger-led activities, such as naturalist discussions, evening programs in the campground amphitheater, and hikes along area trails. ☎ *305/ 242–7700.* ⊙ *Daily 8–4.*

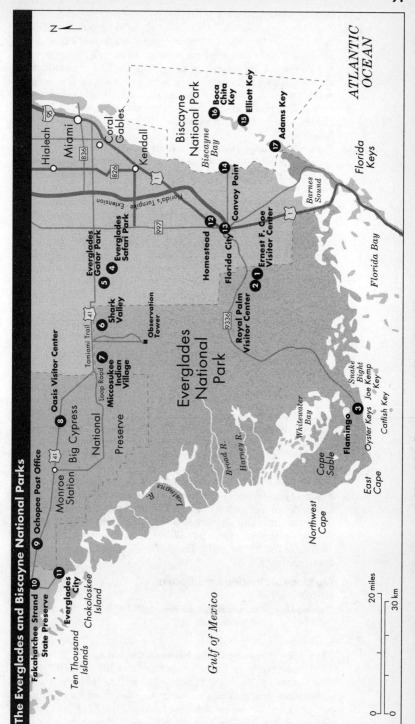

The Everglades and Biscayne National Parks

N

ATLANTIC OCEAN

Hialeah

Miami

Coral Gables

95

836

826

Kendall

Florida's Turnpike Extension

Biscayne National Park

Biscayne Bay

16 Boca Chita Key

15 Elliott Key

17 Adams Key

1

997

14

12 Homestead

13 Florida City

Convoy Point

Barnes Sound

1 Ernest F. Coe Visitor Center

2 1

Florida Keys

Florida Bay

Everglades Gator Park

5

4 Everglades Safari Park

9336

Royal Palm Visitor Center

6 Shark Valley

Tamiami Trail 41

Observation Tower

Everglades National Park

7 Miccosukee Indian Village

Loop Road

Tamiami Trail

8 Oasis Visitor Center

Big Cypress National Preserve

Monroe Station

9 Ochopee Post Office

41

Broad R.

Harney R.

Lostmans R.

Whitewater Bay

Cape Sable

Northwest Cape

East Cape

3 Flamingo

Snake Bight

Oyster Keys Joe Kemp Key

Catfish Key

Gulf of Mexico

Ten Thousand Islands

Chokoloskee Island

10 Fakahatchee Strand State Preserve

11 Everglades City

0   20 miles

0   30 km

Dining and Lodging

$–$$ ✕ **Flamingo Restaurant.** The grand view, convivial lounge, and casual style are great. Big picture windows on the visitor center's second floor overlook Florida Bay, revealing soaring eagles, gulls, pelicans, terns, and vultures. Dine at low tide to see birds flock to the sandbar just offshore. Though the restaurant, which serves palatable seafood, pasta, and grills, is only open in high season, the marina store is open all year for pizza, sandwiches, and salads. ✉ *Flamingo Lodge, 1 Flamingo Lodge Hwy.,* ☎ *941/695–3101. AE, D, DC, MC, V. Closed June–Oct.*

$$$ 🏨 **Flamingo Lodge Marina & Outpost Resort.** This simple low-rise motel is the only lodging inside the park. Accommodations are basic but well kept, and an amiable staff helps you adjust to bellowing alligators, roaming raccoons, and ibis grazing on the lawn. Rooms have contemporary furniture, floral bedspreads, and art prints of bird life. Though they face Florida Bay, they don't necessarily overlook it. Bathrooms are small. Cottages, in a wooded area on the margin of a coastal prairie, have kitchenettes and accommodate up to six people. Reservations are essential in winter; Continental breakfast is included in the summer. Some facilities, like the restaurant, are seasonal. ✉ *1 Flamingo Lodge Hwy., 33034,* ☎ *941/695–3101 or 800/600–3813. 101 rooms, 24 cottages, 1 suite. Restaurant, bar, snack bar, pool, coin laundry. AE, D, DC, MC, V.*

$ ⛺ **Everglades National Park.** Three developed campgrounds and group campsites have drinking water, sewage dump station, and rest rooms. Some also have picnic tables, grills, cold-water showers, and tent and trailer pads. Long Pine Key has 108 drive-up sites; Flamingo has 235 drive-up sites, 60 walk-in sites, and cold showers; and Chekika has 20 sites, warm showers, and a sulphur spring where you can swim. Pets are allowed. All sites are first-come, first served. In addition, deep in the park are 48 backcountry sites, many inland and some on the beach. Two are accessible by land, the others by canoe; 15 have *chickees* (raised wooden platforms with thatch roofs). All have chemical toilets. Several are within an easy day's canoeing of Flamingo; five are closer to Everglades City. Carry your food, water, and supplies in; carry out all trash. You'll need a site-specific permit, available on a first-come, first-served basis from the Flamingo or Gulf Coast Visitor Center (☞ Contacts and Resources *in* Everglades A to Z, *below,* for both). Developed sites are free June–August and $14 the rest of the year, groups pay $28, and backcountry sites cost $10. ☎ *305/242–7700 or 305/251–0371. 471 sites. Picnic areas. No credit cards.*

Outdoor Activities and Sports

BIKING

Flamingo Lodge Marina & Outpost Resort (☎ 941/695–3101) rents bikes for $14 a day and $8 per half day.

BOATING

The marina at **Flamingo Lodge Marina & Outpost Resort** (☎ 941/695–3101) rents power skiffs for $90 per day and $65 per half day, four new Carolina skiffs for $155 per day, as well as fully furnished and outfitted houseboats that sleep up to six. Rates (two-day minimum) run $475 without air-conditioning for two days, $575 with air-conditioning for two days. Several private boats are also available for charter. There are two ramps, one for Florida Bay, the other for Whitewater Bay and the backcountry. The hoist across the plug dam separating Florida Bay from the Buttonwood Canal can take boats 16 ft to 26 ft long. A small store sells food, camping supplies, bait and tackle, propane, and fuel.

CANOEING AND KAYAKING

The Everglades has six well-marked canoe trails in the Flamingo area, including the south end of the 99-mi Wilderness Trail from Everglades City to Flamingo. **Flamingo Lodge Marina & Outpost Resort** (☎ 941/695–3101) rents canoes in two sizes: small (up to two paddlers) and family size (up to four). Small canoes rent for $32 per day and $22 per half day; family-size run $40 and $30, respectively. Single-person kayaks cost $43 per day and $27 per half day; doubles rent for $54 and $38, respectively.

FISHING

Flamingo Lodge Marina & Outpost Resort (☎ 941/695–3101) helps arrange charter fishing trips for two to six persons. The cost is $265 a day for up to two people, $25 each additional person.

Tamiami Trail

141 mi from Miami to Fort Myers.

In 1915, when officials decided to build an east–west highway linking Miami to Fort Myers and continuing north to Tampa, someone suggested calling it the Tamiami Trail. In 1928 the road became a reality, cutting through the Everglades and altering the natural flow of water and the lives of the Miccosukee Indians who eked out a living fishing, hunting, and frogging here.

Today the traffic screams through Everglades National Park, Big Cypress National Preserve, and Fakahatchee Strand State Preserve. The landscape is surprisingly varied, changing from hardwood hammocks to pinelands, then abruptly to tall cypress trees dripping with Spanish moss and back to coastal prairie. Those who slow to take in the scenery can see alligators sunning themselves along the banks of roadside canals and in the shallow waters, hundreds of waterbirds, chickee huts, people fishing, Native American villages, and airboats parked at roadside enterprises.

Businesses along the trail give their addresses either in the distance from Krome Avenue, Florida's Turnpike, and Miami on the east coast or Fort Myers and Naples on the west coast or by mile marker. Between Miami and Fort Myers the road goes by several names, including Tamiami Trail, U.S. 41, and, at the Miami end, Southwest 8th Street.

❹ Attractions at **Everglades Safari Park** include a jungle trail, an educational alligator show and wrestling demonstration, a wildlife museum, airboat rides (included in admission), and a restaurant and gift shop. Climb the observation platform and take in the beauty of the Glades. ⊠ *26700 Tamiami Trail, 9 mi west of Krome Ave.,* ☎ *305/226–6923 or 305/223–3804.* ☞ *$15.* ⊙ *Daily 8:30–5.*

❺ At **Everglades Gator Park,** you can hold a baby alligator while friends snap a photo, squirm in a "reptilium" of venomous and nonpoisonous native snakes, or learn about Native Americans of the Everglades through a reproduction of a Miccosukee village. The park also features airboat tours, fishing charters, and RV campsites as well as a gift shop and restaurant. ⊠ *24050 Tamiami Trail, 12 mi west of Florida's Turnpike,* ☎ *305/559–2255 or 800/559–2205.* ☞ *Free, tours $12.* ⊙ *Daily 10–5, tours 9–5.*

❻ Though **Shark Valley** is the national park's north entrance, no roads here lead to other parts of the park. The only route is a paved 15-mi loop (you can walk, bicycle, or take a tram tour); at the half-way point there's a concrete observation tower built by an oil company in the early 1940s. Climb the ramp that spirals skyward 50 ft. From there everything as far as the eye can see is the vast River of Grass. Expect to see all kinds of waterbirds as well as alligators warming themselves along the banks and on the road (most quickly move out of the way). Just behind the bike rental area, a short boardwalk trail meanders through the saw grass. A small visitor center features rotating exhibits, a bookstore, and park rangers ready to answer questions. ⊠ *23.5 mi west of Florida's Turnpike,* ☎ *305/221–8776.* ⊟ *Park $8 per car, $4 per pedestrian, bicyclist, or motorcyclist.* ⊙ *Visitor center daily 8:30–5:30.*

❼ At the **Miccosukee Indian Village,** Miccosukee families prepare food and make crafts, on sale at the cultural center. Informative alligator-wrestling shows as well as airboat rides and a restaurant are other attractions. The Everglades Music & Craft Festival falls on a July weekend, and the weeklong Indian Arts Festival is in late December. ⊠ *Just west of Shark Valley entrance, 25 mi west of Florida's Turnpike,* ☎ *305/223–8380.* ⊟ *$5, rides $7.* ⊙ *Daily 9–5.*

❽ Pause at the **Oasis Visitor Center** to learn about the national park's northern neighbor, the Big Cypress National Preserve. Through the 1950s and early 1960s, the world's largest cypress-logging industry prospered in the Big Cypress Swamp. The industry died out in the 1960s, and the government began buying parcels. Today part of the swamp, which encompasses more than 729,000 acres, has become this national preserve. Its variegated pattern of wet prairies, ponds, marshes, sloughs, and strands provides a sanctuary for a variety of wildlife, but because of a politically dictated policy of balanced land use—"use without abuse"—the watery wilderness is devoted to research and recreation as well as preservation. The preserve allows—in limited areas—hunting, off-road vehicle (airboat, swamp buggy) use by permit, and cattle grazing. The 8-mi Turner River Canoe Trail begins here and crosses through Everglades National Park before ending in Chokoloskee Bay, near Everglades City. Hikers can join the Florida National Scenic Trail, which runs north–south through the preserve for 31 mi. The visitor center provides a schedule of myriad ranger-led and self-guided activities, such as campfire talks, bike hikes, slough slogs, and canoe excursions. Seven primitive campsites are available on a first-come, first-served basis. ⊠ *50 mi west of Miami, 20 mi west of Shark Valley,* ☎ *941/695–4111.* ⊟ *Free.* ⊙ *Daily 8:30–4:30.*

❾ The tiny **Ochopee post office** is the smallest post office in North America. Buy a picture postcard of the little one-room shack and mail it to a friend, thereby helping to keep this picturesque spot in business. ⊠ *Ochopee, 50 mi west of Miami,* ☎ *941/695–4131.* ⊙ *Weekdays 9:30–noon and 12:30–4, Sat. 9:30–11:30.*

❿ The ½-mi boardwalk at the **Fakahatchee Strand State Preserve** affords an opportunity to see rare plants, bald cypress, and North America's largest stand of native royal palms and largest concentration and variety of epiphytic orchids. ⊠ *Rte. 29 and Tamiami Trail; ranger station 3 mi north of Tamiami Trail on Rte. 29, Box 548, Copeland 34137,* ☎ *941/695–4593.* ⊟ *Admission free.* ⊙ *Daily 8–sunset.*

Dining and Lodging

$–$$ ✕ **Trattoria Creazione.** Kudos to this family-run restaurant a block off the Tamiami Trail and well worth the short detour. Chef Efrain Lopez turns out rich Italian specialties kissed with the flavor of garlic and fresh herbs. Small ravioli stuffed with salmon under a seafood cream sauce, pastas with vegetables, pastas with seafood, stuffed pastas, or the fish of the day are all good choices, especially if the latter is grilled, then sautéed with white wine, herbs, lemon, and butter. Most entrées cost less than $15—a bargain for the quality. ⊠ *Trails Shoppes, 920 S.W. 82nd Ave., at S.W. 9th St., Miami,* ☎ *305/269–9220. AE, DC, MC, V. Beer and wine only.*

$ ✕ **Coopertown Restaurant.** For more than a half century this rustic eatery just into the Everglades west of Miami has been full of Old Florida style—not to mention alligator skulls, stuffed alligator heads, and gator accessories. House specialties are frogs' legs and alligator tail prepared breaded or deep-fried, and they're available for breakfast, lunch, or dinner. You can also order more conventional selections, such as catfish, shrimp, or sandwiches. ⊠ *22700 S.W. 8th St., Miami,* ☎ *305/ 226–6048. MC, V. Beer only.*

$ ✕ **Miccosukee Restaurant.** Murals depict Native American women cooking and men engaged in a powwow in this Native American restaurant at the Miccosukee Indian Village. Favorites are catfish and frogs' legs breaded and deep-fried, Indian fry bread, pumpkin bread, and Indian burgers and tacos. Breakfast is served daily, but weekends bring a breakfast buffet (8–noon) featuring meats, eggs, breads, and lots more. ⊠ *25 mi west of Florida's Turnpike,* ☎ *305/223–8380, ext. 332. MC, V.*

$ ✕ **Pit Bar-B-Q.** The intense aroma of barbecue and blackjack-oak smoke will overwork your salivary glands. Order at the counter, pick up your food when called, and eat at one of the indoor or outdoor picnic tables. Specialties include barbecued chicken and ribs with a tangy sauce, french fries, coleslaw, and a fried biscuit as well as catfish and frogs' legs deep-fried in vegetable oil. Heed the scribbled message on the blackboard menu not to cross the grass median out front. It's an $85 fine if you're caught. ⊠ *16400 Tamiami Trail, Miami,* ☎ *305/226–2272. AE, MC, V.*

$ ⚠ **Everglades Gator Park.** Popular with the RV set, the park has full hookups for as many as 80 vehicles in addition to airboats, Everglades attractions, and a small store. You can rent a campsite by the night ($25), week ($100), or month ($350) or just store your RV. ⊠ *24050 S.W. 8th St., Miami; mailing address:* ⊠ *13800 S.W. 8th St., Box 107, Miami 33184,* ☎ *305/559–2255 or 800/559–2205. 80 sites. Restaurant, lake, fishing. MC, V.*

Outdoor Activities and Sports

Shark Valley Tram Tours (⊠ Shark Valley, ☎ 305/221–8455) rents bikes daily 8:30–4 (last rental at 3) for $3.75 per hour.

Shopping

Clyde Butcher does for the River of Grass what Ansel Adams did for the West, and you can check out his stunning photographs at his **Big Cypress Gallery** (⊠ 52388 Tamiami Trail, 37 mi west of Miami, ☎ 941/695–2428). Working with large-format black-and-white film, Butcher captures every blade of grass, barb of feather, and flicker of light. At the **Miccosukee Indian Village** (⊠ Just west of Shark Valley entrance, 25 mi west of Florida's Turnpike, ☎ 305/223–8380), you can buy Native American crafts, including beadwork, moccasins, dolls, pottery, baskets, and patchwork fabric and clothes, as well as kitschy Florida souvenirs.

Everglades City

⓫ *35 mi southeast of Naples, 83 mi west of Miami.*

The western gateway to Everglades National Park, this community, just off the Tamiami Trail, has been around since the late 19th century. Its biggest draw is the park and the canoe, airboat, fishing, and bird-watching excursions you can take within it. The annual Seafood Festival, held the first weekend of February, attracts 60,000–75,000 visitors to eat seafood, hear nonstop music, and buy crafts.

The **Gulf Coast Visitor Center,** at the Everglades' western entrance, offers interpretive exhibits about local flora and fauna. Backcountry campers can pick up the required free permits, and for those in need of a little more guidance, there are ranger-led boat trips. The center offers access to the Ten Thousand Islands region along the Gulf of Mexico, but there are no roads from here to other sections of the park. ⊠ *Rte. 29,* ☏ *941/695–3311.* ☞ *Park free.* ⊙ *Mid-Nov.–mid-Apr., daily 7–5:30; reduced hours mid-Apr.–mid-Nov.*

OFF THE
BEATEN PATH

SMALLWOOD'S STORE – Ted Smallwood pioneered this last American frontier in 1906 and built a 3,000-square-ft pine trading post raised on pilings in Chokoloskee Bay. Smallwood's granddaughter Lynn McMillin reopened it in 1989, after it had been closed several years, and installed a small gift shop and museum chock-full of original goods from the store; historic photographs; Indian clothing, furs, and hides; and area memorabilia. On the third Saturday in March, a festival celebrates the nearly 100-year relationship the store has had with local Native Americans. ⊠ *360 Mamie St., Chokoloskee Island,* ☏ *941/695–2989.* ☞ *$2.50.* ⊙ *Dec.–May, daily 10–5; May–Nov., daily 10–4.*

Dining and Lodging

$–$$ ✕ **Everglades Seafood Depot.** This new eatery is housed in the old Everglades depot, a 1928 Spanish-style stucco structure on Lake Placid. Once part of the University of Miami, it appeared in the film *Winds Across the Everglades* and has housed several restaurants. Today veteran restaurateur Billy Potter serves up well-prepared seafood—from shrimp and grouper to frogs' legs and alligator—any way you like it, and the staff is eager to please. For big appetites there are generously portioned entrées that include soup or salad, potato or rice, and warm, fresh-baked biscuits. If you aren't very hungry, choose the smaller "lunch-able appetites" portion, which include potato, slaw, and a biscuit. ⊠ *102 Collier Ave.,* ☏ *941/695–0075, MC, V.*

$–$$ ✕ **Oar House Restaurant.** With wood paneling, picnic table–style booths, and a mishmash of fishing and Glades decor, the first full-service eatery in town has the ambience of a diner. The menu features a blend of seafood and such local specialties as frogs' legs, turtle, conch, and gator. To its credit, the service is friendly, prices are very reasonable, the food is fried in canola and corn oils, and most dishes can be grilled or broiled, if you prefer. It's open for breakfast, and there are two lounges. ⊠ *305 Collier Ave.,* ☏ *941/695–3535. D, MC, V.*

$–$$ ✕ **Susie's Station.** Though it was built just several years ago, you'd swear this place dates from Everglades City's heyday. The vintage mood is created by a white-balustered screened porch, gas station memorabilia, an 1898 horse-drawn oil tanker, antiques on all the walls, and replica '20s lamps strung over booths set with beige cloths. Car buffs stop just to see the refurbished antique cars and truck. As for the food, the menu emphasizes local seafood: fried oysters, seafood baskets, crab cakes, and stone-crab claws. The homemade key lime pie sells out daily. Takeout and drive-through service are available. ⊠ *103 S.W. Copeland Ave.,* ☏ *941/695–2002. No credit cards.*

$ ✕ **Ivey House Restaurant.** Home-style meals are served every night at 6 (call for a reservation by 4 if you're not a guest of the hotel). The nightly changing menu features a mix of meat and vegetarian selections. For $11.95 you can dine on barbecued chicken with potatoes, vegetable, salad, pineapple upside-down cake, and coffee or tea, and on Mexican night the fare is chicken fajitas, tortillas, beans, rice, flan, and coffee or tea. ⊠ *107 Camellia St.,* ☎ *941/695–3299. MC, V. Closed May–Oct.*

$$ 🖭 **On the Banks of the Everglades.** Built in 1923, this lodging takes its name from the building it occupies, the former Bank of Everglades. Patty Flick Richards and her father, Bob Flick, created minirooms for single travelers ($35–$40), spacious rooms, suites, and efficiencies with queen- or king-size beds and stylish coordinating linens, wall coverings, and draperies. Suites and efficiencies have private baths and kitchens (the staff does the dishes); a few single rooms share a women's or men's bath. Amenities include hair dryers and in-room ironing boards. At night you can snack on popcorn and watch movies in the parlor. A breakfast of baked goods, cereal, fresh fruit, juices, and coffee and tea is served in the bank's vault. There is no smoking. ⊠ *201 W. Broadway, Box 455, 34139,* ☎ *941/695–3151 or 888/ 431–1977,* ⨎ *941/695–3335. 8 units (3 share baths). Bicycles. AE, D, MC, V.*

$$ 🖭 **Rod and Gun Club.** With a veranda, dark cypress fixtures, and a nautical theme, this landmark inn is like a time-warp trip back to the '20s, when wealthy hunters, anglers, and yachting parties from all over the world came to Florida for the winter season. The old guest rooms above the restaurant and bar aren't open anymore, but you can stay in comfortable cottages (no phone, however). The food is more than passable. Breakfast, lunch, and dinner are still served in the original dining room or on the wide veranda, and as in olden days, if you catch a "keeper," the chef will prepare it for your dinner. ⊠ *200 Riverside Dr., Box 190, 34139,* ☎ *941/695–2101. 17 rooms. Restaurant, bar, pool, 2 tennis courts, fishing. No credit cards.*

$ 🖭 **Ivey House B&B.** This clean, friendly bargain is run by the folks who operate North American Canoe Tours (NACT), David and Sandee Harraden. The shotgun-style cracker house was once a boardinghouse for workers building the Tamiami Trail. Today's guests are well educated, well traveled, and in tune, as evidenced by the new annex, whose rooms have modem connections so "guests can hook up their laptop computers to stay in touch with their families." In the evening people talk about adventures and do jigsaw puzzles in the living room. Family-style dinners ($10–$15) often end with homemade apple pie. Guests save 10% on NACT canoe, kayak, and powerboat rentals. ⊠ *107 Camellia St., 34139,* ☎ *941/695–3299,* ⨎ *941/695–4155. 30 rooms (10 share baths), 1 2-bedroom cottage. Bicycles, recreation room, library. MC, V. Closed May–Oct.*

Outdoor Activities and Sports

BIKING

North American Canoe Tours (⊠ Ivey House, 107 Camellia St., ☎ 941/ 695–4666) rents bikes for $3 per hour, $15 per day (free for Ivey House guests).

BOATING

North American Canoe Tours (⊠ Ivey House, 107 Camellia St., ☎ 941/ 695–4666) rents 16-ft Carolina skiffs with a 25-horsepower outboard, cooler, map, anchor, and safety equipment for $70 for a half day, $110 for a full day.

CANOEING AND KAYAKING

Everglades National Park Boat Tours (⊠ Gulf Coast Visitor Center, ☎ 941/695–2591; 800/445–7724 in FL) rents 17-ft Grumman canoes for day and overnight use. Rates are $18 per day. Car shuttle service is provided for canoeists paddling the Wilderness Trail, and travelers with disabilities can be accommodated. **North American Canoe Tours** (✉ Ivey House, 107 Camellia St., ☎ 941/695–4666) is an established source for canoes, sea kayaks, and guided Everglades trips (November–April). Canoes cost $25 the first day, $20 for each day thereafter, whereas kayaks are $35–$55 per day. Half-day rentals are available. Car shuttles for canoeists paddling the Wilderness Trail are $135 with NACT canoe or $170 with your own, plus the $10 park entrance fee.

GATEWAY TOWNS

The farm towns of Homestead and Florida City, flanked by Everglades National Park on the west and Biscayne National Park to the east, provide the closest visitor facilities to the parks. (The area's better restaurants are in Homestead, but the best lodgings are in Florida City.) The towns date from early in the century, when Henry Flagler extended his railroad to Key West but soon decided that farming would do more for rail revenues than ferrying passengers.

Homestead

⑫ *30 mi southwest of Miami.*

When Hurricane Andrew tore across South Florida with winds approaching 200 mph, it ripped apart lives and the small community of Homestead. The city rebuilt itself, redefining its role as the "Gateway to the Keys" and attracting hotel chains, a shopping center, sports complex, and residential development. The historic downtown area has become a preservation-driven Main Street city. Krome Avenue (Route 997), which cuts through the city's heart, is lined with restaurants and antiques shops.

West of north–south Krome Avenue, miles of fields grow fresh fruits and vegetables. Some are harvested commercially. Others have U-PICK signs, inviting families to harvest their own. Stands that sell farm-fresh produce abound.

In addition to its agricultural legacy, the town has an eclectic flavor, attributable to its population mix: descendants of pioneer Crackers, Hispanic growers, and farmworkers as well as latter-day northern retirees. Until Hurricane Andrew the military had a huge presence at Homestead Air Force Base. The economy still suffers from its loss.

With a saltwater atoll pool that's flushed by tidal action, **Homestead Bayfront Park,** adjacent to Biscayne National Park, is popular among local families as well as anglers and boaters. Highlights include a playground, ramps for people with disabilities (including a ramp that leads into the swimming area), a picnic pavilion with grills, showers, and rest rooms. ✉ *9698 S.W. 328th St.,* ☎ *305/230–3034.* 🎫 *$3.50 per passenger vehicle, $8 per vehicle with boat, $6 per RV.* ☉ *Sunrise–sunset.*

To find out about more area attractions, *see* the South Dade side trip *in* Chapter 3.

Dining

$ ✕ **El Toro Taco.** This family-run area institution features a rustic atmo-
★ sphere, good Mexican food in generous servings, homemade tortilla chips (sometimes a little greasy), and friendly service. Selections range from tasty favorites like beef or chicken fajitas, enchiladas, tamales, burritos, and tacos to more traditional Mexican dishes like *mole de pollo,* which combines cooking chocolate and spices with chicken. Desserts include *tres leches* (a cake soaked in a syrup of three milks—

evaporated, sweetened condensed, and heavy cream) and flan. You can order spicing from mild to tongue challenging. The restaurant is also open for breakfast. ⊠ *1 S. Krome Ave.,* ☎ *305/245–8182. D, MC, V. BYOB.*

$ ✕ **Tiffany's.** What looks like a converted pioneer house with a high-pitched roof and lattice under a big banyan tree is in reality a cluster of shops and this casual restaurant. The decor is frilly nouveau Victorian, with teaberry-color tablecloths and floral place mats, and the atmosphere is quaint but noisy. Featured entrées include hot crabmeat au gratin and asparagus rolled in ham with hollandaise sauce. Among the homemade desserts, choose from a very tall carrot cake, strawberry whipped-cream cake, and a harvest pie with double crust that has layers of apples, cranberries, walnuts, raisins and a caramel topping. Sunday brunch is served, too. ⊠ *22 N.E. 15th St.,* ☎ *305/246–0022. MC, V. Closed Mon. No dinner.*

Outdoor Activities and Sports

AUTO RACING

The **Miami-Dade Homestead Motorsports Complex** (⊠ 1 Speedway Blvd., 33035, ☎ 305/230–7223) is a state-of-the-art facility with two tracks: a 2.21-mi continuous road course and a 1½-mi oval. There's a schedule of year-round manufacturer and race-team testing, club racing, and other national events.

BOATING

Boaters give high ratings to the facilities at **Homestead Bayfront Park.** The 174-slip marina has a ramp, dock, bait-and-tackle shop, fuel station, ice, dry storage, and boat hoist, which can handle vessels up to 25 ft long with lifting rings. The park also has a tidal swimming area. ⊠ *9698 S.W. 328th St.,* ☎ *305/230–3033.* ☞ *$3.50 per passenger vehicle, $8 per vehicle with boat, $6 per RV, $10 hoist.* ☉ *Sunrise–sunset.*

Shopping

In addition to Homestead Boulevard (U.S. 1) and Campbell Drive (Southwest 312th Street and Northeast 8th Street), **Krome Avenue** is popular for shopping. In the heart of old Homestead, it has a brick sidewalk and many antiques stores.

Florida City

⑬ *2 mi southwest of Homestead.*

Florida's Turnpike ends in this southernmost town on the peninsula, spilling thousands onto U.S. 1 and eventually west to Everglades National Park, east to Biscayne National Park, or south to the Florida Keys. As the last civilization before 18 mi of mangroves and water, this stretch of U.S. 1 is lined with fast-food eateries, service stations, hotels, bars, dive shops, and restaurants.

Like Homestead, Florida City has roots planted in agriculture, as evidenced by hundreds of acres of farmland west of Krome Avenue and a huge farmers' market that processes produce to be shipped around the country. Construction is beginning on a new aquarium and IMAX theater, which will eventually show a film on Everglades and Biscayne national parks.

In the **Florida Pioneer Museum,** a former station agent's house, you can pore over a collection of articles from daily life that evokes the area's homestead period on the last frontier of mainland America. Items recall a time when Henry Flagler's railroad vaulted the development of the Florida Keys all the way to Key West, and Homestead and Florida

City were briefly the take-charge supply outposts. A caboose outside, which dates from the days of the old Florida East Coast Railway station, is one of a few wooden cars left in the country. It's staffed by volunteers, so call first. ⊠ *826 N. Krome Ave.,* ☎ *305/246–9531.* ▭ *$1.* ⊙ *Daily 1–5.*

Dining and Lodging

$$–$$$ ✕ **Mutineer Restaurant.** Former Sheraton Hotels builder Allan Bennett created this roadside steak and seafood restaurant with an indoor-outdoor fish and duck pond in 1980, back when Florida City was barely on the map. Etched glass divides the bilevel dining rooms, where striped-velvet chairs, stained glass, and a few portholes set the scene; in the lounge are an aquarium and nautical antiques. The big menu offers 18 seafood entrées plus another half-dozen daily seafood specials, as well as game, ribs, and steaks. There's live music Thursday–Saturday evenings. ⊠ *11 S.E. 1st Ave. (U.S. 1 and Palm Dr.),* ☎ *305/ 245–3377. AE, D, DC, MC, V.*

$–$$$ ✕ **Richard Accursio's Capri Restaurant and King Richard's Room.** Lo-
★ cals have been dining here—one of the oldest family-run restaurants in Miami-Dade County—since 1958. Outside it's a nondescript building in the middle of a big parking lot. Inside there's dark wood paneling and heavy wooden furniture. The tasty fare ranges from pizza with light, crunchy crusts and ample toppings to mild, meaty conch chowder. Mussels come in garlic or marinara sauce, and the yellowtail snapper *française* is a worthy selection. More than a half-dozen early bird entrées are offered 4:30–6:30 for $9.45, including soup or salad and potato or spaghetti. ⊠ *935 N. Krome Ave.,* ☎ *305/247– 1544. AE, MC, V.*

$ ✕ **Farmers' Market Restaurant.** Although it's in the farmers' market and serves fresh vegetables, this restaurant's specialty is seafood. A family of fishermen runs the place, so fish and shellfish are only hours from the sea. Catering to the fishing and farming crowd, it opens at 5:30, serving pancakes, jumbo eggs, and fluffy omelets with home fries or grits. The lunch and dinner menus have shrimp, fish, steaks, and conch baskets, as well as burgers, salads, and sandwiches. Normally the fish comes fried, but you can ask for it broiled or grilled. ⊠ *300 N. Krome Ave.,* ☎ *305/242–0008. No credit cards.*

$$ ⊡ **Best Western Gateway to the Keys.** This two-story motel sits well back from the highway and contains such amenities as full closets, a heat lamp in the bathroom, and complimentary Continental breakfast. Standard rooms have two queen-size beds or one king-size bed. More expensive rooms come with wet bar, refrigerator, microwave, and coffeemaker. Otherwise it's a standard modern motel with floral prints and twin reading lamps. ⊠ *1 Strano Blvd., 33034,* ☎ *305/246–5100,* FAX *305/242–0056. 114 units. Pool, spa, coin laundry, dry cleaning. AE, D, DC, MC, V.*

$$ ⊡ **Hampton Inn.** This two-story motel just off the highway has good clean rooms (including a post–Hurricane Andrew wing) and public-friendly policies, including free Continental breakfast, local calls, and movie channels. All rooms have at least two upholstered chairs, twin reading lamps, and a desk and chair. Units are color-coordinated and carpeted. Baths have tub-showers. ⊠ *124 E. Palm Dr., 33034,* ☎ *305/ 247–8833 or 800/426–7866,* FAX *305/247–6456. 123 units. Pool. AE, D, DC, MC, V.*

Shopping

Florida Keys Factory Shops (⊠ 250 E. Palm Dr.) has 50 discount stores plus a small food court. **Robert Is Here** (⊠ 19200 Palm Dr. [S.W. 344th St.], ☎ 305/246–1592), a remarkable fruit stand, sells vegeta-

Earn Miles With Your MCI Card.

Take the MCI Card along on this trip and start earning miles for the next one. You'll earn frequent flyer miles on all your calls and save with the low rates you've come to expect from MCI. Before you know it, you'll be on your way to some other international destination.

Sign up for MCI by calling
1-800-FLY-FREE

Is this a great time, or what? :-)

Earn Frequent Flyer Miles.

You've read the book. Now book the trip.

For all the best deals on flights, hotels, rental cars, and vacation packages, book them online at www.previewtravel.com. Then click on our Destination Guides featuring content from Fodor's and more. You'll find hotels, restaurants, attractions, and things to do around the globe. There are even interactive maps, videos, and weather forecasts. You'll have everything you need to make your vacation exactly what you want it to be. All it takes is a trip online.

Travel on Your Terms™
www.previewtravel.com
aol keyword: previewtravel

preview travel℠

bles, fresh-fruit milk shakes, 10 flavors of honey, more than 100 flavors of jams and jellies, fresh juices, salad dressings, and some 40 kinds
of tropical fruits, including carambola, litchi, egg fruit, monstera,
sapodilla, soursop, sugar apple, and tamarind. The stand started in 1960,
when seven-year-old Robert sat at this spot selling his father's bumper
crop of cucumbers. Now Robert ships around the world, and everything is first quality. Seconds are given to needy area families. The stand
opens at 8 and never closes earlier than 7.

BISCAYNE NATIONAL PARK

Occupying 180,000 acres along the southern portion of Biscayne Bay,
south of Miami and north of the Florida Keys, this national park is
96% underwater, and its altitude ranges from 4 ft above sea level to
10 fathoms, or 60 ft, below. Contained within it are four distinct
zones. From shore to sea they are mangrove forest along the coast, Biscayne Bay, the undeveloped upper Florida Keys, and coral reefs.

Mangroves line the mainland shore much as they do elsewhere in
South Florida. Biscayne Bay functions as a lobster sanctuary and a nursery for fish, sponges, and crabs. Manatees and sea turtles frequent its
warm, shallow waters. Lamentably, the bay is under assault from
forces similar to those in Florida Bay.

To the east, about 8 mi off the coast, lie 44 tiny keys, stretching 18
nautical mi north–south and accessible only by boat. There is no commercial transportation between the mainland and the islands, and
only a handful can be visited: Elliott, Boca Chita, Adams, and Sands
keys. The rest either are wildlife refuges, are too small, or have rocky
shores or waters too shallow for boats. It's best to explore the Keys
between December and April, when the mosquito population is relatively quiescent.

Another 3 mi east of the Keys, in the ocean, lies the park's main attraction—the northernmost section of Florida's living tropical coral reefs.
Some are the size of a student's desk, others as large as a football field.
You can take a glass-bottom boat ride to see this underwater wonderland,
but you really have to snorkel or scuba dive to appreciate it fully. A
diverse population of colorful fish—angelfish, gobies, grunts, parrot
fish, pork fish, wrasses, and many more—flits through the reefs.

More than 170 species of birds have been seen around the park.
Though all the Keys offer excellent birding opportunities, Jones Lagoon, south of Adams Key, between Old Rhodes Key and Totten Key,
is one of the best. It's approachable only by nonmotorized craft.

Convoy Point

⑭ *9 mi east of Florida City, 30 mi south of downtown Miami.*

Reminiscent of area pioneer homes, the **Convoy Point Visitor Center** is
a wooden building with a metal roof and wide veranda from which
you can look out across mangroves and Biscayne Bay and see the
Miami skyline. Inside is a museum, where hands-on and historical exhibits and videos explore the park's four ecosystems. Among the facilities are a 50-seat auditorium, the park's canoe and tour concessioner,
rest rooms with showers, a ranger information area, and gift shop. A
short trail and boardwalk lead to a jetty and launch ramp. This is the
only area of the park accessible without a boat. ⊠ *S.W. 328th St., Homestead,* ☎ *305/230-7275.* ⌑ *Free.* ⊙ *Park daily 8–sunset; visitor center weekdays 8:30–4:30 (5:30 June–Aug.), weekends 8:30–5.*

Outdoor Activities and Sports

CANOEING

Biscayne National Underwater Park, Inc. (⊠ Convoy Point Visitor Center, ☎ 305/230–1100), the park's official concessioner, has half a dozen canoes for rent on a first-come, first-served basis. Prices are $8 an hour, $22 for four hours.

SCUBA DIVING AND SNORKELING

Biscayne National Underwater Park, Inc. (⊠ Convoy Point Visitor Center, Box 1270, Homestead 33090, ☎ 305/230–1100) rents equipment and conducts snorkel and dive trips aboard the 45-ft *Boca Chita*. Snorkel trips ($27.95) leave daily at 1:30 and include mask, fins, snorkel, and vest. Trips include 1¼ hours on reefs and wrecks. Two-tank scuba trips, which leave at 9 on weekdays, 8:30 on weekends, cost $35. Complete gear rental is $37, and instruction is available. Even with a reservation (recommended), you should arrive 45 minutes before departure.

Elliott Key

⑮ *9 mi east of Convoy Point.*

This key, accessible only by boat (on your own or by special arrangement with the concessioner), has a rebuilt boardwalk made from recycled plastic and two nature trails with tropical plant life. Take an informal, ranger-led nature walk or walk its 7-mi length on your own along a rough path through a hammock. Videos shown at the ranger station describe the island. Facilities include rest rooms, fresh water, showers (cold), grills, and a campground. Pets are allowed on the island but not on trails.

A 30-ft-wide sandy beach about a mile north of the harbor on the west (bay) side of the key is the only one in the national park. Boaters like to anchor off it to swim. For day use only, it has picnic areas and a short trail that follows the shore and cuts through the hammock.

Lodging

$ ⚠ **Biscayne National Park.** Elliott Key has 40 primitive campsites, for which there are neither fees nor reservations. Just bring plenty of insect repellent. The park concessioner runs boats to the key periodically to drop off campers ($21 round-trip) because there is no regular ferry service or boat rental. There is a new $15-per-night charge for docking private vessels.

Boca Chita Key

⑯ *10 mi northeast of Convoy Point.*

This island was once owned by Mark C. Honeywell, former president of Minneapolis's Honeywell Company. Most historical structures damaged by Hurricane Andrew have been repaired and stabilized, and revegetation, harbor repair, and rest-room construction are complete. There is no fresh water, but grills and campsites (details similar to those at Elliott Key) are available. Access is by private boat only. No pets are allowed.

Adams Key

⑰ *9 mi southeast of Convoy Point.*

This small key, a stone's throw off the western tip of Elliott Key, is open for day use and has picnic areas, rest rooms, dockage, and a short trail that runs along the shore and through a hardwood hammock. Access is by private boat.

THE EVERGLADES A TO Z

Arriving and Departing

By Boat

If you're entering the United States by pleasure boat, you must phone **U.S. Customs** (☎ 800/432–1216) either from a marine phone or on first arriving ashore. At their discretion, customs agents will direct you to Dodge Island Seaport (Miami), otherwise rendezvous with you, or clear you by phone.

By Car

From Miami the main highways to the area are U.S. 1, the Homestead Extension of Florida's Turnpike, and Krome Avenue (Route 997 [old U.S. 27]).

By Plane

Miami International Airport (MIA) is 34 mi from Homestead and 83 mi from Flamingo in Everglades National Park.

BETWEEN THE AIRPORT AND TOWNS

Airporter (☎ 800/830–3413) runs shuttle buses three times daily off-season, four times daily in winter, that stop at the Hampton Inn in Florida City on their way between MIA and the Florida Keys. Shuttle service, which takes about an hour, runs 6:10–5:20 from Florida City, 7:30–6 from the airport. Reserve in advance. Pickups can be arranged for all baggage-claim areas. The cost is $20 one-way.

Greyhound Lines (☎ 800/231–2222) buses from MIA to the Keys make a stop in Homestead (✉ 5 N.E. 3rd Rd., ☎ 305/247–2040) four times a day. Buses leave from Concourse E, lower level, and cost $8 one-way, $16 round-trip.

SuperShuttle (☎ 305/871–2000) operates 11-passenger air-conditioned vans to Homestead. Service from MIA is available around the clock; booths are outside most luggage areas on the lower level. For the return to MIA, reserve 24 hours in advance. The one-way cost is $28 per person for the first person, $12 for each additional person at the same address.

Getting Around

By Boat

Bring aboard the proper *NOAA Nautical Charts* before you cast off to explore park waters. The charts run $15–$15.95 at many marine stores in South Florida, at the Convoy Point Visitor Center in Biscayne National Park, and at Flamingo Marina in the Everglades.

The annual *Waterway Guide* (southern regional edition) is widely used by boaters. Bookstores all over South Florida sell it, or you can order it directly from the publisher (✉ Intertec Publishing, Book Department, 6151 Powers Ferry Rd., Atlanta, GA 30339, ☎ 800/233–3359) for $36.95 plus $3 shipping and handling.

By Car

To reach Everglades National Park's Ernest F. Coe Visitor Center and Flamingo, head west on Route 9336 in Florida City and follow signs. From Homestead the Ernest F. Coe Visitor Center is 11 mi; Flamingo is 49 mi.

To get to the south end of Everglades National Park in the Florida Keys, take U.S. 1 south from Homestead. It's 27 mi to the Key Largo Ranger Station (⊠ Between MM 98 and MM 99, BS, Overseas Hwy.), which is not always staffed but has maps and information. From here the park is only accessible by boat.

The north entrance of Everglades National Park at Shark Valley is reached by taking the Tamiami Trail about 20 mi west of Krome Avenue.

To reach the west entrance of Everglades National Park at the Gulf Coast Visitor Center in Everglades City, take Route 29 south from the Tamiami Trail.

To reach Biscayne National Park from Homestead, take U.S. 1 or Krome Avenue to Lucy Street (Southeast 8th Street) and turn east. Lucy Street becomes North Canal Drive (Southwest 328th Street). Follow signs for about 8 mi to the park headquarters.

By Taxi
Cab companies servicing the area include **Action Express Taxi** (☎ 305/743–6800) and **South Dade Taxi** (☎ 305/256–4444).

Contacts and Resources

Car Rentals
Agencies in the area include **A&A Auto Rental** (⊠ 30005 S. Dixie Hwy., Homestead 33030, ☎ 305/246–0974), **Budget Rent a Car** (⊠ 29949 S. Dixie Hwy., Homestead 33030, ☎ 305/246–1000), and **Enterprise Rent-a-Car** (⊠ 29130 S. Dixie Hwy., Homestead 33030, ☎ 305/246–2056 or 800/736–8222).

Emergencies
Dial **911** for police, fire, or ambulance. If you are a TTY caller, tap the space bar or use a voice announcer to identify yourself. In the national parks, rangers answer police, fire, and medical emergencies: **Biscayne** (☎ 305/247–7272) or **Everglades** (☎ 305/247–7272). **Florida Marine Patrol** (☎ 305/795–2145), a division of the Florida Department of Natural Resources, maintains a 24-hour telephone service for reporting boating emergencies and natural-resource violations. **Miami Beach Coast Guard Base** (⊠ 100 MacArthur Causeway, Miami Beach, ☎ 305/535–4300 or 305/535–4314) responds to local marine emergencies and reports of navigation hazards. The base broadcasts on VHF-FM Channel 16. The **National Weather Service** (☎ 305/229–4522) supplies local forecasts.

HOSPITALS
Hospital emergency line (☎ 305/596–6556). **SMH Homestead Hospital** (⊠ 160 N.W. 13th St., Homestead, ☎ 305/248–3232; 305/596–6557 physician referral).

Guided Tours
The National Park Service organizes a variety of free programs, typically focusing on native wildlife, plants, and park history. At Biscayne National Park, for example, rangers give informal tours of Elliott and Boca Chita keys, which you can arrange in advance, depending on ranger availability. Contact the respective visitor centers for details.

AIRBOAT TOURS
In Everglades City, **Captain Doug's Florida Boat Tours** (⊠ 200 Rte. 29, ☎ 941/695–4400; 800/282–9194 in FL) runs 30- to 40-minute backcountry tours ($12.95) aboard custom-designed jet airboats. Even more popular, however, are one-hour tours ($30) through mangrove trails on a six-passenger airboat. The smaller boat allows visitors to

get up close to wild animals, including birds. **Wooten's Everglades Airboat Tours** (✉ Wooten's Alligator Farm, 1½ mi east of Rte. 29 on Tamiami Trail, ☎ 941/695–2781 or 800/282–2781) runs airboat and swamp-buggy tours through the Everglades. (Swamp buggies are giant tractorlike vehicles with oversize rubber wheels.) Tours are approximately 30 minutes.

Southwest of Florida City near the entrance to Everglades National Park, **Everglades Alligator Farm** (✉ 40351 S.W. 192nd Ave., ☎ 305/247–2628 or 800/644–9711) runs a 4-mi, 30-minute tour of the River of Grass with departures 20 minutes after the hour. The tour ($12.50) includes a free hourly alligator, snake, or wildlife show, or you can take in the show only ($7).

From the Shark Valley area, **Buffalo Tiger's Florida Everglades Airboat Ride** (✉ 12 mi west of Krome Ave., 20 mi west of Miami city limits on Tamiami Trail, ☎ 305/559–5250) is led by a former chairman of the Miccosukee tribe. The 35- to 40-minute trip the Everglades includes a stop at an old Native American camp. Tours cost $10 and operate Monday–Thursday and Saturday 10–sunset and Sunday 11–sunset. Reservations are not required. **Coopertown Airboat Ride** (✉ 5 mi west of Krome Ave. on Tamiami Trail, ☎ 305/226–6048) operates the oldest airboat rides in the Everglades (since 1945). The 30- to 35-minute tour visits two hammocks and alligator holes. The charge is $10, with a $24 minimum for the boat. **Everglades Gator Park** (✉ 12 mi west of Florida's Turnpike on Tamiami Trail, ☎ 305/559–2255 or 800/559–2205) offers 45-minute narrated airboat tours ($12). **Everglades Safari Park** (✉ 26700 Tamiami Trail, 9 mi west of Krome Ave., ☎ 305/226–6923 or 305/223–3804) runs 40-minute airboat rides for $15. The **Miccosukee Indian Village** (✉ 25 mi west of Florida's Turnpike on Tamiami Trail, ☎ 305/223–8380) offers 30-minute airboat rides ($7) in addition to its other attractions.

Ray Cramer's Everglades Airboat Tours, Inc. (✉ Coopertown; mailing address: ✉ 1307 Almay St., Key Largo 33037, ☎ 305/852–5339) conducts airboat trips accommodating 6 to 12, for $42.60 per person. Ray Cramer spent his youth fishing, frogging, and hunting in the Everglades with his father and friends. Though daytime trips are offered, a better option is the tour that departs an hour before sundown so you can see birds and fish in daylight and alligators, raccoons, and other nocturnal animals when night falls.

AIR TOURS

Everglades Air Tours (✉ Homestead General Aviation Airport, 28790 S.W. 217th Ave., Homestead, ☎ 305/247–7757) gives bird's-eye tours of the Everglades and Florida Bay that last 30 minutes and cost $45 per person, with a two-passenger minimum.

BOAT TOURS

Tours at Biscayne National Park are run by people-friendly **Biscayne National Underwater Park, Inc.** (✉ Convoy Point, east end of North Canal Dr. [S.W. 328th St.], Box 1270, Homestead 33090, ☎ 305/230–1100). Daily trips (at 10, with a second trip at 1 during high season, according to demand) explore the park's living coral reefs 10 mi offshore on *Reef Rover IV,* a 53-ft glass-bottom boat that carries up to 48 passengers. On days when the weather is unsuitable for reef viewing, an alternative three-hour, ranger-led interpretive tour visits Elliott Key. Reservations are recommended. The cost is $19.95, and you should arrive at least 45 minutes before departure.

Everglades National Park Boat Tours (✉ Gulf Coast Visitor Center, Everglades City, ☎ 941/695–2591; 800/445–7724 in FL) operates tours through the Ten Thousand Islands region ($13) and can accommodate large numbers. (The two biggest boats have drink concessions.) Trips that stop on Sandfly Island include a 30-minute ranger-led tour of the island's flora and fauna. **Majestic Everglades Excursions** (✉ Box 241, Everglades City 34139, ☎ 941/695–2777) are led by exceptionally well informed guides Frank and Georgia Garrett. The 3½- to 4-hour eco-tours, on a 24-ft boat with a covered deck, take in Everglades National Park and the Ten Thousand Islands. Narration focuses on the region's unique flora and fauna and its colorful early residents. Departing from Glades Haven, just shy of a mile south of the circle in Everglades City, tours are limited to six passengers and include brunch or afternoon snacks. The cost is $65.

CANOE AND KAYAK TOURS

North American Canoe Tours (✉ Ivey House, 107 Camellia St., Box 5038, Everglades City 34139, ☎ 941/695–3299) leads one-day to five-night Everglades tours November–April. Highlights include bird and gator sightings, mangrove forests, no-man's-land beaches, relics of the hideouts of infamous and just plain reclusive characters, and spectacular sunsets. Included in the cost of extended tours ($250–$450) are canoes or kayaks, all necessary equipment, a guide, meals, and lodging for the first and last nights at the Ivey House B&B. Day trips by kayak, canoe, or powerboat cost $40–$60.

TRAM TOURS

Starting at the Shark Valley visitor center, **Shark Valley Tram Tours** (✉ Box 1739, Tamiami Station, Miami 33144, ☎ 305/221–8455) follows a 15-mi loop road into the interior, stopping at a 50-ft observation tower especially good for viewing gators. Two-hour narrated tours cost $9 and depart hourly 9–4, except May 1–Christmas, when they run every two hours. Reservations are recommended December–March.

Visitor Information

Big Cypress National Preserve (✉ HCR61, Box 11, Ochopee 34141, ☎ 941/695–4111). **Biscayne National Park:** Convoy Point Visitor Center (✉ 9700 S.W. 328th St., Box 1369, Homestead 33090-1369, ☎ 305/230–7275). **Everglades City Chamber of Commerce** (✉ Rte. 29 and Tamiami Trail, Box 130, Everglades City 34139, ☎ 941/695–3941). **Everglades National Park:** Ernest F. Coe Visitor Center (✉ 40001 Rte. 9336, Homestead 33034-6733, ☎ 305/242–7700), Gulf Coast Visitor Center (✉ Rte. 29, Everglades City 34139, ☎ 941/695–3311), Flamingo Visitor Center (✉ 1 Flamingo Lodge Hwy., Flamingo 33034-6798, ☎ 941/695–2945). **Greater Homestead–Florida City Chamber of Commerce** (✉ 43 N. Krome Ave., Homestead 33030, ☎ 305/247–2332 or 888/352–4891). **Tropical Everglades Visitor Association** (✉ 160 U.S. 1, Florida City 33034, ☎ 305/245–9180 or 800/388–9669, FAX 305/247–4335).

4 Fort Lauderdale and Broward County

From Hollywood north to Fort Lauderdale and beyond, the beach has been transformed. Sidewalk cafés, chic shops, and upscale restaurants bring new energy and excitement to the area.

ALITTLE MORE THAN A DECADE AGO, the Fort Lauderdale beachfront was lined with T-shirt shops, souvenir stores, and fast-food stands, and the downtown area consisted of a few office towers and government buildings. Today, following an enormous renovation program, the beach is home to upscale shops and restaurants, including the popular new Beach Place retail and dining complex, while downtown is in the midst of its own major growth. A long-awaited movie and entertainment complex, Las Olas Riverfront, is complete, and several new office towers have been built, with many others on the drawing boards. In all, more than $1.5 billion in new projects will be finished by the year 2000, including a major airport expansion.

By Herb Hiller

Updated by
Alan Macher

In the years following World War II, sleepy Fort Lauderdale—with miles of inland waterways—promoted itself as the "Venice of America" and the nation's yachting capital. But in 1960 the film *Where the Boys Are* changed everything. The movie described how college students—upward of 20,000—were beginning to swarm to the city for spring break. By 1985 the 20,000 had mushroomed to 350,000. Hotel owners complained of 12 students to a room, the beachfront was littered with tacky bars, and drug trafficking and petty theft were major problems. So city leaders put in place policies and restrictions designed to encourage students to go elsewhere. And they did.

Now the city has been totally transformed into a leading warm-weather vacation destination. This remarkable turnaround has resulted from major investments by both the private and public sectors. Fort Lauderdale has clearly become a city with a mission.

A major beneficiary is Las Olas Boulevard, whose emergence has been credited with creating a whole new identity for Fort Lauderdale. Though it was already famous for its trendy shops, now the sidewalks aren't rolled up when the sun goes down. Nearly two dozen new restaurants have sprung up, and on weekend evenings hundreds of strollers tour the boulevard, taking in the food, the jazz bands, and the scene. On-street parking on weekends has slowed traffic, and the street has a village atmosphere.

Farther west, along New River, is evidence of Fort Lauderdale's cultural renaissance: a new arts and entertainment district and its crown jewel, the Broward Center for the Performing Arts. Still farther west the county enters major-league sports with a new $212 million arena for the National Hockey League's Florida Panthers, in Sunrise.

Of course, what makes Fort Lauderdale and Broward County a major draw for visitors is the beaches. Fort Lauderdale's 2-mi stretch of unobstructed beachfront has been enhanced even further with a sparkling new look designed for the pleasure of pedestrians rather than cars.

Tying this all together is a transportation system that is relatively hassle free, unusual in congested South Florida. A new expressway system, including the long-awaited widening of I–95, connects the city and suburbs and even provides a direct route to the airport and Port Everglades. For a slower and more scenic ride to really see this canal-laced city, cruise aboard the water taxi.

None of this was envisioned by Napoleon Bonaparte Broward, Florida's governor from 1905 to 1909 and for whom the county is named. His drainage schemes opened much of the marshy Everglades region for farming, ranching, and settling (in retrospect, an environmental disaster). Fort Lauderdale's first-known white settler, Charles Lewis, established a plantation along the New River in 1793. But it was for Major William Lauderdale, who built a fort at the river's mouth in 1838 during the Seminole Indian wars, that the city was named.

Incorporated in 1911 with just 175 residents, Fort Lauderdale grew rapidly during the Florida boom of the 1920s. Today its population is 150,000, and its suburbs keep growing—1.3 million live in the county. New homes, offices, and shopping centers have filled in the gaps between older communities along the coastal ridge. Now they're marching west along I–75, I–595, and Route 869 (the Sawgrass Expressway). Broward County is blessed with near-ideal weather, with some 3,000 hours of sunshine a year. The average temperature is 66°F–77°F in winter, 84°F in summer. Once a home for retirees, the county today attracts younger, working-age families. It's always been a sane and pleasant place to live. Now it's also becoming one of Florida's most diverse and dynamic places to vacation.

Pleasures and Pastimes

Beaches
Broward County's beachfront extends for miles without interruption, although the character of the communities behind the beach changes. For example, in Hallandale, the beach is backed by towering condominiums; in Hollywood, by motels and the Broadwalk; and just north of there—blessedly—there's nothing at all.

Dining
Food critics in dining and travel magazines agree that the Greater Fort Lauderdale area offers some of the finest and most varied dining of any U.S. city its size. You can choose from the cuisines of Asia, Europe, or Central and South America—and, of course, good ol' American—and enjoy more than just the food. The ambience, wine, service, and decor can be as varied as the language spoken, and as memorable, too.

Fishing
Four main types of fishing are available in Broward County: bottom or drift-boat fishing from party boats, deep-sea fishing for large sport fish on charters, angling for freshwater game fish, and dropping a line off a pier. For bottom fishing, party boats typically charge between $20 and $22 per person for up to four hours, including rod, reel, and bait. For charters, a half day for as many as six people runs up to $325, six-hour charters up to $495, and full-day charters (eight hours) up to $595. Skipper and crew plus bait and tackle are included. Split parties can be arranged at a cost of about $85 per person for a full day.

Several Broward towns—Dania, Lauderdale-by-the-Sea, Pompano Beach, and Deerfield Beach—have fishing piers that draw anglers for pompano, amberjack, bluefish, snapper, blue runners, snook, mackerel, and Florida lobster.

Golf
More than 50 courses green the landscape in Greater Fort Lauderdale, including famous championship links. Most area courses are inland, in the suburbs west of the city, and there are some great bargains. Off-season (May–October) greens fees range from $15 to $45; peak-season (November–April) charges run from $35 to $75. Fees can be trimmed by working through Next Day Golf, a local service, and many hotels offer golf packages.

Scuba Diving

Good diving can be enjoyed within 20 minutes of shore. Among the most popular of the county's 80 dive sites is the 2-mi-wide, 23-mi-long Fort Lauderdale Reef, the product of Florida's most successful artificial reef–building program. More than a dozen houseboats, ships, and oil platforms have been sunk in depths of from 10 to 150 ft to provide a habitat for fish and other marine life, as well as to help stabilize beaches. The most famous sunken ship is the 200-ft German freighter *Mercedes,* which was blown onto Palm Beach socialite Mollie Wilmot's pool terrace in a violent Thanksgiving storm in 1984; the ship is now underwater a mile off Fort Lauderdale beach.

Exploring Fort Lauderdale and Broward County

Though most activity centers on Fort Lauderdale, there's plenty to see in other parts of Broward County, to the north, south, and, increasingly, west.

The metro area is laid out in a basic grid system, and only the hundreds of canals and waterways interrupt the straight-line path of the streets and roads. Nomenclature is important here. Streets, roads, courts, and drives run east–west. Avenues, terraces, and ways run north–south. Boulevards can run any which way. Las Olas Boulevard is one of the most important east–west thoroughfares, whereas Route A1A—referred to as Atlantic Boulevard and Ocean Boulevard along some stretches—runs along the north–south oceanfront. These names can be confusing to visitors, as there are separate streets called Atlantic and Ocean in Hollywood and Pompano Beach.

The boulevards, those that are paved and those made of water, give Fort Lauderdale its distinct character. Honeycombed with more than 260 mi of navigable waterways, the city is home port for about 40,000 privately owned boats. You won't see the gondolas you'd find in Venice, but you will see just about every other type of craft imaginable docked beside the thousands of homes and businesses that each have a little piece of waterfront. Visitors can tour the canals via the city's water-taxi system, made up of small motor launches that provide transportation and quick, narrated tours. Larger, multideck touring vessels and motorboat rentals for self-guided tours are other options. The Intracoastal Waterway, a massive canal that parallels Route A1A, is the nautical equivalent of an interstate highway. It runs north–south through the metro area and provides easy access to neighboring beach communities; Deerfield Beach and Pompano Beach lie to the north and Dania and Hollywood lie to the south. All are within a 15-mi radius of the city center.

Great Itineraries

Since most Broward County sights are relatively close to each other, it's easy to pack a lot into very little time, but you will probably need a car. You can catch a lot of the history, the museums, and the shops and bistros in Fort Lauderdale's downtown area and along Las Olas Boulevard, and then if you feel like hitting the beach, just take a 10-minute drive east to the intersection of Las Olas and A1A and you're there. Many of the neighboring suburbs, with attractions of their own, are just north or south of Fort Lauderdale. As a result, you can hit most of the high points in 3 days, and with 7 to 10 days, you can see virtually all of Broward's mainstream charms.

Numbers in the text correspond to numbers in the margin and on the Broward County and Fort Lauderdale maps.

IF YOU HAVE 3 DAYS

With a bigger concentration of hotels, restaurants, and sights to see than its suburban neighbors, ⛵ **Fort Lauderdale** ①–⑪ makes a logical base of operations for any visit. On your first day there see the downtown area, especially Las Olas Boulevard between Southeast 6th and Southeast 11th avenues. After enjoying lunch at a sidewalk café, head for the nearby Arts and Science District and the downtown **Riverwalk** ⑤, which you can see at a leisurely pace in half a day. On your second day spend at least some time at the beach, shopping when the hot sun drives you off the sand. Tour the canals on the third day, either on a rented boat from one of the various marinas along Route A1A, or via the water taxi or a sightseeing boat, both of which can be boarded all along the Intracoastal Waterway.

IF YOU HAVE 5 DAYS

With additional time you can see more of the beach and the arts district and still work in some outdoor sports—and you'll be more able to rearrange your plans depending on the weather. On the first day visit the Arts and Science District and the downtown **Riverwalk** ⑤. Set aside the next day for an offshore adventure, perhaps a deep-sea fishing charter or a dive trip to the Fort Lauderdale Reef. On the third day shop, dine, and relax along the **Fort Lauderdale beachfront** ⑨, and at the end of the day, sneak a peak at the Hillsboro Light, at **Lighthouse Point** ⑲. Another good day can be spent at the **Hugh Taylor Birch State Recreation Area** ⑩. Enjoy your fifth day in **Hollywood** ㉑, perhaps combining time on the Broadwalk with a visit to the Anne Kolb Nature Center, at West Lake Park.

IF YOU HAVE 7 DAYS

With a full week you have time for a wider variety of attractions, fitting in beach time around other activities. In fact, enjoy any of the county's public beach areas on your first day. The second day can be spent in another favorite pastime—shopping, either at chic shops or one of the malls. On the next day tour the canals on a sightseeing boat or water taxi. Then shop and dine along Las Olas Boulevard. The fourth day might be devoted to the many museums in downtown Fort Lauderdale and the fifth to an airboat ride at **Sawgrass Recreation Park** ⑮, at the edge of the Everglades. Fort Lauderdale offers plenty of facilities for outdoor recreation; spend the sixth day fishing and picnicking on one of the area's many piers or playing a round at a top golf course. Set aside the seventh day for **Hollywood** ㉑, where you can stroll along the scenic Broadwalk or walk through the aviary at Flamingo Gardens, in **Davie** ㉓, before relaxing in peaceful Hollywood North Beach Park.

When to Tour Fort Lauderdale and Broward County

Tourists visit the area all year long, choosing to come in winter or summer depending on interests, hobbies, and the climate where they live. The winter season, about Thanksgiving through March, still sees the biggest influx of visitors and "snowbirds"—seasonal residents who show up when the snow starts to fly up north. Concert, art, and show seasons are at their height then, and restaurants and highways all show the stress of crowds, Americans and Europeans alike.

Summer has its own fans. Waits at even the most popular restaurants are likely to be reasonable or even nonexistent, but though few services close in the summer, some may establish slightly shorter hours than during the peak season. Summer is the rainy season; the tropics-style rain arrives about mid-afternoon and is usually gone in an hour. When downpours hit, however, driving can be treacherous.

For golfers, almost anytime is great for playing. Just like everywhere else, waits for tee times are longer on weekends year-round.

Remember that sun can cause real scorching burns all year long, especially at midday, marking the tourist from the experienced resident or vacationer. You might want to plan your beach time for morning and late afternoon and go sightseeing or shopping in between.

FORT LAUDERDALE

Like some southeast Florida neighbors, Fort Lauderdale has been revitalizing itself for several years. What's unusual in a state where gaudy tourist zones stand aloof from workaday downtowns is that the city exhibits consistency at both ends of the 2-mi Las Olas corridor. The sparkling look results from a decision to thoroughly improve both beachfront and downtown, as opposed to focusing design attention in town and letting the beach fall prey to development solely by T-shirt retailers. Matching the downtown's new arts district, cafés, and boutiques is an equally inventive beach area with its own share of cafés and shops facing an undeveloped shoreline.

Downtown

The jewel of the downtown area along the New River is a new arts and entertainment district. Pricey tickets are available for Broadway shows at the riverfront Broward Center for the Performing Arts. Clustered within a five-minute walk are the Museum of Discovery and Science, the expanding Fort Lauderdale Historical Museum, and the Museum of Art. Restaurants, sidewalk cafés, delis, and blues, folk, jazz, reggae, and rock clubs flourish. The latest gem is Las Olas Riverfront, a multistory entertainment, dining, and retail complex along several blocks once owned by pioneers William and Mary Brickell.

Tying this district together is the Riverwalk, which extends 1 mi along the New River's north bank and ½ mi along the south. Tropical gardens with benches and interpretive displays fringe the walk on one side, boat landings on the other. East along Riverwalk is Stranahan House, and a block away Las Olas attractions begin. Tropical landscaping and trees separate the traffic lanes in some blocks, setting off fine shops, restaurants, and popular nightspots. From here it's 5 minutes by car or 30 minutes by water taxi back to the beach.

A Good Tour

Start on Southeast 6th Avenue at Las Olas Boulevard, where you'll find **Stranahan House** ①, a turn-of-the-century structure that's now a museum. Between Southeast 6th and 11th avenues, Las Olas has Spanish colonial buildings housing high-fashion boutiques, jewelry shops, and art galleries. If you drive east, you'll cross into the Isles, Fort Lauderdale's most prestigious neighborhood, where homes line canals with large yachts beside the seawalls.

Return west on Las Olas to Andrews Avenue, turn right, and park in one of the municipal garages so you can walk around downtown Fort Lauderdale. First stop is the **Museum of Art** ②, which has a major collection of works from the CoBrA (Copenhagen, Brussels, and Amsterdam) movement. Walk one block north to the **Broward County Main Library** ③ to see works from Broward's Art in Public Places program.

Go west on Southeast 2nd Street to Southwest 2nd Avenue, turn left, and stop at the **Fort Lauderdale Historical Museum** ④, which surveys the city's not-so-recent history. Just to the south is the palm-lined **Riverwalk** ⑤, a good place for a leisurely stroll. Head north toward a cluster of new facilities collectively known as the Arts and Science District. The district contains the outdoor Esplanade, whose exhibits include a hands-on display of the science and history of navigation, and the major science attraction, the **Museum of Discovery and Science** ⑥. The adjacent Broward Center for the Performing Arts, a massive glass-and-concrete structure by the river, opened in 1991.

Finally, go west along Las Olas Boulevard to Southwest 7th Avenue and the entrance to **Sailboat Bend** ⑦. You can return to the start of the tour by traveling east along Las Olas Boulevard.

TIMING

Depending on how long you like to linger in museums and how many hours you want to spend in the quaint shops on Las Olas Boulevard, you can spend anything from half a day to an entire day on this tour.

Sights to See

❸ Broward County Main Library. This distinctive building was designed by Marcel Breuer. Works on display from Broward's Art in Public Places program include a painting by Yaacov Agam; a wooden construction by Marc Beauregard; an outdoor aluminum-and-steel sculpture by Dale Eldred; and ceramic tile by Ivan Chermayeff. (Art in Public Places displays more than 200 works—painting, sculpture, photographs, weaving—by nationally renowned and Florida artists. Pieces can be found at 13 major sites, including the main bus terminal and the airport.) Productions from theater to poetry readings are presented in a 300-seat auditorium. ⊠ *100 S. Andrews Ave.,* ☎ *954/357–7444 or 954/357–7457 for self-guided Art in Public Places walking tour brochure.* ⊑ *Free.* ☉ *Mon.–Thurs. 9–9, Fri.–Sat. 9–5, Sun. noon–5:30.*

❹ Fort Lauderdale Historical Museum. In 1996 this museum expanded into several historic buildings, including the King-Cromartie House and the New River Inn. The complex surveys city history from the Seminole era to World War II. A model in the lobby depicts old Fort Lauderdale. There's also a research library and bookstore. ⊠ *219 S.W. 2nd Ave.,* ☎ *954/463–4431.* ⊑ *$2.* ☉ *Tues.–Fri. 10–4.*

★ ❷ Museum of Art. Housed in an Edward Larrabee Barnes–designed building that's considered an architectural masterpiece, this museum has Florida's largest art exhibition space. The impressive permanent collection features 20th-century European and American art, including works by Picasso, Calder, Moore, Dalí, Rivers, Warhol, and Stella, as well as a notable collection of works by celebrated Ashcan School artist William Glackens. Opened in 1986, the museum launched a revitalization of the downtown district and nearby Riverwalk area. ⊠ *1 E. Las Olas Blvd.,* ☎ *954/763–6464.* ⊑ *$6.* ☉ *Tues.–Thurs. and Sat. 10–5, Fri. 10–8, Sun. noon–5.*

★ ☺ ❻ Museum of Discovery and Science. Forget those old, cheesy 3-D movies. The new IMAX theater—converted to 3-D in a $2.5 million project—uses the latest film technology; regularly changing features shown on a five-story screen will astound you. The museum also features interactive exhibits on ecology, health, and outer space. Many displays focus on the local environment, including a replica of an oak forest complete with mosses, lichens, and air plants, which grow without soil. Another unusual exhibit offers a cutaway of an Indian shell mound. For a sunny respite from the labyrinth of indoor displays, check out the exhibits on the Esplanade. ⊠ *401 S.W. 2nd St.,* ☎ *954/467–6637 for museum or 954/463–4629 for IMAX.* ⊑ *Museum $6, IMAX $9, both $12.50.* ☉ *Mon.–Sat. 10–5, Sun. noon–6.*

Broward County

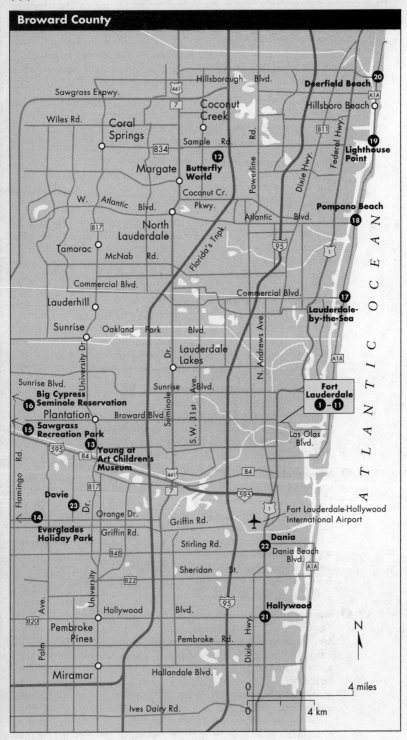

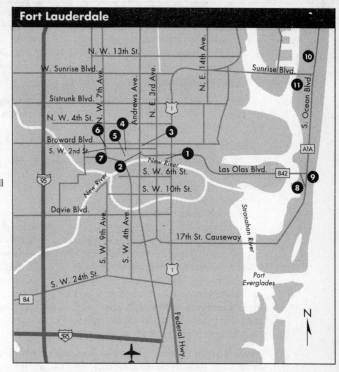

★ ❺ **Riverwalk.** This lovely, paved promenade on the north bank of the New River is great for entertainment as well as views. On the first Sunday of every month a jazz brunch attracts visitors. The walk is being extended 2 mi on both sides of the beautiful urban stream, connecting the facilities of the Arts and Science District.

❼ **Sailboat Bend.** Between Las Olas and the river, as well as just across the river, lies a neighborhood with much of the character of Old Town in Key West and historic Coconut Grove in Miami. No shops or services are located here.

Stranahan House. The oldest standing structure in the city was once the home of pioneer businessman Frank Stranahan. Stranahan arrived in 1892 and, with his wife, Ivy, befriended the Seminole Indians, traded with them, and taught them "new ways." In 1901 he built a store and later made it his home. Now it's a museum with many of his original furnishings on display. ✉ *1 Stranahan Pl. (S.E. 6th Ave. at Las Olas Blvd.),* ☎ *954/524–4736.* 💲 *$5.* ☺ *Wed.–Sat. 10–4, Sun. 1–4.*

Along the Beach

Fort Lauderdale's beachfront offers the best of all possible worlds, with easy access to restaurants and shops. For 2 mi beginning just north of the welcome center and the Bahia Mar yacht basin, strollers and café goers along Route A1A enjoy clear views, typically across rows of colorful beach umbrellas, to the sea and ships passing in and out of nearby Port Everglades. Those on the beach can look back on an exceptionally graceful promenade.

Pedestrians rank ahead of cars in Fort Lauderdale. Broad walkways line both sides of the beach road, and traffic has been trimmed to two gently curving northbound lanes, where in-line skaters dance alongside slow-moving cars. On the beach side, a low masonry wall, which serves as an extended bench, extends the promenade. At night the wall is wrapped in ribbons of fiber-optic color. The most crowded portion of beach is between Las Olas and Sunrise boulevards. This onetime strip—famous from the *Where the Boys Are* era of spring-break madness—is now but a memory.

North of the redesigned beachfront is another 2 mi of open and natural coastal landscape. Much of the way parallels the Hugh Taylor Birch State Recreation Area, which preserves a patch of primeval Florida.

A Good Tour

Go east on Southeast 17th Street across the Brooks Memorial Causeway over the Intracoastal Waterway and bear left onto Seabreeze Boulevard (Route A1A). You will pass through a neighborhood of older homes set in lush vegetation before emerging at the south end of Fort Lauderdale's beachfront strip. On your left is the Radisson Bahia Mar Beach Resort, where novelist John McDonald's fictional hero, Travis McGee, is honored with a plaque at marina slip F-18, where he docked his houseboat. Three blocks north, visit the **International Swimming Hall of Fame Museum and Aquatic Complex** ⑧, which celebrates its 34th anniversary in 1999. As you approach Las Olas Boulevard, you will see the lyrical styling that has given a distinctly European flavor to the **Fort Lauderdale beachfront** ⑨. Plan to break for lunch and perhaps a bit of shopping at Beach Place, the new $50 million, 100,000-square-ft entertainment, retail, and dining complex just north of Las Olas.

Turn left off Route A1A at Sunrise Boulevard, then right into **Hugh Taylor Birch State Recreation Area** ⑩, where many outdoor activities can be enjoyed amid picturesque flora and fauna. Cross Sunrise Boulevard and visit the **Bonnet House** ⑪ to marvel at both the mansion and the surrounding subtropical 35-acre estate.

TIMING

The beach is all about recreation and leisure. To enjoy it as it's meant to be, allow at least a day to loll about, or rent a fishing boat.

Sights to See

★ ⑪ **Bonnet House.** A 35-acre oasis in the heart of the beach area, this subtropical estate is a tribute to the history of old South Florida. The charming mansion was the winter residence of Frederic and Evelyn Bartlett, artists whose personal touches and small surprises are evident throughout. Whether you're interested in architecture, artwork, or the natural environment, this is a special place. ✉ *900 N. Birch Rd.,* ☎ *954/563–5393.* 🎟 *$9.* ☉ *Wed.–Fri. 10–2, weekends noon–2.*

★ ⑨ **Fort Lauderdale beachfront.** A wave theme unifies the setting—from the low, white wave wall between the beach and widened beachfront promenade to the widened and bricked inner promenade in front of shops, restaurants, and hotels. Alone among Florida's major beachfront communities, Fort Lauderdale's beach remains open and uncluttered. More than ever, the boulevard is worth promenading.

⑩ **Hugh Taylor Birch State Recreation Area.** Amid the tropical greenery of this 180-acre park you can stroll along a nature trail, visit the Birch House Museum, picnic, play volleyball, pitch horseshoes, and paddle a rented canoe. ✉ *3109 E. Sunrise Blvd.,* ☎ *954/564–4521.* 🎟 *$3.25 per vehicle with up to 8 people.* ☉ *Daily 8–sunset; ranger-guided nature walks Fri. at 10:30.*

★ ⑧ **International Swimming Hall of Fame Museum and Aquatic Complex.** This monument to underwater accomplishments has two 10-lane, 50-meter pools and an exhibition building featuring photos, medals, and other souvenirs from major swimming events around the world, as well as a theater that shows films of onetime swimming stars Johnny Weissmuller and Esther Williams. ⊠ *1 Hall of Fame Dr.,* ☎ *954/462–6536 for museum or 954/468–1580 for pool.* ⊠ *$3 museum, $3 pool.* ☉ *Museum and pro shop daily 9–7; pool weekdays 8–4 and 6–8, weekends 8–4; closed mid-Dec.–mid-Jan.*

Dining

American

$$–$$$ ✕ **Burt & Jack's.** At the far end and most scenic lookout of Port Everglades, this local favorite has been operated by veteran restaurateur Jack Jackson and actor Burt Reynolds since 1984. Behind the heavy mission doors and bougainvillea, guests are presented with Maine lobster, steaks, and chops, and the waitstaff displays the main ingredients in the raw before orders are taken. The two-story gallery of hacienda-like dining rooms surrounded by glass has views of both Port Everglades and John U. Lloyd Beach State Recreation Area. Come for cocktails in early evening on Saturday or Sunday and watch the cruise ships steam out. The dining area is no-smoking. ⊠ *Berth 23, Port Everglades,* ☎ *954/522–2878 or 954/525–5225. Jacket required. AE, D, DC, MC, V. No lunch.*

Cajun/Creole

$$–$$$ ✕ **Evangeline.** Set inside and out on the ocean drive just south of its sister restaurant Mistral (☞ *below*), Evangeline celebrates Acadian Louisiana in decor and food. The mood is created by paneled wainscoting and plank floors—a tankard and tavern look—highlighted by verse from Longfellow's legendary poem inscribed along the turn of the ceiling. Traditional favorites include smoked rabbit gumbo with andouille sausage, a crawfish Caesar salad, jambalaya (clams, mussels, shrimp, and chicken andouille with a creole sauce), sautéed alligator in a meunière sauce topped with flash-fried oysters, and crisp roasted duckling with poached plums and prunelle brandy. There's music nightly, and a Dixieland band plays weekends, including Sunday afternoon. ⊠ *211 S. Atlantic Blvd. (Rte. A1A),* ☎ *954/522–7001. AE, MC, V.*

Contemporary

$$–$$$ ✕ **Mark's Las Olas.** Chef Mark Militello is in command at this popu-
★ lar restaurant, where metallic finishes bounce the hubbub around the room. Entrées change daily, but typical choices include Gulf shrimp, dolphinfish, yellowtail snapper, grouper, swordfish, Florida lobster, and callaloo (a West Indian spinach), chayote (cho-cho on Mark's menu), ginger, jícama, and plantain, all brilliantly presented and combined in sauces that tend to be low fat. Pastas and full-size dinner pizzas are thoughtful offerings. ⊠ *1032 E. Las Olas Blvd.,* ☎ *954/463–1000. AE, DC, MC, V. No lunch weekends.*

$$–$$$ ✕ **Sheffield's.** You might expect dishes like beef Wellington, chateaubriand, and rack of lamb at this formal oceanfront restaurant in Fort Lauderdale's most upscale luxury hotel, but skillful preparation keeps them from becoming Continental clichés. An extensive seafood selection includes salmon, grouper, swordfish, tuna, tilapia, red snapper, dolphinfish, and lobster; all can be ordered sautéed, grilled, blackened, poached, or broiled. A curried mango glaze and fresh raisin butter are two of the excellent toppings from which you can choose, and the symphony of shellfish, made with lobster, shrimp, and scallops, is excellent eating. ⊠ *Marriott's Harbor Beach Resort, 3030 Holiday Dr.,* ☎ *954/525–4000. AE, D, DC, MC, V. No lunch.*

$$ ✕ **Mistral.** This dining room, surrounded by tropical art and pottery,
★ rates high in both taste and looks. The kitchen staff turns out hearty
pastas, such as a *primavera* redolent with garlic and herbs and *tagli-
olini* (an angel-hair pasta) with prosciutto, pine nuts, and tomatoes.
Other favorites are grilled shrimp and black-bean cakes as well as pan-
seared dolphinfish. Pizzas, big salads, and a strong selection of affordable
wines, available by the bottle and by the glass, are also served. ⊠ *201
S. Atlantic Blvd. (Rte. A1A),* ☏ *954/463–4900. AE, MC, V.*

French

$$ ✕ **French Quarter.** This 1920 building, formerly a Red Cross headquarters, sits on a quiet street, just off bustling Las Olas Boulevard.
The French-style architecture has a touch of New Orleans style, and
the food captures both creole and traditional French elements. Interior rooms are small and intimate, watched over by the friendly, excellent waitstaff. Among the favorites are shrimp *maison* (large shrimp
sautéed with carrots and mushrooms in beurre blanc), bouillabaisse,
crab cakes, and escargot appetizers. French baking is done on site, and
fresh bread and all pastry desserts are made daily. A fixed-price three-
course pretheater dinner ($18.95) is served until 6:30. ⊠ *215 S.E. 8th
Ave.,* ☏ *954/463–8000. AE, MC, V. Closed Sun. No lunch Sat.*

$$ ✕ **La Coquille.** Although this country-French restaurant sits at the
edge of busy Sunrise Boulevard, it seems worlds away thanks to French
doors, pastel coral and green, faux open beams, and a tropical garden.
The friendly and helpful service comes with a delightful French accent,
and the cuisine is equally authentic: Dubonnet and vermouth cassis aper-
itifs are a prelude to seared sea scallops with spring vegetables, honey-
glazed duckling with lingonberry sauce and wild rice, sweetbreads in
a morel and truffle sauce, or veal with shallots and sweet bell peppers.
There's always a soufflé among the desserts as well as a multicourse
dinner special most nights. ⊠ *1619 E. Sunrise Blvd.,* ☏ *954/467–3030.
AE, MC, V. Closed Mon. No lunch Sat.–Thurs.*

$$ ✕ **Studio One French Bistro.** More like an art gallery—intimate, black-
★ and-white, mirrored—this restaurant serves up bountiful portions at
low prices. About 30 choices are offered nightly as part of the $20 fixed-
price dinner. Food is thoughtfully presented, from high-gluten breads
through a dozen or so appetizers, dinner-size salads, and entrées that
include a grilled salmon in puff pastry with lobster sauce, Camembert-
stuffed chicken breast with French cranberry sauce, and crispy roasted
duckling with vanilla sauce. Chef Bernard Asendorf has charge of the
kitchen, and his wife, Roberta, carries on the tradition of greeting by
name the locals who return time and again, often bringing out-of-town
guests. ⊠ *2447 E. Sunrise Blvd.,* ☏ *954/565–2052. AE, DC, MC, V.
Closed Mon. mid-May–mid-Dec. No lunch.*

Italian

$$–$$$ ✕ **Primavera.** Northern Italian food is the specialty at this lovely find
in the middle of an ordinary shopping plaza. Elegant floral arrangements enhance the fine dining experience. In addition to interesting pasta
and risotto entrées, there is a wide variety of creative fish, poultry, veal,
and beef dinners. One of the chef's favorites is veal chop Boscaiola (with
shallots, wild mushrooms, and bordelaise sauce). Primavera is renowned
for its spectacular assortment of both appetizers and desserts. ⊠ *830
E. Oakland Park Blvd.,* ☏ *954/564–6363. AE, D, DC, MC, V. No
lunch.*

Mexican

$$ ✕ **Eduardo de San Angel.** Forget tacos and burritos, which aren't even
available here, and try the classic Mexican dishes served up by Eduardo
Pria and his family. Authentic chilies, spices, and herbs enhance an array

of seafood, meat, and poultry dishes. Typical specialties are beef tenderloin tips sautéed with Portobello mushrooms and onions with a chipo-
tle chili sauce, and a marvelous mesquite-grilled red snapper flavored
with jalapeños and mango salsa. The gourmet dishes are matched by
a sophisticated setting. ⊠ *2822 E. Commercial Blvd.,* ☎ *954/772–4731.
AE, MC, V. Closed Sun. No lunch.*

Seafood

$–$$ ✕ **Rustic Inn Crabhouse.** Wayne McDonald started with a cozy one-
room roadhouse in 1955, when this was a remote service road just west
of the little airport. Now, the plain, rustic place is huge. Steamed crabs
seasoned with garlic and herbs, spices, and oil are eaten with mallets
on tables covered with newspapers; peel-and-eat shrimp are served either with garlic and butter or spiced and steamed with Old Bay sea-
soning. The big menu includes other seafood items as well. Pies and
cheesecakes are offered for dessert. ⊠ *4331 Ravenswood Rd.,* ☎ *954/
584–1637. AE, D, DC, MC, V.*

$–$$ ✕ **Shirttail Charlie's.** Diners look out on the New River from the out-
door deck or upstairs dining room of this restaurant, named for a
yesteryear Seminole Indian who wore his shirttails out. A free 30- to
40-minute after-dinner cruise on *Shirttail Charlie's Express* chugs up-
river past an alleged Al Capone speakeasy or across the river to and
from the Broward Center. Charlie's is built to look old, with a 1920s
tile floor that leans toward the water. Florida-style seafood includes
conch served four ways, crab balls, blackened tuna with Dijon mustard sauce, crunchy coconut shrimp with a not-too-sweet piña colada
sauce, and three fresh catches nightly. A children's menu is available.
⊠ *400 S.W. 3rd Ave.,* ☎ *954/463–3474. AE, MC, V. Closed Mon. June–
Sept.*

Lodging

On the Beach

$$$$ 🏨 **Marriott's Harbor Beach Resort.** If you look down from the upper
stories (14 in all) at night, this 16-acre property south of the big public beach shimmers like a jewel. Spacious guest rooms are done in tropical colors, lively floral prints, rattan, wicker, and wood. Each has a
balcony facing the ocean or the Intracoastal Waterway, and there are
in-room minibars. Sheffield's is one of the city's top restaurants. No
other hotel gives you so many options. ⊠ *3030 Holiday Dr., 33316,*
☎ *954/525–4000 or 800/222–6543,* ℻ *954/766–6152. 588 rooms,
36 suites. 5 restaurants, 3 bars, pool, massage, saunas, 5 tennis courts,
health club, beach, windsurfing, boating, parasailing, children's program (ages 5–12). AE, DC, MC, V.*

$$$–$$$$ 🏨 **Lago Mar Resort Hotel & Club.** The sprawling Lago Mar has been
★ owned by the Banks family since the early 1950s. In recent years
they've poured $11 million into renovations, including those in 1998
that upgraded bathrooms and kitchens in the 25 deluxe suites in the
north building. The lobby is still luxurious, with fanlight surrounds,
a coquina-rock fireplace, and an eye-popping saltwater aquarium be-
hind the registration desk. Allamanda trellises and bougainvillea plant-
ings edge the swimming lagoon, and guests have use of the broadest
beach in the city. Lago Mar is less a big resort than a small town—
and, in its way, a slice of Old Florida. ⊠ *1700 S. Ocean La., 33316,*
☎ *954/523–6511 or 800/524–6627,* ℻ *954/524–6627. 32 rooms, 123
1-bedroom suites, 15 2-bedroom suites. 4 restaurants, 2 pools, minia-
ture golf, 4 tennis courts, shuffleboard, volleyball. AE, DC, MC, V.*

$$$ 🏨 **Bahia Cabana Beach Resort.** *Boating Magazine* ranks the waterfront
bar and restaurant here among the world's 10 best, but it's far enough
from guest rooms so that nightly entertainment is not disturbing. A

video bar yields a sweeping view of the marina. Rooms are spread among five buildings furnished in tropical-casual style. Those in the 500 building are more motel-like and overlook the parking lot, but rates here are lowest. ⊠ *3001 Harbor Dr., 33316,* ☎ *954/524–1555 or 800/922–3008; 800/232–2437 in FL;* FAX *954/764–5951. 52 rooms, 37 efficiencies, 10 suites. Restaurant, 2 bars, café, 3 pools, hot tub, saunas, shuffleboard. AE, D, DC, MC, V.*

$$$ 🔛 **La Casa Del Mar.** This is a Florida rarity: a true bed-and-breakfast
★ inn located at the beach. Co-owners Larry Ataniso and Lee Prellwitz took the plunge two years ago, and guests have been delighted ever since. Rooms have names like Stolen Kiss, Monet, and Southwest. The full American breakfast might consist of orange-flavored French toast, buttermilk pancakes, poached eggs, and mushroom-sausage casserole, among other treats, and guests can indulge again in the late afternoon at the poolside wine and cheese party. ⊠ *3003 Granada St., 33304,* ☎ *954/467–2037,* FAX *954/467–7439. 10 units. Pool. AE, MC, V.*

$$ 🔛 **Nina Lee Motel.** This is typical of the modest, affordable 1950s-style lodgings that can be found within a block or two of the ocean along Fort Lauderdale beach. Be prepared for plain rooms—homey and clean, but not tiny, with at least a toaster, coffeepot, and refrigerator; efficiencies have gas kitchens, large closets, and tub-showers. The pool is set in a garden, and the entire property is just removed enough from the beach causeway to be quiet. ⊠ *3048 Harbor Dr., 33316,* ☎ *954/524–1568. 14 units. Pool. MC, V.*

Downtown and Beach Causeways

$$$$ 🔛 **Hyatt Regency Pier Sixty-Six.** The trademark of this high-rise re-
★ sort on the Intracoastal Waterway is its rooftop Pier Top Lounge, which revolves every 66 minutes and is reached by an exterior elevator. The 17-story tower dominates a 22-acre spread that includes the Spa LXVI. Tower and lanai lodgings are tops from the ground up. In the early evening, guests try to perch at the Pelican Bar; at 6:06 a cannon is fired, and anybody around the bar gets a drink on the house. When you want to swim in the ocean, hail the water taxi at the resort's dock for a three-minute trip to the beach. ⊠ *2301 S. 17th St., 33316,* ☎ *954/525–6666 or 800/327–3796,* FAX *954/728–3541. 380 rooms, 8 suites. 3 restaurants, 3 bars, pool, hot tub, spa, 2 tennis courts, dock, snorkeling, boating, parasailing, waterskiing, fishing. AE, D, MC, V.*

$$$ 🔛 **Riverside Hotel.** This six-story hotel was built in 1936 and has been steadily upgraded. A sidewalk café fronts Bob Jenny's tropical murals, one of which is a New Orleans–style work that stretches across 725 square ft of the hotel's facade. Old Fort Lauderdale photos grace the hallways, and rooms are outfitted distinctively, with antique oak furnishings, framed French prints, and European-style baths. The poolside bar in back offers a great view of the New River, as do the best guest rooms; the least desirable are the 36 series, from which you can hear the elevator. No-smoking rooms are available. An attentive staff includes many who have been with the hotel for two decades or more. ⊠ *620 E. Las Olas Blvd., 33301,* ☎ *954/467–0671 or 800/325–3280,* FAX *954/462–2148. 109 rooms, 7 suites. Restaurant, bar, pool, dock. AE, DC, MC, V.*

$$–$$$ 🔛 **Banyan Marina Apartments.** These outstanding waterfront apart-
★ ments, on a residential island just off Las Olas Boulevard, are set amid imaginative landscaping that includes a walkway through the upper branches of a banyan tree. Featuring leather sofas, springy carpets, real potted plants, sheer curtains, custom drapes, high-quality art, French doors, and jalousies for sweeping the breeze in, the luxurious units are as comfortable as any first-class hotel—but for half the price. Also in-

cluded are a full kitchen, dining area, beautiful gardens, dockage for
eight yachts, and exemplary housekeeping. ✉ *111 Isle of Venice,
33301,* ☎ *954/524–4430,* FAX *954/764–4870. 10 rooms, 1 efficiency,
4 1-bedroom apartments, 2 2-bedroom apartments. Dining room,
pool, dock. MC, V.*

Nightlife and the Arts

For the most complete weekly listing of events, read the **"Showtime!"**
entertainment insert and events calendar in the Friday *Fort Lauderdale News/Sun Sentinel.* **"Weekend,"** in the Friday edition of the *Herald,* the Broward edition of the *Miami Herald,* carries listings of area
happenings. The weekly *City Link* is principally an entertainment and
dining paper with a relic "underground" look. A 24-hour **Arts & Entertainment Hotline** (☎ 954/357–5700) provides updates on art, attractions, children's events, dance, festivals, films, literature, museums,
music, opera, and theater.

Tickets are sold at individual box offices and through **Ticketmaster** (☎
954/523–3309); there is a service charge.

The Arts

Broward Center for the Performing Arts (✉ 201 S.W. 5th Ave., ☎ 954/
462–0222) is the waterfront centerpiece of Fort Lauderdale's new cultural arts district. More than 500 events a year are scheduled at the
2,700-seat architectural masterpiece, including Broadway musicals, plays,
dance, symphony and opera, rock, film, lectures, comedy, and children's
theater.

Nightlife

BARS AND LOUNGES

Baja Beach Club (✉ Coral Ridge Mall, 3200 N. Federal Hwy., ☎ 954/
561–2432) offers trendy entertainment: karaoke, lip synching, virtual
reality, performing bartenders, temporary tatoos—plus a 40-ft free buffet. The newest hot spot is **Beach Place** (✉ 17 S. Atlantic Blvd.), on
Route A1A. An assortment of clubs is mingled among the shops, making it *the* weekend place to be. **Cheers** (✉ 941 E. Cypress Creek Rd.,
☎ 954/771–6337) is an action-filled nightspot with a wide variety of
rock bands, two bars, and a dance floor. **O'Hara's Pub & Sidewalk Cafe**
(✉ 722 E. Las Olas Blvd., ☎ 954/524–1764) features live jazz and blues
nightly. It's packed for TGIF, though usually by the end of each day
the trendy crowd spills onto this prettiest of downtown streets. The
Parrot Lounge (✉ 911 Sunrise La., ☎ 954/563–1493) is a loony feast
for the eyes, with a casual, friendly local crowd. Fifteen TVs and frequent sing-alongs add to the fun. A jukebox jams all night. **Squeeze**
(✉ 2 S. New River Dr., ☎ 954/522–2151) is a favorite of alternative-
music fans.

COMEDY

New York Comedy Cafe (✉ 1432 N. Federal Hwy., ☎ 954/565–1369)
features nationally touring headline acts at 8:30 Friday and 8:30 and
10:45 Saturday.

COUNTRY AND WESTERN

Desperado (✉ 2520 S. Miami Rd., ☎ 954/463–2855) offers a mechanical bull and free line-dance lessons. The club is open from Wednesday through Sunday.

Outdoor Activities and Sports

Baseball

From mid-February to March the **Baltimore Orioles** (⊠ Fort Lauderdale Stadium, N.W. 12th Ave., ☎ 954/776–1921) are in spring training.

Biking

Some of the most popular routes are Route A1A and Bayview Drive, especially early in the morning before traffic builds, and a 7-mi bike path that parallels Route 84 and the New River and leads to Markham Park, which has mountain-bike trails. For a free bicycle map, contact **County Bicycle Coordinator** (⊠ 115 S. Andrews Ave., 33301, ☎ 954/357–6661). Most area bike shops also have cycling maps.

Fishing

If you're interested in a saltwater charter, check out the **Radisson Bahia Mar Beach Resort** (⊠ 801 Seabreeze Blvd., ☎ 954/764–2233). **Captain Bill's** (⊠ South dock, Radisson Bahia Mar Beach Resort, 801 Seabreeze Blvd., ☎ 954/467–3855) offers bottom fishing.

Scuba Diving and Snorkeling

Lauderdale Diver (⊠ 1334 S.E. 17th St. Causeway, ☎ 954/467–2822 or 800/654–2073), which is PADI affiliated, arranges dive charters throughout the county. Dive trips typically last four hours. Nonpackage reef trips are open to divers for $38; scuba gear is extra.

Pro Dive (⊠ Radisson Bahia Mar Beach Resort, 801 Seabreeze Blvd., ☎ 954/761–3413 or 800/772–3483), a PADI five-star facility, is the area's oldest diving operation and offers packages with Radisson Bahia Mar Beach Resort, from where its 60-ft boat departs. Snorkelers can go out for $25 on the four-hour dive trip or $20 on the two-hour snorkeling trip, which includes snorkel equipment but not scuba gear. Scuba divers pay $35 using their own gear or $85 with all rentals included.

Soccer

A new major-league soccer team, the **Fusion** (⊠ 5301 N.W. 12th Ave., ☎ 954/717–2200), calls the newly renovated Lockhart Stadium home. Their season, which begins in March, includes 20 home games.

Tennis

With 21 courts, 18 of them lighted clay courts, **Holiday Park Tennis Center** is Fort Lauderdale's largest public tennis facility. Chris Evert, one of the game's greatest players, learned the sport here under the watchful eye of her father, James Evert, who recently retired after 37 years as the tennis professional here. ⊠ *701 N.E. 12th Ave.,* ☎ *954/761–5378.* ☞ *$4 per person per hr.* ☉ *Weekdays 8 AM–9:15 PM, weekends 8–7.*

Shopping

Malls

Just north of Las Olas Boulevard on Route A1A is the happening, new **Beach Place** (⊠ 17 S. Atlantic Blvd.). Here you can browse through such shops as the Gap, Bath & Body Works, and Banana Republic; have lunch or dinner at an array of restaurants, from casual Caribbean to elegant American; or carouse at a selection of nightspots—all open late. By and large, eateries on the lower level are more upscale, whereas on the upper level, the prices are lower and the ocean view is better.

With a convenient in-town location just west of the Intracoastal Waterway, the split-level **Galleria Mall** (⊠ 2414 E. Sunrise Blvd.) contains more than 1 million square ft of space. It's anchored by Neiman-Marcus, Lord & Taylor, Dillards, and Saks Fifth Avenue and features 150 world-class specialty stores with an emphasis on fashion and sporting goods.

Shopping Street

If only for a stroll and some window-shopping, don't miss the **Shops of Las Olas** (⊠ 1 block off New River east of U.S. 1). The city's best boutiques plus top restaurants (many affordable) and art galleries line a beautifully landscaped street.

Side Trips

The Western Suburbs and Beyond

West of Fort Lauderdale is an ever-growing mass of suburbs flowing one into the other. They're home to most of the city's golf courses as well as some attractions and large malls. As you head farther west, the terrain becomes more Everglades-like, and you'll occasionally see an alligator sunning itself on a canal bank. No matter how dedicated developers are to building over this natural resource, the Everglades keeps trying to assert itself. Waterbirds, fish, and other creatures are found in canals and lakes, even man-made ones, throughout the western areas.

⓬ Thousands of caterpillars representing as many as 150 species pupate and emerge as butterflies in the walk-through laboratory that is **Butterfly World,** on 3 acres inside Tradewinds Park. A screened aviary called North American Butterflies is reserved for native species. The Tropical Rain Forest is a 30-ft-high construction, with observation decks, waterfalls, ponds, and tunnels where colorful butterflies flit and shift about. ⊠ *3600 W. Sample Rd., Coconut Creek,* ☎ *954/977–4400.* *$10.95.* ☉ *Mon.–Sat. 9–5, Sun. 1–5.*

⓭ At the **Young at Art Children's Museum,** kids can work in paint, graphics, sculpture, and crafts according to themes that change three times a year. Then they take their masterpieces home with them. ⊠ *801 S. University Dr., in Fountains Shoppes, Plantation,* ☎ *954/424–0085.* *$3.* ☉ *Tues.–Sat. 11–5, Sun. noon–5.*

⓮ The 30-acre **Everglades Holiday Park** provides a good glimpse of the Everglades. Here you can take an airboat tour, look at an 18th-century-style Native American village, or watch an alligator-wrestling show. A souvenir shop, TJ's Grill, a convenience store, and a campground with RV hookups and a tent are all on site. ⊠ *21940 Griffin Rd.,* ☎ *954/434–8111.* *Free, $12.50 airboat tour.* ☉ *Daily 9–5.*

⓯ To understand and enjoy the Everglades, take an airboat ride at **Sawgrass Recreation Park.** You'll probably see all sorts of plants and wildlife, such as birds, alligators, turtles, snakes, and fish. Included in the entrance fee along with the airboat ride is admission to an Everglades nature exhibit, a native Seminole Indian village, and exhibits about alligators, other reptiles, and birds of prey. A souvenir and gift shop, food service, and an RV park with hookups are also at the park. ⊠ *U.S. 27 north of I–595,* ☎ *954/426–2474.* *$13.85.* ☉ *Daily 6–6, airboat rides 8–5.*

⓰ Some distance from Fort Lauderdale's tranquil beaches but worth the one-hour drive, is the **Big Cypress Seminole Reservation** and its two very different attractions. At the **Billie Swamp Safari,** you can experience the majesty of the Everglades firsthand. Daily tours of the wetlands and hammocks, where wildlife abound, yield sightings of deer, water buffalo, bison, wild hogs, hawks, eagles, alligators, and even the rare Florida panther. Tours are provided aboard swamp buggies—customized motor vehicles specially designed to provide visitors with an elevated view of the frontier. ⊠ *Snake Rd., 19 mi north of I–75 Exit 14,* ☎ *941/983–6101 or 800/949–6101.* ⊡ *Free, $38 swamp buggy ecotour/alligator and snake education show/airboat ride package.* ☉ *Daily 8–5.*

Not far away from the Billie Swamp Safari is the **Ah-Tha-Thi-Ki Museum,** whose name means "a place to learn, a place to remember." It is just that. The new $12 million facility honors the culture and tradition of the Seminoles through artifacts and reenactments of rituals and ceremonies. ⊠ *Snake Rd., 17 mi north of I–75 Exit 14,* ☎ *954/792–0745.* ⊡ *$6.* ☉ *Tues.–Sun. 9–5.*

LODGING

$$$$ 🏨 **Wyndham Resort & Spa Fort Lauderdale.** As its name suggests, this resort offers the luxury, amenities, and facilities of a resort with the health-consciousness of a spa. Spacious guest rooms and suites are done in tropical colors with rattan seating and overlook a lake or golf course. Oversize baths have dressing areas. In the morning complimentary caffeine-free herbal teas are offered; in the afternoon it's fresh fruit. The staff nutritionist follows American Heart Association and American Cancer Society guidelines and can accommodate macrobiotic and vegetarian diets. Also on site and open to the public is a full-service beauty salon. The resort offers combination spa-tennis and spa-golf packages. ⊠ *250 Racquet Club Rd., 33326,* ☎ *954/389–3300 or 800/327–8090,* 𝔽𝔸𝕏 *954/384–0563. 493 units. 4 restaurants, 2 bars, 5 pools, beauty salon, spa, 2 golf courses, 24 tennis courts, bowling, horseback riding, roller-skating rink, shops. AE, D, MC, V.*

NIGHTLIFE AND THE ARTS

Sunrise Musical Theatre (⊠ 5555 N.W. 95th Ave., Sunrise, ☎ 954/741–7300) is a 4,000-seat theater featuring everything from ballet to top-name pop, rock, and country artists.

OUTDOOR ACTIVITIES AND SPORTS

Fishing. The marina at **Everglades Holiday Park** (⊠ 21940 Griffin Rd., ☎ 954/434–8111) caters to freshwater fishing. For $52.50 for five hours, you can rent a 14-ft johnboat (with a 9.9-horsepower Yamaha outboard) that carries up to four people. A rod and reel rent for $10 a day, and bait is extra. For two people, a fishing guide for a half day (four hours) is $140; for a full day (eight hours), $190. A third person adds $35 for a half day, $70 for a full day. You can also buy a freshwater fishing license (mandatory) here; a seven-day nonresident license is $17. Freshwater fishing with a guide out of **Sawgrass Recreation Park** (⊠ U.S. 27 north of I–595, ☎ 954/426–2474) costs $175 for two people for a half day, $225 for a full day. Resident and nonresident fishing licenses and live bait are available.

Golf. Next Day Golf (☎ 954/772–2582) provides access at no extra fee to private courses normally limited to members and arranges bookings up to 12 months in advance—a big advantage for golfers planning trips during the busy winter months. And they also offer last-minute discount tee times (call 12 hours in advance). **Bonaventure Country Club** (⊠ 200 Bonaventure Blvd., ☎ 954/389–2100) has 36 holes. **Broken Woods Country Club** (⊠ 9000 Sample Rd., Coral Springs, ☎ 954/752–2140) has 18 holes. **Colony West Country Club** (⊠ 6800 N.W. 88th Ave., Tamarac, ☎ 954/726–8430) offers play on 36 holes. Just west of Florida's Turnpike, the **Inverrary Country Club** (⊠ 3840 Inverrary Blvd., Lauderhill, ☎ 954/733–7550) has three 18-hole courses. **Jacaranda Golf Club** (⊠ 9200 W. Broward Blvd., Plantation, ☎ 954/472–5855) has 18 holes to play. **Sabal Palms Golf Course** (⊠ 5101 W. Commercial Blvd., Tamarac, ☎ 954/731–2600) has 18 holes. **Sunrise**

Country Club (⌖ 7400 N.W. 24th Pl., Sunrise, ☎ 954/742–4333) provides 18 holes.

Ice Hockey. The new $200 million Broward Arena opens for the 1999 season of the National Hockey League's **Florida Panthers** (⌖ 13611 Green Toad Rd., Sunrise, ☎ 954/523–3309), who previously played at the Miami Arena.

SHOPPING

Broward's shopping extravaganza, **Fashion Mall at Plantation** (⌖ University Dr. north of Broward Blvd., Plantation) is a jewel of a mall. The three-level complex includes such department stores as Macy's, Lord & Taylor, and Burdines; a Sheraton Suites Hotel; and more than 100 specialty shops. In addition to a diverse food court, the Brasserie Max restaurant offers gourmet dining.

Containing more than 270 stores, the huge (2 million square ft) **Sawgrass Mills Mall** (⌖ Flamingo Rd. and Sunrise Blvd., Sunrise) is a destination in itself. Travelers and locals alike come for the shopping, restaurants, food courts, entertainment, and great prices, and the place teems on weekends and holidays. Shops, many of which are outlets, include Neiman-Marcus, Loehmann's, JCPenney, Ann Taylor, Alfred Angelo Bridal, Levi's, TJ Maxx, Donna Karan, Saks Fifth Avenue, and Kenneth Cole.

NORTH ON SCENIC A1A

North of Fort Lauderdale's Birch Recreation Area, Route A1A edges back from the beach through the section known as the Galt Ocean Mile, and a succession of ocean-side communities line up against the sea. Traffic can line up, too, as it passes through a changing pattern of beach-blocking high-rises and modest family vacation towns and back again. Here and there a scenic lighthouse or park punctuates the landscape, while other attractions and recreational opportunities are found inland.

Lauderdale-by-the-Sea

⑰ *5 mi north of Fort Lauderdale.*

Tucked just north of Fort Lauderdale's northern boundary, this low-rise family resort town bans construction of more than three stories. You can drive along lawn-divided El Mar Drive, lined with garden-style motels a block east of Route A1A. In actuality, however, you don't need a car in Lauderdale-by-the-Sea. Dozens of good restaurants and shops are in close proximity to hotels and the beach.

Where Commercial Boulevard meets the ocean, you can walk out onto **Anglin's Fishing Pier,** stretching 875 ft into the Atlantic. Here you can fish, stop in at any of the popular restaurants clustered around the seafront plaza, or just soak up the scene.

Dining and Lodging

$$ ✕ **Sea Watch.** It's set back from the road and easy to miss, but after 25 years, this nautical-theme restaurant right on Lauderdale-by-the-Sea's beach stays packed during lunch and dinner. Waits can be as long as 30 minutes, but time passes quickly in the sumptuous upstairs lounge with comfy sofas and high-back rattan chairs. The menu has all the right appetizers: oysters Rockefeller, Gulf shrimp, clams casino, and Bahamian conch fritters. Typical daily specials might be sautéed yellowtail snapper, oat-crusted with roasted red bell pepper sauce and basil, or a charbroiled dolphinfish fillet marinated with soy sauce, garlic, black pepper, and lemon juice. Desserts include a cappuccino

brownie and strawberries Romanoff. Good early bird specials are offered off-season. ⊠ *6002 N. Ocean Blvd. (Rte. A1A), Fort Lauderdale,* ☎ *954/781–2200. AE, MC, V.*

$ ✕ **Aruba Beach Cafe.** This is your best bet at the pier. A big beachside barn of a place—very casual, always crowded, always fun—it serves large portions of Caribbean conch chowder, Cuban black-bean soup, fresh tropical salads, burgers, sandwiches, and seafood. ⊠ *1 E. Commercial Blvd.,* ☎ *954/776–0001. AE, D, DC, MC, V.*

$$$ ☷ **A Little Inn by the Sea.** French, German, and English are spoken at this inn, which caters to a very international clientele. Innkeeper Uli Brandt and his family maintain tropical charm and bed-and-breakfast style, and since taking over the property in 1994, they have continued to make upgrades. Adding to the flavor are fountains and classical background music at breakfast. The inn is directly on the ocean, and rooms have nice views from private balconies. Some efficiencies and one- and two-bedroom suites are available. ⊠ *4546 El Mar Dr., 33308,* ☎ *954/772–2450 or 800/492–0311,* FAX *954/938–9354. 10 rooms, 7 suites, 12 efficiencies. Pool, beach, bicycles. AE, D, DC, MC, V.*

$$$ ☷ **Tropic Seas Resort Inn.** It's only a block off A1A, but it's a million-dollar location—directly on the beach and two blocks from municipal tennis courts. Built in the 1950s, units are plain but clean and comfortable, with tropical rattan furniture and ceiling fans. Managers Sandy and Larry Lynch tend to the largely repeat, family-oriented clientele. The complimentary Sunday brunch and weekly wiener roast and rum swizzle party are good opportunities to mingle with other guests. ⊠ *4616 El Mar Dr., 33308,* ☎ *954/772–2555 or 800/952–9581,* FAX *954/771–5711. 16 rooms, 6 efficiencies, 7 apartments. Pool, beach. AE, D, DC, MC, V.*

$$ ☷ **Blue Seas Courtyard.** Bubbly innkeeper Cristie Furth runs this one- and two-story motel with her husband, Marc, and small as it is, they keep investing their future in it. Lattice fencing and gardens of cactus and impatiens were added in front for more privacy around the brick patio and garden-set pool. Guest quarters feature kitchenettes, terra-cotta tiles, bright Haitian and Peruvian art, and generally Tex-Mex and Danish furnishings, whose woody textures work well together. Handmade painted shutters and indoor plants add to the look. This remains an excellent buy in a quiet resort area just a block from the beach. ⊠ *4525 El Mar Dr., 33308,* ☎ *954/772–3336 or 877/225–8373,* FAX *954/772–6337. 12 units. Pool, coin laundry. MC, V.*

Outdoor Activities and Sports

Anglin's Fishing Pier (☎ 954/491–9403) is open for fishing 24 hours a day. Fishing costs $3 for adults and $2 for children up to 12, tackle rental is an additional $10 (plus $10 deposit), and bait averages $2.

Pompano Beach

⑱ *3 mi north of Lauderdale-by-the-Sea.*

As Route A1A enters this town directly north of Lauderdale-by-the-Sea, the high-rise procession begins again. Sportfishing is big in Pompano Beach, as its name implies, but there's more to beachside attractions than the popular Fisherman's Wharf. Behind a low coral-rock wall, Alsdorf Park extends north and south of the wharf along the road and beach.

Dining and Lodging

$$$ ✕ **Cafe Maxx.** New-wave epicurean dining had its South Florida start
★ here in the early 1980s, and Cafe Maxx remains popular among re-
gional food lovers. The setting is ordinary, in a little strip of stores, but
inside there's a holiday glow year-round. Chef Oliver Saucy demon-
strates ritual devotion to the preparation of fine cuisine. The menu
changes nightly but always showcases foods from the tropics: jumbo
stone-crab claws with honey-lime mustard sauce and black bean and
banana pepper chili with Florida avocado. Desserts, too, reflect a trop-
ical theme, from praline macadamia mousse over chocolate cake with
butterscotch sauce to candied ginger with pears poached in muscatel
and sun-dried cherry ice cream. More than 200 wines are offered by
the bottle, another 20 by the glass. ✉ *2601 E. Atlantic Blvd.,* ☎ *954/
782–0606. AE, D, DC, MC, V. No lunch.*

$$$$ 🏨 **Palm-Aire Spa Resort.** This 750-acre health, fitness, and stress-re-
duction spa offers exercise activities, personal treatments, and calorie-
controlled meals. Separate men's and women's pavilions have private
sunken Roman baths, Swiss showers, and some of the most experienced
hands in the massage business. There are 166 spacious rooms and 18
golf villas with private terraces. All have separate dressing rooms, and
some have two baths. You can have use of the spa for $96 for a half
day or $220 for the whole day, including lunch, massage, facial, and
fitness classes. ✉ *2601 Palm-Aire Dr. N, 33069,* ☎ *954/972–3300 or
800/272–5624. 184 units. Restaurant, pools, hot tubs, massage, saunas,
spa, steam rooms, 3 golf courses, 37 tennis courts, aerobics, exercise
room, racquetball, squash. AE, D, MC, V.*

$$$ 🏨 **Beachcomber.** This Best Western property has been completely ren-
ovated, and its beach location is central to most Broward County at-
tractions. Ocean views are everywhere, from the oversize guest room
balconies to the dining rooms. Though there are also villas and penthouse suites atop the eight-story structure, standard rooms are spacious.
The multilingual staff seems attentive to guest requests. ✉ *1200 S. Ocean
Blvd., 33062,* ☎ *954/941–7830 or 800/231–2423. 134 rooms, 9 villas, 4 suites. Restaurant, bar, 2 pools, beach. AE, D, MC, V.*

Outdoor Activities and Sports

FISHING

Pompano Pier (☎ 954/943–1488) extends 1,080 ft into the Atlantic.
The cost is $2.65 for adults, $1.06 for children under 10; rod-and-reel
rental is $10.07 (including admission and initial bait).

For drift fishing try *Fish City Pride* (✉ Fish City Marina, 2621 N. Riverside Dr., ☎ 954/781–1211). You can arrange for a saltwater charter
boat through the **Hillsboro Inlet Marina** (✉ 2629 N. Riverside Dr., ☎
954/943–8222).

GOLF

Crystal Lake South Course (✉ 3800 Crystal Lake Dr., ☎ 954/943–2902)
has 18 holes. The **Oaks Golf & Racquet Club** (✉ 3701 Oaks Clubhouse
Dr., ☎ 954/978–1737; 954/975–6244 for tee line), part of the Palm-
Aire Spa Resort, has 94 holes of golf, including a course with an extra
4 holes.

HORSE RACING

Pompano Harness Track, Florida's only harness track, features world-
class trotters and pacers during its October–August meet. The Top o'
the Park restaurant overlooks the finish line. ✉ *1800 S.W. 3rd St.,* ☎
954/972–2000. 🎫 *Grandstand $1, clubhouse $2.* ☉ *Racing Mon., Wed.,
Fri., and Sat. 7:30.*

ICE-SKATING

Visitors from the North who miss ice and cold can skate at the **Gold Coast Ice Arena** during morning, afternoon, or evening sessions. You can also watch the NHL Florida Panthers practice mornings during the hockey season. ✉ *4601 N. Federal Hwy.,* ☎ *954/943–1437.* ✑ *Sessions $5 ($5.50 weekend evenings), skate rental $2.* ⊙ *Daily 8:30–4 plus Tues. 8:15 PM–10 PM, Fri.–Sat. 8:15 AM–11 PM.*

Shopping

The old Pompano Fashion Square has been reborn as **Pompano Square** (✉ 2001 N. Federal Hwy.) and now features a tropical motif. This comfortably sized city mall has 110 shops, four department stores, and a few places for food.

Lighthouse Point

⑲ *2 mi north of Pompano Beach.*

A big attraction here is the view across Hillsboro Inlet to **Hillsboro Light,** the brightest lighthouse in the Southeast. Mariners have used this landmark for decades. From the ocean you can see the light almost halfway to the Bahamas. Although the lighthouse is on private property and is inaccessible to the public, it's well worth a peek.

Dining

$$–$$$ ✕ **Cafe Arugula.** Chef Dick Cingolani draws upon the culinary tradi-
★ tions of warm climates from Italy to the American Southwest. The decor, too, blends southwestern with Mediterranean looks—a row of mauve-velvet booths beneath steamboat-wheel windows surrounds an entire wall of chili peppers, corn, cactus, and garlic cloves. A frequently changing menu may include succulent fresh hogfish with capers and shaved almonds over fettuccine or a free-range loin of venison with juniper–wild mushroom sauce, quesadilla, and stir-fried vegetables. ✉ *3110 N. Federal Hwy.,* ☎ *954/785–7732. AE, D, DC, MC, V. No lunch.*

$$ ✕ **Place.** On an island that was once a bootlegger's haunt, this seafood
★ restaurant is reached by launch and has served such luminaries as Winston Churchill, FDR, and John F. Kennedy. "Cap" was Captain Theodore Knight, born in 1871, who, with partner-in-crime Al Hasis, floated a derelict barge to the area in the 1920s. Today the rustic restaurant, built on the barge, is run by descendants of Hasis. Baked wahoo steaks are lightly glazed and meaty, the long-cut french fries arouse gluttony, hot and flaky rolls are baked fresh several times a night, and tangy lime pie is a great finishing touch. Turn east off Federal Highway onto Northeast 24th Street (two blocks north of Pompano Square); follow the double yellow line to the launch. ✉ *Cap's Dock, 2765 N.E. 28th Ct.,* ☎ *954/941–0418. AE, MC, V. No lunch.*

En Route   To the north, Route A1A traverses the so-called Hillsboro Mile (actually more than 2 mi), a millionaire's row of some of the most beautiful and expensive homes in Broward County. The road runs along a narrow strip of land between the Intracoastal Waterway and the ocean, with bougainvillea and oleanders edging the way and yachts docked along both banks. In winter the traffic often creeps at a snail's pace, as vacationers and retirees gawk at the views.

Deerfield Beach

⑳ *3½ mi north of Lighthouse Point.*

☾ The name **Quiet Waters Park** belies what's in store for kids here. Splash Adventure is a high-tech water-play system with swings, slides, and tunnels, among other activities. There's also cable waterskiing and boating on the park's lake. ⊠ *6601 N. Powerline Rd.,* ☎ *954/360–1315.* ⊠ *$1 weekends, free weekdays; Splash Adventure $2.* ☉ *Daily 8–6.*

Deerfield Island Park, an 8½-acre island that can only be reached by boat, is a paradise of coastal hammock, or tree islands. Officially designated an urban wilderness area along the Intracoastal Waterway, it contains mangrove swamp that provides critical habitat for gopher tortoises, gray foxes, raccoons, and armadillos. ⊠ *1 Deerfield Island; boat landing at Riverview Restaurant, Riverview Rd.,* ☎ *954/360–1320.* ⊠ *Free.* ☉ *Boat shuttles Wed. and Sun.; call for times.*

Dining and Lodging

$$ ✕ **Brooks.** This is one of the city's better restaurants, thanks to a
★ French perfectionist, Bernard Perron. Meals are served in a series of rooms filled with replicas of old masters, cut glass, antiques, and tapestrylike floral wallpapers, though the shedlike dining room still feels very Florida. Fresh ingredients go into distinctly Floridian cuisine. Main courses include red snapper in papillote, broiled fillet of pompano with seasoned root vegetables, and a sweet lemongrass linguine with bok choy and julienned crisp vegetables. ⊠ *500 S. Federal Hwy.,* ☎ *954/427–9302. AE, D, MC, V.*

$ ✕ **Whale's Rib.** If you're looking for a casual, almost funky, nautical
★ setting near the beach, look no farther. For 18 years the Williams family has been serving up excellent seafood and good cheer. Fish specials are offered daily, along with Whale Fries—thinly sliced potatoes that look like hot potato chips. Those with smaller appetites can choose from a good selection of salads and fish sandwiches. Other favorites are specials from the raw bar and a popular fish dip for starters. The place is crowded on weekends, and parking is limited. ⊠ *2031 N.E. 2nd St.,* ☎ *954/421–8880. AE, MC, V.*

$$$–$$$$ ☲ **Ocean Terrace Suites.** This four-story motel is in one of the quieter sections of north Broward, just south of the Palm Beach county line, across the narrow shore road from the beach. Large units—efficiencies and one- and three-bedroom apartments—all have big balconies overlooking the sea. Colors vary from shore washed to bright; pink and green pastels tint the bedrooms. The furniture is rattan, and units are clean and neat. Art is throwaway, flowers are artificial, and materials are bargain quality. Still, for size, location, and price this is a good buy. An outdoor barbecue grill is available. ⊠ *2080 E. Hillsboro Blvd., 33441,* ☎ *954/427–8400,* FAX *954/427–0555. 30 units. Pool. AE, D, DC, MC, V.*

$$$–$$$$ ☲ **Royal Flamingo Villas.** This small community of houselike villas, built in the 1970s, reaches from the Intracoastal Waterway to the ocean. The roomy and comfortable one- and two-bedroom villas are all condominium owned, so they're fully furnished the way owners want them. All are so quiet that you hear only the soft click of ceiling fans and kitchen clocks. The development is wisely set back a bit from the beach, which is scheduled to be restored. If you don't need lavish public facilities, this is your upscale choice at a reasonable price. ⊠ *1225 Hillsboro Mile (Rte. A1A), Hillsboro Beach 33062,* ☎ *954/427–0669, 954/427–0660, or 800/241–2477,* FAX *954/427–6110. 41 villas. Pool, putting green, shuffleboard, beach, dock, boating, coin laundry. D, MC, V.*

$$–$$$ ☲ **Carriage House Resort Motel.** This clean and tidy motel sits one block from the ocean. Run by a French-American couple, the white, two-story Colonial-style motel with black shutters is actually two buildings connected by a second-story sundeck. Steady improvements have been made

to the facility, including the addition of Bahama beds that feel and look like sofas. Kitchenettes are equipped with good-quality utensils. Rooms are self-contained and quiet and have walk-in closets and room safes. ⊠ *250 S. Ocean Blvd., 33441,* ☎ *954/427–7670,* ℻ *954/428–4790. 6 rooms, 14 efficiencies, 10 apartments. Pool, shuffleboard, coin laundry. AE, MC, V.*

Outdoor Activities and Sports

FISHING

The **Cove Marina** (⊠ Hillsborough Blvd. and the Intracoastal Waterway, ☎ 954/360–9343) is home to a deep-sea charter fleet. During the winter season there are excellent runs of sailfish, kingfish, dolphinfish, and tuna. A half-day charter costs about $325 for six people. Enter the marina through the Cove Shopping Center.

GOLF

Off Hillsborough Boulevard west of I–95, **Deer Creek Golf Club** (⊠ 2801 Country Club Blvd., ☎ 954/421–5550) has 18 holes.

SCUBA DIVING

One of the area's most popular dive boats, the 43-ft *Get Down* (⊠ Cove Marina, Hillsborough Blvd. and the Intracoastal Waterway, ☎ 954/ 421–2601) goes on morning and afternoon dives, plus evening dives on weekends. Divers can explore the marine life of nearby reefs and shipwrecks. The cost is $39 for a two-tank dive, and riders are welcome for $18.

SOUTH BROWARD

From Hollywood's Broadwalk, a 27-ft-wide thoroughfare paralleling 2 mi of palm-fringed beach, to the western reaches of Old West–flavored Davie, this region has a personality all its own. South Broward's roots are in early Florida settlements. Thus far it has avoided some of the glitz and glamour of its neighbors to the north and south, and folks here like it that way. Still, there's plenty to see and do—excellent restaurants in every price range, world-class pari-mutuels, and a new focus on the arts.

Hollywood

㉑ *7 mi south of Fort Lauderdale.*

Hollywood is a city undergoing a revival. New shops, restaurants, and art galleries are opening at a rate that rivals that of Miami's South Beach. The city recently spiffed up its Broadwalk, a wide pedestrian walkway along the beach, where Rollerbladers are as common as visitors from the North. Trendy sidewalk cafés have opened, vying for space with mom-and-pop T-shirt shops. Downtown, along Harrison Street, jazz clubs and still more fashionable restaurants are drawing young professionals to the scene.

In 1921 Joseph W. Young, a California real estate developer, began developing the community of Hollywood from the woody flatlands. It quickly became a major tourist magnet, home to casino gambling and everything else that made Florida hot. Reminders of the glory days of the Young era remain in places like Young Circle (the junction of U.S. 1 and Hollywood Boulevard) and the stately old homes that line east Hollywood streets.

The **Art and Culture Center of Hollywood** is a visual and performing arts center with an art reference library, outdoor sculpture garden, arts school, and museum store. It's just east of Young Circle. ⊠ *1650 Har-*

rison St., ☎ *954/921–3274.* 🖃 *Wed.–Sat. $3, Sun. $5 (including classical or jazz concert); donation welcome Tues.* ☉ *Tues.–Sat. 10–4, Sun. 1–4.*

With the Intracoastal Waterway to its west and the beach and ocean to the east, the 2.2-mi paved promenade known as the **Broadwalk** has been popular with pedestrians and cyclists since 1924. Expect to hear French spoken along this scenic stretch, especially during the winter; Hollywood Beach has been a favorite winter getaway for Québecois ever since Joseph Young hired French-Canadians to work here in the 1920s.

Hollywood North Beach Park is at the north end of the Broadwalk. No high-rises overpower the scene, nothing hip or chic, just a laid-back old-fashioned place for enjoying the sun, sand, and sea. ⊠ *Rte. A1A and Sheridan St.,* ☎ *954/926–2444.* 🖃 *Free; parking $5 until 2, $3 after.* ☉ *Daily 8–6.*

☾ Comprising 1,500 acres at the Intracoastal Waterway, **West Lake Park** is one of Florida's largest urban nature facilities, providing a wide range of recreational activities. You can rent a canoe, kayak, or boat with an electric motor (no fossil fuels are allowed in the park) or take the 40-minute environmental boat tour. Extensive boardwalks traverse a mangrove community, where endangered and threatened species abound. A 65-ft observation tower allows views of the entire park. More than $1 million in exhibits are on display at the **Anne Kolb Nature Center,** named after the late county commissioner who was a leading environmental advocate. A great place to take youngsters, the center's exhibit hall features 27 interactive displays, an ecology room, and a trilevel aquarium. ⊠ *1200 Sheridan St.,* ☎ *954/926–2410.* 🖃 *Weekends $1, weekdays free; exhibit hall $3.* ☉ *Daily 8–6.*

At the edge of Hollywood lies **Seminole Native Village,** a reservation where Seminole Indians both sell their arts and crafts and run a high-stakes bingo parlor and low-stakes poker tables. ⊠ *4150 N. Rte. 7,* ☎ *954/961–5140 or 954/961–3220.* ☉ *Daily 9–5.*

☾ In addition to displaying a collection of artifacts from the Seminoles and other tribes, Joe Dan and Virginia Osceola sell contemporary Native American arts and crafts at the **Anhinga Indian Museum and Art Gallery.** It's just across the street from the Seminole Native Village, though that technically puts it over the Fort Lauderdale border. ⊠ *5791 S. Rte. 7, Fort Lauderdale,* ☎ *954/581–0416.* ☉ *Daily 9–5.*

Dining and Lodging

$$$ ✕ **Martha's.** Although upstairs is more informal, the downstairs is dressy—tables adorned with orchid buds, fanned napery, etched-glass dividers, brass, rosewood, and an outdoor patio surrounded by a wild floral mural. Piano music accompanies dinner downstairs, and later a band plays for dancing, setting a supper-club mood. Both floors offer similar menus, however—chiefly Florida seafood: flaky dolphinfish in a court bouillon; shrimp dipped in a piña colada batter, rolled in coconut, and panfried with orange mustard sauce; and snapper prepared 17 ways. For dessert try sorbet and vanilla and chocolate ice cream topped with meringue and hot fudge brandy sauce. ⊠ *6024 N. Ocean Dr.,* ☎ *954/923–5444. Reservations essential. AE, D, DC, MC, V.*

$$ ✕ **Las Brisas.** There's a wonderful bistro atmosphere at this small and cozy restaurant with Mexican tiles and blue-and-white checked tablecloths beneath paddle fans. Right next to the beach, Las Brisas offers eating inside or out, and food is Argentine with an Italian flair. Antipasto salads are prepared for two; the roasted vegetables are crunchy and flavorful. A small pot sits on each table filled with *chimichurri* (a paste made of oregano, parsley, olive oil, salt, garlic, and crushed pepper), for spreading on steaks. Grilled or deep-fried fish are favorites, as are pork chops, chicken, and pasta entrées. Desserts include a rum cake, a flan like *mamacita* used to make, and a *dulce con leche* (a sweet milk pudding). The wine list is predominantly Argentine. ⊠ *600 N. Surf Rd.,* ☎ *954/923–1500. AE, MC, V. Closed Mon. No lunch.*

$–$$ ✕ Revolution 2029. This brightest new star in Hollywood was voted best new restaurant by many South Florida critics. It takes its name from a combination of the address and its role in revolutionizing (i.e., reviving) the area. The kitchen is topflight, the young staff experienced, and the atmosphere decidedly trendy. On offer is creative American cuisine, including such typical appetizers as saffron-herb-seared tuna and jumbo lump crab cake. Entrées feature ginger-plum-seared Atlantic salmon, pasta with mesquite chicken, and bourbon-glazed beef tenderloin. ⊠ *2029 Harrison St.,* ☎ *954/920–4748. AE, MC, V. Closed Mon. No lunch weekends.*

$–$$ ✕ Sushi Blues Cafe. First-class Japanese food, accompanied by live music from Thursday through Saturday evenings, is served up in a cubicle setting that's so jammed you wonder where this hip group goes by day. Chef Yozo Masuda prepares conventional and macrobiotic-influenced dishes that range from a variety of sushi and rolls (California, tuna, and the the Yozo roll, with snapper, flying-fish eggs, asparagus, and Japanese mayonnaise) to steamed veggies with tofu and steamed snapper with miso sauce. Also available are a few wines by the glass or bottle, a selection of Japanese beers, and some very un-Japanese desserts—fried banana and Swiss chocolate mousse cake. ⊠ *1836 S. Young Circle,* ☎ *954/929–9560. No credit cards. Closed Sun. No lunch.*

$ ✕ Istanbul. The owners of this Turkish delight take pride in preparing everything from scratch: hummus, tabbouleh, *adana* kebab (partially grilled, chopped lamb on skewers on a bed of yogurt-soaked pita squares, oven-finished with hot butter sauce), pizza, salads, soups, and phyllo-pie fingers filled with spinach, chicken, or meat. At lunch blue-suited attorney types dine alongside beachgoers. You should also consider getting takeout. After all, how often can you lounge on the beach with a reasonably priced Turkish picnic? ⊠ *707 N. Broadwalk,* ☎ *954/921–1263. No credit cards.*

$ ✕ Le Tub. Formerly a Sunoco gas station, this place is now a quirky waterside saloon with a seeming affection for claw-foot bathtubs. Hand-painted tubs are everywhere—under ficus, sea grape, and palm trees. The eatery is highly favored by locals for affordable food: mostly shrimp, burgers, and barbecue. ⊠ *1100 N. Ocean Dr.,* ☎ *954/921–9425. No credit cards.*

$$–$$$ 🏨 Greenbriar Beach Club. In a neighborhood of Hollywood Beach known for its flowered streets, this oceanfront all-suites hotel has been completely renovated. Though it retains its 1950s style outside, inside the rooms have been upgraded and feature full kitchens. The staff is multilingual, and the TVs even feature four Spanish and two French channels. Fronting on a 200-ft stretch of beach, the hotel bills itself as "Florida's best-kept secret," and it just could be. ⊠ *1900 S. Surf Rd., 33019,* ☎ *954/922–2606,* 𝖥𝖠𝖷 *954/923–0897. 47 suites. Pool, volleyball, beach, coin laundry. AE, MC, V.*

$$–$$$ 🏨 Manta Ray Inn. Canadians Donna and Dwayne Boucher run this
★ exemplary two-story lodging on the beach and have kept the place immaculate and the rates affordable. Dating from the 1940s, the inn offers the casual, comfortable beachfront for which vacations in Hollywood are famous. Nothing's fussy—white spaces with burgundy trim and

rattan furniture—and everything's included. Kitchens are equipped with pots, pans, and mini-appliances that make housekeeping convenient. All apartments have full closets, and all except for two-bedroom units with stalls have tub-showers. Grills are available. ⊠ *1715 S. Surf Rd., 33019,* ☎ *954/921–9666,* ℻ *954/929–8220. 12 units. Beach. No credit cards.*

$$–$$$ ⊡ **Sea Downs.** This three-story lodging directly on the Broadwalk is a good choice for efficiency or apartment living (one-bedroom apartments can be joined to make two-bedroom units). Views vary from full on the beach to rear-of-the-house prospects of neighborhood motels. Luck of the draw determines what you get. All units are comfortably done in chintz, however, with blinds, not drapes. Kitchens are fully equipped, and most units have tub-showers and closets. Housekeeping is provided once a week. In between, guests receive fresh towels daily and sheets on request, but they make their own beds. ⊠ *2900 N. Surf Rd., 33019-3704,* ☎ *954/923–4968,* ℻ *954/923–8747. 5 efficiencies, 8 1-bedroom apartments. Pool. No credit cards.*

$$ ⊡ **Driftwood on the Ocean.** This attractive late-'50s-era resort motel faces the beach at the secluded south end of Surf Road. The setting is what draws guests, but attention to maintenance and frequent refurbishing are what make it a value. Most units have a kitchen, one-bedroom apartments have a daybed, and standard rooms have a queen-size Murphy bed. All have balconies. ⊠ *2101 S. Surf Rd., 33019,* ☎ *954/923–9528,* ℻ *954/922–1062. 10 rooms, 39 efficiencies. Pool, shuffleboard, beach, bicycles, coin laundry. AE, MC, V.*

Outdoor Activities and Sports

BIKING

The 2-mi **Broadwalk,** which has its own bike path, is popular with cyclists.

DOG RACING

Hollywood Greyhound Track has dog-racing action during its December–May season. There is a clubhouse dining room. ⊠ *831 N. Federal Hwy., Hallandale,* ☎ *954/454–9400.* ⊡ *Grandstand $1, clubhouse $2.* ☉ *Racing Tues., Thurs., and Sat. 12:30 and 7:30; Sun.–Mon., Wed., and Fri. 7:30.*

FISHING

Sea Leg's III (⊠ 5400 N. Ocean Dr., ☎ 954/923–2109) runs drift-fishing trips from 8 to 12:30 and 1:30 to 6 at a cost of $23, and bottom-fishing trips from 7 PM to midnight for $25. Both trips include fishing gear.

GOLF

The **Diplomat Country Club** (⊠ 501 Diplomat Pkwy., Hallandale, ☎ 954/457–2082), with 18 holes, is south of town. The course at **Emerald Hills** (⊠ 4100 Hills Dr., ☎ 954/961–4000) has 18 holes.

HORSE RACING

Gulfstream Park Race Track is the winter home of some of the nation's top Thoroughbreds. The park greatly improved its facilities during the past few years: Admission costs have been lowered, time between races shortened, and the paddock ring elevated for better viewing by fans. The season is capped by the $500,000 Florida Derby, which always features Kentucky Derby hopefuls. Racing is held from January through mid-March. ⊠ *901 S. Federal Hwy., Hallandale,* ☎ *954/454–7000.* ⊡ *$3, including parking and program; clubhouse $5 plus $2 for reserved seat or $1.75 for grandstand.* ☉ *Racing Wed.–Mon. 1.*

Dania

㉒ *3 mi north of Hollywood, 4 mi south of Fort Lauderdale.*

This town at the south edge of Fort Lauderdale is probably best known for its antiques dealers, but there are other attractions as well.

The **Graves Museum of Archaeology & Natural History,** a little-known treasure, has the goal of becoming the "Smithsonian of the South." Its wide-ranging collections feature everything from pre-Columbian art and Greco-Roman materials to underwater artifacts from the St. Thomas harbor and a 9,000-square-ft dinosaur hall. Also on display are a 3-ton quartz crystal and dioramas on Tequesta Indian life and jaguar habitat. Monthly lectures, conferences, field trips, and a summer archaeological camp are offered. The museum bookstore is one of the best in Florida. ⊠ *481 S. Federal Hwy.,* ☎ *954/925–7770.* ☒ *$6.* ☉ *Tues.–Sat. 10–4, Sun. 1–5.*

★ The **John U. Lloyd Beach State Recreation Area** is a pleasant plot of land with a pine-shaded beach, a jetty pier where you can fish, a marina, nature trails, and canoeing on Whiskey Creek. This is a great spot to watch cruise ships entering and departing Port Everglades, to the west across the waterway. ⊠ *6503 N. Ocean Dr.,* ☎ *954/923–2833.* ☒ *$4 per vehicle with up to 8 people.* ☉ *Daily 8–sunset.*

Outdoor Activities and Sports

FISHING

The 920-ft **Dania Pier** (☎ 954/927–0640) is open around the clock. Fishing is $3 for adults (including parking), tackle rental is $6, bait is about $2, and spectators pay $1.

JAI ALAI

Dania Jai-Alai Palace has one of the fastest games on the planet, scheduled year-round. ⊠ *301 E. Dania Beach Blvd.,* ☎ *954/428–7766.* ☒ *$1, reserved seats $1.50–$7.* ☉ *Games Tues. and Sat. noon and 7:15, Wed.–Fri. 7:15; closed Wed. in June.*

Shopping

More than 75 **antiques** dealers line Federal Highway (U.S. 1), ½ mi south of the Fort Lauderdale airport and ½ mi north of Hollywood. Take the Stirling Road or Griffin Road East exit off I–95.

Davie

㉓ *4 mi west of Dania.*

This town's horse farms and estates are the closest thing to the Old West in South Florida. Folks in western wear ride their fine horses through downtown and order up takeout at "ride-through" windows. A weekly rodeo is Davie's most famous activity.

☾ Gators, crocodiles, river otters, and birds of prey can be seen at **Flamingo Gardens,** as can a 23,000-square-ft walk-through aviary, a plant house, and an Everglades museum in the pioneer Wray Home. Admission includes a half-hour guided tram ride through a citrus grove and wetlands area. ⊠ *3750 Flamingo Rd.,* ☎ *954/473–2955.* ☒ *$8.* ☉ *Daily 9:30–5:30.*

Dining

$$ ✕ **Armadillo Cafe.** Eve Montella and Kevin McCarthy have created a
★ restaurant whose southwestern theme, casual decor, and award-winning food make it worth the drive from anywhere in Broward County. It has been named to best-restaurant lists in local and national publi-

cations, and visitors from around the world have feasted on its south-western-style South Florida seafood. Though some exotic dishes are prepared, everything is served in a creative and fun atmosphere. ⊠ *4630 S.W. 6th Ave.,* ☎ *954/791–5104. AE, D, DC, MC, V. No lunch.*

Nightlife and the Arts

THE ARTS

Bailey Concert Hall (⊠ Central Campus of Broward Community College, 3501 S.W. Davie Rd., ☎ 954/475–6884) is a popular place for classical music concerts, dance, drama, and other performing arts activities, especially October–April.

NIGHTLIFE

Uncle Funny's Comedy Club (⊠ 9160 Rte. 84, ☎ 954/474–5653) has national and local comics in two shows Friday and Saturday.

Outdoor Activities and Sports

BIKING

Bicycle enthusiasts can ride at the **Brian Piccolo Park velodrome** (⊠ Sheridan St. and N.W. 101st Ave., Cooper City), south of Davie.

GOLF

Rolling Hills (⊠ 3501 Rolling Hills Circle, ☎ 954/475–3010) has 18 holes.

RODEO

The local **rodeo** (⊠ 6591 S.W. 45th St., ☎ 954/475–9787) is held every Wednesday night. Special national rodeos come to town some weekends.

FORT LAUDERDALE AND BROWARD COUNTY A TO Z

Arriving and Departing

By Bus

Greyhound Lines (☎ 800/231–2222) buses stop in Fort Lauderdale (⊠ 515 N.E. 3rd St., ☎ 954/764–6551).

By Car

Access to Broward County from north or south is via Florida's Turnpike, I–95, U.S. 1, or U.S. 441. I–75 (Alligator Alley) connects Broward with Florida's west coast and runs parallel to Route 84 within the county.

By Plane

Fort Lauderdale–Hollywood International Airport (FLHIA) (☎ 954/359–6100), 4 mi south of downtown Fort Lauderdale and just off U.S. 1, is one of Florida's busiest, serving more than 11 million passengers a year. Because the airport is a hub for Southwest Airlines and has seen an increase in international carriers, numbers continue to grow. Scheduled airlines include Air Canada (☎ 800/776–3000), Air Jamaica (☎ 800/523–5585), AirTran (☎ 800/825–8538), American (☎ 800/433–7300), Carnival (☎ 800/824–7386), Comair (☎ 800/354–9822), Continental (☎ 800/525–0280), Delta (☎ 800/221–1212), Icelandair (☎ 954/359–2735), Island Express (☎ 954/359–0380), Laker (☎ 888/525–3724), Midway (☎ 800/446–4392), Northwest (☎ 800/225–2525), Pan Am (☎ 800/359–7262), Southwest (☎ 800/435–9792), TWA (☎ 800/221–2000), United (☎ 800/241–6522), and US Airways (☎ 800/428–4322).

Broward Transit (☎ 954/357–8400) operates bus route No. 1 between the airport and its main terminal at Broward Boulevard and Northwest 1st Avenue, in the center of Fort Lauderdale. Service from the airport begins daily at 5:30 AM; the last bus from the downtown terminal to the airport leaves at 9:50 PM. The fare is $1 (50¢ for senior citizens). **Gray Line** (☎ 954/561–8886) provides limousine service to all parts of Broward County. Fares to most Fort Lauderdale beach hotels are in the $8–$10 range.

By Train

Amtrak (☎ 800/872–7245) provides daily service to the Fort Lauderdale station (⊠ 200 S.W. 21st Terr., ☎ 954/463–8251) as well as other Broward County stops at Hollywood and Deerfield Beach.

Tri-Rail (☎ 954/728–8445) operates train service daily 5 AM–11 PM (more limited on weekends) through Broward, Miami-Dade, and Palm Beach counties. There are six Broward stations west of I–95: Hillsboro Boulevard in Deerfield Beach, Cypress Creek, Fort Lauderdale, Fort Lauderdale Airport, Sheridan Street in Hollywood, and Hollywood Boulevard.

Getting Around

By Boat

Water Taxi (☎ 954/467–6677) provides service along the Intracoastal Waterway between Port Everglades and Commercial Boulevard 10 AM– 1 AM and between Atlantic Boulevard in Pompano Beach and Hillsboro Boulevard in Deerfield Beach noon–midnight. Boats stop at more than 30 restaurants, hotels, shops, and nightclubs; the fare is $7 one-way, $12 round-trip, and $15 for an all-day pass. Children under 12 accompanied by an adult pay half fare.

By Bus

Broward County Mass Transit (☎ 954/357–8400) bus service covers the entire county. The fare is $1 plus 15¢ for a transfer. Service on all beach routes starts before 6 AM and continues past 10 PM except on Sunday. Call for route information. Special seven-day tourist passes, which cost $9, are good for unlimited use on all county buses. These are available at some hotels, at Broward County libraries, and at the main bus terminal (⊠ Broward Blvd. at N.W. 1st Ave., Fort Lauderdale).

Fort Lauderdale has replaced its motorized trolley service with expanded, free **TMAX** (☎ 954/761–3543) bus service. Routes cover both the downtown loop and the beach area, with the Las Olas/Beach Line connecting major tourist sites in both places. Buses run every 30 minutes, weekdays 11:15 –3:15 and Friday and Saturday nights 7–2.

By Car

Except during rush hour, Broward County is a fairly easy place in which to drive. East–west I–595 runs from westernmost Broward County and links I–75 with I–95 and U.S. 1, providing handy access to Fort Lauderdale–Hollywood International Airport. The scenic but slow Route A1A generally parallels the beach.

By Taxi

It's difficult to hail a cab on the street. Sometimes you can pick one up at a major hotel. Otherwise, phone ahead. Fares are not cheap; meters run at a rate of $2.45 for the first mile and $1.75 for each additional mile; waiting time is 25¢ per minute. The major company serving the area is **Yellow Cab** (☎ 954/565–5400).

Contacts and Resources

Car Rentals

Agencies in the airport include **Avis** (☎ 954/359–3255), **Budget** (☎ 954/359–4700), **Dollar** (☎ 954/359–7800), **Hertz** (☎ 954/359–5281), and **National** (☎ 954/359–8303).

Emergencies

Dial **911** for police or ambulance.

Florida Poison Information Center (☎ 800/282–3171).

HOSPITALS

The following hospitals have a 24-hour emergency room: **Broward General Medical Center** (⊠ 1600 S. Andrews Ave., Fort Lauderdale, ☎ 954/355–4400; 954/355–4888 physician referral), **Columbia Plantation General Hospital** (⊠ 401 N.W. 42nd Ave., Plantation, ☎ 954/797–6470; 954/587–5010 physician referral), **Coral Springs Medical Center** (⊠ 3999 Coral Hills Dr., Coral Springs, ☎ 954/344–3000; 954/355–4888 physician referral), **Florida Medical Center South** (⊠ 6701 W. Sunrise Blvd., Plantation, ☎ 954/581–7800; 954/730–2700 physician referral), **Hollywood Medical Center** (⊠ 3600 Washington St., Hollywood, ☎ 954/966–4500; 800/237–8701 physician referral), **Holy Cross Hospital** (⊠ 4725 N. Federal Hwy., Fort Lauderdale, ☎ 954/771–8000; 954/771–9082 physician referral), **Imperial Point Medical Center** (⊠ 6401 N. Federal Hwy., Fort Lauderdale, ☎ 954/776–8500; 954/355–4888 physician referral), and **North Broward Medical Center** (⊠ 201 E. Sample Rd., Pompano Beach, ☎ 954/786–6400; 954/355–4888 physician referral).

LATE-NIGHT PHARMACIES

The following are open 24 hours: **Eckerd Drug** (⊠ 1385 S.E. 17th St., Fort Lauderdale, ☎ 954/525–8173; ⊠ 1701 E. Commercial Blvd., Fort Lauderdale, ☎ 954/771–0660; ⊠ 154 University Dr., Pembroke Pines, ☎ 954/432–5510) and **Walgreens** (⊠ 2855 Stirling Rd., Fort Lauderdale, ☎ 954/981–1104; ⊠ 5001 N. Dixie Hwy., Oakland Park, ☎ 954/772–4206; ⊠ 289 S. Federal Hwy., Deerfield Beach, ☎ 954/481–2993).

Guided Tours

BOAT TOURS

Carrie B. (⊠ Riverwalk at S.E. 5th Ave., Fort Lauderdale, ☎ 954/768–9920), a 300-passenger day cruiser, gives 90-minute tours up the New River and Intracoastal Waterway.

Jungle Queen III and IV (⊠ Radisson Bahia Mar Beach Resort, 801 Seabreeze Blvd., Fort Lauderdale, ☎ 954/462–5596) are 175-passenger and 527-passenger tour boats that take day and night cruises up the New River through the heart of Fort Lauderdale. The sightseeing cruises at 10 and 2 cost $10.95, whereas the evening dinner cruise costs $23.95. You can also take a daylong trip to Miami's Bayside Marketplace ($14.95), on Biscayne Bay, for shopping and sightseeing.

Professional Diving Charters (⊠ Radisson Bahia Mar Beach Resort, 801 Seabreeze Blvd., Fort Lauderdale, ☎ 954/761–3413) operates the 60-ft glass-bottom boat *Pro Diver II*. On Tuesday through Saturday mornings and Sunday afternoon, two-hour sightseeing trips take in offshore reefs, and snorkeling can be arranged.

ECOTOURS

National Audubon Society Education Dept. (⊠ 2514 Hollywood Blvd., Suite 400, Box 222145, Hollywood 33020-2145, ☎ 954/371–6399 or 800/498–8129), a not-for-profit organization, conducts dry-land field trips throughout South Florida and one-day, overnight, and longer boat tours as part of its program. Call in advance for availability.

HORSE TOURS

Las Olas Horse and Carriage (✉ 600 S.E. 4th St., Fort Lauderdale, ☎ 954/763–7393) operates in-town tours and transportation to and from the performing arts center Thursday through Saturday from 8 until midnight.

WALKING TOURS

Cosponsored by the Fort Lauderdale Historical Society, **Walking Tours** (✉ 219 S.W. 2nd Ave., Fort Lauderdale, ☎ 954/463–4431) traces the New River by foot.

Visitor Information

Chamber of Commerce of Greater Fort Lauderdale (✉ 512 N.E. 3rd Ave., Fort Lauderdale 33301, ☎ 954/462–6000). **Davie/Cooper City Chamber of Commerce** (✉ 4185 S.W. 64th Ave., Davie 33314, ☎ 954/581–0790). **Greater Deerfield Beach Chamber of Commerce** (✉ 1601 E. Hillsboro Blvd., Deerfield Beach 33441, ☎ 954/427–1050). **Greater Fort Lauderdale Convention & Visitors Bureau** (✉ 1850 Eller Dr., Suite 303, Fort Lauderdale 33301, ☎ 954/765–4466). **Hollywood Chamber of Commerce** (✉ 330 N. Federal Hwy., Hollywood 33019, ☎ 954/923–4000). **Lauderdale-by-the-Sea Chamber of Commerce** (✉ 4201 N. Ocean Dr., Lauderdale-by-the-Sea 33308, ☎ 954/776–1000). **Pompano Beach Chamber of Commerce** (✉ 2200 E. Atlantic Blvd., Pompano Beach 33062, ☎ 954/941–2940). **Visitors Information Center** (✉ 600 Seabreeze Blvd., Fort Lauderdale), on the beach three blocks south of Las Olas Boulevard.

5 Palm Beach and the Treasure Coast

Long stretches of golden beaches are the unifying theme along this part of the Florida coast. The southern end is anchored by the sophisticated beach towns of Boca Raton and Delray Beach. Just north is wealthy and glitzy Palm Beach, internationally known for power shopping and pricey dining. Then comes the Treasure Coast, a collection of quaint, rustic, and uncrowded beach towns and peaceful nature preserves.

THIS SECTION OF ATLANTIC COAST defies categorization. Though it's easy to affix labels—the stretch from Palm Beach to Boca Raton is considered the northern reaches of the Gold Coast (which in its entirety extends all the way to Miami), while north of Palm Beach is called the Treasure Coast—the individual communities along this section of the Florida coastline all have their own personalities. Here you'll find the center-stage glitziness of Palm Beach and the low-key quiet of Hutchinson Island. The unifying attraction is compelling—golden beaches bordered by luxuriant palms. The arts also flourish here. In town after town you will find a profusion of museums, galleries, theaters, and groups committed to historic preservation.

By Herb Hiller

Updated by
Pamela
Acheson

The focus of the region is indisputably Palm Beach. Although tourists may go to Delray Beach or Jupiter Island or scores of other towns to catch some rays and feel sand between their toes, most stop in Palm Beach for a completely different pastime: gawking. The gold on this stretch of coast is the kind you put in a vault, and for a century now the island town has been a hotbed of conspicuous consumption. Palm Beach is the richest city in Florida and would easily compete for honors with places like Monaco and Malibu as the most affluent community in the world. It has long been the winter address for families with names such as Rockefeller, Vanderbilt, Kennedy, and Trump.

It all started with Henry Morrison Flagler, cofounder of Standard Oil, who, in addition to bringing the railroad to Florida in the 1890s, brought his own view of civilization. The poor and middle-class fishermen and laborers who inhabited the place in the pre-Flagler era were moved a mile west or so to West Palm Beach. Still a proletariat cousin, West Palm is home to those who serve Flagler's successors on the island.

The town of Palm Beach represents only 1% of the land area in Palm Beach County, however. The rest is given over to sprawling West Palm Beach, classic Florida beach towns, malls, and to the west, citrus farms, the Arthur R. Marshall–Loxahatchee National Wildlife Refuge, and Lake Okeechobee, the largest lake in Florida and one of the country's hot spots for bass-fishing devotees.

Also worth exploring is the Treasure Coast, which encompasses the northernmost part of Palm Beach County plus Martin, St. Lucie, and Indian River counties. Although late to develop, the Treasure Coast now has its share of malls and beachfront condominiums, and yet much of its shoreline is laid-back and peaceful. Inland is largely devoted to citrus and sugar production and cattle ranching in rangelands of pine and palmetto scrub.

Along the coast the broad tidal lagoon called the Indian River separates the barrier islands from the mainland. In addition to sheltering boaters on the Intracoastal Waterway and playing nursery for many saltwater game fish, it's a natural radiator, keeping frost away from the tender orange and grapefruit trees that grow near its banks. Sea turtles come ashore at night from April to August to lay their eggs on the beaches.

Pleasures and Pastimes

Beaches

Half the towns in the area include the word *beach* in their name, and for good reason. Here are miles of golden strands—some relatively remote and uncrowded, some buzzing with activity, and all blessed with the kind of blue-green waters you just won't find farther north. Among the least crowded are those at Hobe Sound National Wildlife Refuge and Fort Pierce Inlet State Recreation Area. Boca Raton's three beaches are among the most popular.

Dining
Not surprisingly, numerous elegant establishments offer Continental and contemporary cuisine that stacks up well among foodies, but the area also has many good, casual waterfront watering holes that serve up a mean fried or blackened grouper. Just an hour west, on Lake Okeechobee, you can dine on panfried catfish a few hundred yards from where it was caught. Lower-price early bird menus, a Florida hallmark, are offered by most restaurants.

Fishing
Within a 50-mi radius of Palm Beach, you'll find virtually every form of fishing except, of course, ice fishing. If it involves a hook and a line, you can do it here—year-round. Charter a boat for deep-sea fishing out of towns from Boca Raton to Sebastian Inlet. West of Vero Beach, there's tremendous marsh fishing for catfish, bass, and perch. Lake Okeechobee is one of the world's bass-fishing capitals.

Golf
Palm Beach County is to golf what Saudi Arabia is to oil. For openers, there's the Professional Golfing Association (PGA) headquarters at the PGA National Resort & Spa in Palm Beach Gardens (a mere five golf courses). In all, there are approximately 150 public, private, and semiprivate golf courses in Palm Beach County. A Golf-A-Round program, in which more than 100 hotels participate, lets you play at one of 10 courses each day, with no greens fees.

Shopping
Some of the most expensive stores in the United States cluster on Worth Avenue, which is comparable to Rodeo Drive in Beverly Hills as an upscale shopper's nirvana. But there's also plenty of middle-American shopping nearby, including the likes of the Palm Beach Mall and the Manufacturers Outlet Center. You can browse in art galleries and antiques shops in Vero Beach, Delray Beach, and Boca Raton's Mizner Park.

Exploring Palm Beach and the Treasure Coast

The center of most any visit to the area is Palm Beach proper (and it certainly is!). Not only is it within an hour's drive of most of the region, but its Gatsby-era architecture, stunning mansions, and highbrow shopping make it unlike any other place in Florida. From there you can head in any of three directions: south along the Gold Coast toward Boca Raton, north to the mainland and barrier-island treasures of the Treasure Coast, or west for some inland delights.

Great Itineraries
Tucked into an island 12 mi long and about ¼ mi wide, Palm Beach is easy to cover thoroughly in just a day or two. If you have several days, you can take in a lot of varied sights, exploring everything from galleries to subtropical wildlife preserves, and with a week you'll easily be able to see the whole area. Of course you could just do what a lot of visitors prefer—laze around soaking up the rays and the atmosphere.

Numbers in the text correspond to numbers in the margin and on the Gold Coast and Treasure Coast and the Palm Beach and West Palm Beach maps.

IF YOU HAVE 3 DAYS

With a short amount of time, make ⊞ **Palm Beach** ①–⑪ your base. On the first day start in the middle of downtown, **Worth Avenue** ⑦, to do some window-shopping and gallery browsing. After you've refreshed yourself with a *très* chic bistro lunch, head for that other must-see on even the shortest itinerary: the **Henry Morrison Flagler Museum** ②. Your second day is for the beach; two good options are Lantana Public Beach, which has great food concessions, and Oceanfront Park, in **Boynton Beach** ㉔. Spend the better part of your last day exploring attractions you wouldn't expect to find in South Florida, such as the Morikami Museum and Japanese Gardens in nearby **Delray Beach** ㉖. Trite as it may sound, it's like a one-day visit to Japan.

IF YOU HAVE 5 DAYS

With five days you can be more contemplative at the galleries and museums, more leisurely at the beaches, and have time for more serendipitous exploring. Stay in ⊞ **Palm Beach** ①–⑪ for two nights. The first day visit the **Henry Morrison Flagler Museum** ② and the luxury hotel known as the **Breakers** ④, another Flagler legacy. Then head to **Worth Avenue** ⑦ for a leisurely lunch and an afternoon of window-shopping. On the second day drive over to **West Palm Beach** ⑫–㉑ and the **Norton Gallery of Art** ⑬, which has an extensive collection of 19th-century French Impressionists. On day three, choose between making an overnight visit to ⊞ **Lake Okeechobee,** the bass-fishing capital of the world, and staying in Palm Beach another night and driving a half hour to explore the Arthur R. Marshall–Loxahatchee National Wildlife Refuge. Head south to ⊞ **Boca Raton** ㉗ on the fourth day, and check into a beachfront hotel before spending the rest of the afternoon wandering through Mizner Park's shops. On your fifth day meander through the Boca Raton Museum of Art in the morning and get some sun at South Beach Park after lunch.

IF YOU HAVE 7 DAYS

With an entire week you can see the Gold and Treasure coasts thoroughly, with time left to fit in such recreational pursuits as taking sailboard or croquet lessons, catching a polo match, or going deep-sea fishing or jet skiing. Stay two nights in ⊞ **Palm Beach** ①–⑪, spending your first day taking in its best sights, mentioned above. On day two, rent a bicycle and follow the 10-mi path along Lake Worth, providing a great look at the backyards of many of Palm Beach's big mansions. Drive north on day three, across Jerry Thomas Bridge to Singer Island and John D. MacArthur Beach State Park. Spend the third night farther north, on ⊞ **Hutchinson Island** ㉝, and relax the next morning on the beach in front of your hotel. On your way back south, explore **Stuart** ㉜ and its tiny but interesting historic downtown area, and pause at the Arthur R. Marshall–Loxahatchee National Wildlife Refuge before ending up in ⊞ **Boca Raton** ㉗, for three nights at a beachfront hotel. Split day five between shopping at Mizner Park and beaching it at South Beach Park. Day six is for cultural attractions: the Boca Raton Museum of Art followed by the galleries and interesting Japanese museum in **Delray Beach** ㉖. If you have time on your last day, take in one of Boca Raton's other two beaches, Spanish River and Red Reef parks.

When to Tour Palm Beach and the Treasure Coast

The weather is optimum November through May, but the trade-off is that facilities are more crowded and prices somewhat higher. In summer you'll need a tolerance for heat and humidity if you want to spend time outside; also watch for frequent afternoon downpours. If you're set on watching the sea turtles come ashore to nest, make sure to visit between late April and August, and remember that nesting occurs at night. No matter when you visit, bring insect repellent if you plan outdoor outings.

PALM BEACH

78 mi north of Miami.

Setting the tone in this incredibly wealthy town is the baroque architecture of developer Addison Mizner, who began building homes, stores, and public buildings here in the 1920s and whose Moorish-Gothic style has influenced virtually all the landmarks of the community. Thanks to Mizner and those influenced by him, Palm Beach looks like a kind of neo-Camelot, the perfect backdrop for a playground of the rich and famous.

Exploring Palm Beach

You can get a taste of what this town is all about when you squeeze into a parking place on Worth Avenue, among the Mercedes and Bentleys, and head to its boutiques to rub Versace-covered shoulders with shoppers whose credit card limits likely exceed the gross national product of Liechtenstein. Away from downtown, along County Road and Ocean Boulevard (the shore road, also designated as Route A1A), are Palm Beach's other defining landmarks: mansions. In some parts they're fronted by thick 20-ft hedgerows and topped by the seemingly de rigueur barrel-tile roofs. The low wall that separates the dune-top shore road from the sea hides a badly eroded beach in many places. Here and there, where the strand deepens a bit, homes are built directly on the beach.

A Good Tour

Start on the north end of the island with a quick look at the sandstone and limestone minicanyon that is the **Canyon of Palm Beach** ①, on Lake Way Road. Drive south, across Royal Poinciana Way, to the **Henry Morrison Flagler Museum** ②, in a 73-room palace that was once Flagler's home. From here backtrack to Royal Poinciana Way, turn right, and follow the road until it ends at North County Road and the Spanish-style **Palm Beach Post Office** ③. Here County Road changes from north to south designations. Take it southbound and look for the long, stately driveway on the left that leads to the **Breakers** ④, a famous hotel built in the style of an Italian Renaissance palace. Continue south on South County Road about ¼ mi farther to **Bethesda-by-the-Sea** ⑤, a Spanish Gothic Episcopal church. Keep driving south on South County Road until you reach Royal Palm Way; turn right, then right again on Cocoanut Row. In just a few blocks you'll see the gardens of the **Society of the Four Arts** ⑥.

Head south on Cocoanut Row until you reach famed **Worth Avenue** ⑦, where you can park and walk around—that is, if the prices in the art galleries and designer shops haven't knocked your socks off. After taking in the sights, drive south on South County Road for a peek at some magnificent estates, including **El Solano** ⑧, built by Addison Mizner, and **Mar-A-Lago** ⑨, now owned by Donald Trump. At this point you might want to get out of the car for some sun and fresh air, so continue south on South County Road until you reach **Phipps Ocean Park** ⑩ and its stretch of sandy beach, or head back toward town along South Ocean Boulevard to the popular **Mid-Town Beach** ⑪.

TIMING

You'll need half a day minimum to see these sights. A few of the destinations are closed Sunday or Monday, so be sure to do your sightseeing during daytime business hours. In winter be prepared for heavy traffic, and consider touring in the morning and when roads are less congested.

Sights to See

⑤ Bethesda-by-the-Sea. This Spanish Gothic Episcopal church was built in 1927 by the first Protestant congregation in southeast Florida. Next to it are the formal, ornamental **Cluett Memorial Gardens.** ⊠ *141 S. County Rd.,* ☏ *561/655–4554.* ☉ *Church and gardens daily 8–5; services Sept.–May, Sun. 8, 9, and 11; June–Aug., Sun. 8 and 10; call for weekday schedule.*

★ **④ The Breakers.** Originally built by Henry Flagler in 1895 and rebuilt by his descendants after a fire in 1925, this luxury hotel was one of the starting points of Florida tourism. It resembles an ornate Italian Renaissance palace and was renovated to the tune of $150 million not long ago. Walk into the lobby and take a look at the painted arched ceilings hung with crystal chandeliers, and peek into the ornate Florentine Dining Room with its 15th-century Flemish tapestries. ⊠ *1 S. County Rd.,* ☏ *561/655–6611.*

① Canyon of Palm Beach. A road cut about 25 ft deep through a ridge of reddish-brown sandstone and oolite limestone gives you a brief feeling of being in the desert Southwest. ⊠ *Lake Way Rd.*

⑧ El Solano. Perhaps no Palm Beach mansion represents the town's ongoing generations of flashbulb fame better than this one. The Spanish-style home was built by Addison Mizner for himself in 1925. Mizner then sold it to Harold Vanderbilt, and the property made the rounds of socialites, photo shoots, and expansions until it was bought by John Lennon and Yoko Ono 10 months before Lennon's death. Now owned by a banking executive, El Solano is not open to the public. ⊠ *721 S. County Rd.*

★ **② Henry Morrison Flagler Museum.** The opulence of Florida's Gilded Age is still apparent at Whitehall, the palatial 73-room mansion Henry Flagler had built in 1901 for his third wife, Mary Lily Kenan, and now home to a museum. Then-famous architects John Carrère and Thomas Hastings were instructed to spare no expense in creating the finest home they could imagine. They did as they were told, and Whitehall rivals some of the fine palaces of Europe. In 1960 Flagler's granddaughter, Jean Flagler Matthews, bought the building and made it a museum. On display are many of the original furnishings, an art collection, a 1,200-pipe organ, and exhibits on the history of the Florida East Coast Railway. Flagler's personal railroad car, the *Rambler,* is parked behind the building. A tour by well-informed guides takes about an hour. ⊠ *1 Whitehall Way,* ☏ *561/655–2833.* ☐ *$7.* ☉ *Tues.–Sat. 10–5, Sun. noon–5.*

⑨ Mar-A-Lago. Still one of the grandest of homes along Ocean Boulevard, the former estate of breakfast-food heiress Marjorie Meriweather Post has Italianate towers silhouetted against the sky. It's currently owned by real estate magnate Donald Trump, who first turned it into a membership club and is continuing with plans to subdivide the property, which curves for ⅓ mi along the road. ⊠ *1100 S. Ocean Blvd.*

⑪ Mid-Town Beach. This small beach south of Worth Avenue is especially popular because it's so close to town. But be warned: The only parking meters along Ocean Boulevard—ergo, the only convenient public

Gold Coast and Treasure Coast

Palm Beach and West Palm Beach

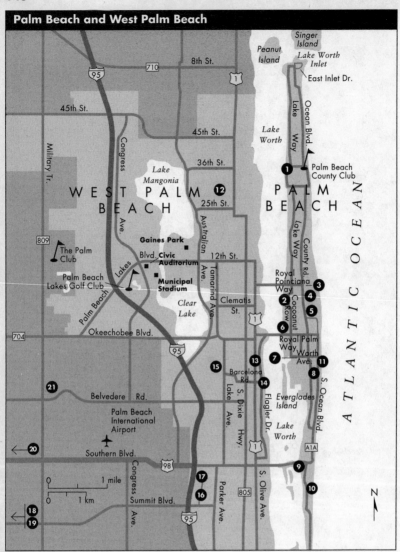

Ann Norton Sculpture
Gardens, **14**

Armory Arts
Center, **15**

Bethesda-by-
the-Sea, **5**

The Breakers, **4**

Canyon of Palm
Beach, **1**

Dreher Park Zoo, **16**

El Solano, **8**

Henry Morrison
Flagler Museum, **2**

Lion Country
Safari, **20**

Mar-A-Lago, **9**

Mid-Town Beach, **11**

Mounts Horticultural
Learning Center, **21**

Norton Gallery of
Art, **13**

Okeeheelee Nature
Center, **19**

Old Northwood
Historic District, **12**

Palm Beach Post
Office, **3**

Phipps Ocean
Park, **10**

Pine Jog
Environmental
Education Center, **18**

Society of the Four
Arts, **6**

South Florida
Science Museum,
Planetarium, and
Aquarium, **17**

Worth Avenue, **7**

beach access—are found between Worth Avenue and Royal Palm Way. ⊠ *400 S. Ocean Blvd.,* ☎ *no phone.* 🅿 *Parking 25¢ for 15 mins.* ☉ *Daily 8–8.*

❸ Palm Beach Post Office. Spanish-style architecture defines the exterior, while inside murals depict Seminole Indians in the Everglades and stately royal and coconut palms. ⊠ *95 N. County Rd.,* ☎ *561/832–1867.*

❿ Phipps Ocean Park. Besides the ubiquitous beautiful beach, some picnic tables, and grills, this park contains a Palm Beach County landmark in the **Little Red Schoolhouse.** Dating from 1886, it was the first schoolhouse in what was then Dade County and is open Monday–Saturday 8–8. ⊠ *2145 S. Ocean Blvd.,* ☎ *no phone.* 🅿 *Parking 25¢ for 20 mins.*

❻ Society of the Four Arts. In addition to presenting cultural events, this privately endowed arts and educational institution incorporates an exhibition hall, library, 13 distinct gardens, and the Philip Hulitar Sculpture Garden. ⊠ *Four Arts Plaza,* ☎ *561/655–7226.* 🅿 *$3.* ☉ *Galleries Dec.–mid-Apr., Mon.–Sat. 10–5, Sun. 2–5; library, children's library, and gardens Nov.–May, weekdays 10–5, Sat. 9–1.*

★ ❼ Worth Avenue. This ¼-mi-long street is synonymous with posh, pricey shopping. A stroll amid the Moorish architecture of its scores of top-drawer shops—Cartier, Charles Jourdan, and Giorgio Armani, to name a few—gives you a taste of what the good life must be like. ⊠ *Between Cocoanut Row and S. Ocean Blvd.*

Dining and Lodging

$$$–$$$$ ✕ **Café L'Europe.** This is one of the most popular and elegant restau-
★ rants in Palm Beach. Sumptuous oak paneling, dim lighting, and elaborate flower bouquets set the mood. Ladies-who-lunch can enjoy spa cuisine, whereas evening guests dine expensively on specialty pastas such as *orecchiette* with broccoli rapini, Italian sausage, tomato, and ricotta; seafood dishes like sautéed pompano with herbal mustard crust; or a traditional Wiener schnitzel with spinach spaëtzle and red cabbage. Veal chops and steaks are on the menu, too. Apple pancake with lingonberries is the signature dessert, and a caviar bar has a wide assortment of the delicacy, with prices to match. ⊠ *331 S. County Rd.,* ☎ *561/655–4020. Reservations essential. Jacket required. AE, DC, MC, V. No lunch Sun.*

$$$–$$$$ ✕ **Janeiro.** Versace-designed Rosenthall china and Reidel crystal on
★ black-on-black tablecloths provide the setting for a spectacularly elegant contemporary French dining experience. Wild mushrooms sautéed with garlic, scallopini of goose liver with shredded turnips and port wine, and baked goat cheese with tomatoes in a pastry shell are some of the appetizers. Entrées, brought to the table under silver domes, include Mediterranean bouillabaisse, lemon sole fillets with tomato and black squid and spinach lasagna, boneless rack of lamb stuffed with spinach and wild mushrooms wrapped in puff pastry, and a beef fillet with green peppercorn sauce. Save room for the chocolate soufflé dessert. It's topped with edible 24-carat gold leaf! ⊠ *191 Bradley Pl.,* ☎ *561/659–5223. Reservations essential. Jacket required. AE, DC, MC, V. No lunch Sun.*

$$–$$$$ ✕ **Amici.** Night after night a steady stream of six-figure automobiles
★ pulls into the valet parking spot of this trendy eatery. Inside, the lighting is dim, and tables are close together but never empty. The northern Italian menu features such house specialties as antipasti of cold marinated and grilled vegetables, rigatoni with spicy tomato sauce and

roasted eggplant, potato gnocchi with grilled chicken and roasted peppers, grilled veal chops, risottos, and a long list of pizzas cooked in the wood-burning oven. There are nightly pasta and fresh fish specials as well. If you want to avoid the crowds, stop by for a late lunch. ⊠ 228 S. County Rd., ☎ 561/832–0201. Reservations essential. AE, D, DC, MC, V.

$$–$$$$ ✕ **Chuck & Harold's.** Ivana Trump, Larry Holmes, Brooke Shields, and Michael Bolton are among the celebrities who have eaten at this combination power-lunch bar, sidewalk café, and jazz–big band garden, which is popular day and night. Locals who want to be part of the scenery and tourists hot to people-watch catch a seat and linger in the outdoor café, next to pots of red and white begonias mounted on the sidewalk rail. Specialties include conch chowder, terrific hamburgers, an onion-crunchy gazpacho, grilled steaks, and tangy key lime pie. A big blackboard lists daily specials and celebrity birthdays. ⊠ 207 Royal Poinciana Way, ☎ 561/659–1440. AE, DC, MC, V.

$$$ ✕ **Bice Ristorante.** This dining establishment is so thoroughly Italian that it's easy to be disappointed when the parking attendant speaks to you in English. Brilliant flower arrangements and lots of brass accent a dark beige-and-yellow color scheme. Aromas of basil, chives, and oregano fill the air as waiters bring out the divine home-baked focaccia accompanying such house favorites as *Robespierre alla moda della bice* (sliced steak topped with arugula salad) and *costoletta di vitello impanata alla milanese* (breaded veal cutlet with a tomato salad). The name is short for Beatrice, mother of Roberto Ruggeri, who founded the original in Milan in 1926 and has opened branches here and in other smart places since then. ⊠ 313¼ Worth Ave., ☎ 561/835–1600. Jacket required. AE, DC, MC, V.

$$–$$$ ✕ **Jo's.** With 150 seats and a full bar, this pastel, latticed, and mirrored French restaurant, decorated with lavish fresh flower arrangements, occupies a prominent corner on South County Road. Chef Richard Kline, son of the owner, Jo, holds sway in the kitchen. Look for the three-soup sampler (lobster bisque, green pea soup, and beef consommé) as well as osso buco and boned half roast duckling with orange—always moist but never rare. For dessert try the tart Tatin (upside-down apple pie) or fresh raspberries. ⊠ 375 S. County Rd., ☎ 561/659–6776. AE, MC, V.

$$–$$$ ✕ **Ta-boó.** Dressed in gorgeous pinks, greens, and florals, the spaces
★ of this Worth Avenue landmark are divided into discreet salons: One resembles a courtyard, another an elegant living room with a fireplace, and a third a skylighted gazebo. The Tiki Tiki bar makes an elegant salon for the neighborhood crowd. Appetizers range from a very proletariat nachos grande with chili to Beluga caviar; dinners include chicken and arugula from the grill, prime rib, steaks, frogs' legs, and main course salads. White pizza with goat and mozzarella cheeses, pesto, and sweet roasted red peppers is a favorite. Drop in late at night during the season, and you're bound to spot a famous face or two. ⊠ 221 Worth Ave., ☎ 561/835–3500. AE, MC, V.

$$ ✕ **Dempsey's.** This New York–style Irish pub under the palms comes complete with paisley table covers, plaid café curtains, burgundy banquettes, horse prints, and antique coach lanterns. When major sports events are on the big TV, this place is always packed, noisy, and as electric as a frenzied Friday at the stock exchange. Along with much socializing, people enjoy Maine lobster, fresh seafood, chicken hash Dempsey (with a dash of Scotch), and Welsh rarebit, followed by hot apple pie. ⊠ 50 Cocoanut Row, ☎ 561/835–0400. AE, MC, V.

$ ✕ **TooJay's.** New York deli food served in a bright California-style setting—what could be more Florida? The menu at this spot, one of nine TooJay's in the Sunshine State, includes matzo ball soup, corned beef on rye, and a killer cake made with five kinds of chocolate and topped with whipped cream. A salami-on-rye sandwich layered with onions, Muenster cheese, coleslaw, and Russian dressing is a house favorite. On the High Holidays look for carrot tzimmes (a sweet vegetable compote), brisket, and roast chicken. Wisecracking waitresses keep the pace fast. ⊠ *313 Royal Poinciana Plaza,* ☎ *561/659–7232. AE, DC, MC, V. Beer and wine only.*

$$$$ 🏨 **Brazilian Court.** Spread out over half a block, the yellow-stucco Span-
★ ish-style facade with a red-tile roof reminds you of this hotel's Roaring '20s origins. Thanks to a multimillion-dollar renovation completed in 1997 this terrific spot has undergone a luxurious transformation. Rooms and spacious suites are now decorated in soft, muted tones, and original art hangs on the walls. Remodeled bathrooms are marble and completely modernized. The closets, however, are still big enough for people who once brought trunks for the entire season (some still do). Outside, stone fountains and private courtyards (one with a wishing well) offer peaceful oases. ⊠ *301 Australian Ave., 33480,* ☎ *561/655–7740, 800/552–0335; 800/228–6852 in Canada;* 🖷 *561/655–0801. 63 rooms, 40 suites. Restaurant, bar, pool, beauty salon, exercise room, library. AE, D, DC, MC, V.*

$$$$ 🏨 **The Breakers.** Dating from 1926 and enlarged in 1969, this opu-
★ lent seven-story Italian Renaissance–style resort sprawls over 140 splendidly manicured acres. Cupids frolic in the Florentine fountain at the main entrance, while majestic ceiling vaults and frescoes grace the lobby and the long hallways that lead to restaurants and ballrooms. Balancing formality with casualness, the hotel no longer *requires* men to wear jackets and ties everywhere after 7 PM. A recent $75 million renovation completely modernized the rooms and bathrooms and enhanced the resort's elegance without sacrificing old-world luxury. Many rooms have been enlarged, and all have been redecorated. ⊠ *1 S. County Rd., 33480,* ☎ *561/655–6611 or 800/833–3141,* 🖷 *561/659–8403. 572 rooms, 48 suites. 5 restaurants, 2 bars, pool, saunas, 2 18-hole golf courses, putting green, 14 tennis courts, croquet, health club, jogging, shuffleboard, beach, boating, children's programs. AE, D, DC, MC, V.*

$$$$ 🏨 **The Colony.** What distinguishes this legendary pale, pale yellow Georgian-style hotel only steps from Worth Avenue is its attentive staff, who are youthful yet experienced. There's a buzz of competence and a true desire to please. Cool and classical guest rooms have fluted blond cabinetry and matching draperies and bedcovers in deep floral prints. As in many older hotels, bathrooms are small. The "scene" for glitterati after charity balls at the Breakers, this is where Roxanne Pulitzer retreated after her infamous seven-week marriage in 1992. ⊠ *155 Hammon Ave., 33480,* ☎ *561/655–5430 or 800/521–5525,* 🖷 *561/832–7318. 63 rooms, 39 suites and apartments, 7 villas. Restaurant, bar, pool, spa. AE, D, DC, MC, V.*

$$$$ 🏨 **Four Seasons Ocean Grand.** This 6-acre property at the south end
★ of town is coolly elegant but warm in detail. Marble, art, fanlight windows, swagged drapes, chintz, and palms create a serene atmosphere. Rooms are spacious, with a separate seating area and private balcony, and many have gorgeous ocean views. On weekend evenings year-round, piano music accompanies cocktails in the Living Room lounge. On some weekend nights in season, jazz groups perform, and there are classical recitals on Sunday afternoon. Although its name suggests grandeur, this four-story hotel with a long beach is more like a small jewel. ⊠ *2800 S. Ocean Blvd., 33480,* ☎ *561/582–2800 or 800/432–2335,* 🖷 *561/547–1557. 210 rooms and suites. 2 restaurants, bar, pool, saunas, 3 tennis courts, health club, beach. AE, D, DC, MC, V.*

$$$–$$$$ ☒ **Palm Beach Historic Inn.** Longtime hoteliers Harry and Barbara Kehr manage this delightfully unexpected inn in the heart of downtown. The setting, tucked between Town Hall and a seaside residential block, combines town and vacationland. B&B touches include flowers, wine and fruit, snacks, seasonal turndown, tea and cookies in rooms, and a generous Continental breakfast. Guest rooms tend to the frilly with lots of lace, ribbons, and scalloped edges. Most are furnished with Victorian antiques and reproductions (some out of old mansions, others more secondhand than authentic) and chiffon wall drapings above the bed. A 1944 Coke machine still supplies an 8-ounce bottle for a dime. Bath towels are as thick as parkas. ☒ *365 S. County Rd., 33480,* ☎ *561/832–4009,* ℻ *561/832–6255. 9 rooms, 4 suites. Library. AE, D, DC, MC, V.*

$$$–$$$$ ☒ **Palm Beach Sea Lord Hotel.** If you don't need glamour or brand names, and you're not the B&B type, this garden-style hideaway is for you. Choose from accommodations that overlook Lake Worth, the pool, or the ocean; the reasonably priced café adds to the at-home, comfy feeling and attracts repeat customers. Units are plain but not cheap in season and come with carpet, at least one comfortable chair, small or large refrigerator, and tropical print fabrics. ☒ *2315 S. Ocean Blvd., 33480,* ☎ ℻ *561/582–1461. 23 rooms, 11 apartments, 6 efficiencies. Restaurant, pool, beach. D, MC, V.*

$$$–$$$$ ☒ **Plaza Inn.** This three-story hotel, Deco-designed from the 1930s,
★ operates B&B style; a full breakfast is included. The pool, gardens, and piano bar have the intimate charm of a trysting place for the likes of Cary Grant and Katharine Hepburn. Inn owner Ajit Asrani is a retired Indian army officer who raises show horses and polo ponies. The courteous staff and location in the heart of Palm Beach are pluses, and the uncluttered, individually decorated rooms with phone and refrigerator provide a welcome change from other B&Bs. So, too, does the appealing courtyard with waterfalls and a pool. ☒ *215 Brazilian Ave., 33480,* ☎ *561/832–8666 or 800/233–2632,* ℻ *561/835–8776. 50 rooms and suites. Bar, pool, hot tub. AE, MC, V.*

Nightlife and the Arts

The Arts
The **Royal Poinciana Playhouse** (☒ 70 Royal Poinciana Plaza, ☎ 561/659–3310) presents seven productions each year between December and April. **Society of the Four Arts** (☒ Four Arts Plaza, ☎ 561/655–7226) offers concerts, lectures, and Friday films December–March. Movie tickets can be purchased at time of showing; other tickets may be obtained a week in advance.

Nightlife
Cheek-to-cheek dancers head to the **Colony** (☒ 155 Hammon Ave., ☎ 561/655–5430) for a spin around the dance floor. A trio plays Thursday, Friday, and Saturday nights. As the weekend dinner crowd thins out, late-night party seekers fill up **Ta-boó** (☒ 221 Worth Ave., ☎ 561/835–3500), where a DJ keeps everyone on their feet.

Outdoor Activities and Sports

Biking
Bicycling is an excellent way to get a good look at Palm Beach, which is as small and flat as the top of a billiard table (and just as green). The wonderful, 10-mi, palm-fringed **Palm Beach Bicycle Trail** (☒ Parallel to Lake Way) skirts the backyards of many palatial mansions and the edge of Lake Worth. Just a block from the bike trail, the **Palm Beach**

Trail Bicycle Shop (⊠ 223 Sunrise Ave., ☎ 561/659–4583) rents bikes by the hour or day.

Dog Racing

Since 1932 the hounds have been racing year-round at the 4,300-seat **Palm Beach Kennel Club.** There are also simulcasts of jai alai and horse racing, as well as wagering on live and televised sports. ⊠ *1111 N. Congress Ave.,* ☎ *561/683–2222.* ▣ *50¢, terrace level $1, parking free.* ☉ *Racing Mon. 12:30; Wed.–Thurs. and Sat. 12:30 and 7:30; Fri. 7:30; Sun. 1; simulcasts Mon. and Fri. noon, Tues. 12:30.*

Golf

Breakers Hotel Golf Club (⊠ 1 S. County Rd., ☎ 561/655–6611 or 800/833–3141) has 36 holes. The **Palm Beach Par 3** (⊠ 2345 S. Ocean Blvd., ☎ 561/547–0598) has 18 holes, including 4 on the Atlantic and 3 on the inland waterway.

Shopping

One of the world's showcases for high-quality shopping, **Worth Avenue** runs ¼-mi east–west across Palm Beach, from the beach to Lake Worth. The street has more than 250 shops, and many upscale stores (Cartier, Gucci, Hermès, Pierre Deux, Saks Fifth Avenue, and Van Cleef & Arpels) are represented, their merchandise appealing to the discerning tastes of Palm Beach clientele. The six blocks of **South County Road** north of Worth Avenue have appealing stores. For specialty items (out-of-town newspapers, health foods, and books), try the shops along the north side of **Royal Poinciana Way.**

WEST PALM BEACH

2 mi west of Palm Beach.

Long considered Palm Beach's impoverished cousin, West Palm is now economically vibrant in its own right. Far larger in area than its upper-crust neighbor to the east, it has become the cultural, entertainment, and business center of the county and of the region to the north. Sparkling government buildings like the mammoth $124 million Palm Beach County Judicial Center and Courthouse and the State Administrative Building exemplify the health of the city's corporate life, and facilities such as the $60 million Kravis Center for the Performing Arts attest to the strength of the arts and entertainment community.

Downtown

The heart of revived West Palm Beach is an attractive downtown area, which has been spurred on by an active historic preservation movement. Along beautifully landscaped Clematis Street, you'll find boutiques and restaurants in charmingly restored buildings and exuberant nightlife that mimics that of South Beach. Even at the downtown's fringes, you'll encounter sights of cultural interest. There's a free downtown shuttle by day and free on-street parking at night and on weekends.

A Good Tour

From a geographical perspective, the best place to start is at the north end of the city with a walk through the **Old Northwood Historic District** ⑫, on the National Register of Historic Places. Drive south on U.S. 1, take a left onto 12th Street, and then a right onto South Olive Avenue to view the exceptional art collection at the **Norton Gallery of Art** ⑬. From here it is just a few blocks farther south to the peaceful **Ann Norton Sculpture Gardens** ⑭. Finally, drive west across Barcelona Road to the **Armory Arts Center** ⑮ and check out the current exhibit.

Late morning is a good time to start this tour, so you can walk through the historic neighborhood before having lunch on Clematis Street. In the afternoon you'll need about three hours at the various arts-oriented sights. It's important to take this tour during daytime business hours.

Sights to See

⑭ Ann Norton Sculpture Gardens. This monument to the late American sculptor Ann Weaver Norton, second wife of Norton Gallery founder Ralph H. Norton, consists of charming 3-acre grounds displaying seven granite figures and six brick megaliths. The plantings were designed by Norton, an environmentalist, to attract native bird life. ⊠ *253 Barcelona Rd.,* ☎ *561/832–5328.* ☜ *$3.* ◷ *Tues.–Sat. 10–4 (call ahead; schedule is not always observed) or by appointment.*

⑮ Armory Arts Center. Built by the WPA in 1939, the facility is now a complete visual arts center. Its gallery hosts rotating exhibitions, and classes are held throughout the year. ⊠ *1703 S. Lake Ave.,* ☎ *561/ 832–1776.* ☜ *Free.* ◷ *Weekdays 9–5, Sun. 10–2.*

★ ⑬ Norton Gallery of Art. Constructed in 1941 by steel magnate Ralph H. Norton, this museum boasts an extensive permanent collection of 19th- and 20th-century American and European paintings with special emphasis on 19th-century French Impressionists. There are also Chinese bronze and jade sculptures, a sublime outdoor patio with sculptures on display in a tropical garden, and a library housing more than 3,000 art books and periodicals. Nine galleries showcase traveling exhibits as well as art from the permanent collection. ⊠ *1451 S. Olive Ave.,* ☎ *561/832–5194.* ☜ *$5.* ◷ *Tues.–Sat. 10–5, Sun. 1–5.*

⑫ Old Northwood Historic District. This 1920s-era neighborhood, on the National Register of Historic Places, hosts special events and Sunday walking tours (☞ Guided Tours *in* Palm Beach and the Treasure Coast A to Z, *below*). ⊠ *West of Flagler Dr. between 26th and 35th Sts.*

Away from Downtown

At its outskirts, West Palm Beach sprawls. Flat, straight stretches lined with fast-food outlets and car dealerships may not be pretty to drive past, but it's worth it to reach some of the interesting attractions scattered around the southern and western reaches of the city. Several are especially rewarding for children and other animal- and nature lovers.

A Good Tour

Head south from downtown and turn right on Southern Boulevard, left onto Parker Avenue, and right onto Summit Boulevard to reach the **Dreher Park Zoo** ⑯. In the same area (just turn right onto Dreher Trail) and also appealing to kids, the **South Florida Science Museum, Planetarium, and Aquarium** ⑰ is full of hands-on exhibits.

Backtrack to Summit Avenue and go west to the 150-acre **Pine Jog Environmental Education Center** ⑱. For more natural adventure, head farther west on Summit until you reach Forest Hills Boulevard, where you turn right to reach the **Okeeheelee Nature Center** ⑲ and its miles of wooded trails.

Now retrace your steps to Summit Boulevard, drive east until you reach Military Trail, and take a left. Drive north to Southern Boulevard and turn west to reach **Lion Country Safari** ⑳, a 500-acre cageless zoo. For the last stop on this tour, backtrack to Military Trail and travel north to the gardens of the **Mounts Horticultural Learning Center** ㉑.

You could easily spend most of a day at some of these sights, so you'll want to pick and choose based on your interests, creating your own subtour. During morning and afternoon rush hours and in the winter, be prepared for heavy traffic; sightseeing in the morning (not *too* early) will help somewhat.

Sights to See

🐾 ⑯ **Dreher Park Zoo.** This wild kingdom is a 22-acre complex with more than 500 animals representing more than 100 species, including Florida panthers, red kangaroos, and Bengal tigers. Also of note are a nature trail, an Australian Outback exhibit, and a children's zoo. ⊠ *1301 Summit Blvd.,* ☎ *561/533–0887 or 561/547–9453.* ⊡ *$6, boat rides $1.* ⊙ *Daily 9–5 (until 7 on spring and summer weekends), boat rides every 15 mins.*

🐾 ⑳ **Lion Country Safari.** Drive (with car windows closed) on 8 mi of paved roads through a 500-acre cageless zoo where 1,300 wild animals roam. Lions, elephants, white rhinoceroses, giraffes, zebras, antelopes, chimpanzees, and ostriches are among those in residence. New exhibits include the Kalahari Bushvelt, designed after a South African plateau and featuring water buffalo and Nilgai (the largest type of Asian antelope), and the Gir Forest, modeled after a game forest in India and showcasing a pride of lions. ⊠ *Southern Blvd. W,* ☎ *561/793–1084.* ⊡ *$14.95, car rental $6 per hr.* ⊙ *Daily 9:30–5:30.*

㉑ **Mounts Horticultural Learning Center.** Take advantage of balmy weather by walking among the tropical and subtropical plants here. Free tours are given. ⊠ *531 N. Military Trail,* ☎ *561/233–1749.* ⊡ *Free.* ⊙ *Mon.–Sat. 8:30–5, Sun. 1–5; tours Sat. 11, Sun. 2:30.*

⑲ **Okeeheelee Nature Center.** At this popular spot, you can explore 5 mi of trails through 90 acres of native pine flat woods and wetlands. A spacious visitor center–gift shop has hands-on exhibits. ⊠ *7715 Forest Hill Blvd.,* ☎ *561/233–1400.* ⊡ *Free.* ⊙ *Visitor center Tues.–Fri. 1–4:45, Sat. 8:15–4:45; trails open daily.*

⑱ **Pine Jog Environmental Education Center.** The draw here is 150 acres of mostly undisturbed Florida pine flat woods with two self-guided ½-mi trails. Formal landscaping around the five one-story buildings features an array of native plants, and dioramas and displays show native ecosystems. Trails are reserved for the classes that are given here during the week but are open to the public on Sunday. ⊠ *6301 Summit Blvd.,* ☎ *561/686–6600.* ⊡ *Free.* ⊙ *Sun. 2–5.*

🐾 ⑰ **South Florida Science Museum, Planetarium, and Aquarium.** Here you'll find hands-on exhibits, aquarium displays with touch tanks, planetarium shows, and a chance to observe the heavens Friday nights through the most powerful telescope in South Florida (weather permitting). ⊠ *4801 Dreher Trail N,* ☎ *561/832–1988.* ⊡ *$5, planetarium $1.75 extra, laser show $2 extra.* ⊙ *Sat.–Thurs. 10–5, Fri. 10–10.*

Dining and Lodging

$$–$$$ ✕ **Café Protégé.** The restaurant of the Florida Culinary Institute, this is the place to come to sample superb cuisine at less than astronomical prices. The contemporary Continental menu changes frequently, and patrons can watch students at work slicing, dicing, and sautéing in the unique observation kitchen. ⊠ *2400 Metrocentre Blvd.,* ☎ *561/687–2433. AE, MC, V.*

$$ ✕ **Rain Dancer Steak House.** Steak lovers stop by this dark and cozy establishment to indulge in thick and juicy filet mignons, giant 24-ounce porterhouse steaks, sizzling sirloins for two, and grilled lean flank steaks. You'll also find chicken and pork chops on the menu and a bountiful salad bar. ⊠ *2300 Palm Beach Lakes Blvd.,* ☎ *561/684–2811. AE, MC, V.*

$–$$ ✕ **Pescatore Seafood and Oyster Bar.** When you want to rest your feet after wandering around Clematis Street, slip through the handsome French doors of this trendy spot for a light lunch, an afternoon snack, or a leisurely dinner. Tables are close together, and there's a sophisticated bustle. Naturally, fresh oysters and clams are on the menu, but you'll also find a variety of grilled fish, including mahimahi, tuna, and salmon; steamed Maine lobster; grilled shrimp; assorted pasta dishes; and a grilled Black Angus burger. ⊠ *200 Clematis St.,* ☎ *561/837–6633. AE, DC, MC, V.*

$$–$$$ 🏠 **Hibiscus House.** Few Florida B&B hosts work harder at hospital-
  ★ ity and at looking after their neighborhood than Raleigh Hill and Colin Rayner. As proof, since the inn opened in the late 1980s, 11 sets of guests have bought houses in Old Northwood, which is listed on the National Register of Historic Places thanks to Hill and Rayner's efforts. Their Cape Cod–style B&B is full of the antiques Hill has collected during decades of in-demand interior designing: a 150-year-old four-square piano, a gorgeous green and cane planter chair, and Louis XV pieces in the living room. Outstanding, too, is the landscaped, tropical pool-patio area. Both Hill and Rayner are informed about the best—and most affordable—dining in the area. ⊠ *501 30th St., 33407,* ☎ *561/863–5633 or 800/203–4927. 8 rooms. Pool. AE, DC, MC, V.*

$$ 🏠 **Tropical Bed & Breakfast.** More informal and Key West–like than most of Old Northwood, this tiny cottage-style B&B has a clump of rare paroutis palms out front. The three cozy rooms are individually decorated, but the splashy poolside carriage house and the brightly striped cottage with the fruity fabrics and Peter Max–style posters are where you want to be. ⊠ *419 32nd St., 33407,* ☎ *561/848–4064 or 800/736–4064,* 𝔽𝔸𝕏 *561/842–1688. 3 rooms, carriage house, cottage. Pool, bicycles. AE, MC, V.*

Nightlife and the Arts

The Arts

Part of the treasury of arts attractions is the **Raymond F. Kravis Center for the Performing Arts** (⊠ 701 Okeechobee Blvd., ☎ 561/832–7469), a $60 million, 2,200-seat glass, copper, and marble showcase occupying the highest ground in West Palm Beach. Its 250-seat Rinker Playhouse includes a space for children's programming, family productions, and other special events. Some 300 performances of drama, dance, and music—everything from gospel and bluegrass to jazz and classical—are scheduled each year.

Palm Beach Opera (⊠ 415 S. Olive Ave., ☎ 561/833–7888) stages four productions each winter at the Kravis Center. The **Carefree Theatre** (⊠ 2000 S. Dixie Hwy., ☎ 561/833–7305) is Palm Beach County's premier showcase of foreign and art films.

Nightlife

The **Respectable Street Cafe** (⊠ 518 Clematis St., ☎ 561/832–9999) explodes in high energy like an indoor Woodstock. It's open until 4 AM Tuesday–Saturday (Thursday night features the best in underground alternative sound) and for special concerts on other days. **Underground Coffeeworks** (⊠ 105 S. Narcissus Ave., ☎ 561/835–4792), a retro '60s spot, has "something different going on" (but always live music) Tuesday–Saturday. The cover charge varies, depending on the performers.

Outdoor Activities and Sports

The plush **Emerald Dunes Golf Club** (✉ 2100 Emerald Dunes Dr., ☎ 561/684–4653) has 18 holes of golf. **Palm Beach Polo and Country Club** (✉ 13198 Forest Hill Blvd., Wellington, ☎ 561/798–7000 or 800/327–4204) has 45 holes with an excellent overall layout. The **West Palm Beach Country Club** (✉ 7001 Parker Ave., ☎ 561/582–2019) offers 18 holes with no water hazards, unusual for Florida.

Shopping

As good as the malls are, they're sterile compared to the in-the-midst-of-things excitement—the mix of food, art, performance, landscaping, and retailing—that has renewed downtown West Palm around **Clematis Street.** Water-view parks, outdoor performing areas, and attractive plantings and lighting—including fanciful palm tree sculptures—add to the pleasure of browsing, window-shopping, and resting at an outdoor café. For those single-mindedly bent on mall shopping, the **Palm Beach Mall** (✉ Palm Beach Lakes Blvd. at I–95) has a Burdines, JCPenney, Lord & Taylor, and Sears.

Side Trip

Lake Okeechobee
40 mi west of West Palm Beach.

Rimming the western shore of Palm Beach and Martin counties, this second-largest freshwater lake in the United States is girdled by 120 mi of roads; yet for almost its entire circumference, it remains hidden from sight. The Seminole's Big Water and the heart of the great Everglades watershed, Lake Okeechobee measures 730 square mi—roughly 33 mi north–south and 30 mi east–west—with an average natural depth of only 10 ft (flood control brings the figure up to 12 ft and deeper). Six major lock systems and 32 separate water-control structures manage the water.

Encircling the lake is a 30-ft-high grassy levee, known locally as "the wall," and the Lake Okeechobee Scenic Trail, a coarse track that has been integrated into the Florida National Scenic Trail. Inside the wall, on the big lake itself, fisherfolk come from everywhere for reputably the best bass fishing in North America.

Small towns dot the lakeshore in an area that's still largely agricultural. To the southeast is Belle Glade, whose motto—"Her soil is her fortune"—results from the town's role as the eastern hub of the 700,000-acre Everglades Agricultural Area, the crescent of farmlands lying south and east of the lake. To the west lies Clewiston, the most prosperous lake town. It's known as "the sweetest town in America" thanks to the resident headquarters of the United States Sugar Corporation. At the north end of the lake, around Okeechobee, citrus production has outgrown cattle ranching as the principal economy, while dairying, though still important, is diminishing as the state acquires land in its efforts to reduce water pollution. Somewhat set back from the lake, Indiantown is the western hub of Martin County, noteworthy for citrus production, cattle ranching, and timbering. The town reached its apex in 1927, when the Seaboard Airline Railroad briefly established its southern headquarters and a model town here.

Grouped together in Belle Glade's **Municipal Complex** are the public library and the **Lawrence E. Will Museum**, both with materials on the town's history. On the front lawn is a Ferenc Verga sculpture of a family fleeing the wall of water that rose from the lake during the catastrophic hurricane of 1928. More than 2,000 people lost their lives and 15,000 families were left homeless by the torrential flood. ⊠ *530 Main St., Belle Glade,* ☎ *561/996–3453.* ⌸ *Free.* ☉ *Mon.–Tues. and Fri. 9–4, Wed. and Sat. 9–1, Thurs. 9–8.*

The **Clewiston Museum** details the history of the city, with stories not only of sugar and of the Herbert Hoover Dike construction, but also of a ramie crop grown here to make rayon, of World War II RAF pilots who trained at the Clewiston airfield, and of a German POW camp. ⊠ *112 S. Commercio St., Clewiston,* ☎ *941/983–1493.* ⌸ *Free.* ☉ *Tues.–Fri. 10–4.*

The Florida Power and Light Company's Martin Power Plant maintains the **Barley Barber Swamp,** a 400-acre freshwater cypress swamp preserve. A 5,800-ft-long boardwalk enables you to walk through this vestige of what near-coastal Florida was largely like before vast water-control efforts began in the 19th century. Dozens of birds, reptiles, and mammals inhabit these wetlands and lowlands, with an outstanding reserve of bald cypress trees, land and swamp growth, and slow-flowing coffee-color water. Reservations are required at least one week in advance for tours. During certain times of the year there are manatee and turtle walks. Call for schedules. ⊠ *Rte. 710, Indiantown,* ☎ *800/ 552–8440.* ⌸ *Free.* ☉ *Tours Fri.–Wed. 8:30 and 12:30.*

DINING AND LODGING

$–$$ ✗ **Colonial Dining Room.** The Clewiston Inn's restaurant has ladder-back chairs, chandeliers, and fanlight windows, and though the food is good, the attitude's not fancy. Southern regional and Continental dishes—chicken, pork, steak, and the ubiquitous catfish—are served. ⊠ *108 Royal Palm Ave., at U.S. 27, Clewiston,* ☎ *941/983–8151. MC, V.*

$–$$ ✗ **Lightsey's.** The pick of the lake, this beautiful lodgelike restaurant at the Okee-Tantie Recreation Area started closer to town as a fish company with four tables in a corner. Now everybody comes out here. You can get most items fried, steamed, broiled, or grilled. The freshest are the catfish, cooter (freshwater turtle), frogs' legs, and gator. ⊠ *10430 Rte. 78W, Okeechobee,* ☎ *941/763–4276. MC, V. Beer and wine only.*

$$ ⌸ **Clewiston Inn.** This classic antebellum-style country hotel in the heart of town was built in 1938. Its cypress-panel lobby, wood-burning fireplace, Colonial Dining Room, and Everglades Lounge with a wraparound Everglades mural are standouts. Rooms are pleasant but basic, with reproduction furniture. Still it's worth a stay to soak up the lore and take advantage of the excellent value (full breakfast included). A pool is across the street in the park. ⊠ *108 Royal Palm Ave., at U.S. 27, Clewiston 33440,* ☎ *941/983–8151 or 800/749–4466,* ℻ *941/983– 4602. 48 rooms, 5 suites. Restaurant, bar, 6 tennis courts, jogging. AE, MC, V.*

$$ ⌸ **Seminole Country Inn.** This two-story, Mediterranean Revival inn,
★ once the southern headquarters of the Seaboard Airline Railroad, was restored by longtime Indiantown patriarch the late Holman Wall. It's now being run for the second time (other innkeepers didn't get it right) by his daughter, Jonnie Wall Williams, a fifth-generation native, who is devoted to the inn's restoration. Rooms are done in country ruffles and prints, with full carpeting and comfy beds. There are rocking

chairs on the porch, Indiantown memorabilia in the lobby, a sitting area on the second floor, and good local art throughout. ⊠ *15885 S.W. Warfield Blvd., Indiantown 34956,* ☎ *561/597–3777. 21 rooms. 2 restaurants, pool. AE, D, MC, V.*

$ 🏨 **Okeechobee Days Inn Pier II.** This modern two-story motel on the
★   rim canal has a five-story observation tower for looking over the levee to the lake. Large, clean, motel-plain rooms are well maintained. Out back there's a 600-ft fishing pier and the Oyster Bar, one of the best hangouts on the lake for shooting a game of pool or watching a game on TV. It attracts a good mix of locals and out-of-towners. ⊠ *2200 S.E. U.S. 441, Okeechobee 34974,* ☎ *941/763–8003 or 800/874–3744,* ☏ *941/763–2245. 89 rooms. Bar, fishing. AE, D, DC, MC, V.*

$ 🏨 **Okeechobee Inn.** Rooms in this simple, two-story L-shape motel, 2 mi west of Belle Glade, are furnished in green floral prints. Large windows let in plenty of light. All rooms have balconies that overlook the pool, and fishing and boat ramps are just a mile away. ⊠ *265 N. U.S. 27, South Bay 33493,* ☎ *561/996–6517. 115 rooms. Pool, playground. MC, V.*

$ ⚲ **Belle Glade Marina Campground.** Just a few miles north of downtown Belle Glade, just offshore in Lake Okeechobee is Torry Island. Campsites have water and electrical hookups; some have sewer hookups and docking facilities. ⊠ *Torry Island 33493,* ☎ *561/996–6322. 350 campsites. Picnic area, horseshoes, shuffleboard, dock, boating, fishing. MC, V.*

$ ⚲ **Okee-Tantie Recreation Area.** In addition to its recreational facilities, the park offers 215 RV sites, 38 tent sites, picnic spots, rest rooms, showers, Lightsey's restaurant, and a shop from which you can buy groceries and sandwiches. ⊠ *10430 Rte. 78W, Okeechobee 34974,* ☎ *941/763–2622. Restaurant, grocery, picnic area, dock, boating, fishing, playground. MC, V.*

OUTDOOR ACTIVITIES AND SPORTS

Biking. Euler's Cycling & Fitness (⊠ 50 S.E. U.S. 441, Okeechobee, ☎ 941/357–0458) is the only source for bicycle rentals and repairs on the lake.

Fishing. In addition to operating the bridge to Torry Island (the last remaining swing bridge in Florida, it is cranked open and closed by hand, swinging at right angles to the road), brothers Charles and Gordon Corbin run **Slim's Fish Camp** (⊠ Torry Island, ☎ 561/996–3844). Here you'll find a complete tackle shop, guides, camping facilities, fully equipped bass boats, and even the name of a good taxidermist to mount your trophy. **J-Mark Fish Camp** (⊠ Torry Island, ☎ 561/996–5357) provides fully equipped bass boats, fishing guides, tackle, bait, and licenses. Since the **Okee-Tantie Recreation Area** (⊠ 10430 Rte. 78W, Okeechobee, ☎ 941/763–2622) has direct access to the lake, it's a popular place for fishing. There are two public boat ramps, fish-cleaning stations, a marina, picnic areas and a restaurant, a playground, rest rooms, showers, and a bait shop (☎ 941/763–9645) that stocks groceries.

Golf. Belle Glade Municipal Country Club (⊠ Torry Island Rd., Belle Glade, ☎ 561/996–6605) has an 18-hole golf course and restaurant open to the public.

SOUTH TO BOCA RATON

Strung together by Route A1A, the towns between Palm Beach and Boca Raton are notable for their variety. Though the glamour of Palm Beach has rubbed off on many towns, there are pockets of modesty and unpretentiousness alongside the well-established high and mighty. In one town you might find a cluster of sophisticated art galleries and fancy eateries, whereas the very next town could have a few hamburger stands and mom-and-pop "everything" stores.

Lake Worth

㉒ *2 mi south of West Palm Beach.*

Tourists are mainly interested in this mainland town for its inexpensive lodging in close proximity to Palm Beach, which is accessible via a nearby bridge.

Lake Worth Municipal Park, also known as Casino Park, has a beach, Olympic-size swimming pool, fishing pier, picnic areas, shuffleboard, restaurants, and shops. ⊠ *Rte. A1A at end of Lake Worth Bridge,* ☎ *561/533–7367.* ☞ *Pool $2, parking 25¢ for 15 mins.* ☼ *Daily 9–4:45.*

The Arts

Klein Dance Company (⊠ 3208 2nd Ave. N, No. 10, 33461, ☎ 561/586–1889) is a nationally acclaimed, world-touring, professional troupe that also gives local performances.

Dining and Lodging

$ ✕ **John G's.** About the only time the line lets up is when the restaurant closes at 3 PM. The menu is as big as the crowd: big fruit platters, sandwich-board superstars, grilled burgers, seafood, and eggs every which way, including a United Nations omelets. Breakfast is served until 11. ⊠ *Lake Worth Casino,* ☎ *561/585–9860. No credit cards. No dinner.*

$$ ▥ **Holiday House.** Standing out from its motel strip, a five-minute walk from the heart of town, is this uncommercial-looking lodging with bougainvillea-entwined balconies and rich tropical gardens. The motel rooms, efficiencies, and one-bedroom apartments live up to expectations. In two adjacent two-story buildings dating from the late 1940s but kept up nicely, each is warmly furnished, clean, and fitted out with refrigerator and microwave. Maid service is provided weekly for efficiencies and apartments (one-week stay minimum) and daily for rooms. ⊠ *320 N. Federal Hwy., 33460,* ☎ *561/582–3561,* 🖷 *561/582–3561. 30 units. Pool, coin laundry. MC, V.*

$ ▥ **New Sun Gate Motel.** Each room is dedicated to a famous movie star of a bygone era—Cary Grant, Rita Hayworth, James Dean—in this simple establishment near downtown. Units are decorated in art deco style, and some have microwaves. ⊠ *901 S. Federal Hwy., 33460,* ☎ *561/588–8110,* 🖷 *561/588–8041. 31 rooms. Restaurant, pool, coin laundry. AE, MC, V.*

Outdoor Activities and Sports

The **Gulfstream Polo Club,** the oldest club in the Palm Beach area, began in the 1920s and plays medium-goal polo (for teams with handicaps of 8–16 goals). There are six polo fields. ⊠ *4550 Polo Rd.,* ☎ *561/965–2057.* ☞ *Free.* ☼ *Games Dec.–Apr.*

Lantana

㉓   *2 mi south of Lake Worth.*

Like Lake Worth, Lantana has inexpensive lodging and a bridge connecting the town to Palm Beach's barrier island. It's just a bit farther away from Palm Beach. A closer island neighbor is **Manalapan,** a tiny residential community with a luxury beach resort.

Lantana Public Beach has one of the best food concessions around. You'll find fresh fish on weekends and breakfast and lunch specials every day outdoors under beach umbrellas. ✉ *100 N. Ocean Ave.,* ☏ *no phone.* 🅿 *Parking 25¢ for 15 mins.* ☉ *Daily 9–4:45.*

Dining and Lodging

$$ ✕ **Old House.** Overlooking the Intracoastal Waterway, the 1889 Lyman House has grown in spurts over the years and is now a patchwork of shedlike spaces. Partners Wayne Cordero and Captain Bob Hoddinott have turned it into an informal Old Florida seafood house that serves not only local seafood but also, incongruously, Baltimore steamed crab—the specialty. Although there's air-conditioning, dining is still open-air most evenings and in cooler weather. ✉ *300 E. Ocean Ave.,* ☏ *561/ 533–5220. AE, MC, V.*

$$$$ 🏨 **Ritz-Carlton, Palm Beach.** Despite its name, this hotel is actually in
★   Manalapan, halfway between Palm Beach and Delray. The bisque-color, triple-tower landmark may look like the work of Addison Mizner, but in fact it was built in 1991. Dominating the lobby is a huge double-sided marble fireplace, foreshadowing the luxury of the guest rooms' marble tubs and upholstered furniture. Most rooms have ocean views, and oceanfront rooms have balconies. Not to be outdone by the fabulous beaches, a large pool and courtyard area has more than 100 coconut palms. Bikes and scuba and snorkeling equipment can be rented. ✉ *100 S. Ocean Blvd., Manalapan 33462,* ☏ *561/533–6000 or 800/ 241–3333,* ℻ *561/588–4555. 5 restaurants, 2 bars, pool, beauty salon, massage, sauna, spa, steam room, 7 tennis courts, beach, bicycles. AE, D, DC, MC, V.*

$ 🏨 **Super 8 Motel.** There's nothing special about this sprawling one-story motel except the price—a real bargain, considering the proximity to Palm Beach. Efficiencies and rooms (some with refrigerators) are clean but basically furnished. ✉ *1255 Hypoluxo Rd., 33462,* ☏ *561/ 585–3970,* ℻ *561/586–3028. 129 rooms, 11 efficiencies. Pool, coin laundry. AE, DC, MC, V.*

Outdoor Activities and Sports

B-Love Fleet (✉ 314 E. Ocean Ave., ☏ 561/588–7612) offers three deep-sea fishing excursions daily: 8–noon, 1–5, and 7–11. No reservations are needed; just show up 30 minutes before the boat is scheduled to leave. The cost is $23 per person.

Boynton Beach

㉔   *3 mi south of Lantana.*

This town is far enough from Palm Beach to have kept its laid-back, low-key atmosphere. Its two parts, on the mainland and the barrier island, are connected by a causeway.

Knollwood Groves dates from the 1930s, when it was planted by the partners of the *Amos & Andy* radio show. You can take a 30-minute, 30-acre tram tour through the orange groves and a processing plant and visit the **Hallpatee Seminole Indian Village,** where there's an alligator exhibit and crafts shop. During the busy season, special guest Martin Twofeather gives a weekly one-hour alligator-handling show. ✉ *8053 Lawrence Rd.,* ☎ *561/734–4800.* 🎟 *Tour $1, show $5.* ☉ *Daily 8:30–5:30, show Sat. 2.*

The **Puppetry Arts Center** provides shows and educational programs from the home of the Gold Coast Puppet Guild. ✉ *3633 S. Federal Hwy.,* ☎ *561/687–3280.* 🎟 *Shows $2.50.* ☉ *Call for schedule.*

Oceanfront Park has a beach, boardwalk, concessions, grills, a jogging trail, and playground. Parking is expensive if you're not a Boynton resident. ✉ *Ocean Ave. at Rte. A1A,* ☎ *no phone.* 🎟 *Parking $10 per day in winter, $5 per day rest of year.* ☉ *Daily 9 AM–midnight.*

<table>
<tr><td>OFF THE
BEATEN PATH</td><td>**ARTHUR R. MARSHALL–LOXAHATCHEE NATIONAL WILDLIFE REFUGE** – The most robust part of the Everglades, this 221-square-mi refuge is one of three huge water-retention areas that account for much of the Everglades outside the national park. These areas are managed less to protect natural resources, however, than to prevent flooding to the south. Start from the visitor center, where there are two walking trails: a boardwalk through a dense cypress swamp and a marsh trail to a 20-ft-high observation tower overlooking a pond. There is also a 5½-mi canoe trail, recommended for more experienced canoeists because it's rather overgrown. Wildlife viewing is good year-round, and you can fish for bass and panfish. ✉ *10119 Lee Rd., off U.S. 441 between Boynton Beach Blvd. (Rte. 804) and Atlantic Ave. (Rte. 806), west of Boynton Beach,* ☎ *561/734–8303.* 🎟 *$5 per vehicle, $1 per pedestrian.* ☉ *Daily 6 AM–sunset; visitor center weekdays 8–4, weekends 8–4:30.*</td></tr>
</table>

Outdoor Activities and Sports

FISHING

You can fish the canal at the **Arthur R. Marshall–Loxahatchee National Wildlife Refuge** (☎ 561/734–8303). There's a boat ramp, and the waters are decently productive, but bring your own equipment.

GOLF

Boynton Beach Municipal Golf Course (✉ 8020 Jog Rd., ☎ 561/969–2200) has 27 holes.

Gulf Stream

㉕ *2 mi south of Boynton Beach.*

This beautiful little beachfront community was also touched by Mizner. As you pass the bougainvillea-topped walls of the Gulf Stream Club, a private police officer may stop traffic for a golfer to cross.

Lodging

$$ 🏨 **Riviera Palms Motel.** Hans and Herter Grannemann have owned this small two-story motel dating from the 1950s since 1978. It has two primary virtues: It's clean, and it's well located. Across Route A1A from mid-rise apartment houses on the water, it has three wings surrounding a grassy front yard and heated pool. Rooms are done in Danish modern and a blue, brown, and tan color scheme; all have at least a refrigerator but no phone. ✉ *3960 N. Ocean Blvd., 33483,* ☎ *561/ 276–3032. 17 rooms, efficiencies, and suites. Pool. No credit cards.*

Delray Beach

㉖ *2 mi south of Gulf Stream.*

What began as an artists' retreat and a small settlement of Japanese farmers is now a sophisticated beach town with a successful local historic-preservation movement. Atlantic Avenue, the main drag, has been transformed into a 1-mi stretch of palm-dotted brick sidewalks, almost entirely lined with stores, art galleries, and dining establishments. Running east–west and ending at the beach, it's a pleasant place for a stroll day or night. Another lovely pedestrian way begins at the edge of town, across Northeast 8th Street (George Bush Boulevard), along the big broad swimming beach that extends north and south of Atlantic Avenue.

Municipal Beach (⊠ Atlantic Ave. at Rte. A1A) has a boat ramp and volleyball court.

The chief landmark along Atlantic Avenue is the Mediterranean Revival **Colony Hotel** (⊠ 525 E. Atlantic Ave., ☎ 561/276–4123), still open only for the winter season as it has been for more than 60 years.

Cason Cottage, a restored Victorian-style home that dates from about 1915, now serves as offices of the Delray Beach Historical Society. The house is filled with relics of the Victorian era, including an old pipe organ donated by descendants of one of the original families to settle Delray Beach. Periodic displays celebrate the town's architectural evolution. The cottage is a block north of the cultural center. ⊠ 5 N.E. 1st St., ☎ 561/243–0223. ☞ Free. ☉ Tues.–Fri. 11–4.

The **Old School Square Cultural Arts Center,** just off Atlantic Avenue, houses several museums in restored school buildings dating from 1913 and 1926. The **Cornell Museum of Art & History** offers an ever-changing array of art exhibits. ⊠ 51 N. Swinton Ave., ☎ 561/243–7922. ☞ Donation welcome. ☉ Tues.–Sat. 11–4, Sun. 1–4.

★ Florida seems an odd place for the **Morikami Museum and Japanese Gardens.** At this 200-acre cultural and recreational facility, a display in a building modeled after a Japanese imperial villa recalls the Yamato Colony, an agricultural community of Japanese settlers who came to Florida in 1905. Gardens include the only known collection of bonsai Florida plants. There are also programs and exhibits in a lakeside museum and theater, as well as a nature trail, picnic pavilions, a library and audiovisual center, and snack bar. ⊠ 4000 Morikami Park Rd., ☎ 561/495–0233. ☞ $4.25, free Sun. 10–noon. ☉ Park daily sunrise–sunset; museum Tues.–Sun. 10–5.

Dining and Lodging

$–$$ ✕ **Blue Anchor.** Unbelievably, this pub was actually shipped from En-
★ gland, where it stood for 150 years as the old Blue Anchor Pub, in London's historic Chancery Lane. There it was a regular watering hole for many famous Englishmen, including Winston Churchill. The Delray Beach incarnation still cooks up authentic British pub fare: ploughman's lunch (a chunk of cheddar or Stilton cheese, a chunk of bread, and English pickled onions), steak-and-kidney pie, fish-and-chips, and bangers (sausage) and mash, to name just a few. You can also get delicious hamburgers, sandwiches, and salads. The dessert menu includes an English sherry trifle and a Bailey's Irish Cream pie. English beers and ales are available on tap and in the bottle. ⊠ 804 E. Atlantic Ave., ☎ 561/272–7272. AE, MC, V.

$–$$ ✕ **Boston's on the Beach.** Often a restaurant that's facing a beach re-
★ lies on its location to fill the place up and doesn't worry enough about the food. Not so with Boston's, which is just across the street from the public beach. As you might expect from the name, you'll find good New England clam chowder and several lobster dishes, as well as fresh fish grilled, fried, or prepared just about any other way. All this is presented in an ultra-informal setting. Tables are old and wooden, and walls are decorated with traffic signs and other conversation stoppers,

most notably paraphernalia from the Boston Bruins, New England Patriots, and Boston Red Sox, including a veritable shrine to Ted Williams. An outdoor deck upstairs is a terrific place to catch ocean breezes. After dark the place becomes a casual club with live music. ⊠ *40 S. Ocean Blvd. (Rte. A1A)*, ☎ *561/278–3364. AE, MC, V.*

$$$–$$$$ 🛏 **Seagate Hotel & Beach Club.** One of the best garden hotels in Palm Beach County, this property offers value, comfort, style, and personal attention. The one-bedroom suite is all chintz and rattan, with many upholstered pieces. All units have at least kitchenettes. The less expensive studios have compact facilities behind foldaway doors, whereas more expensive units have a separate living room and a larger kitchen. You can dress up and dine in a smart little mahogany- and lattice-trimmed beachfront salon or have the same Continental fare in casual attire in the equally stylish bar. Guests enjoy privileges at the private beach club. ⊠ *400 S. Ocean Blvd., 33483,* ☎ *561/276-2421 or 800/233–3581. 70 1- and 2-bedroom suites. Restaurant, bar, kitchenettes, freshwater and saltwater pools, beach. AE, DC, MC, V.*

$$$ 🛏 **Harbor House.** These white, two-story 1950s buildings have a privileged location in a quiet residential enclave three blocks east of U.S. 1 and across from the Delray Marina. In addition to two tiny motel rooms, there are 23 efficiencies and one- and two-bedroom apartments with kitchens and a mix of seating generally done in white, beige, tan, and blue. Everything retains a 1950s look, but carpets and upholstery are replaced before they look tired. In a nice touch, matching fabrics are changed by the season: solid blue in summer, blue florals in winter. ⊠ *124 Marine Way, 33483,* ☎ *561/276–4221. 25 units. Pool, shuffleboard, coin laundry. MC, V.*

Nightlife and the Arts

THE ARTS

The **Crest Theater** (⊠ 51 N. Swinton Ave., ☎ 561/243–7922), in the Old School Square Cultural Arts Center, presents productions in dance, music, and theater.

NIGHTLIFE

The **Back Room Blues Lounge** (⊠ 303 W. Atlantic Ave., ☎ 561/243–9110), behind Westside Liquors, has comedy night on Wednesday and live bands Thursday–Saturday. **Boston's on the Beach** (⊠ 40 S. Ocean Blvd., ☎ 561/278–3364) presents live reggae music Monday and rock and roll Tuesday–Sunday.

Outdoor Activities and Sports

BIKING

There is a bicycle path in Barwick Park and a special oceanfront lane along Route A1A. **Rich Wagen's Bicycle Shop** (⊠ 217 E. Atlantic Ave., ☎ 561/276–4234) rents bikes by the hour or day.

SCUBA DIVING AND SNORKELING

Scuba and snorkeling equipment can be rented from longtime family-owned **Force E** (⊠ 660 Linton Blvd., ☎ 561/276–0666). It has PADI affiliation, provides instruction at all levels, and offers charters.

TENNIS

Each winter the **Delray Beach Tennis Center** (⊠ 201 W. Atlantic Ave., ☎ 561/243–7380) hosts a professional women's tournament that attracts players like Steffi Graf. The center is also a great place to practice or learn; it has 14 clay courts and 5 hard courts and offers individual lessons and clinics.

WATERSKIING

Lake Ida Park (⊠ 2929 Lake Ida Rd., ☎ 561/964–4420) is an excellent place to water-ski, whether you're a beginner or a veteran. The park has a boat ramp, slalom course, and trick ski course.

Shopping

Street-scaped **Atlantic Avenue** is a showcase for art galleries, shops, and restaurants. In addition to serving lunch and a traditional afternoon tea, the charmingly old-fashioned **Sundy House** (⊠ 106 S. Swinton Ave., ☎ 561/278–2163 or 561/272–3720) sells antiques and gifts in the former home of onetime Flagler foreman and first Delray mayor John Shaw Sundy. The structure's beautiful gardens and five gingerbread gables complement Delray's finest wraparound porch.

Boca Raton

㉗ *6 mi south of Delray Beach.*

This upscale town at the south end of Palm Beach County, 30 minutes south of Palm Beach, has a lot in common with its ritzy cousin. For one thing, both reflect the unmistakable architectural presence of Addison Mizner, their principal developer in the mid-1920s. Mizner Park, an important Boca Raton shopping district, bears his name.

Built in 1925 as the headquarters of the Mizner Development Corporation, the structure at **2 East El Camino Real** is a good example of Mizner's characteristic Spanish Revival architectural style, with its wrought-iron grills and handmade tiles.

☾ Championed by *Beetle Bailey* cartoonist Mort Walker, the **International Museum of Cartoon Art** is the only museum of its kind in the world. It showcases more than 160,000 pieces of art created over two centuries by more than 1,000 artists from more than 50 countries—everything from turn-of-the-century Buster Brown cartoons to the *Road Runner* to Charles Schulz's *Peanuts.* ⊠ *201 Plaza Real,* ☎ *561/391–2200.* ▦ *$6.* ◷ *Tues.–Sat. 10–6, Sun. noon–5.*

Containing whimsical metal sculptures on the lawn, the **Boca Raton Museum of Art** is a must. The permanent collection includes works by Picasso, Degas, Matisse, Klee, and Modigliani as well as notable pre-Columbian art. ⊠ *801 W. Palmetto Park Rd.,* ☎ *561/392–2500.* ▦ *$3.* ◷ *Weekdays 10–4, weekends noon–4.*

The residential area behind the Boca Raton Museum of Art is known as **Old Floresta.** Developed by Addison Mizner starting in 1925 and landscaped with many varieties of palms and cycads, it includes houses that are mainly in a Mediterranean style, many with upper balconies supported by exposed wood columns.

☾ A big draw for kids, the **Gumbo Limbo Nature Center** has four huge saltwater sea tanks and a long boardwalk through dense forest with a 50-ft tower you can climb to overlook the tree canopy. In the spring and early summer, staff members lead nighttime turtle walks to see nesting females come ashore and lay their eggs. ⊠ *1801 N. Ocean Blvd.,* ☎ *561/338–1473.* ▦ *Donation welcome; turtle tours $3 (tickets must be obtained in advance).* ◷ *Mon.–Sat. 9–4, Sun. noon–4; turtle tours late May–mid-July, Mon.–Thurs. 9 PM–midnight.*

Red Reef Park (⊠ 1400 N. Rte. A1A) offers a beach and playground plus picnic tables and grills. In addition to its beach, **Spanish River Park** (⊠ 3001 N. Rte. A1A) has picnic tables, grills, and a large playground. Popular **South Beach Park** (⊠ 400 N. Rte. A1A) has a concession stand along with its sand and ocean.

The Arts

Caldwell Theatre Company (✉ 7873 N. Federal Hwy., ☎ 561/241–7432), an Equity regional theater, hosts the multimedia Mizner Festival each April and May and stages four productions each winter. **Jan McArt's Royal Palm Dinner Theatre** (✉ 303 S.E. Mizner Blvd., Royal Palm Plaza, ☎ 561/392–3755 or 800/841–6765), an Equity theater, presents five or six musicals a year.

Dining and Lodging

$$–$$$$ ✕ **La Vieille Maison.** This French restaurant remains one of the tem-
★ ples of haute cuisine along the Gold Coast. Featuring a stunning court-
yard, it occupies a 1920s-era dwelling believed to be an Addison
Mizner design. Closets and cubbyholes have been transformed into in-
timate private dining rooms. Fixed-price, à la carte, Temptations, and
Grand menus are available, and all feature Provençale dishes, includ-
ing *soupe au pistou* (vegetable soup with basil and Parmesan cheese)
and venison chop with red currant pepper sauce and roasted chestnuts.
Health-conscious selections are available on all menus. Dessert choices
include French sponge cake with lemon cream and strawberries, French
apple tart, and a chocolate lover's delight called *L'Indulgence de
Chocolat.* ✉ 770 E. Palmetto Park Rd., ☎ 561/391–6701 or 561/737–
5677. AE, D, DC, MC, V. Closed early July–Aug.

$$–$$$$ ✕ **Ristorante La Finestra.** Belle Epoque lithographs decorate the walls,
★ and though the formal interior is just this side of austere, the cuisine
itself is an extravaganza of taste treats. Start with the Portobello mushroom with garlic or the roasted red peppers and anchovies. For a main
course try a pasta dish, such as ricotta ravioli with vodka or rigatoni
Bolognese (with ground veal, marinara sauce, and Parmesan). Or
order the scallopini of veal stuffed with crabmeat, lobster, and Gor-
gonzola; the Tuscan fish stew; or the baked jumbo shrimp wrapped in
bacon and stuffed with Swiss cheese. ✉ 171 E. Palmetto Rd., ☎ 561/
392–1838. AE, DC, MC, V.

$$–$$$ ✕ **Kasha.** Those in the know come to this small and quiet restaurant
to experience the culinary talents of chef Jose Garcia, formerly chef at
the Gazebo Café. He's kept many of his specialties on the new menu,
including fresh lump crabmeat glazed with an excellent Mornay sauce
on a marinated artichoke bottom, a robust bouillabaisse that includes
Maine lobster, fresh Dover sole flown in from Holland and prepared
amandine or meunière, and strawberries with a Grand Marnier–
sabayon sauce. Bay scallops, rack of lamb, and veal chops with morel
sauce are other popular entrées. ✉ 287 E. Indiantown Rd., ☎ 561/
745–5609. AE, MC, V. No lunch.

$ ✕ **Tom's Place.** "This place is a blessing from God," says the sign over
★ the fireplace, and after braving the long lines and sampling the superb
menu, you will add, "Amen!" That's in between mouthfuls of Tom
Wright's soul food—sauce-slathered ribs, pork chop sandwiches,
chicken cooked in peppery mustard sauce over hickory and oak, sweet
potato pie. Buy a bottle or two of Tom's barbecue sauce ($2.25 a pint)
just as Lou Rawls, Ben Vereen, Sugar Ray Leonard, and a rush of NFL
players have before you. ✉ 7251 N. Federal Hwy., ☎ 561/997–0920.
MC, V. Closed Sun., also Mon. May–mid-Nov.

$$$$ 🏨 **Boca Raton Resort & Club.** Addison Mizner built the Mediterranean-
★ style Cloister Inn here in 1926; it has been added to several times since
to create this sprawling, elegant resort, which counts a golf school run
by Dave Pelz among its facilities. Rooms in the Cloister tend to be small
and warmly traditional; those in the 27-story Tower are in a similar
style but larger, while rooms in the Beach Club are light, airy, and contemporary. The concierge staff speaks at least 12 languages. Rates dur-

ing the winter season don't include meals, but you can pay extra for MAP (including breakfast and dinner). ✉ *501 E. Camino Real, 33431-0825,* ☎ *561/395–3000 or 800/327–0101. 963 rooms, suites, studios, and villas. 7 restaurants, 3 bars, 5 pools, 2 golf courses, 34 tennis courts, basketball, 3 health clubs, beach, boating, fishing. AE, DC, MC, V.*

Outdoor Activities and Sports

BIKING

Plenty of bike trails and quiet streets make for pleasant pedaling in the area; for current information contact the city of Boca Raton's **Bicycle Coordinator** (☎ 561/393–7910).

BOATING

If you ever wanted the thrill of blasting across the water at up to 80 mph, check out **Air and Sea Charters** (✉ 490 E. Palmetto Park Rd., Suite 330, ☎ 561/368–3566). For $80 per person (four-person minimum), you can spend a wild-eyed hour holding on to your life vest aboard an 800-horsepower offshore racing boat. For a more leisurely trip go for Air and Sea's 55-ft catamaran or 45-ft sailboat.

GOLF

Two championship courses and a golf school are available at **Boca Raton Resort & Club** (✉ 501 E. Camino Real, ☎ 561/395–3000 or 800/327–0101).

POLO

Royal Palm Polo, founded in 1959 by Oklahoma oilman John T. Oxley and now home to the $100,000 International Gold Cup Tournament, has seven polo fields within two stadiums. ✉ *6300 Old Clint Moore Rd.,* ☎ *561/994–1876.* ✍ *$6, box seats $10–$25.* ☉ *Games Jan.–Apr., Sun. 1 and 3.*

SCUBA DIVING AND SNORKELING

Information about dive trips, as well as rental scuba and snorkeling equipment, can be obtained at **Force E** (✉ 877 E. Palmetto Park Rd., ☎ 561/368–0555).

Shopping

Mizner Park (✉ Federal Hwy. between Palmetto Park Rd. and Glades Rd.) is a distinctive 30-acre shopping village with apartments and town houses among its gardenlike spaces. Some three dozen retail stores include the excellent Liberties Fine Books & Music, a Jacobson's specialty department store, seven restaurants with sidewalk cafés, and 12 movie screens. **Town Center** (✉ 6000 W. Glades Rd.) combines a business park with ritzy shopping and great dining. Major retailers include Bloomingdale's, Burdines, Lord & Taylor, Saks Fifth Avenue, and Sears—201 stores and restaurants in all.

THE TREASURE COAST

From south to north, the Treasure Coast encompasses the top end of Palm Beach County plus Martin, St. Lucie, and Indian River counties. Though dotted with towns, this section of coastline is one of Florida's quietest. Most towns are small and laid-back, and there's lots of undeveloped land between them. Vero is the region's most sophisticated town and the one place you'll find clusters of fine dining establishments and upscale shops. The beaches along here are sought out by nesting sea turtles; you can join locally organized watches, which go out to view the turtles laying their eggs in the sand between April and August.

Palm Beach Shores

28   *7 mi north of Palm Beach.*

This residential town rimmed by mom-and-pop motels is at the southern tip of Singer Island, across Lake Worth Inlet from Palm Beach. To get between the two, however, you must cross over to the mainland before returning to the beach. The main attraction of this unpretentious middle-class community is its affordable beachfront lodging and its proximity to several nature parks.

OFF THE
BEATEN PATH

JOHN D. MACARTHUR BEACH STATE PARK – Here you will find almost 2 mi of beach, good fishing and shelling, and one of the finest examples of subtropical coastal habitat remaining in southeast Florida. To learn about what you see, take an interpretive walk to a mangrove estuary along the upper reaches of Lake Worth. Or visit the **William T. Kirby Nature Center** (☎ 561/624–6952), open Wednesday–Monday from 9 to 5, which has exhibits on the coastal environment. ⊠ *10900 Rte. A1A, North Palm Beach,* ☎ *561/624–6950.* ⊡ *$3.25 per vehicle with up to 8 people.* ⊙ *8–sunset.*

LOGGERHEAD PARK MARINE LIFE CENTER OF JUNO BEACH – Established by Eleanor N. Fletcher, "the turtle lady of Juno Beach," the center focuses on the natural history of sea turtles. Also on view are displays of coastal natural history, sharks, whales, and shells. ⊠ *1200 U.S. 1 (entrance on west side of park), Juno Beach,* ☎ *561/627–8280.* ⊡ *Donation welcome.* ⊙ *Tues.–Sat. 10–4, Sun. noon–3.*

Dining and Lodging

$$ ✕ **The Galley.** Don't overlook this open-air waterfront restaurant. After a hot day of mansion gawking or beach bumming, there's no better place to chill out. The blender seems to run nonstop, churning out tropical drinks like piña coladas and Goombay Smashes. Old Florida favorites like grouper and conch chowder are mainstays, but there are also a few highbrow entrées (this is Palm Beach County, after all), such as lobster tail or baby sea scallops sautéed in garlic and lemon butter. This is also a good spot for breakfast. ⊠ *98 Lake Dr.,* ☎ *561/848–1492. MC, V. No dinner Mon.–Tues.*

$$–$$$ ☷ **Sailfish Marina.** This long-established one-story motel has a marina
★   with 94 deep-water slips and 15 rooms and efficiencies that open to landscaped grounds. None is directly on the water, but units 9–11 have ocean views across the blacktop drive. Rooms have peaked ceilings, carpeting, king-size or twin beds, and stall showers; many have ceiling fans. From the seawall you can see fish through the clear inlet water. The motel's staff is informed and helpful, and the proprietors are as promotional as they are friendly. ⊠ *98 Lake Dr., 33404,* ☎ *561/844–1724 or 800/446–4577,* ⨳ *561/848–9684. 15 units. Restaurant, bar, grocery, pool, dock. AE, MC, V.*

Palm Beach Gardens

29   *5 mi north of West Palm Beach.*

About 15 minutes northwest of Palm Beach is this relaxed, upscale residential community widely known for its high-profile golf complex, the PGA National Resort & Spa. Although the town is not on the beach, the ocean is just a 15-minute drive away.

Dining and Lodging

$$–$$$ ✕ **Arezzo.** The pungent smell of fresh garlic tips you off that the food's
★ the thing at this outstanding Tuscan grill at the PGA National Resort
& Spa. In this unusually relaxed, upscale resort setting, you can dine
in shorts or in jacket and tie. Families are attracted by the affordable
prices (as well as the food), so romantics might be tempted to pass Arezzo
up. Their loss. Dishes include the usual variety of chicken, veal, fish,
and steaks, but there are a dozen pastas, including rigatoni Bolognese
(a specialty), and almost as many pizzas. The decor, too, has the right
idea: an herb garden in the center of the room, slate floors, upholstered
banquettes to satisfy the upscale mood, and butcher paper over yellow table covers to establish the light side. ⊠ *400 Ave. of the Cham-
pions,* ☎ *561/627–2000. AE, MC, V. No lunch. Closed Mon.*

$$ ✕ **River House.** People keep returning to this waterfront restaurant for
the large portions of straightforward American fare; the big salad bar
and fresh, slice-it-yourself breads; the competent service; and, thanks
to the animated buzz of a rewarded local clientele, the feeling that you've
come to the right place. Choices include seafood (always with a daily
catch), steaks, chops, and seafood-steak combo platters. Booths and
freestanding tables are surrounded by lots of blond wood, high ceil-
ings, and nautical art under glass. The wait on Saturday night in sea-
son can be 45 minutes. Reserve one of the 20 upstairs tables, available
weekends only; the upstairs is a little more formal and doesn't have a
salad bar (bread comes from below), but it does possess a cathedral
ceiling. ⊠ *2373 PGA Blvd.,* ☎ *561/694–1198. AE, MC, V. No lunch.*

$$$$ ⊡ **PGA National Resort & Spa.** Outstanding mission-style rooms are
decorated in deep, almost somber florals, and the rest of the resort is
equally richly detailed, from lavish landscaping to limitless sports fa-
cilities to excellent dining. The spa is housed in a building styled after
a Mediterranean fishing village. Its six outdoor therapy pools, dubbed
"Waters of the World," are joined by a collection of imported mineral
salt pools; there are 22 private treatments. Golf courses and croquet
courts are adorned with 25,000 flowering plants amid a 240-acre na-
ture preserve. Two-bedroom, two-bath cottages with fully equipped
kitchens and no-smoking rooms are available, too. ⊠ *400 Ave. of the
Champions, 33418,* ☎ *561/627–2000 or 800/633–9150. 275 rooms,
60 suites, 85 cottages. 4 restaurants, 2 bars, kitchenettes, no-smoking
rooms, lake, pool, hot tubs, saunas, spa, 5 18-hole golf courses, 19 ten-
nis courts, croquet, racquetball, boating. AE, D, DC, MC, V.*

Nightlife

Irish Times (⊠ 9920 Alternate A1A, Promenade Shopping Plaza, ☎
561/624–1504) is a four-leaf-clover find, featuring a microbrewery. There
are live music and live Irish acts Wednesday–Saturday.

Outdoor Activities and Sports

AUTO RACING

Weekly ¼-mi drag racing; monthly 2¼-mi, 10-turn road racing; and
monthly AMA motorcycle road racing take place year-round at the **Mo-
roso Motorsports Park** (⊠ 17047 Beeline Hwy., ☎ 561/622–1400).

GOLF

PGA National Resort & Spa (⊠ 1000 Ave. of the Champions, ☎ 561/
627–1800) offers a reputedly tough 90 holes.

Shopping

The Gardens mall (⊠ 3101 PGA Blvd.) contains the standards if you
want to make sure you're not missing out on anything at home: Bloom-
ingdale's, Burdines, Macy's, Saks Fifth Avenue, and Sears.

Jupiter

③0   *12 mi north of Palm Beach Shores.*

This little town is on one of the few parts of the east coast of Florida that do not have an island in front of them. Beaches here are part of the mainland, and Route A1A runs for almost 4 mi along the beachfront dunes, offering a great ocean view.

Take a look at how life once was in the **Dubois Home,** a modest pioneer home dating from 1898. Sitting atop an ancient Jeaga Indian mound 20 ft high and looking onto Jupiter Inlet, it features Cape Cod as well as Cracker design. Even if you arrive when the house is closed, surrounding **Dubois Park** is worth the visit for its lovely beaches and swimming lagoons. ⊠ *Dubois Rd.,* ☎ *no phone.* ⊡ *Donation welcome.* ☉ *Wed. 1–4.*

Permanent exhibits at the **Florida History Center and Museum** review not only modern-day development along the Loxahatchee River but also shipwrecks, railroads, and Seminole, steamboat-era, and pioneer history. ⊠ *805 N. U.S. 1, Burt Reynolds Park,* ☎ *561/747–6639.* ⊡ *$4.* ☉ *Tues.–Sat. 10–4, Sun. 1–5.*

Carlin Park (⊠ 400 Rte. A1A) provides beachfront picnic pavilions, hiking trails, a baseball diamond, playground, six tennis courts, fishing sites, and, naturally, a beach. The Park Galley, serving snacks and burgers, is usually open daily 9–5.

Dining and Lodging

$$–$$$$ ✕ **Charley's Crab.** The grand view across the Jupiter River complements
★   the soaring ceiling and striking interior architecture of this marina-side restaurant. You'll have great water views whether you choose to dine inside or out, and if you eat after dark, you can watch the searching beam of the historic Jupiter Light House. Come here for expertly prepared seafood, including outstanding pasta choices: *pagliara* with scallops, fish, shrimp, mussels, spinach, garlic, and olive oil; fettuccine *verde* with lobster, sun-dried tomatoes, fresh basil, and goat cheese; and shrimp and tortellini boursin with cream sauce and tomatoes. Consider also such fresh fish as black grouper, Florida pompano, red snapper, or Gulf Stream yellowfin tuna. Other branches of Charley's are in Boca Raton, Deerfield Beach, Fort Lauderdale, Palm Beach, and Stuart. ⊠ *1000 N. U.S. 1,* ☎ *561/744–4710. AE, D, DC, MC, V.*

$$–$$$ ✕ **Sinclairs Ocean Grill & Rotisserie.** In the Jupiter Beach Resort, this popular spot, where you can dine inside or on the terrace, looks out over the ocean. The menu features a daily selection of fresh locally caught fish, which you can have grilled, blackened, baked, or fried. Landlubbers can choose thick juicy steaks (filet mignon is the house specialty) and a variety of chicken dishes, plus pastas and salads. Sunday brunch is a big draw. ⊠ *5 N. Rte. A1A,* ☎ *561/746–2551. AE, MC, V.*

$ ✕ **Lighthouse Restaurant.** Low prices match the plain decor in this coffee shop–style building, but the menu and cuisine are a delightful surprise. You can get chicken breast stuffed with sausage and fresh vegetables, burgundy beef stew, and king crab cakes, and a full-time pastry chef is at work, too. The same people-pleasing formula has been employed for more than 60 years: round-the-clock service (except 10 PM Sunday–6 AM Monday) and a menu that changes daily to take advantage of the best market buys. Those looking for something less "stick-to-the-ribs" can order one of the affordable "lite dinners." ⊠ *1510 U.S. 1,* ☎ *561/746–4811. D, DC, MC, V.*

$$$$ ⚅ **Jupiter Beach Resort.** Management can say without equivocation that this is the best beachfront resort in Jupiter—of course, it's the only beachfront resort in Jupiter. Nevertheless, this unpretentious, elegant hotel would bear up well even against Palm Beach properties. Most guest rooms have balconies, the restaurant is worth staying in for, and the resort takes full advantage of its location. In season sign up for the turtle watch, when you can see newly hatched turtles make their way to the water for the first time. Snorkeling and scuba equipment are available for rent. ⊠ *5 N. Rte. A1A, 33477,* ☎ *561/746–2511 or 800/228–8810,* ☒ *561/747–3304. 187 rooms, 28 suites. Restaurant, 3 bars, pool, tennis court, beach, dive shop, recreation room, children's programs, coin laundry, business services. AE, D, MC, V.*

Outdoor Activities and Sports

BASEBALL

Both the **St. Louis Cardinals** and **Montreal Expos** (⊠ 4751 Main St., ☎ 561/684–6801) train at the new $28 million Roger Dean Stadium, which has seating for 7,000 fans and 12 practice fields.

CANOEING

Canoe Outfitters of Florida (⊠ 4100 W. Indiantown Rd., ☎ 561/746–7053) runs trips along 8 mi of the Loxahatchee River, Florida's only designated Wild and Scenic River. Canoe rental for two people, with drop-off and pickup, costs $28 plus tax. You can also just paddle around for an hour.

GOLF

The **Indian Creek Golf Club** (⊠ 1800 Central Blvd., ☎ 561/747–6262) has 18 holes of varying difficulty. **Jupiter Dunes Golf Club** (⊠ 401 Rte. A1A, ☎ 561/746–6654) has 18 holes and a putting green.

Jupiter Island and Hobe Sound

③ *5 mi north of Jupiter.*

Northeast across the Jupiter Inlet from Jupiter is the southern tip of Jupiter Island, which includes a carefully planned community of the same name. Here estates often retreat from the road behind screens of vegetation, while at the north end of the island, turtles come to nest in a wildlife refuge. To the west, on the mainland, is the little community of Hobe Sound.

The **Jupiter Inlet Lighthouse,** a redbrick Coast Guard navigational beacon, has operated here since 1866. Tours of the 105-ft-tall local landmark are given every half hour, and there is also a small museum. ⊠ *Rte. 707, Jupiter Island,* ☎ *561/747–8380.* ☜ *Tour $5.* ◷ *Sun.–Wed. 10–4, last tour 3:30.*

Within **Blowing Rocks Preserve,** a 73-acre Nature Conservancy holding, you'll find plant communities native to beachfront dune, coastal strand (the landward side of the dunes), mangrove, and hammock (tropical hardwood forests). The best time to visit is when high tides and strong offshore winds coincide, causing the sea to blow spectacularly through holes in the eroded outcropping. Park in the lot; police ticket cars parked along the road. ⊠ *Rte. 707, Jupiter Island,* ☎ *561/744–6668.* ☜ *$3 donation.* ◷ *Daily 6–5.*

The **Hobe Sound National Wildlife Refuge** actually consists of two tracts: 232 acres of sand pine and scrub oak forest in Hobe Sound and 735 acres of coastal sand dune and mangrove swamp on Jupiter Island. Trails are open to the public in both places. Turtles nest and shells wash ashore on the 3½-mi beach, which has been severely eroded by high tides and strong winds during winter high tides. ✉ *13640 S.E. Federal Hwy., Hobe Sound,* ☎ *561/546–6141;* ✉ *Beach Rd. off Rte. 707, Jupiter Island.* *$4 per vehicle.* ⏲ *Daily sunrise–sunset.*

Though on the Hobe Sound National Wildlife Refuge, the appealing **Hobe Sound Nature Center** is an independent organization. Its museum, which has baby alligators, baby crocodiles, and a scary-looking tarantula, is a child's delight. Interpretive exhibits focus on the environment, and a ½-mi trail winds through a forest of sand pine and scrub oak—one of Florida's most unusual and endangered plant communities. A classroom program on environmental issues is for preschool-age children to adults. ✉ *13640 S.E. Federal Hwy., Hobe Sound,* ☎ *561/546–2067.* *Free.* ⏲ *Trail daily sunrise–sunset; nature center weekdays 9–11 and 1–3, call for Sat. hrs, group tours by appointment.*

Once you've gotten to the **Jonathan Dickinson State Park,** follow signs to Hobe Mountain. An ancient dune topped with a tower, it yields a panoramic view across the park's 10,285 acres of varied terrain, as well as the Intracoastal Waterway. The Loxahatchee River, part of the federal government's Wild and Scenic Rivers program, cuts through the park and harbors manatees in winter and alligators year-round. Two-hour boat tours of the river leave four times daily. Among amenities here are bicycle and hiking trails, a campground, and a snack bar. ✉ *16450 S.E. Federal Hwy., Hobe Sound,* ☎ *561/546–2771.* *$3.25 per vehicle with up to 8 people, boat tours $10.* ⏲ *Daily 8–sunset.*

Outdoor Activities and Sports

Jonathan Dickinson's River Tours (✉ Jonathan Dickinson State Park, ☎ 561/746–1466) rents canoes for use around the park.

Stuart

32 *7 mi north of Hobe Sound.*

This compact little town on a peninsula that juts out into the St. Lucie River has a remarkable amount of river shoreline for its size as well as a charming historic district. The ocean is about 5 mi east.

Strict architectural and zoning standards guide civic renewal projects ★ in **historic downtown Stuart,** which now claims eight antiques shops, eight restaurants, and more than 50 specialty shops within a two-block area. The old courthouse has become the **Cultural Court House Center** (✉ 80 E. Ocean Blvd., ☎ 561/288–2542), which features art exhibits. The George W. Parks General Store is now the **Stuart Heritage Museum** (✉ 101 S.W. Flagler Ave., ☎ 561/220–4600). On the National Register of Historic Places, the **Lyric Theatre** (✉ 59 S.W. Flagler Ave., ☎ 561/220–1942) has been revived for performing and community events; a gazebo features free music performances. For information on downtown, contact the **Stuart Main Street Office** (✉ 151 S.W. Flagler Ave., 34994, ☎ 561/286–2848).

Dining and Lodging

$$ ★ ✕ **The Ashley.** Since expanding in 1993, this restaurant has more tables, more art, and more plants than before. However, it still has elements of the old bank that was robbed three times early in the century by the Ashley Gang (hence the name). The big outdoor mural in the French Impressionist style was paid for by downtown revivalists, whose names are duly inscribed on wall plaques inside. The Continental menu appeals, with lots of salads, fresh fish, and pastas. Crowds head to the lounge for a popular happy hour. ✉ *61 S.W. Osceola St.,* ☎ *561/221–9476. AE, MC, V. Closed Mon. in off-season.*

$$ ✕ **Jolly Sailor Pub.** In an old historic-district bank building, this eatery is owned by a 27-year British Merchant Navy veteran, which may account for the endless ship paraphernalia. A veritable Cunard museum, it has a model of the *Brittania,* prints of 19th-century side-wheelers, and a big bar painting of the *QE2.* There's a wonderful brass-railed wood bar, a dartboard, and such pub grub as fish-and-chips, cottage pie, and bangers and mash, with Guinness and Double Diamond ales on tap. You can also get hamburgers and salads. ⊠ *1 S.W. Osceola St.,* ☎ *561/221–1111. AE, MC, V.*

$$–$$$ 🏠 **HarborFront.** On a quiet site that slopes to the St. Lucie River, this
★ B&B combines an unusual mix of accommodations and imaginative extras, including picnic baskets and conciergelike custom planning. Rooms and cottages are cozy and eclectic, ranging from a spacious chintz-covered suite to a cozy apartment with full kitchen, from rooms that are tweedy and dark to those that are airy and bright with a private deck. Furnishings mix wicker and antiques. From hammocks in the yard you can watch pelicans and herons, or take a full- or half-day sail on the 33-ft sailboat that's tied up to the dock. ⊠ *310 Atlanta Ave., 34994,* ☎ *561/288–7289. 8 rooms, suites, cottages, and apartments. Dock, boating. MC, V.*

$$ 🏠 **The Homeplace.** The house was built in 1913 by pioneer Sam Matthews, who contracted much of the early town construction for railroad developer Henry Flagler. Hardwood floors have been restored, and rooms are individually and quaintly decorated with antiques. The fern-filled dining room and Victorian parlor, full of cushioned wicker, overlook a pool, heated spa, and patio. A full breakfast is included. ⊠ *501 Akron Ave., 34994,* ☎ *561/220–9148. 4 rooms. Pool, hot tub. MC, V.*

Outdoor Activities and Sports

Deep-sea charters are available at the **Sailfish Marina** (⊠ 3565 S.E. St. Lucie Blvd., ☎ 561/283–1122).

Shopping

More than 60 restaurants and shops featuring antiques, art, and fashions have opened along **Osceola Street** in the restored downtown area, with hardly a vacancy.

Hutchinson Island (Jensen Beach)

㉝ *5 mi northeast of Stuart.*

Unusual care limits development here and prevents the commercial crowding found to the north and south, although there are some high-rises here and there along the shore. The small town of Jensen Beach, part of which is in the central part of the island, actually stretches across both sides of the Indian River. Citrus farmers and fishermen still play a big role in the community, giving the area a down-to-earth feel. Its most notable population is that of the sea turtles; in summer more than 600 turtles come to nest along the town's Atlantic beach.

Built in 1875, the **House of Refuge Museum** is the only remaining building of nine such structures erected by the U.S. Life Saving Service (a predecessor of the Coast Guard) to aid stranded sailors. Exhibits include antique lifesaving equipment, maps, artifacts from nearby wrecks, and boat-making tools. ⊠ *301 S.E. Mac Blvd.,* ☎ *561/225–1875.* 🎫 *$2.* ☉ *Tues.–Sun. 11–4.*

Run by the Florida Oceanographic Society, the **Coastal Science Center** consists of a coastal hardwood hammock and mangrove forest. Expansion has yielded a visitor center, a science center with interpretive exhibits on coastal science and environmental issues, and a ½-mi interpretive boardwalk. Guided nature walks are offered. ⊠ *890 N.E. Ocean Blvd.,* ☎ *561/225–0505.* ⌸ *$3.50.* ⊘ *Mon.–Sat. 10–5, nature walks Mon.–Sat. 10:30 and by request.*

The pastel-pink **Elliott Museum** was built in 1961 in honor of Sterling Elliott, inventor of an early automated addressing machine and a four-wheel bicycle. The museum features antique automobiles, dolls and toys, and fixtures from an early general store, blacksmith shop, and apothecary shop. ⊠ *825 N.E. Ocean Blvd.,* ☎ *561/225–1961.* ⌸ *$6.* ⊘ *Daily 11–4.*

Bathtub Beach (⊠ MacArthur Blvd. off Rte. A1A), at the north end of the Indian River Plantation, is ideal for children because the waters are shallow for about 300 ft offshore and usually calm. At low tide bathers can walk to the reef. Facilities include rest rooms and showers.

Dining and Lodging

$$–$$$ ✗ **11 Maple Street.** This 16-table restaurant is as good as it gets on
★ the Treasure Coast. Run by Margee and Mike Perrin, it offers a Continental menu that changes nightly. The soft recorded jazz and the earnest, friendly staff satisfy as fully as the brilliant food served in ample portions. Appetizers might include walnut bread with melted fontina cheese or sautéed conch with balsamic vinegar; among entrées are salmon with leeks, lobster, and blue-crab cake, and porcini mushroom risotto. For dessert look out for cherry *clafouti* (like a bread pudding) and white-chocolate custard with blackberry sauce. ⊠ *3224 Maple Ave.,* ☎ *561/334–7714. Reservations essential. MC, V. Closed Mon.–Tues. No lunch.*

$$–$$$ ✗ **Scalawags.** The look is plantation tropical—coach lanterns, gingerbread, wicker, slow-motion paddle fans—but the top-notch buffets are aimed at today's resort guests. Standouts are the all-you-can-eat Wednesday evening Seafood Extravaganza, with jumbo shrimp, Alaskan crab legs, clams on the half shell, marinated salmon, and fresh catch. A regular menu with a big selection of fish, shellfish, and grills plus a big salad bar is also offered. The main dining room in this second-floor restaurant at the Indian River Plantation Marriott Beach Resort overlooks the Indian River; there is also a private 20-seat wine room and a terrace that looks out on the marina. ⊠ *555 N.E. Ocean Blvd.,* ☎ *561/225–6818. AE, DC, MC, V.*

$$ ✗ **Conchy Joe's.** This classic Florida stilt house full of antique fish mounts, gator hides, and snakeskins dates from the late 1920s—but Conchy Joe's, like a hermit crab sliding into a new shell, only moved up from West Palm Beach in 1983. Under a huge Seminole-built *chickee* (raised wood platform) with a palm through the roof, you find a super-casual atmosphere and the freshest Florida seafood from a menu that changes daily. Staples, however, are the grouper marsala, broiled sea scallop, and fried cracked conch. Try the rum drinks with names like Goombay Smash and Bahama Mama, while listening to steel-band calypso or reggae Wednesday–Sunday. Happy hour is 3–6 daily and during all NFL games. ⊠ *3945 N. Indian River Dr.,* ☎ *561/334–1130. AE, D, MC, V.*

$ ✗ **The Emporium.** Indian River Plantation Marriott Beach Resort's coffee shop is an old-fashioned soda fountain and grill that also serves hearty breakfasts. Specialties include eggs Benedict, omelets, deli sandwiches, and salads. ⊠ *555 N.E. Ocean Blvd.,* ☎ *561/225–3700. AE, DC, MC, V.*

$$$$ ⊞ **Indian River Plantation Marriott Beach Resort.** With a wealth of recreational activities and facilities as well as many restaurants and bars, this 200-acre, sprawling yet self-contained resort is an excellent choice for families. Reception, some of the restaurants, and many rooms are in three yellow four-story buildings that form an open courtyard with a large swimming pool. Additional rooms and apartments with kitchens are in numerous other buildings spread around the property. Some overlook the Intracoastal Waterway and the resort's 77-slip marina, while other rooms look out to the ocean or onto tropical gardens. Complimentary tram service runs to key points around the property day and night. ⊠ *555 N.E. Ocean Blvd., Hutchinson Island, Stuart 34996,* ☎ *561/225–3700 or 800/775–5936. 326 rooms and suites, 150 condominiums. 5 restaurants, 4 bars, 4 pools, spa, 18-hole golf course, 13 tennis courts, beach, boating, children's program. AE, DC, MC, V.*

$$–$$$ ⊞ **Hutchinson Inn.** Sandwiched among the high-rises, this modest and affordable two-story motel from the mid-1970s has the feel of a B&B thanks to pretty canopies at the entrance and management's friendly attitude. An expanded Continental breakfast is served in the well-appointed lobby or on little tables outside, and you can borrow a book or a stack of magazines to take to your room, where homemade cookies are delivered in the evenings. On Saturday there's a noon barbecue. Motel-style rooms range from small but comfortable to fully equipped efficiencies and seafront suites with private balconies. ⊠ *9750 S. Ocean Dr., 34957,* ☎ *561/229–2000,* ℻ *561/229–8875. 21 units. Pool, tennis court, beach. MC, V.*

Outdoor Activities and Sports

BASEBALL

The **New York Mets** (⊠ 525 N.W. Peacock Blvd., Port St. Lucie, ☎ 561/871–2115) train at the St. Lucie County Sport Complex.

GOLF

Indian River Plantation Marriott Beach Resort (⊠ 555 N.E. Ocean Blvd., ☎ 561/225–3700 or 800/444–3389) has 18 holes.

Fort Pierce

㉞ *11 mi north of Stuart.*

This community, about an hour north of Palm Beach, has a distinctive rural feel, focusing on ranching and citrus farming rather than tourism. It has several worthwhile stops for visitors, including those easily seen while following Route 707.

Once a reservoir, 550-acre **Savannahs Recreation Area** has been returned to its natural state. Today the semiwilderness has campsites, a petting zoo, botanical garden, boat ramps, and trails. ⊠ *1400 E. Midway Rd.,* ☎ *561/464–7855.* ☞ *$1 per vehicle.* ☉ *Daily 8 AM–8:30 PM.*

At the **Heathcote Botanical Gardens,** a self-guided tour takes in a palm walk, Japanese garden, and subtropical foliage. ⊠ *210 Savannah Rd.,* ☎ *561/464–4672.* ☞ *$2.50.* ☉ *Tues.–Sat. 9–5, also Sun. 1–5 Nov.–Apr.*

As the home of the Treasure Coast Art Association, the **A. E. "Bean" Backus Gallery** displays the works of one of Florida's foremost landscape artists. The gallery also mounts changing exhibits and offers exceptional buys on work by local artists. ⊠ *500 N. Indian River Dr.,* ☎ *561/465–0630.* ☞ *Donation welcome.* ☉ *Tues.–Sun. 1–5.*

Highlights at the **St. Lucie County Historical Museum** include historic photos, early 20th-century memorabilia, vintage farm tools, a restored

1919 American La France fire engine, replicas of a general store and the old Fort Pierce railroad station, and the restored 1905 Gardner House. ✉ *414 Seaway Dr.,* ☎ *561/462–1795.* ⊡ *$3.* ☉ *Tues.–Sat. 10–4, Sun. noon–4.*

The 340-acre **Fort Pierce Inlet State Recreation Area** contains sand dunes and a coastal hammock. The park offers swimming, surfing, picnicking, hiking, and walking along a self-guided nature trail. ✉ *905 Shorewinds Dr.,* ☎ *561/468–3985.* ⊡ *$3.25 per vehicle with up to 8 people.* ☉ *Daily 8–sunset.*

The **UDT-Seal Museum** commemorates the site where more than 3,000 navy frogmen trained during World War II. Weapons and equipment are on view, and exhibits depict the history of the UDTs (Underwater Demolition Teams). Numerous patrol boats and vehicles are displayed outdoors. ✉ *3300 N. Rte. A1A,* ☎ *561/595–5845.* ⊡ *$3.25.* ☉ *Mon.–Sat. 10–4, Sun. noon–4.*

Accessible only by footbridge, the **Jack Island Wildlife Refuge** contains 4⅓ mi of trails. The 1½-mi Marsh Rabbit Trail across the island traverses a mangrove swamp to a 30-ft observation tower overlooking the Indian River. ✉ *Rte. A1A,* ☎ *561/468–3985.* ⊡ *Free.* ☉ *Daily 8–sunset.*

The **Harbor Branch Oceanographic Institution** is an internationally recognized diversified research and teaching facility that offers a glimpse into the high-tech world of marine research. Its fleet of research vessels—particularly its two submersibles—operates around the world for NASA, NOAA, and NATO, among other contractors. Visitors can take a 90-minute tour of the 500-acre facility, including aquariums of sea life indigenous to the Indian River Lagoon, exhibits of marine technology, and other learning facilities. There are also lifelike and whimsical bronze sculptures created by founder J. Seward Johnson Jr., and a gift shop with imaginative sea-related items. ✉ *5600 Old Dixie Hwy.,* ☎ *561/465–2400.* ⊡ *$6.* ☉ *Tours Mon.–Sat. 10, noon, and 2.*

Dining and Lodging

$–$$ ✗ **Mangrove Mattie's.** Since its opening in the late 1980s, this upscale but rustic spot on Fort Pierce Inlet has provided dazzling waterfront views and imaginative nautical decor with delicious seafood. Dine outdoors on the terrace or inside in the cool air-conditioning, and try the coconut-fried shrimp or the chicken and scampi. Or come by during happy hour (weekdays 5–8) for a free buffet of snacks. ✉ *1640 Seaway Dr.,* ☎ *561/466–1044. AE, D, DC, MC, V.*

$–$$ ✗ **Theo Thudpucker's Raw Bar.** Businesspeople dressed for work mingle here with people fresh from the beach wearing shorts. On squally days everyone piles in off the jetty. Specialties include oyster stew, smoked fish spread, conch salad and conch fritters, fresh catfish, and alligator tail. ✉ *2025 Seaway Dr. (South Jetty),* ☎ *561/465–1078. No credit cards.*

$$$ ⊞ **Mellon Patch Inn.** This little B&B has an excellent location—across the shore road from a beach park, at the end of a canal leading to the Indian River Lagoon. One side of the canal has a bank of attractive new homes; the other has the Jack Island Wildlife Refuge. Images of split-open melons permeate the house—on pillows, crafts, and candies on night tables. Each of the guest rooms has imaginative accessories, art, and upholstery appropriate to its individual theme. The cathedral-ceiling living room features a wood-burning fireplace, and full breakfast is included. ✉ *3601 N. Rte. A1A, North Hutchinson Island 34949,* ☎ *561/461–5231. 4 rooms. Dock, fishing. MC, V.*

$$–$$$ ⊞ **Harbor Light Inn.** The pick of the pack of lodgings lining the Fort Pierce Inlet along Seaway Drive is this modern nautical, blue-trimmed motel. Spacious units on two floors feature kitchen or wet bar and routine but well-cared-for furnishings. Half the rooms have a waterfront porch or balcony. In addition to the motel units there is a set of four apartments across the street (off the water), where in-season weekly rates are $360. ⊠ *1156–1160 Seaway Dr., 34949,* ☎ *561/468–3555 or 800/433–0004. 21 units. Pool, fishing, coin laundry. AE, D, DC, MC, V.*

Outdoor Activities and Sports

FISHING

For charter boats and fishing guides, try the **Dockside Inn** (⊠ 1152 Seaway Dr., ☎ 561/461–4824).

JAI ALAI

Fort Pierce Jai Alai operates seasonally for live jai alai and year-round for off-track betting on horse-racing simulcasts. ⊠ *1750 S. Kings Hwy., off Okeechobee Rd.,* ☎ *561/464–7500 or 800/524–2524.* ☑ *$1.* ☉ *Games Jan.–Apr., Wed. and Sat. 12:30 and 7, Thurs.–Fri. 7, Sun. 1; call to double-check schedule; simulcasts Wed.–Mon. noon and 7.*

SCUBA DIVING

Some 200 yards from shore and ¼ mi north of the UDT-Seal Museum on North Hutchinson Island, the **Urca de Lima Underwater Archaeological Preserve** features the remains of a flat-bottom, round-bellied storeship. Once part of a treasure fleet bound for Spain, it was destroyed by a hurricane. Dive boats can be chartered through the **Dockside Inn** (⊠ 1152 Seaway Dr., ☎ 561/461–4824).

Shopping

One of Florida's best discount malls, the **Manufacturer's Outlet Center** (⊠ Rte. 70, off I–95 at Exit 65) contains 41 stores offering such brand names as American Tourister, Jonathan Logan, Aileen, Polly Flinders, Van Heusen, London Fog, Levi Strauss, and Geoffrey Beene.

En Route To reach Vero Beach, you have two options—Route A1A, along the coast, or Route 605 (often called Old Dixie Highway), on the mainland. As you approach Vero on the latter, you'll pass through an ungussied landscape of small farms and residential areas. On the beach route, part of the drive is through an unusually undeveloped section of the Florida coast. Both trips are very relaxing.

Vero Beach

③⑤ *12 mi north of Fort Pierce.*

There's a tranquility to this Indian River County seat, an affluent town with a strong commitment to the environment and the arts. Retirees make up about half the winter population. In the exclusive Riomar Bay area of town, "canopy roads" are shaded by massive live oaks, and a popular cluster of restaurants and shops is just off the beach.

At the **Indian River Citrus Museum,** photos, farm tools, and videos tell about a time when oxen hauled the citrus crop to the railroads, when family fruit stands dotted the roadsides, and when gorgeous packing labels made every crate arriving up north an enticement to visit the Sunshine State. You can also book free citrus tours of actual groves. ⊠ *2140 14th Ave.,* ☎ *561/770–2263.* ☑ *Donation welcome.* ☉ *Tues.– Sat. 10–4, Sun. 1–4.*

In Riverside Park's Civic Arts Center, the **Center for the Arts** presents a full schedule of exhibitions, art movies, lectures, workshops, and other events, with a focus on Florida artists. ⊠ *3001 Riverside Park Dr.,* ☎ *561/231–0707.* 🖭 *Free.* ⊙ *Fri.–Wed. 10–4:30, Thurs. 10–8.*

In addition to a wet lab containing aquariums filled with Indian River Lagoon life, the outstanding 51-acre **Environmental Learning Center** has a 600-ft boardwalk through mangrove shoreline and a 1-mi canoe trail. The center is on the north edge of Vero Beach, on Wabasso Island, but it's a pretty drive and worth the trip. ⊠ *255 Live Oak Dr.,* ☎ *561/589–5050.* 🖭 *Free.* ⊙ *Weekdays 9–5, weekends 1–4.*

Humiston Park is just one of the beach-access parks along the east edge of town that have boardwalks and steps bridging the foredune. It has a large children's play area and picnic tables and is across the street from shops. ⊠ *Ocean Dr. below Beachland Blvd.,* ☎ *no phone.* 🖭 *Free.* ⊙ *Daily 7 AM–10 PM.*

The Arts

The **Civic Arts Center** (⊠ Riverside Park), a cluster of cultural facilities, includes the Riverside Theatre (⊠ 3250 Riverside Park Dr., ☎ 561/231–6990), which stages six productions each season in its 633-seat performance hall; the Agnes Wahlstrom Youth Playhouse (⊠ 3280 Riverside Park Dr., ☎ 561/234–8052), which mounts children's productions; and the Center for the Arts (⊠ 3001 Riverside Park Dr., ☎ 561/231–0707), which presents art movies and lectures in addition to its other offerings. **Riverside Children's Theatre** (⊠ 3280 Riverside Park Dr., ☎ 561/234–8052) offers a series of professional touring and local productions, as well as acting workshops at the Agnes Wahlstrom Youth Playhouse.

Dining and Lodging

$$–$$$ ✕ **Black Pearl.** This intimate and sophisticated restaurant with deep pink walls and pink-and-green Art Deco furnishings is one of Vero's trendiest dining picks. The menu emphasizes fresh local ingredients. Specialties include chilled leek-and-watercress soup, local fish in parchment paper, and panfried veal with local shrimp and vermouth. ⊠ *2855 Ocean Dr.,* ☎ *561/234–4426. AE, MC, V. No lunch weekends.*

$$–$$$ ✕ **Ocean Grill.** Opened by Waldo Sexton as a hamburger shack in 1938, ★ the oceanfront Ocean Grill is now furnished with Tiffany lamps, wrought-iron chandeliers, and Beanie Backus paintings of pirates and Seminole Indians. The menu includes black-bean soup, jumbo lump-crabmeat salad, and at least three kinds of fish every day. The house drink, the Leaping Limey, a curious blend of vodka, blue curaçao, and lemon, commemorates the 1894 wreck of the *Breconshire* that occurred just offshore and from which 34 British sailors escaped. The bar and some tables look over the water. ⊠ *1050 Sexton Plaza (Beachland Blvd. east of Ocean Dr.),* ☎ *561/231–5409. AE, D, DC, MC, V. Closed 2 wks following Labor Day. No lunch weekends.*

$–$$ ✕ **Pearl's Bistro.** Island-style cuisine is the draw at this laid-back and less expensive sister restaurant to the Black Pearl (☞ Dining and Lodging, *above*). For starters try the pasta Rasta, the seafood chowder, or the Jamaican jerk shrimp. Then move on to grilled Yucatán-spiced local fish, barbecued ribs, Bahamian shrimp and grouper pepper pot, or blackened New York strip with peppery rum sauce. ⊠ *56 Royal Palm Blvd.,* ☎ *561/778–2950. AE, MC, V. No lunch Sun.*

$$$$ 🏨 **DoubleTree Guest Suites.** This five-story rose-color stucco hotel is conveniently located—right on the beach and near restaurants, specialty shops, and boutiques. One- and two-bedroom suites have patios opening onto a pool or balconies and excellent ocean views. ⊠ *3500 Ocean*

Dr., 32963, ☎ *561/231–5666. 55 suites. Bar, 2 pools, wading pool, hot tub. AE, D, DC, MC, V.*

$$$–$$$$ 🏨 **Disney's Vero Beach Resort.** Built on 71 oceanfront acres, this sprawling vacation getaway, which operates both as a time-share and a hotel, is the classiest resort in Vero Beach. The main four-story building, three freestanding villas, and six beach cottages are nestled among tropical greenery. Buildings are painted in pale pastels and sport steeply pitched gables, and many units have balconies. Bright interiors feature rattan furniture and tile floors. ⊠ *9235 Rte. A1A, 32963,* ☎ *561/234–2000. 175 units. 2 restaurants, bar, pool, wading pool, 6 tennis courts, basketball, bicycles, video games. AE, D, DC, MC, V.*

$$–$$$ 🏨 **Captain Hiram's Islander Motel.** Across from the beach, the aqua-and-white-trim Islander has a snoozy Key West style that contrasts stylishly with the smart shops it's tucked between. Jigsaw-cut brackets and balusters and beach umbrellas dress up the pool. All rooms feature white wicker, paddle fans hung from vaulted ceilings, and fresh flowers. It's just right for beachside Vero. ⊠ *3101 Ocean Dr., 32963,* ☎ *561/231–4431 or 800/952–5886. 16 rooms, 1 efficiency. Pool. AE, DC, MC, V.*

Outdoor Activities and Sports

The **Los Angeles Dodgers** (⊠ 4101 26th St., ☎ 561/569–4900) train at Dodgertown, actually in Vero Beach.

Shopping

Along **Ocean Drive** near Beachland Boulevard, a specialty shopping area includes art galleries, antiques shops, and upscale clothing stores.

Sebastian

③⑥ *7 mi north of Vero Beach.*

One of only a few sparsely populated areas on Florida's east coast, this little fishing village has as remote a feeling as you'll find anywhere between Jacksonville and Miami Beach. That remoteness adds to the appeal of the recreation area around Sebastian Inlet, where you can walk for miles along quiet beaches.

The **McLarty Treasure Museum,** designated a National Historical Landmark, features displays dedicated to the 1715 hurricane that sank a fleet of Spanish treasure ships. ⊠ *13180 N. Rte. A1A,* ☎ *561/589–2147.* 🎫 *$1.* ☼ *Daily 10–4:30.*

You've really come upon hidden loot when you step into **Mel Fisher's Treasure Museum.** You can view some of what was recovered from the Spanish treasure ship *Atocha* and its sister ships of the 1715 fleet. Fisher operates a similar museum in Key West. ⊠ *1322 U.S. 1,* ☎ *561/589–9875.* 🎫 *$5.* ☼ *Mon.–Sat. 10–5, Sun. noon–5.*

Because of the highly productive fishing waters of Sebastian Inlet, at the north end of Orchid Island, the 578-acre **Sebastian Inlet State Recreation Area** is one of the best-attended parks in the Florida state system. On both sides of the high bridge that spans the inlet—from which the views are spectacular—the recreation area attracts plenty of anglers as well as those eager to enjoy the fine sandy beaches (both within the recreation area and outside it), which are known for having the best waves in the state. A concession stand on the north side of the inlet sells short-order food, rents various craft, and has an apparel and surf shop. A boat ramp is available. Not far away along the sea is a dune area that's part of the **Archie Carr National Wildlife Refuge,** a haven for sea turtles and other protected Florida wildlife. ⊠ *9700 S. Rte. A1A, Melbourne Beach,* ☎ *407/984–4852;* ⊠ *1300 Rte. A1A,*

Melbourne Beach, ☎ *561/589–9659.* 🖾 *$3.25.* ⊙ *Daily 24 hrs, bait and tackle shop daily 7:30–6, concession stand daily 8–5.*

Dining and Lodging

$–$$ ✕ **Capt. Hiram's.** This family-friendly restaurant on the Indian River Lagoon is easygoing, fanciful, and fun—definitely not purposefully hip. As the sign says, NECKTIES ARE PROHIBITED. The place is "real"—full of wooden booths, stained glass, umbrellas on the open deck, and ceiling fans. Don't miss Capt. Hiram's Sandbar, where kids can play while parents enjoy a drink at stools set in an outdoor shower or a beached boat. Choose among seafood brochette, New York strip steak, the fresh catch, and lots of other seafood dishes as well as raw-bar items. The full bar has a weekday happy hour and free hot hors d'oeuvres Friday 5–6. There's nightly entertainment in season. 🖾 *1606 N. Indian River Dr.,* ☎ *561/589–4345. AE, D, MC, V.*

$–$$ ✕ **Hurricane Harbor.** Built in 1927 as a garage and used during Prohibition as a smugglers' den, Hurricane Harbor now draws a year-round crowd of retirees and locals. Guests love the waterfront window seats on stormy nights, when sizable waves break outside in the Indian River Lagoon. The menu features seafood, steaks, and grills, along with lighter fare. On Friday and Saturday nights the Antique Dining Room is opened, with linen, stained glass, and a huge antique breakfront. There's also live music nightly. 🖾 *1540 Indian River Dr.,* ☎ *561/589–1773. AE, D, MC, V. Closed Mon.*

$$ 🏨 **Captain's Quarters Riverfront Motel.** Five units—four overlooking the Indian River Lagoon and the marina at Capt. Hiram's restaurant and one two-room suite—are all Key West cute. Painted in bright colors with matching fabrics, the rooms have pine and white-wicker furniture and pine plank floors with grass rugs. The adequate bathrooms have large stall showers. Glass doors open to a plank porch, but the porches are all within sight of each other. 🖾 *1606 Indian River Dr., 32958,* ☎ *561/589–4345. 4 rooms, 1 suite. Restaurant. AE, D, MC, V.*

$$ 🏨 **Davis House Inn.** Vero native Steve Wild modeled his two-story inn after the clubhouse at Augusta National, and, perhaps surprisingly, it fits right in with Sebastian's fishing-town look. Wide overhung roofs shade wraparound porches. In a companion house that Steve calls the Gathering Room, he serves a complimentary expanded Continental breakfast. Rooms are huge—virtual suites, with large sitting areas—though somewhat underfurnished. Overall, it's a terrific value. 🖾 *607 Davis St., 32958,* ☎ *561/589–4114. 12 efficiencies. Bicycles. MC, V.*

Outdoor Activities and Sports

CANOEING AND KAYAKING

Bill Rogers Outdoor Adventures (🖾 1541 DeWitt La., ☎ 561/564–9600) outfits canoe trips down the Sebastian River, along Indian River Lagoon, and through Pelican Island Wildlife Refuge, as well as more distant locations. The concession stand at **Sebastian Inlet State Recreation Area** (🖾 9700 S. Rte. A1A, Melbourne Beach, ☎ 561/984–4852) rents canoes, kayaks, and paddleboats.

FISHING

The best inlet fishing in the region is at **Sebastian Inlet State Recreation Area** (🖾 9700 S. Rte. A1A, Melbourne Beach), where the catch includes bluefish, flounder, jack, redfish, sea trout, snapper, snook, and Spanish mackerel. For deep-sea fishing try *Miss Sebastian* (🖾 Sembler Dock, ½ block north of Capt. Hiram's restaurant, ☎ 561/589–3275); $25 for a half day covers rod, reel, and bait. **Sebastian Inlet Marina at Capt.**

Hiram's (⊠ 1606 Indian River Dr., ☎ 561/589–4345) offers half- and full-day fishing charters.

WINDSURFING

The **Sailboard School** (⊠ 9125 U.S. 1, ☎ 561/589–2671 or 800/253–6573) provides year-round one-day, weekend, and five-day programs of windsurfing instruction, including boards, for $120 a day, $575 for five days.

PALM BEACH AND THE TREASURE COAST A TO Z

Arriving and Departing

By Bus

Greyhound Lines (☎ 800/231–2222) buses arrive at the station in West Palm Beach (⊠ 100 Banyan Blvd., ☎ 561/833–8534).

By Car

I-95 runs north–south, linking West Palm Beach with Miami and Fort Lauderdale to the south and with Daytona, Jacksonville, and the rest of the Atlantic coast to the north. To get to central Palm Beach, exit at Belvedere Road or Okeechobee Boulevard. Florida's Turnpike runs up from Miami through West Palm Beach before angling northwest to reach Orlando.

By Plane

Palm Beach International Airport (PBIA) (⊠ Congress Ave. and Belvedere Rd., West Palm Beach, ☎ 561/471–7400) is served by Air Canada (☎ 800/776–3000), American/American Eagle (☎ 800/433–7300), American Trans-Air (☎ 800/225–2995), Canadian Holidays (☎ 800/661–8881), Carnival Airlines (☎ 800/824–7386), Comair (☎ 800/354–9822), Continental (☎ 800/525–0280), Delta (☎ 800/221–1212), KIWI International Airlines (☎ 800/538–5494), Northwest (☎ 800/225–2525), Paradise Island (☎ 800/432–8807), Republic Air Travel (☎ 800/233–0225), TWA (☎ 800/221–2000), United (☎ 800/241–6522), and US Airways/US Airways Express (☎ 800/428–4322).

BETWEEN THE AIRPORT AND THE TOWNS

Route 10 of **Tri-Rail Commuter Bus Service** (☎ 800/874–7245) runs from the airport to Tri-Rail's nearby Palm Beach airport station daily. **CoTran** (☞ Getting Around by Bus, *below*) Route 4-S operates from the airport to downtown West Palm Beach every two hours at 35 minutes after the hour from 7:35 until 5:35. The fare is $1.

Palm Beach Transportation (☎ 561/689–4222) provides taxi and limousine service from PBIA. Reserve at least a day in advance for a limousine. The lowest fares are $1.50 per mile, with the meter starting at $1.25. Depending on your destination, a flat rate (from PBIA only) may save money. Wheelchair-accessible vehicles are available.

By Train

Amtrak (☎ 800/872–7245) connects West Palm Beach (⊠ 201 S. Tamarind Ave., ☎ 561/832–6169) with cities along Florida's east coast and the Northeast daily and via the *Sunset Limited* to New Orleans and Los Angeles three times weekly. Included in Amtrak's service is transport from West Palm Beach to Okeechobee (⊠ 801 N. Parrott Ave.); the station is unmanned.

Getting Around

The **Downtown Transfer Facility** (⊠ Banyan Blvd. and Clearlake Dr., West Palm Beach), off Australian Avenue at the west entrance to downtown, links the downtown shuttle, Amtrak, Tri-Rail (the commuter line of Miami-Dade, Broward, and Palm Beach counties), CoTran (the county bus system), Greyhound, and taxis.

By Bus

CoTran (Palm Beach County Transportation Authority) buses require exact change. The cost is $1.50, $1 for students, senior citizens, and people with disabilities (with reduced-fare ID); transfers are 20¢. Service operates 5 AM–8:30 PM, though pickups on most routes are 5:30 AM–7 PM. For details call 561/233–1111 (Palm Beach) or 561/930–5123 (Boca Raton–Delray Beach).

Palmtran (☎ 561/833–8873) is a shuttle system that provides free transportation around downtown West Palm Beach, weekdays 6:30 AM–7:30 PM.

By Car

U.S. 1 threads north–south along the coast, connecting most coastal communities, while the more scenic Route A1A ventures out onto the barrier islands. The interstate, I–95, runs parallel to U.S. 1 but a bit farther inland.

A nonstop four-lane route, Okeechobee Boulevard carries traffic from west of downtown West Palm Beach, near the Amtrak station in the airport district, directly to the Flagler Memorial Bridge and into Palm Beach. Flagler Drive will be turned over for pedestrian use before the end of the century.

The best way to get to Lake Okeechobee from West Palm is to drive west on Southern Boulevard from I–95 past the cutoff road to Lion Country Safari. From there the boulevard is designated U.S. 98/441.

By Taxi

Palm Beach Transportation (☎ 561/689–4222) has a single number serving several cab companies. Meters start at $1.25, and the charge is $1.25 per mile within West Palm Beach city limits; if the trip at any point leaves the city limits, the fare is $1.50 per mile. Some cabs may charge more. Waiting time is 25¢ per 75 seconds.

By Train

Tri-Rail (☎ 305/728–8445 or 800/874–7245), the commuter rail system, has six stations in Palm Beach County (13 stops altogether between West Palm Beach and Miami). The round-trip fare is $5, $2.50 for students and senior citizens.

Contacts and Resources

Emergencies

Dial **911** for police or ambulance.

HOSPITALS

The following hospitals have 24-hour emergency rooms: **Good Samaritan Hospital** (⊠ Flagler Dr. and Palm Beach Lakes Blvd., West Palm Beach, ☎ 561/655–5511; 561/650–6240 physician referral), **JFK Medical Center** (⊠ 5301 S. Congress Ave., Atlantis, ☎ 561/965–7300; 561/642–3628 physician referral), **Palm Beaches Medical Center** (⊠ 2201 45th St., West Palm Beach, ☎ 561/881–2670; 561/881–2661 physician referral), **Palm Beach Regional Hospital** (⊠ 2829 10th Ave. N, Lake Worth, ☎ 561/967–7800; 800/237–6644 physician referral), and **St.**

Mary's Hospital (⊠ 901 45th St., West Palm Beach, ☎ 561/844–6300; 561/881–2929 physician referral).

Eckerd Drug (⊠ 3343 S. Congress Ave., Palm Springs, ☎ 561/965–3367) and **Walgreens** (⊠ 1688 S. Congress Ave., Palm Springs, ☎ 561/968–8211; ⊠ 7561 N. Federal Hwy., Boca Raton, ☎ 561/241–9802; ⊠ 1634 S. Federal Hwy., Boynton Beach, ☎ 561/737–1260; ⊠ 1208 Royal Palm Beach Blvd., Royal Palm Beach, ☎ 561/798–9048; ⊠ 6370 Indiantown Rd., Jupiter, ☎ 561/744–6822; ⊠ 20 E. 30th St., Riviera Beach, ☎ 561/848–6464).

Guided Tours

Capt. Doug's (⊠ Sebastian Marina, Sebastian, ☎ 561/589–2329) offers three-hour lunch and dinner cruises along the Indian River on board a 35-ft sloop. Cost is $100 per couple, including meal, tips, beer, and wine. **J-Mark Fish Camp** (⊠ Torry Island, ☎ 561/996–5357) has 45- to 60-minute airboat rides for $20 per person, with a minimum of two people and a maximum of six; 90- to 120-minute rides for $30 per person include a look at an active eagle's nest. **Jonathan Dickinson's River Tours** (⊠ Jonathan Dickinson State Park, 16450 S.E. Federal Hwy., Hobe Sound, ☎ 561/746–1466) runs two-hour guided riverboat cruises daily at 9, 11, 1, and 3 and once a month, at the full moon, at 7. The cost is $10. **Loxahatchee Everglades Tours** (⊠ 10400 Loxahatchee Rd., ☎ 561/482–6107) operates airboat tours year-round from west of Boca Raton through the marshes between the built-up coast and Lake Okeechobee. The *Manatee Queen* (⊠ Jonathan Dickinson State Park, 16450 S.E. Federal Hwy., Hobe Sound, ☎ 561/744–2191), a 49-passenger catamaran, offers day and evening cruises November–May on the Intracoastal Waterway and into the park's cypress swamps.

Ramblin' Rose Riverboat (⊠ 1 N.E. 1st St., Delray Beach, ☎ 561/243–0686) operates luncheon, dinner-dance, and Sunday brunch cruises along the Intracoastal Waterway. *The Spirit of St. Joseph* (⊠ 109 Myrtle St., Fort Pierce, ☎ 561/467–2628) offers seven lunch and dinner cruises weekly on the Indian River, leaving from alongside the St. Lucie County Historical Museum. Atlantic Cruises' *Star of Palm Beach* (⊠ Phil Foster Park, 900 E. Blue Heron Rd., Palm Beach, ☎ 561/842–0882) runs year-round from Singer Island, each day offering one dinner-dance and three sightseeing cruises on the Intracoastal Waterway. **Water Taxi Scenic Cruises** (⊠ Sailfish Marina and Riviera Beach Marina, Palm Beach, ☎ 561/775–2628) offers several different daily tours in a 16-person launch designed to let you get a close-up look at the mansions of the rich and famous. The southern tour includes the mansions of Palm Beach, while the northern tour includes the North Palm Beach Canal. There's also a one-hour BYOB sunset cruise.

Contact the **Audubon Society of the Everglades** (⊠ Box 16914, West Palm Beach 33461, ☎ 561/588–6908) for field trips and nature walks. **Swampland Tours** (⊠ 103 75th Hwy. 78W, Okeechobee 34974, ☎ 941/467–4411), on Lake Okeechobee, operates interpretive boat tours through the National Audubon Society Wildlife Sanctuary.

The **Boca Raton Historical Society** (⊠ 71 N. Federal Hwy., Boca Raton, ☎ 561/395–6766) offers afternoon tours of the Boca Raton Resort & Club on Tuesday year-round and to other South Florida sites. The **Fort Pierce Historical Society** (⊠ 131 Main St., Fort Pierce, ☎ 561/466–3880) gives walking tours of the town's historic section, past buildings built by early settlers. The **Indian River County Historical Society** (✉ 2336 14th Ave., Vero Beach, ☎ 561/778–3435) conducts walking tours of downtown Vero on Wednesday at 11 and 1 (by reservation). **Old Northwood Historic District Tours** (✉ 501 30th St., West Palm Beach, ☎ 561/863–5633) leads two-hour walking tours that include visits to historic home interiors. They leave Sundays at 2, and a $5 donation is requested. Tours for groups of six or more can be scheduled almost any day.

Visitor Information

Belle Glade Chamber of Commerce (✉ 540 S. Main St., Belle Glade 33430, ☎ 561/996–2745). **Chamber of Commerce of the Palm Beaches** (✉ 401 N. Flagler Dr., West Palm Beach 33401, ☎ 561/833–3711). **Clewiston Chamber of Commerce** (✉ 544 W. Sugarland Hwy., Clewiston 33440, ☎ 941/983–7979). **Glades County Chamber of Commerce** (✉ U.S. 27 and 10th St., Moore Haven 33471, ☎ 941/946–0440). **Indian River County Tourist Council** (✉ 1216 21st St., Box 2947, Vero Beach 32961, ☎ 561/567–3491). **Indiantown Chamber of Commerce** (✉ 15518 S.W. Osceola St., Indiantown 34956, ☎ 561/597–2184). **Okeechobee County Chamber of Commerce** (✉ 55 S. Parrott Ave., Okeechobee 34974, ☎ 941/763–6464). **Pahokee Chamber of Commerce** (✉ 115 E. Main St., Pahokee 33476, ☎ 561/924–5579). **Palm Beach Chamber of Commerce** (✉ 45 Cocoanut Row, Palm Beach 33480, ☎ 561/655–3282). **Palm Beach County Convention & Visitors Bureau** (✉ 1555 Palm Beach Lakes Blvd., Suite 204, West Palm Beach 33401, ☎ 561/471–3995). **St. Lucie County Tourist Development Council** (✉ 2300 Virginia Ave., Fort Pierce 34982, ☎ 561/462–1535 or 800/344–8443). **Stuart/Martin County Chamber of Commerce** (✉ 1650 S. Kanner Hwy., Stuart 34994, ☎ 561/287–1088). For more information on the Okeechobee area, contact the **U.S. Army Corps of Engineers** (✉ South Florida Operations Office, 525 Ridgelawn Rd., Clewiston 33440-5399, ☎ 941/983–8101).

6 The Florida Keys

The Keys are one of America's last frontiers. Here both humans and nature seek refuge in a verdant island chain that stretches raggedly west-southwest across a deep blue-green seascape at the base of the Florida peninsula.

THE FLORIDA KEYS ARE A WILDERNESS of flowering jungles and shimmering seas, a jade necklace of mangrove-fringed islands dangling toward the tropics. The Florida Keys are also a 110-mi traffic jam lined with garish billboards, hamburger stands, shopping centers, motels, and trailer courts. Unfortunately, in the Keys you can't have one without the other. A river of tourist traffic gushes along U.S. 1 (also called the Overseas Highway), the main artery between Key Largo and Key West. Residents of Monroe County live by diverting that river's flow of green dollars to their own pockets. In the process, the fragile beauty of the Keys—or at least the 45 that are inhabited and linked to the mainland by 43 bridges—has paid the environmental price.

By Herb Hiller

Updated by
Diane P.
Marshall

Despite designation as "an area of critical state concern" in 1975 and a subsequent state-mandated development slowdown, rapid growth has continued, and the Keys' natural resources are still in peril. In 1990 Congress established the Florida Keys National Marine Sanctuary, covering 2,800 square nautical mi of coastal waters. Adjacent to the Keys landmass are spectacular, unique, and nationally significant marine environments, including sea-grass meadows, mangrove islands, and extensive living coral reefs. These fragile environments support rich and diverse biological communities possessing extensive conservation, recreational, commercial, ecological, historical, research, educational, and aesthetic values.

The Florida Keys National Marine Sanctuary and Protection Act is intended to protect the coral reefs and restore worsening water quality. But problems continue. Increased salinity in Florida Bay causes large areas of sea grass to die and drift in mats out of the bay. These mats then block sunlight from reaching the reefs, stifling their growth and threatening both the Keys' recreational diving economy and tourism in general.

Other threats to the Keys' charm also loom. As government officials with one hand sign the national marine sanctuary into effect, with the other they bring about the four-laning of U.S. 1 to the mainland, opening the floodgates to increased traffic, population, and tourism. Observers wonder if the four-laning of the rest of U.S. 1 throughout the Keys can be far away and if a trip to paradise will then be worth it.

For now, however, take pleasure as you drive down U.S. 1 along the islands. Most days you can gaze over the silvery blue and green Atlantic and its still-living reef, with Florida Bay, the Gulf of Mexico, and the backcountry on your right (the Keys extend east–west from the mainland). At a few points the ocean and gulf are as much as 10 mi apart. In most places, however, they are within 1–4 mi, and on the narrowest landfill islands, they are separated only by the road.

Things to do and see are everywhere, but first you have to remind yourself to get off the highway. Once you do, rent a boat and find a secluded anchorage and fish, swim, or marvel at the sun, sea, and sky. In the Atlantic you can dive to spectacular coral reefs or pursue dolphin, blue marlin, and other deep-water game fish. Along the Florida Bay coastline you can seek out the bonefish, snapper, snook, and tarpon that lurk in the grass flats and in the shallow, winding channels of the backcountry.

Along the reefs and among the islands are more than 600 kinds of fish. Diminutive deer and pale raccoons, related to but distinct from their mainland cousins, inhabit the Lower Keys. And throughout the islands you'll find such exotic West Indian plants as Jamaica dogwood, pigeon plum, poisonwood, satin leaf, and silver and thatch palms, as well as tropical birds, including the great white heron, mangrove cuckoo, roseate spoonbill, and white-crowned pigeon. Mangroves, with their gracefully bowed prop roots, appear to march out to sea. Day by day they busily add more keys to the archipelago.

With virtually no distracting air pollution or obstructive high-rises, sunsets are a pure, unadulterated spectacle that each evening attracts thousands of tourists and locals to waterfront parks, piers, restaurants, bars, and resorts throughout the Keys.

Another attraction is the weather: In the winter it's typically 10°F warmer than on the mainland; in the summer it's usually 10°F cooler. The Keys also get substantially less rain, around 30 inches annually, compared to 55–60 inches in Miami and the Everglades. Most rain falls in quick downpours on summer afternoons, except in June, September, and October, when tropical storms can dump rain for two to four days. In winter continental cold fronts occasionally stall over the Keys, dragging overnight temperatures down to the 40s.

The Keys were only sparsely populated until the early 20th century. In 1905, however, railroad magnate Henry Flagler began building the extension of his Florida railroad south from Homestead to Key West. His goal was to establish a rail link to the steamships that sailed between Key West and Havana, just 90 mi across the Straits of Florida. The railroad arrived at Key West in 1912 and remained a lifeline of commerce until the Labor Day hurricane of 1935 washed out much of its roadbed. For three years thereafter, the only way in and out of Key West was by boat. The Overseas Highway, built over the railroad's old roadbeds and bridges, was completed in 1938, and many sections and bridges have recently been widened or replaced.

Pleasures and Pastimes

Biking

Cyclists are now able to ride all but a tiny portion of the bike path that runs along the Overseas Highway from MM 106 south to the Seven Mile Bridge. The state plans to extend the route throughout the Keys.

Boating

If it floats, local marinas rent it. For up-close exploration of the mangroves and near-shore islands in Florida Bay, nothing beats a kayak or canoe. You can paddle within a few feet of a flock of birds without disturbing them. Visiting the backcountry islands and inlets of Everglades National Park requires a shallow-draft boat: A 14- to 17-ft skiff with a 40- to 50-horsepower outboard is sufficient. For diving the reef or fishing on the open ocean, you'll need a larger boat with greater horsepower. Houseboats are ideal for cruising the Keys.

Only experienced sailors should attempt to navigate the shallow waters surrounding the Keys with deep-keeled sailboats. On the other hand, small shallow-draft, single-hulled sailboats and catamarans are ideal. Personal water vehicles, such as Wave Runners and Jet Skis, rent by the half hour or hour but are banned in many areas. Flat, stable pontoon boats are a good choice for anyone with seasickness. Those interested in experiencing the reef without getting wet can take a glass-bottom boat trip.

Dining

A number of talented young chefs have settled in the Keys—especially Key West—contributing to the area's image as one of the nation's points of culinary interest. Restaurants' menus, rum-based fruit beverages, and music reflect the Keys' tropical climate and their proximity to Cuba and other Caribbean islands. Better restaurants serve imaginative and tantalizing fusion cuisine that draws on traditions from all over the world.

Florida citrus, seafood, and tropical fruits figure prominently, and Florida lobster and stone crab should be local and fresh from August to March. Also keep an eye out for authentic key lime pie. The real McCoy has a yellow custard in a graham-cracker crust and tastes like nothing else.

Restaurants may close for a two- to four-week vacation during the slow season—between mid-September and mid-November. Check local newspapers or call ahead, especially if driving any distance.

Fishing

These sun-bathed waters are home to 100 species of game fish as well as lobster, shrimp, and crabs. Flats fishing and backcountry fishing are Keys specialties. In flats fishing, a guide poles a shallow-draft outboard boat through the shallow, sandy-bottomed waters while sighting for bonefish and snook to be caught on light tackle, spin, and fly. Backcountry fishing may include flats fishing or fishing in the channels and basins around islands in Florida Bay. Charter boats fish the reef and Gulf Stream for deep-sea fish. Party boats, which can be crowded, carry up to 50 people to fish the reefs for grouper, kingfish, and snapper. Some operators boast a guarantee, or "no fish, no pay" policy.

Scuba Diving and Snorkeling

Diving in the Keys is spectacular. In shallow and deep water with visibility up to 120 ft, you can explore sea canyons and mountains covered with waving sea plumes, brain and star coral, historic shipwrecks, and sunken submarines. The colors of the coral are surpassed only by the brilliance of the fish that live around it. There's no best season for diving, but occasional storms in June, September, and October cloud the waters and make seas rough.

You can dive the reefs with scuba, snuba, or snorkeling gear, using your own boat, renting a boat, or booking a tour with a dive shop. Tours depart two or three times a day, stopping at two sites on each trip. The first trip of the day is usually the best. It's less crowded—vacationers like to sleep in—and visibility is better before the wind picks up in the afternoon. There's also night diving.

If you want to scuba dive but are not certified, take an introductory resort course. Though it doesn't result in certification, it allows you to scuba with an instructor in the afternoon following morning classroom and pool instruction.

Nearly all the waters surrounding the Keys are part of the Florida Keys National Marine Sanctuary and thus are protected. Signs, brochures, tour guides, and marine enforcement agents remind visitors that the reef is fragile and shouldn't be touched.

Exploring the Florida Keys

Finding your way around the Keys isn't hard once you understand the unique address system. Many addresses are simply given as a mile marker (MM) number. The markers themselves are small, green rectangular signs along the side of the Overseas Highway (U.S. 1). They begin with MM 126 a mile south of Florida City and end with MM 0, in Key West. Keys residents use the abbreviation BS for the bay side of U.S. 1 and OS for the ocean side.

The Keys are divided into four areas: the Upper Keys, from Key Largo to the Long Key Channel (MM 106–65) and Ocean Reef and North Key Largo, off Card Sound Road and Route 905, respectively; the Middle Keys, from Conch (pronounced *konk*) Key through Marathon to the south side of the Seven Mile Bridge, including Pigeon Key (MM 65–40); the Lower Keys, from Little Duck Key south through Big Coppitt Key (MM 40–9); and Key West, from Stock Island through Key West (MM 9–0). The Keys don't end with the highway, however; they stretch another 70 mi west of Key West to the Dry Tortugas.

Numbers in the text correspond to numbers in the margin and on the Florida Keys and Key West maps.

Great Itineraries

IF YOU HAVE 3 DAYS

You can fly and then dive; but if you dive, you can't fly for 24 hours, so spend your first morning diving or snorkeling at John Pennekamp Coral Reef State Park in ⊞ **Key Largo** ②. If you aren't certified, take a resort course, and you'll be exploring the reefs by afternoon. Afterward, breeze through the park's visitor center. The rest of the afternoon can be whiled away either lounging around a pool or beach or visiting the Maritime Museum of the Florida Keys. Dinner or cocktails at a bay-side restaurant or bar will give you your first look at a fabulous Keys sunset. On day two, get an early start to savor the breathtaking views on the way to Key West. Along the way make stops at the natural history museum that's part of the Museums of Crane Point Hammock, in **Marathon** ⑧, and Bahia Honda State Park, on **Bahia Honda Key** ⑨, where you can stretch your legs on a forest trail or snorkel on an offshore reef. Once in ⊞ **Key West** ⑫–㉝, you can watch the sunset before dining at one of the island's first-class restaurants. Spend the next morning exploring beaches or taking a walking or trolley tour of Old Town before driving back to the mainland.

IF YOU HAVE 4 DAYS

Spend the first day as you would above, overnighting in ⊞ **Key Largo** ②. Start the second day by renting a kayak and exploring the mangroves and small islands of Florida Bay or take an ecotour of the islands in Everglades National Park. In the afternoon stop by the Florida Keys Wild Bird Rehabilitation Center before driving down to ⊞ **Islamorada** ④. Pause to read the inscription on the Hurricane Monument, and before day's end, make plans for the next day's fishing. After an early dinner on day three—perhaps at one of the many restaurants that will prepare your catch for you—set off for ⊞ **Key West** ⑫–㉝ and spend the last day as you would above.

IF YOU HAVE 7 DAYS

Spend your first three days as you would in the four-day itinerary, but stay the third night in ⊞ **Islamorada** ④. In the morning catch a boat to Lignumvitae Key State Botanical Site, before heading to ⊞ **Marathon** ⑧, where you can visit the natural history museum that's part of the Museums of Crane Point Hammock and walk or take a train across the Old Seven Mile Bridge to Pigeon Key. The next stop is just 10 mi away at Bahia Honda State Park, on ⊞ **Bahia Honda Key** ⑨. Take a walk on a wilderness trail, go snorkeling on an offshore reef, wriggle your toes in the beach's soft sand, and spend the night in a waterfront cabin, letting the waves lull you to sleep. Your sixth day starts with either a half day of fabulous snorkeling or diving at Looe Key National Marine Sanctuary or a visit to the National Key Deer Refuge, on **Big Pine Key** ⑩. Then continue on to ⊞ **Key West** ⑫–㉝, and get in a little sightseeing before watching the sunset. The next morning take a walking, bicycling, or trolley tour of town or catch a ferry or sea-plane to Dry Tortugas National Park before heading home.

When to Tour the Florida Keys

High season in the Keys is mid-December through March, and traffic on the Overseas Highway is inevitably heavy. From November to the middle of December, crowds are thinner, and the weather is superlative. Summer, which is hot and humid, is becoming a second high season, especially among families and Europeans. Key West's annual Fantasy Fest is the last week in October; if you plan to attend this popular event, reserve at least six months in advance. Rooms are also scarce the first few weekends of lobster season, which starts in August.

THE UPPER KEYS

The tropical coral reef tract that runs a few miles off the seaward coast accounts for most of the Upper Keys' reputation. This is a diving heaven, thanks to scores of diving options, accessible islands and dive sites, and an established tourism infrastructure.

Yet although diving is king here, fishing, kayaking, and nature touring draw an enviable number of tourists. Within 1½ mi of the bay coast lie the islands of Everglades National Park; here naturalists lead eco-tours to see one of the world's only saltwater forests, endangered manatees, dolphins, roseate spoonbills, and tropical bird rookeries. Though the number of birds has dwindled since John James Audubon captured their beauty on a visit to the Keys, bird-watchers won't be disappointed. At sunset flocks take to the skies, and in spring and autumn migrating birds add their numbers. Tarpon and bonefish teem in the shallow waters surrounding the islands, providing food for birds and a challenge to light-tackle fishermen. These same crystal-clear waters attract windsurfers, sailors, and powerboaters.

Dining in the Upper Keys used to be, with one or two exceptions, ho hum. However, within the last five years, half a dozen fine restaurants have opened and are thriving on repeat local customers and word-of-mouth tourist business.

Accommodations are as varied as they are plentiful. The majority are in small waterfront resorts, whose efficiency and one- or two-bedroom units are decorated in tropical colors. They offer dockage and either provide or will arrange boating, diving, and fishing excursions. In high season, expect to pay $65–$165 for an efficiency (in low season, $45–$145). Campground and RV park rates with electricity and water run $22–$48. Some properties require two- or three-day minimum stays during holidays and on weekends in high season. Conversely, discounts are given for midweek, weekly, and monthly stays, and rates can drop 20%–40% April–June and September–October. Keep in mind that salty winds and soil play havoc with anything man-made, and constant maintenance is a must; inspect your accommodations before checking in.

Key Largo

56 mi south of Miami International Airport.

The first Key reachable by car, 30-mi-long Key Largo—named Cayo Largo (long key) by the Spanish—is also the largest island in the chain. Comprising three areas—North Key Largo, Key Largo, and Tavernier—it runs northeast–southwest between Lake Surprise and Tavernier Creek, at MM 95. Most businesses are on the four-lane divided highway (U.S. 1) that runs down the middle, but away from the overdevelopment and generally suburban landscape you can find many areas of pristine wilderness.

❶ One such area is **North Key Largo,** which still contains a wide tract of virgin hardwood hammock and mangrove as well as a crocodile sanctuary (not open to the public). To reach North Key Largo, take Card Sound Road just south of Florida City, or from within the Keys, take Route 905 north.

The 2,005-acre **Key Largo Hammocks State Botanical Site** is the largest remaining stand of the vast West Indian tropical hardwood hammock and mangrove wetland that once covered most of the Keys' upland areas. Among the site's 84 species of protected plants and animals are the endangered American crocodile and the Key Largo wood rat. Concrete skeletons of defunct developments remain but are slowly disappearing under vegetation. To protect the land from further development, state and federal governments are acquiring as much of the hammock as they can. You can take a self-guided tour by picking up a brochure at the park entrance. Better still are the biweekly tours led by Ranger Joseph Nemec, who points out rare species, tells humorous nature stories, and encourages visitors to taste the fruits of native plants. Pets are welcome, if on a 6-ft leash. ⊠ *1 mi north of U.S. 1 on Rte. 905, OS, North Key Largo,* ☎ *305/451–1202.* ▣ *Free.* ☉ *Daily 8–5, tours Thurs. and Sun. 10.*

Taking the Overseas Highway from the mainland lands you closer to
❷ **Key Largo** proper, abounding with shopping centers, chain restaurants, and, of course, dive shops.

The small but earnest not-for-profit **Maritime Museum of the Florida Keys** depicts the local history of shipwrecks and salvage efforts through retrieved treasures, reconstructed wreck sites, and artifacts in various stages of preservation. Some of the more notable exhibits have come from a fleet of treasure ships wrecked by a hurricane in 1715. A bottle exhibit tells Keys history through more than 200 salvaged bottles, dating from as early as the 1600s. The museum is a labor of love, and its primary purpose is preservation. ⊠ *MM 102.5, BS,* ☎ *305/451–6444.* ▣ *$5.* ☉ *Mon.–Wed. and Fri.–Sat. 10–5; Sun. noon–5.*

★ **John Pennekamp Coral Reef State Park** encompasses 78 square mi of coral reefs, sea-grass beds, and mangrove swamps. Its reefs contain 40 of the 52 species of coral in the Atlantic Reef System and more than 650 varieties of fish, and the diving and snorkeling here are famous. A concessioner rents canoes and sailboats and offers boat trips to the reef. Even a landlubber can appreciate the superb interpretive aquarium, exhibits, and video in the visitor center. The park also includes a nature trail through a mangrove forest, two man-made beaches, picnic shelters, a snack bar, and a campground. ⊠ *MM 102.5, OS, Box 487, 33037,* ☎ *305/451–1202.* ▣ *$2.50 per vehicle, $1.50 per pedestrian or bicyclist, plus 50¢ per person county surcharge.* ☉ *Daily 8–sunset.*

The *African Queen*—the steam-powered workboat on which Katharine Hepburn and Humphrey Bogart rode in the movie of the same name— is moored at the **Key Largo Harbor Marina** (⊠ MM 99.7, OS, 305/451–4655), next to the Holiday Inn Key Largo Resort. Also on display is the *Thayer IV,* a 22-ft mahogany Chris Craft used by Hepburn and Henry Fonda in *On Golden Pond.* Both vessels are in demand at boat shows and occasionally vacate their moorings.

❸ The southernmost part of Key Largo is **Tavernier.** Wood-carver and teacher Laura Quinn brought the **Florida Keys Wild Bird Rehabilita-**

190

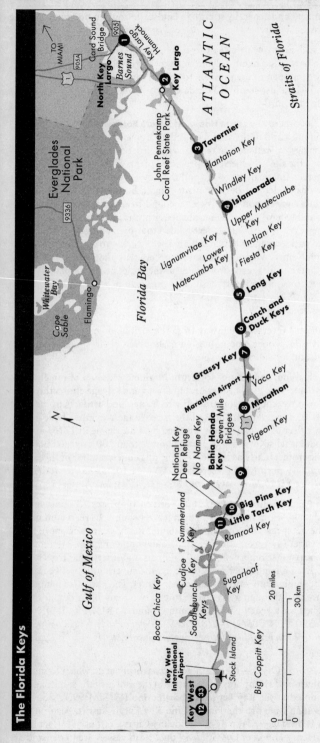

tion Center here in 1991, and nowhere else in the Keys can you see birds so close up. Many are kept for life because of injuries that can't be healed, whereas others are brought for rehabilitation and then set free. At any time the residents can include ospreys, hawks, pelicans, cormorants, terns, and herons of various types. A short nature trail runs into the mangrove forest (bring bug spray May–October), and a video explains the center's mission. *MM 93.6, BS, Tavernier,* ☎ *305/852–4486.* 🖃 *Donation welcome.* ☺ *Daily sunrise–sunset.*

Harry Harris County Park (🖂 MM 93, OS, Burton Dr., Tavernier, ☎ 305/852–7161 or 888/227–8136) has play equipment, a small swimming lagoon, a boat ramp, ball fields, barbecue grills, and rest rooms. Though the turnoff is clearly marked on the Overseas Highway, the road to the ocean is circuitous.

Dining and Lodging

$–$$$ ★ ✕ **The Fish House.** Behind the screened, diner-style facade are display cases filled with the freshest catches, which are then baked, blackened, broiled, fried, sautéed, steamed, or stewed as if every night were the finals of a seafood competition (in fact, the Fish House wins many such competitions). The dining room—festooned with nets and fishy Christmas ornaments—is as redolent of the Keys as a Bogart movie. Generous portions come with corn on the cob, new potatoes or rice, and coleslaw; the key lime pie is homemade. You can't beat the fast service and great eats. 🖂 *MM 102.4, OS,* ☎ *305/451–4665. AE, D, MC, V. Closed early Sept.–early Oct.*

$–$$$ ★ ✕ **Frank Keys Cafe.** This contemporary restaurant is hidden in a natural hardwood hammock except at night, when little white lights in the branches mark the spot. The wooden, Victorian-style house has a deep porch for dining alfresco. Chef-owner Frank Graves III and executive chef Mark Dixon do wonderful things with fresh fish. The pan-sautéed catch is washed in egg, lightly coated, then given a kiss of sherry. Opt for delicate seafood entrées like seafood Mediterranean (sautéed fresh seafood over pesto linguine with a marinara cream sauce). 🖂 *MM 100, OS,* ☎ *305/453–0310. AE, MC, V. Closed Tues., plus Wed. Easter–Christmas.*

$–$$ ✕ **Anthony's Italian Restaurant & Lounge.** The portly proprietor greets guests at the door or their tables, making sure they are enjoying his hospitality. There's little to be concerned about; the food, faithful to Italian tradition, speaks for itself. The solid kitchen serves veal, chicken, and home-style pasta dishes in a comfortable setting. Spicy mussels marinara are so good you'll want an order to go. Friday and Saturday nights bring live music. 🖂 *MM 97.6, in the median,* ☎ *305/853–1177. AE, D, MC, V.*

$–$$ ★ ✕ **Cafe Largo.** Soothing jazz plays in this intimate bistro-style Italian restaurant. Dinner starts with a basket of focaccia bread and garlic rolls. Next choose one of the chef's specials; they won't disappoint. The chicken garlic—two thin breast cutlets lightly coated and sautéed, then covered in a light sauce of garlic and rosemary—is divine. The penne with shrimp and broccoli has tender shrimp, al dente broccoli, and a hint of garlic. A more than ample wine list, international beers, Italian bottled waters, and, of course, espresso and cappuccino are offered, and the dessert list is short but sweet. 🖂 *MM 99.5, BS,* ☎ *305/451–4885. AE, MC, V. No lunch.*

$–$$ ✕ **Crack'd Conch.** For serious beer connoisseurs, there isn't a better choice than this seafood restaurant. The food's good, the staff loves to tease customers, and more than 100 different imported and domestic brews are poured along with seafood sandwiches and entrées like fried alligator and blackened fish. As you might guess, conch figures prominently in salads and sandwiches or just plain fried. Portions are big, but you can get takeout. ⊠ *MM 105, OS,* ☎ *305/451–0732. AE, D, MC, V. Closed Wed.*

$–$$ ✕ **Mrs. Mac's Kitchen.** Hundreds of beer cans, beer bottles, and expired license plates from all over the world decorate the walls of this wood-paneled, screened, open-air restaurant, which offers traditional American sandwiches, burgers, barbecue, and seafood. At breakfast and lunch, the counter and booths fill up early with locals. Regular nightly specials are worth the stop: meat loaf on Monday, Italian on Wednesday, and seafood Thursday–Saturday. The chili is always good, and the beer of the month is $1.50 a bottle. ⊠ *MM 99.4, BS,* ☎ *305/451–3722. No credit cards. Closed Sun.*

$ ✕ **Alabama Jack's.** In 1953 Alabama Jack Stratham opened his open-air seafood restaurant on two barges in an old fishing community 13 mi southeast of Homestead. The spot, something of a no-man's-land, belongs to the Keys in spirit thanks to Card Sound Road. Regular customers include Keys fixtures, Sunday cyclists, local retirees, and boaters, who come to admire tropical birds in nearby mangroves, the occasional crocodile in the canal, the live band on weekends, or simply the food. Favorites include peppery crab cakes, crispy-chewy conch fritters, crunchy breaded shrimp, and homemade tartar sauce. The place closes by 7 or 7:30, when the skeeters come out. ⊠ *58000 Card Sound Rd., Card Sound,* ☎ *305/248–8741. No credit cards.*

$ ✕ **Harriette's Restaurant.** If you're looking for a traditional American eatery, this is it. Owner Harriette Mattson takes the trouble to know many of her guests by name and remember what they eat. Wisecracking waitresses will tell you that the three-egg omelet usually has six eggs because Harriette has a heavy hand. Harriette's is famous for breakfast: steak and eggs with hash browns or grits and toast and jelly for $6.95, or old-fashioned hotcakes with whipped butter and syrup and sausage or bacon for $3.75. A Keys mural, a little paneling, and some carpet touch things up, but a homey style, punctuated with local crafts and photos on consignment, pervades. ⊠ *MM 95.7, BS,* ☎ *305/852–8689. No credit cards. No dinner.*

$ ✕ **Chad's Deli & Bakery.** Each morning Chad, the owner, bakes eight kinds of fresh breads that he uses to make sandwiches ($5–$6) large enough to feed two hungry adults. Residents recently voted them the best sandwiches in the Upper Keys. If you're not in the mood for one of the regular sandwiches, ranging from certified Angus roast beef to veggie, try the daily special. The menu also features salads, sides, soft drinks, and a choice of two cookies—white-chocolate macadamia nut and chocolate chip—with a whopping 8-inch diameter (75¢–$1). Most orders in this four-table establishment are takeout. ⊠ *MM 92.3, BS,* ☎ *305/853–5566. No credit cards. Closed Sun. No dinner.*

$$$$ ⊞ **Jules' Undersea Lodge.** In the "not for everyone" category, this novel accommodation caters to well-finned visitors who want a total Keys diving experience. The hotel, a former underwater research lab, is 5 fathoms (30 ft) below the surface. Hence, to be one of the six guests, you have to be a certified diver or take the hotel's three-hour introductory course (an additional $75). Rooms have a shower, telephone, VCR and stereo (no TV), and galley. The lodge is popular with honeymooners. Rates include breakfast, dinner, snacks, beverages, and diving gear. Because of the length of stay underwater, once back on terra firma, you can't fly or make deep dives for 24 hours. ⊠ *MM 103.2, OS, 51 Shoreland Dr., 33037,* ☎ *305/451–2353,* ☎ *305/451–4789. 2 bedrooms, sleeps up to 6. Dining room, in-room VCRs. AE, D, MC, V.*

$$$$ 🏨 **Marriott's Key Largo Bay Beach Resort.** This 17-acre bay-side resort's five lemon-yellow, grill-balconied, and spire-topped stories are
sliced between highway and bay and give off an air of warm, indolent
days. The facilities are as good as the guest rooms, which feature rattan, paddle fans, and balconies. From some you can watch the sunset
sweep across the bay. ✉ *MM 103.8, BS, 103800 Overseas Hwy.,
33037,* ☎ *305/453–0000 or 800/932–9332,* FAX *305/453–0093. 153
rooms, 20 2-bedroom suites, 6 3-bedroom suites, 1 penthouse suite.
Restaurant, 3 bars, pool, beauty salon, hot tub, massage, beach, dive
shop, fishing, meeting rooms. AE, D, DC, MC, V.*

$$$–$$$$ 🏨 **Kona Kai Resort.** A narrow sidewalk winds between beautifully land-
★ scaped cottages to a sandy beach and marina. The garden alone, fea-
turing fruits and rare and native plants, makes this one of the best places
to stay in the Keys, but owners Joe and Ronnie Harris go farther. They
redecorated with beautiful tropical furnishings and added special toi-
letries made from fruits and flowers; some services are left to guests,
however. Studios and one- and two-bedroom suites—with full kitchens
and original art by prominent Florida artists—are spacious and light-
filled. Beachfront hammocks and a pool make it easy to while away
the day, but there's plenty for those who want more activity. Try a pad-
dleboat or kayak, or visit the art gallery, with works by major South
Florida artists. ✉ *MM 97.8, BS, 97802 Overseas Hwy., 33037,* ☎ *305/
852–7200 or 800/365–7829. 11 units. Pool, tennis court, basketball,
volleyball, boating, beach, dock. AE, D, MC, V.*

$$$–$$$$ 🏨 **Westin Beach Resort, Key Largo.** This pink-and-turquoise gem is
★ tucked away in a hardwood hammock. A $7 million upgrade is evi-
dent from the lush landscaping to the waterfront restaurant, Tree
Tops. Fourth-floor bay-side rooms afford marvelous water views,
whereas units on the first three floors overlook the woods, except the
230, 330, and 430 series, which face the landscaped parking lot. All
rooms are spacious and comfortable, with new tropical decor. Lighted
nature trails and boardwalks wind through the woods to a beach. Two
pools, one for adults only, are separated by a coral rock wall and wa-
terfall. ✉ *MM 96.9, BS, 97000 Overseas Hwy., 33037,* ☎ *305/852–
5553 or 800/826–1006,* FAX *305/852–8669. 190 rooms, 10 suites. 2
restaurants, 2 bars, 2 pools, hot tub, 2 tennis courts, beach, dock, wind-
surfing, boating, fishing. AE, D, DC, MC, V.*

$$$ 🏨 **Marina Del Mar Resort and Marina.** This two- to four-story resort
on a deep-water marina caters to sailors and divers. Heavy use does-
n't show, as owner Scott Marr renovates rooms year-round. Units
have original watercolors by Keys artist Mary Boggs, as well as refrigerators. Suites 502–504 have kitchens (as do studios) and plenty
of room for groups. There's live entertainment nightly in the restaurant and bar, a free Continental breakfast in the lobby, and spectacular sunrise and sunset views from the fourth-floor observation deck.
✉ *MM 100, OS, 527 Caribbean Dr., 33037,* ☎ *305/451–4107 or 800/
451–3483,* FAX *305/451–1891. 52 rooms, 8 suites, 16 studios. Restaurant, bar, refrigerators, pool, 2 tennis courts, exercise room, boating,
fishing. AE, D, DC, MC, V.*

$$ 🏨 **Frank's Key Haven Resort.** In a quiet neighborhood under a canopy
of graceful, towering gumbo-limbo trees, this lodge, made of beams
from Flagler's railroad tracks and imported German concrete, was built
in the 1930s to withstand hurricane-force winds. The original owner
ran bird-watching tours, and though the enlarged property still offers
ecotours, it now caters more to divers. The resort has its own dive boat,
waterfront, and training pool and offers diving certification as well as
diving-lodging packages that include night dives. Screened porches
have racks for dive equipment. Rooms vary from one-room efficien-

cies to one- and two-bedroom apartments and family units. A public area has a TV, half kitchen, and comfy seating. ⊠ *MM 92, BS, 198 Harborview Dr., Tavernier 33070,* ☎ *305/852–3017 or 800/765–5397,* FAX *305/852–3880. 14 units. Pool, docks. MC, V.*

$$ ⊞ **Largo Lodge.** No two rooms are the same in this 1950s-vintage re-
★ sort, but all are cozy and fully equipped with kitchens, rattan furniture, and screened porches but no phones. The prettiest palm alley you've ever seen sets the mood, while tropical gardens with more palms, sea grapes, and orchids surround the guest cottages. There's 200 ft of bay frontage. Late in the day, wild ducks, pelicans, herons, and other birds come looking for a handout from longtime owner Harriet "Hat" Stokes. If you want a top-value tropical hideaway not too far down the Keys, this is it. ⊠ *MM 101.5, BS, 101740 Overseas Hwy., 33037,* ☎ *305/451–0424 or 800/468–4378. 6 apartments, 1 efficiency. Beach, dock. MC, V.*

$$ ⊞ **Popp's Motel.** For 45 years and four generations, Popp family members have welcomed guests to this small and private motel. Rooms are just yards from a sandy beach, and you can take part in activities galore or relax in a hammock while the kids play on swings. All bedroom units and efficiencies have a kitchen. Though the place is clean and has been updated several times, dark wood paneling and terrazzo floors in some rooms reveal their age. Other than that, it's a gem of a resort. ⊠ *MM 95.5, BS, 95500 Overseas Hwy., 33037,* ☎ *305/852–5201,* FAX *305/852–5200. 9 units. Picnic area, beach, dock, playground. AE, MC, V.*

$ ⚠ **America Outdoors.** Reserve early to camp here, especially around holidays and from January to mid-March. A waterfront location and woodsy setting, security, boat ramps and rentals, a sandy beach, store, bait shop, bathhouse, and an adult recreation center make it popular with snowbirds and South Floridians, who come back year after year and weekend after weekend. It's also very clean, orderly, and well managed. Rates are the same for tents and RVs year-round: $35 for water and electric, $40 for full hookups ($50 on the beach). ⊠ *MM 97.5, BS, 97450 Overseas Hwy., 33037,* ☎ *305/852–8054. 154 sites. Grocery, beach, dock, boating, fishing, coin laundry, recreation room. AE, D, MC, V.*

Nightlife

The semiweekly *Keynoter* (Wednesday and Saturday), weekly *Reporter* (Thursday), and Friday to Sunday editions of the *Miami Herald* are the best sources of information on entertainment and nightlife.

Breezers Tiki Bar (⊠ MM 103.8, BS, ☎ 305/453–0000), in Marriott's Key Largo Bay Beach Resort (☞ Dining and Lodging, *above*), is popular with the smartly coiffed crowd. Office workers join guests for cocktails to toast the sun going down. Walls plastered with Bogart memorabilia remind customers that the classic 1948 Bogart-Bacall flick *Key Largo* was shot in the **Caribbean Club** (⊠ MM 104, BS, ☎ 305/451–9970). An archetype of a laid-back Keys bar, it also was the setting for *Blood & Wine,* with Jack Nicholson and Michael Caine. It draws a hairy-faced, down-home group to shoot the breeze while shooting pool but is friendlier than you might imagine. It also has postcard-perfect sunsets. **Coconuts** (⊠ MM 100, OS, 528 Caribbean Dr., ☎ 305/453–9794), in Marina Del Mar Resort (☞ Dining and Lodging, *above*), has nightly entertainment year-round. The cabana bar and waterfront terrace of the **Italian Fisherman** (⊠ MM 104, BS, ☎ 305/451–4471) are ideal spots to watch the sunset while nibbling snacks and sipping drinks. It's big with families.

Outdoor Activities and Sports

BIKING

Equipment Locker Sport & Cycle (⊠ Tradewinds Plaza, MM 101, OS, ☎ 305/453–0140) rents single-speed adult and children's bikes. Cruisers go for $10 a day, $50 a week. No helmets are available.

FISHING

Sailors Choice (⊠ MM 99.7, OS, ☎ 305/451–1802 or 305/451–0041) runs a party boat daily plus a night trip on Friday and Saturday. The ultramodern 60-ft, 49-passenger boat with air-conditioned cabin leaves from the Holiday Inn docks.

SCUBA DIVING AND SNORKELING

American Diving Headquarters (⊠ MM 105.5, BS, ☎ 305/451–0037) offers certification and dive tours on request, not a schedule, and a Water-Tight Guarantee ensures you'll get your money's worth. The staff is concerned about guests and the environment, the latter evidenced by a reef ecology and fish identification course. Before getting their toes wet, divers attend lectures and slide presentations to help them get more out of the dive experience. The cost is $55 for a two-tank dive with tank and weight rental, $75 if you need everything.

Captain Slate's Atlantis Dive Center (⊠ MM 106.5, OS, 51 Garden Cove Dr., ☎ 305/451–3020 or 800/331–3483) is a full-service dive shop (NAUI, PADI, SSI, and YMCA certified) that also performs underwater weddings. **Coral Reef Park Co.** (⊠ John Pennekamp Coral Reef State Park, MM 102.5, OS, ☎ 305/451–1621) offers scuba and snorkeling tours of the park. **Quiescence Diving Service, Inc.** (⊠ MM 103.5, BS, ☎ 305/451–2440) sets itself apart in two ways: It limits groups to six to ensure personal attention and offers twilight dives an hour before sundown, the time when sea creatures are most active. Two day and night dives are also available.

WATER SPORTS

Coral Reef Park Co. (⊠ John Pennekamp Coral Reef State Park, MM 102.5, OS, ☎ 305/451–1621) rents boats and equipment for sailing, canoeing, and windsurfing. You can rent a canoe or a one- or two-person sea kayak, even camping equipment, from **Florida Bay Outfitters** (⊠ MM 104, BS, ☎ 305/451–3018). Real pros, they match the right equipment to the right skill level, so even novices feel confident paddling off. Rentals are by the hour, half day, or full day. They also sell lots of accessories.

Islamorada

❹ *MM 90.5–70.*

Early settlers named Islamorada after their schooner, the *Island Home,* but to make the name more romantic, they translated it into Spanish— "Isla Morada." The local chamber of commerce prefers to say it means "the purple isles." Early maps show Islamorada as only Upper Matecumbe Key. Historians refer to it as the group of islands between Tavernier Creek at MM 90 and Fiesta Key at MM 70, including Plantation Key, Upper Matecumbe Key, Lower Matecumbe Key, Craig Key, and Fiesta Key. In addition, two islands—Indian Key, in the Atlantic Ocean, and Lignumvitae Key, in Florida Bay—belong to the group.

Claiming they were fed up with a county government more interested in the needs of Key West than the Upper Keys, residents voted for self-incorporation in a controversial election in fall 1997. Though it's now officially the Village of Isles, some things haven't changed. The area remains a great place to fish. For nearly 100 years, seasoned anglers have recognized these sun-bathed waters as home to a huge variety of game fish as well as lobster, shrimp, and crabs. The rich, the famous, the powerful have all fished here, including Lou Gehrig, Ted Williams, Zane Grey, and presidents Hoover, Truman, Carter, and Bush. More than 150 backcountry guides and 400 offshore captains operate out of this 20-mi stretch.

Activities range from fishing tournaments to historic reenactments. During September and October, Heritage Days feature free lectures on Islamorada history, a golf tournament, and the Indian Key Festival. Holiday Isle Resort sponsors boating, fishing, car, and golf tournaments, as well as bikini and body-building contests.

Between 1885 and 1915 settlers earned good livings growing pineapples on **Plantation Key** (⊠ MM 90.5–86), using black Bahamian workers to plant and harvest their crops. The plantations are gone, replaced by a dense concentration of homes and businesses.

At 16 ft above sea level, **Windley Key** (⊠ MM 86–84) is the highest point in the Keys. Originally two islets, the area was first inhabited by Native Americans, who left middens and other remains, and then by settlers, who farmed and fished in the mid-1800s and called the islets the Umbrella Keys. The Florida East Coast Railway bought the land from homesteaders in 1908, filled in the inlet between the two islands, and changed the name. They quarried rock for the rail bed and bridge approaches in the Keys—the same rock used in many historic South Florida structures, including Miami's Vizcaya and the Hurricane Monument on Upper Matecumbe. Though the Quarry Station stop was destroyed by the 1935 hurricane, quarrying continued until the 1960s. Today a few resorts and attractions occupy the island.

When the Florida East Coast Railway drilled, dynamited, and carved Windley Key's limestone bed, it exposed the once-living fossilized coral reef that was laid down about 125,000 years ago, now visible at the **Windley Key Fossil Reef State Geologic Site.** Five trails lead to old quarrying equipment and cutting pits, where you can stand within a petrified reef and take rubbings of beautifully fossilized brain coral and sea ferns. Volunteers give tours once a month, but you can sign out a brochure and gate key at Long Key State Recreation Area (☞ Long Key, *below*) and follow a self-guided tour or stop in when the gates are open Tuesday mornings. ⊠ *MM 85.5, BS,* ☎ *305/664–4815 or 305/664–5574.* ⊠ *Free.* ⊙ *Gates open Tues. 8:30–9:30, tours 3rd Sat. of month 9 and 11.*

At the **Theater of the Sea,** 12 dolphins, three sea lions, and an extensive collection of tropical fish swim in the 1907 Windley Key railroad quarry, whose huge blasted holes are now filled with seawater. Allow at least two hours to attend the dolphin and sea-lion shows and visit all the exhibits, which include an injured birds of prey display, a "bottomless" boat ride, a shell-life touch tank, a pool where sharks are fed by a trainer, and several small-fish aquariums. For an additional fee, you can even swim with dolphins for 30 minutes, after a 30-minute orientation, and arrange for video or still photos of your experience. ⊠ *MM 84.5, OS, Box 407, 33036,* ☎ *305/664–2431.* ⊠ *$15.75; swim with dolphins $85, reservations required with 50% deposit.* ⊙ *Daily 9:30–4.*

Upper Matecumbe Key (⊠ MM 84–79) was one of the earliest in the Upper Keys to be permanently settled. Homesteaders were so successful at growing pineapples and limes in the rocky soil that at one time the island had the largest U.S. pineapple crop; however, Cuban pineapples and the hurricane of 1935 killed the industry. Today life centers on fishing and tourism, and the island is lively with homes, charter fishing boats, bait shops, restaurants, stores, nightclubs, marinas, nurseries, and offices.

Somewhere in Time is a small, unlikely combination museum and antiques and jewelry shop crowded with hundreds of interesting artifacts. Nearly every inch of wall and counter space is filled with objects salvaged from merchant and slave ships that plied Florida's waters. There are coins from the *Atocha,* rare ceramic containers, original 18th-century maps, cannon, solid silver bars, slave artifacts, religious medallions, rare bottles, and a corny diorama of two infamous English women who were pirates. The owner tells marvelous stories about the objects' provenance. ⊠ *MM 82.7, OS,* ☎ *305/664–9699.* 🎫 *Free.* ☉ *Daily 9–5.*

Home to the local chamber of commerce, a **red train caboose** sits at the site where the Florida East Coast Railway had a station and living quarters, before they washed away with the hurricane of 1935. Artifacts ranging from dishes and flatware to uniform buttons and medicine bottles were excavated and are on display. ⊠ *MM 82.5, BS.* 🎫 *Free.* ☉ *Weekdays 9–5, Sat. 9–4.*

Beside the highway, the **Hurricane Monument** (⊠ MM 81.6, OS) marks the mass grave of 423 victims of the 1935 Labor Day hurricane. Many of those who perished were World War I veterans who had been working on the Overseas Highway and died when a tidal surge overturned a train sent to evacuate them. The 65-ft by 20-ft Art Deco–style monument, built of Keys coral limestone with a ceramic map of the Keys, depicts wind-driven waves and palms bowing before the storm's fury. Note that the trees bend in the wrong direction.

Tucked away behind the Islamorada library is a small beach on a creek at **Islamorada County Park** (⊠ MM 81.5, BS, ☎ 305/852–7161 or 888/227–8136). The water isn't very deep, but it is crystal clear. Currents are swift, making swimming unsuitable for young children, but they can enjoy the playground as well as picnic tables, grassy areas, and rest rooms.

OFF THE BEATEN PATH

INDIAN KEY STATE HISTORIC SITE – On the ocean side of the Matecumbe islands, 10½-acre Indian Key was inhabited by Native Americans for several thousand years before Europeans arrived, as archaeological excavations here show. The islet was a county seat and base for early 19th-century shipwreck salvagers until an Indian attack wiped out the settlement in 1840. Dr. Henry Perrine, a noted botanist, was killed in the raid. Today his plants overgrow the town's ruins. On the first weekend in October the Indian Key Festival celebrates the Key's heritage. Guided tours are available most days, but even when they're not, you can roam among the marked trails and sites. The island is reachable only by boat—either your own, a rental, or a ferry. Robbie's Marina (☞ *below*), the official concessioner, rents kayaks and boats and operates twice-daily ferry service coordinated with the tours. To arrange for a ranger-led tour if you're using your own or a rental boat, contact Long Key State Recreation Area (☞ *Long Key, below*). Locals like to kayak out from Indian Key Fill (⊠ MM 78.5, BS). ⊠ MM 78.5, OS, ☎ 305/664–9814 for ferry service or 305/664–4815 for Long Key State Recreation Area. 🎫 *Free, tour $1, ferry (includes tour) $15, $25 with Lignumvitae Key.* ☉ Tours Thurs.–Mon. 9 and 1.

LIGNUMVITAE KEY STATE BOTANICAL SITE – A virgin hardwood forest still cloaks this 280-acre bay-side island, punctuated by the home and gardens that chemical magnate William Matheson built as a private retreat in 1919. Access is only by boat—either your own, a rental, or a ferry operated by the official concessioner, Robbie's Marina (☞ *below*). which also rents kayaks and boats. (Kayaking out from Indian Key Fill, at MM 78.5, is popular with locals.) Once on the key you can take a tour with the resident ranger, from whom you can request a list of native and well-naturalized plants. As a courtesy, you should arrange for a tour in advance with Long Key State Recreation Area (☞ *Long Key below*) if you're using your own or a rental boat. ⊠ *MM 78.5, BS,* ☎ *305/664–9814 for ferry service or 305/664–4815 for Long Key State Recreation Area.* ☒ *Free, tour $1, ferry (includes tour) $15, $25 with Indian Key.* ⊙ *Tours Thurs.–Mon. 10 and 2.*

Though tarpon are known for the exciting fight they put up when hooked, you'd never know it judging by the 50 or so prehistoric-looking specimens that gather around the docks at **Robbie's Marina,** on Lower Matecumbe Key. These fish—some as long as 5 ft—literally eat out of the hands of children who buy a $2 bucket of bait fish. Both kids and adults enjoy watching them. ⊠ *MM 77.5, BS,* ☎ *305/664–9814 or 305/664–4196.* ☒ *Dock access $1.* ⊙ *Daily 8–5:30.*

Anne's Beach (⊠ MM 73.5, OS, ☎ 305/852–7161 or 888/227–8136), on Lower Matecumbe Key, has a ½-mi elevated wooden boardwalk that meanders through a natural wetland hammock. Covered picnic areas along the boardwalk provide a place to rest and enjoy the view. Rest rooms are at the north end.

Dining and Lodging

$$–$$$ ✕ **Morada Bay.** The owners of the tony Moorings resort opened this
  ★   new restaurant, which has a bay-front location perfect for sunset watching. Conch architecture is enhanced by the black-and-white Everglades photos of Clyde Butcher, which line the walls. The contemporary menu features a died-and-gone-to-heaven shrimp bisque, Portobello burger, and cumin-seared snapper with roasted red peppers and a spinach quesadilla. It's a small place (there's often a wait to be seated), with half a dozen tables inside and a dozen on the porch overlooking a sandy beach dotted with Adirondack chairs. Here the melodic tunes of a guitar player waft out to sea on the breezes Friday to Sunday nights. ⊠ *MM 81, BS,* ☎ *305/664–0604. AE, MC, V.*

$–$$ ✕ **Grove Park Cafe.** French doors on a renovated Conch house,
  ★   Provençal tablecloths, paintings, and pastel-color walls give this place a light, airy feel. Nibble on freshly baked focaccia bread set in a pool of olive oil and balsamic vinegar while looking over the bistro-style menu. Caribbean conch chowder followed by grilled vegetable antipasto with couscous is satisfying. Crab cake on mixed greens or as a sandwich on focaccia bread is outstanding. For dinner try steamed mussels in a white wine and garlic broth or the yellowtail snapper encrusted, sautéed, and served with a mango-and-papaya salsa. The desserts, except ice cream, are made in-house. ⊠ *MM 81.7, OS, 81701 Old Hwy.,* ☎ *305/664–0116. AE, D, MC, V. Closed Sun.*

$–$$ ✕ **Islamorada Fish Company.** When the sun starts to set, this very casual seafood restaurant is one of the prettiest spots in the Keys to have dinner. Small umbrella-covered tables and family-style awning-covered picnic benches are arranged inches from the water, overlooking several islets and the calm waters of Florida Bay. At the fish market's dock, boats unload the fresh catch, which minutes later is served fried, grilled, blackened, or broiled. The food is good, satisfying, and simple for lunch or dinner. There's wine, and the beer, soda, and pink lemonade are served icy cold. A recent expansion created more waterfront seating, but during inclement weather you can eat in a small dining area inside. ⊠ *MM 81.5, BS,* ☎ *305/664–9271. MC, V.*

$–$$ ✕ **Manny & Isa's.** Fewer than a dozen tables are squeezed into the simple room, where the namesake owners serve always perfect Cuban and Spanish cuisine. The regular menu is split between traditional Cuban dishes and local seafood, and there are several fish, chicken, and pork chop specials, all served with salad and Cuban bread. Succulent fish fingers served with black beans and rice will set you back only $8.95. Manny's key lime pies are legendary. On any evening a parade of customers comes through to get them takeout, and speaking of takeout, many people call ahead for meals to go, to avoid lines on weekends and in high season. ✉ *MM 81.6, OS, 81610 Old Hwy.,* ☎ *305/664–5019. AE, D, MC, V. Closed Tues. and mid-Oct.–mid.-Nov.*

$–$$ ✕ **Squid Row.** This affable roadside seafood eatery serves the freshest
★ fish possible, courtesy of the seafood wholesalers who own it. Grouper comes grilled, divinely flaky, or in bread crumbs and sautéed, served with citrus butter, and the nightly special bouillabaisse ($23.95) is simply wonderful. If you finish it by yourself—no cheating—you get a free slice of key lime pie. The waitstaff will brew a fresh pot of coffee and volunteer to wrap what's left of the flavorful, airy banana bread that comes at the start of the meal but is best as dessert. There's also a bar with happy hour 4–7. ✉ *MM 81.9, OS,* ☎ *305/664–9865. AE, D, DC, MC, V.*

$$$$ 🏨 **Cheeca Lodge.** This 27-acre low-rise resort sits amid tranquil fish-filled lagoons and gardens. Recently refurbished with high-grade fabrics, carpets, and furniture, units are washed in oh-so-tropical blue and rich sand. Suites have kitchens and screened balconies; fourth-floor rooms in the main lodge have ocean or bay views. The resort is the local leader in green activism with everything from recycling efforts to ecotours. Camp Cheeca for kids is fun and educational. ✉ *MM 82, OS, Box 527, 33036,* ☎ *305/664–4651 or 800/327–2888,* 🖷 *305/664–2893. 139 rooms, 64 suites. 2 restaurants, lobby lounge, 2 pools, saltwater tidal pool, 9-hole golf course, 6 lighted tennis courts, boating, parasailing, fishing, children's programs, playground. AE, D, DC, MC, V.*

$$$ 🏨 **The Moorings.** This onetime coconut plantation on 18 acres is one
★ of the finest places to stay in the Keys. Tucked in a tropical forest, one-, two-, three-, and four-bedroom cottages and town houses are furnished with wicker and artistic African fabrics and have pristine white kitchens. Peaked roofs rise behind French doors, lighting is soft, and there are many exquisite touches, from thick towels to extradeep, cushiony bedcovers. The beach has a scattering of Adirondack chairs and hammocks, complimentary windsurfing and kayaking, and a swimming dock (no Jet Skis allowed). There's a two-night minimum on one-bedrooms and a one-week minimum on other lodgings. ✉ *MM 81.6, OS, 123 Beach Rd., 33036,* ☎ *305/664–4708,* 🖷 *305/664–4242. 18 cottages and town houses. Pool, tennis court, beach, dock, windsurfing, boating. MC, V.*

$$ 🏨 **Ragged Edge Resort.** People come to the Keys to get away. The fortunate ones find the Ragged Edge, a come-as-you-are, be-who-you-are kind of place. There are lots of regulars, some of whom have been coming for 20 years. Clean rooms feature pine paneling, chintz, and a tile bath suite, and most have kitchens with irons. Most downstairs units have screened porches, whereas upper units have large decks, more windows, and beam ceilings. Though the place feels expensive, it's affordable due to a lack of staff and things like in-room phones. Amenities take the form of a thatch-roof observation tower, picnic areas, barbecue pits, and free bikes. There's not much of a beach, but you can swim off the dock—a virtual rookery when boats don't disturb the pelicans, herons, anhingas, and terns. ✉ *MM 86.5, OS, 243 Treasure Harbor Rd.,*

33036, ☎ 305/852–5389. 10 units. Picnic area, pool, shuffleboard, dock, bicycles. MC, V.

Nightlife

Holiday Isle Beach Resorts & Marina (⊠ MM 84, OS, ☎ 305/664–2321) is the liveliest spot in the Upper Keys. On weekends, especially during spring break and holidays, the resort's three entertainment areas are mobbed, primarily with the under-30 set, whose IDs are carefully scrutinized. Live bands play everything from reggae to heavy metal. Behind the larger-than-life mermaid is the Keys-easy, over-the-water cabana bar the **Lorelei** (⊠ MM 82, BS, ☎ 305/664–4656). Live nightly sounds are mostly reggae and light rock.

Outdoor Activities and Sports

BIKING

Pete's Bike Shop (⊠ MM 82.9, BS, ☎ 305/664–1910) rents adult, children's, and tandem bikes—single-speed bicycles with coaster brakes and multispeed mountain bikes. Helmets and locks are included in the price: $10 a day, $50 a week. Repairs are available.

BOATING

To experience the Keys as they were before the highway intruded, rent a houseboat from **Houseboat Vacations of the Florida Keys** (⊠ MM 85.9, BS, 85944 Overseas Hwy., 33036, ☎ 305/664–4009). The 40- and 42-ft boats accommodate eight people and come fully outfitted with safety equipment and necessities—except food—as well as an AM/FM cassette stereo. You can rent by the day, with a three-day minimum; a week costs $975—$1,195. **Robbie's Boat Rentals & Charters** (⊠ MM 77.5, BS, 77520 Overseas Hwy., 33036, ☎ 305/664–9814 or 305/664–4196) rents a 14-ft skiff with a 25-horsepower outboard (the smallest you can charter) for $25 an hour, $60 for four hours, and $80 for the day. Boats up to 27 ft are also available. Other than clothes and food, Captains Pam and Pete Anderson of **Treasure Harbor Marine** (⊠ MM 86.5, OS, 200 Treasure Harbor Dr., 33036, ☎ 305/852–2458 or 800/352–2628) provide everything you'll need for a vacation at sea—linens, safety gear, and, best of all, advice on where to find the best beaches, marinas, and lobster sites. You can rent a vessel bareboat or crewed, with sail or with power. Boats include a 19-ft Cape Dory, 41-ft custom-built ketch, 35-ft Mainship, and 35-ft Chenhwa trawler, as well as Morgans, Watkins, and Hunters. Rates start at $95 a day, $395 a week. Most business is repeat customers. Marina facilities are basic—water, electric, ice machine, laundry, picnic tables, and shower/rest rooms—and dockage is only $1 a foot.

FISHING

The 65-ft party boat **Gulf Lady** (⊠ Bud 'n' Mary's Marina, MM 79.8, OS, ☎ 305/664–2628 or 305/664–2451) operates full-day and night fishing trips. Party boats can be crowded, so call about loads in advance. For almost 40 years Captain Ken Knudsen of the **Hubba Hubba** (⊠ Bud 'n' Mary's Marina, MM 79.8, OS, ☎ 305/664–9281) has fished the waters around Islamorada, first taking out guests at his family's hotel when he was 12, later as a licensed backcountry guide. His expertise earned him ranking as one of the top 10 guides in Florida by national fishing magazines, and he fishes what he knows best: bonefish, permit, and tarpon. Unlike most guides, he offers four-hour sunset trips for tarpon ($300) and two-hour sunset trips for bonefish ($175), as well as half- ($275) and full-day ($375) outings. Prices are for two anglers, $50 extra for a third. Tackle and bait are included. On **Tag 'Em** (⊠ Holiday Isle Marina, MM 84, OS, ☎ 305/852–8797 or 305/664–2321, ext. 642), Captain John Magursky runs one of the best charters in the Keys. The crew is refreshingly knowledgeable, clean, friendly, and hardworking, whether they're doing light tackle and fly-fishing or going after deep-sea game fish like dolphin, sailfish, tuna, or marlin. The 40-ft vessel has a four-chair cockpit and well-maintained custom tackle. For off-shore and reef fishing, half- and full-day trips ($400 and $600, respectively, for six anglers) include everything but food and beverages.

SCUBA DIVING AND SNORKELING

Florida Keys Dive Center (⊠ MM 90.5, OS, Box 391, Tavernier 33070, ☏ 305/852–4599 or 800/433–8946) organizes dives from John Pennekamp Coral Reef State Park to Alligator Light. The center has two Coast Guard–approved dive boats, offers scuba training, and is one of few Keys dive centers to offer Nitrox (mixed gas) diving. For more than 15 years **Lady Cyana Divers** (⊠ MM 85.9, BS, Box 1157, 33036, ☏ 305/664–8717 or 800/221–8717), a PADI five-star training resort, has operated dives on deep and shallow wrecks and reefs between Molasses and Alligator reefs. The 40- and 55-ft boats provide everything a diver needs, including full bathrooms.

TENNIS

The four clay and two hard courts at **Islamorada Tennis Club** (⊠ MM 76.8, BS, ☏ 305/664–5340) are busiest December–March, and reservations are essential to play between 9 and 11. It's popular partly because it's cheap ($7 an hour) and partly because it's well run. Amenities include tension stringing, ball machines, private lessons, a pro shop, night games, and partner pairing.

Shopping

Two former Miami teachers knocked down walls, added a coffee bar, and turned the once tiny **Cover to Cover Books** (⊠ MM 90.1, OS, 90130 Old Hwy., ☏ 305/852–1415) into one of the best bookstores in the Keys. They also sell gifts and jewelry and hold book signings and readings for kids. There is an extensive selection of books, cards, and maps on Florida and the Keys. There's chic shopping at the **Gallery at Morada Bay** (⊠ MM 81.6, BS, ☏ 305/664–3650), stocked with blown glass and glassware, furniture and home furnishings, original paintings and lithographs, sculptures, and hand-painted scarves and earrings by top South Florida artists. **H. T. Chittum & Co.** (⊠ MM 82.7, BS, ☏ 305/664–4421) carries informal clothing from Timberland and Nautica, specialty knives, and smart ready-to-wear. There are branches in Marathon (⊠ MM 48.5, OS, ☏ 305/743–4171) and Key West (⊠ 725 Duval St., ☏ 305/292–9002). At **Island Silver & Spice** (⊠ MM 82, OS, ☏ 305/664–2714), the first floor is devoted to women's and men's resort wear, a large jewelry section with high-end Swiss watches and marine-theme jewelry, tropical housewares, cards, and toys and games. Climb the wooden stairway to the second floor to browse through tropical bedding and bath goods and a sale section.

A 20-year-old crafts village set in a tropical garden of native plants and orchids, **Rain Barrel** (⊠ MM 86.7, BS, ☏ 305/852–3084) represents works by numerous local and national artists and has eight resident artists in separate studios. On the third weekend in March, the largest arts show in the Keys takes place here; some 20,000 visitors view the work of 100 artists and listen to live jazz. Such nationally and internationally recognized outdoor artists as sculptor Kendall Van Sant; watercolorists Chet Reneson, Jeanne Dobie, and Kathleen Denis; and painters C. D. Clarke and Tim Borski are represented at the **Redbone Gallery** (⊠ MM 81, OS, 200 Industrial Dr., ☏ 305/664–2002). At **Treasure Village** (⊠ MM 86.7, OS, 86729 Old Hwy., ☏ 305/852–0511), salvage master Art McKee ran McKee's Treasure Museum in the 1950s.

An enormous fabricated lobster by artist Richard Blaes stands in front of the center, where a dozen crafts and specialty shops plus the excellent little Made to Order eat-in and carryout restaurant operate. George Hommell Jr., who's served as fishing guide to President George Bush, General Norman Schwarzkopf, and numerous celebrities, opened **World Wide Sportsman** (✉ MM 82.5, BS, ☎ 305/664–4615) in 1967. He sold it to Missouri-based Bass Pro, which spared no expense in turning it into a two-level attraction, lounge, and retail center selling very upscale fishing equipment. It has a pricey art gallery, marina, and departments for clothing and gifts. Black-and-white photos of former U.S. presidents, celebs, and record holders beaming alongside their catches adorn the walls.

Long Key

❺ *MM 70–65.5.*

This island is best known for the **Long Key State Recreation Area.** On the main, ocean side, the Golden Orb Trail leads onto a boardwalk through a mangrove swamp alongside a lagoon, where waterbirds congregate. The park has a campground, picnic area, rest rooms and showers, a canoe trail through a tidal lagoon, and a not-very-sandy beach fronting a broad expanse of shallow grass flats. Bring a mask and snorkel to observe the marine life in this rich nursery area. Across the road, near a historical marker partially obscured by foliage, is the **Layton Nature Trail** (✉ MM 67.7, BS), which takes 20–30 minutes to walk and leads through tropical hardwood forest to a rocky Florida Bay shoreline overlooking shallow grass flats. A marker relates the history of the Long Key Viaduct, the first major bridge on the rail line, and the exclusive Long Key Fishing Camp, which Henry Flagler established nearby in 1906 and which attracted sportsman Zane Grey, the noted western novelist and conservationist, who served as its first president. The camp was washed away in the 1935 hurricane and never rebuilt. For Grey's efforts, the creek running near the recreation area was named for him. ✉ *MM 67.5, OS, Box 776, 33001, ☎ 305/664–4815. ▨ $3.25 for 1 person, plus 50¢ each additional person; canoe rental $4 per hr; Layton Nature Trail free. ☉ Daily 8–sunset.*

Dining and Lodging

$–$$ ✕ **Little Italy.** The hearty Italian and seafood dishes here are a great value. Lunches like fried fish fingers, snapper almandine, baked grouper, lasagna, and a 21-shrimp basket run $4.50–$6.95 including salad, french fries, and bread. Dinner selections are equally tasty and well priced—chicken, seafood, veal, and steak for $8.50–$13.95. Don't miss the rich, dreamy hot chocolate pecan pie. Breakfast, too, is served, and a children's menu is available. ✉ *MM 68.5, BS, ☎ 305/664–4472. AE, D, MC, V.*

$$–$$$ ▣ **Lime Tree Bay Resort Motel.** This popular 2½-acre hideaway has attractive wicker- and rattan-furnished guest rooms, tropical art, and cottages with kitchens along with a little beach, nice landscaping, a beautiful pool deck, hammocks, a gazebo, and a covered walkway. The best units are the cottages out back (no bay views) and four deluxe rooms upstairs, which have cathedral ceilings and skylights. The upstairs Tree House, the best bet for two couples traveling together, has a palm tree growing through its private deck. You can swim and snorkel in the shallow grass flats offshore. An on-site concessioner offers water sports, available separately or with an accommodation package. ✉ *MM 68.5, BS, Box 839, Layton 33001, ☎ 305/664–4740 or 800/723–4519, ⅻ 305/664–0750. 29 rooms. Restaurant, picnic area,*

pool, hot tub, tennis court, horseshoes, shuffleboard, beach, dive shop, snorkeling, windsurfing, boating, jet skiing. AE, D, DC, MC, V.

$ ⚠ **Long Key State Recreation Area.** Situated along the park's narrow, semi-sandy beach are tent and RV sites under tall, shady trees. Fishing in the near-shore flats is superb, yielding bonefish, permit, and tarpon. A new reservation system went into effect in early 1998 (you can reserve up to 11 months in advance by phone or in person) along with major upgrades. All sites now have water and electricity, signage has been improved, and campground hostesses are available to answer questions and help out. Sites cost $17, plus $2 for electricity. ✉ *MM 67.5, OS, Box 776, 33001,* ☎ *305/664–4815. 60 sites. Picnic area, hiking, beach, fishing. D, MC, V.*

Outdoor Activities and Sports

Based at Lime Tree Bay Resort, Captain Elizabeth Jolin's **Lime Tree Water Sports** (✉ MM 68.5, BS, ☎ 305/664–0052) provides a wide variety of recreational opportunities, including sunset cruises; sailboat, powerboat, kayak, sailboard, and Wave Runner rentals; backcountry fishing trips; and snorkeling and scuba. She also offers PADI diving certification and windsurfing and sailing lessons.

En Route As you cross Long Key Channel, look beside you at the old **Long Key Viaduct.** The second-longest bridge on the former rail line, this 2-milong structure has 222 reinforced-concrete arches.

THE MIDDLE KEYS

Stretching from Conch Key to the far side of the Seven Mile Bridge, the Middle Keys contain U.S. 1's most impressive stretch, MM 65–40, bracketed by the Keys' two longest bridges—Long Key Bridge and Seven Mile Bridge, both historic landmarks. Activity centers on the town of Marathon, the Keys' third-largest metropolitan area.

Fishing and diving are the main attractions. In both bay and ocean, the deep-water fishing is superb at places like the Marathon West Hump, whose depth ranges from 500 to more than 1,000 ft. Anglers successfully fish from a half-dozen bridges, including Long Key Bridge, the old Seven Mile Bridge, and both ends of Toms Harbor. There are also many beaches and natural areas to enjoy in the Middle Keys.

Conch and Duck Keys

❻ *MM 63–61.*

This stretch of islands is rustic. Fishing dominates the economy, and many residents are descendants of immigrants from the mainland South. Across a causeway from Conch Key, a tiny fishing and retirement village, lies Duck Key, an upscale community and resort.

Dining and Lodging

$–$$$ ✕ **Watersedge.** A collection of historic photos on the walls depicts the railroad era, the development of Duck Key, and many of the notables who have visited this eatery at the Hawk's Cay Resort (☞ *below*). Dine indoors or under the dockside canopy. Soup and a 40-item salad bar are included with dinners. The menu emphasizes seafood, and specialties range from spicy conch chowder, chicken Key West (stuffed with crab and shrimp), and Florida stone-crab claws (in season) to mud pie and coconut ice cream. ✉ *MM 61, OS, Duck Key,* ☎ *305/743–7000. AE, D, DC, MC, V. No lunch.*

$$$$ ⊞ **Hawk's Cay Resort.** This rambling West Indies–style resort opened
in 1959, and over the years it has entertained film stars and politicians.
Decor features wicker, a sea-green-and-salmon color scheme, and contemporary artwork. Many rooms face the water, and two-bedroom town
houses are available, with more on the way. Guests can use a nearby
golf course, take a dive trip, play volleyball on a sand court overlooking
the Atlantic, or swim in the smooth saltwater lagoon or in one of two
pools. Dolphin Discovery is an interactive, in-the-water educational
program. ⊠ *MM 61, OS, 33050,* ☎ *305/743–7000 or 800/432–2242,*
FAX *305/743–5215. 160 rooms, 15 suites, 120 two-bedroom town
houses. 4 restaurants, 2 bars, 2 pools, golf privileges, 8 tennis courts,
health club, volleyball, boating, fishing, video games, children's programs. AE, D, DC, MC, V.*

$$$ ⊞ **Conch Key Cottages.** This happy hideout on its own island bridged
by a pebbly causeway has a castaway, live-and-let-live mood. Allamanda,
bougainvillea, and hibiscus jiggle colorfully, and the beach curves
around a mangrove-edged cove. Lattice-trimmed cottages with kitchens,
some with two bedrooms, rise up on pilings, old-fashioned in Dade
County pine. Cool tile floors, hammocks, and furnishings of reed, rat-
tan, and wicker create an island look. Three cottages face the beach.
Though not on the water, the small honeymoon cottage is very charm-
ing. If you need a coffee fix, bring your own to prepare, as the closest
source is 1½ mi away. Highway noise can be distracting. ⊠ *MM 62.3,
OS, R.R. 1, Box 424, Marathon 33050,* ☎ *305/289–1377 or 800/330–
1577,* FAX *305/743–8207. 12 units. Pool, beach. D, MC, V.*

Grassy Key

❼ *MM 60–57.*

Local lore has it that this sleepy little key was named not for its vege-
tation—mostly native trees and shrubs—but for an early settler. It's pri-
marily inhabited by a few families who operate small fishing camps
and motels.

The former home of Milton Santini, creator of the original *Flipper* movie,
the **Dolphin Research Center** is now home to a colony of about 15 dol-
phins. A not-for-profit organization offers a half-day program called
Dolph*Insight,* which teaches dolphin biology and human–dolphin
communications and allows you to touch the dolphins out of the
water. A 2½-hour instruction-education program aptly called Dolphin
Encounter enables you to do just that in the water for 20 minutes. Tips
on Training, a new daily program, allows visitors to sit on the dock
with a trainer and interact with the marine mammals. ⊠ *MM 59, BS,
Box 522875, Marathon Shores 33052,* ☎ *305/289–1121.* ▣ *$12.50,
DolphInsight $75, Dolphin Encounter $90, Tips on Training $30–$35.*
☉ *Daily 9–4, walking tours daily 10, 11, 12:30, 2, and 3:30. Children
5–12 must swim with accompanying, paying adult. Reserve 30 days
in advance for all programs.*

Dining

$–$$ ✗ **Grassy Key Dairy Bar.** Tables, counters, and even white shirts in the
kitchen are now found at this ever-improving little seafood and steak
landmark, which dates from 1959. Locals and construction workers
stop here for quick lunches. The broiled dolphin with black beans and
rice and cheese sauce is a local favorite. Owner-chefs George and
Johnny Eigner are also especially proud of their broiled or grilled fish
with wasabi, as well as the fresh-daily homemade bread and fresh-cut
beef. In fall their OctoberFest features German foods, beers, and live

entertainment. ⊠ *MM 58.5, OS,* ☎ *305/743–3816. MC, V. Closed Sun.–Mon. No lunch Sat.*

Marathon

⑧ *MM 53–47.5.*

This community is the commercial hub of the Middle Keys. Commercial fishing—still a big local industry—began here in the early 1800s. Pirates, salvers, fishermen, spongers, and later farmers eked out a living, traveling by boat between islands. About half the population were blacks, who burned charcoal for a living. According to local lore, Marathon was renamed after a 1906 hurricane, when a worker commented that it was a marathon task to rebuild railway across the 6-mi island.

The railroad brought businesses and a hotel, and today Marathon is a bustling town by Keys standards. Yet the town remains laid-back. Fishing, diving, and boating are the primary attractions.

The small **Museums of Tropical Crane Point Hammock**—part of a 63-acre tract that includes the last-known undisturbed thatch-palm hammock—is owned by the Florida Keys Land Trust, a private, nonprofit conservation group. In the **Museum of Natural History of the Florida Keys,** behind a stunning bronze-and-copper door crafted by Roy Butler of Plantation, are a few dioramas, a shell exhibit, and displays on Keys geology, wildlife, and cultural history. Also here is the **Florida Keys Children's Museum,** which has iguanas, fish, and a pirate dress-up room. Outside, on the 1-mi indigenous loop trail, you can visit the remnants of a Bahamian village, site of the restored **George Adderly House,** the oldest surviving example of Conch-style architecture outside Key West. From November to Easter, docent-led tours, included in the price, are available; bring good walking shoes and bug repellent. ⊠ *MM 50.5, BS, 5550 Overseas Hwy., Box 536, 33050,* ☎ *305/743–9100.* ☜ *$7.50.* ☺ *Mon.–Sat. 9–5, Sun. noon–5; tours weekdays 10, 11, 1:30, 2:30 (call to confirm).*

Sombrero Beach has separate areas for swimmers, jet boats, and windsurfers, as well as a grassy park with barbecue grills, picnic kiosks, showers, rest rooms, a baseball diamond, large playground, and volleyball court. The park is accessible for travelers with disabilities. Turn left at the traffic light in Marathon and follow signs to the end. ⊠ *MM 50, OS, Sombrero Rd.,* ☎ *305/289–6077 or 888/227–8136.* ☜ *Free.* ☺ *Daily 8–sunset.*

OFF THE BEATEN PATH

PIGEON KEY – This 5-acre island under the Seven Mile Bridge was once the site of a railroad work camp and, later, a fish camp, park, and government administration building. In 1993 the nonprofit Pigeon Key Foundation leased this National Historic District from Monroe County and started developing it as a center focusing on Florida Keys culture, environmental education, and marine research. Its first project was the restoration of the old railroad work-camp buildings, the earliest of which dates from 1908. A museum recalls the history of the railroad and the Keys, and a 28-minute video chronicles the life and projects of railroad baron Henry M. Flagler. To reach the island, you can either take the shuttle, which departs from the depot on Knight's Key (⊠ MM 47), or walk across a 2.2-mi stretch of the Old Seven Mile Bridge. Families bring picnics and stay the day. ⊠ *MM 45, OS, Box 500130, Pigeon Key 33050,* ☎ *305/289–0025.* ☜ *$7.50.* ☺ *Daily 10–5.*

Dining and Lodging

$$-$$$ ✕ **Kelsey's.** This steak and seafood eatery at the Faro Blanco Marine Resort (☞ *below*) is hung with boat paddles inscribed by charter-boat captains and other frequent diners. Entrées like Maryland-style crab cakes and horseradish-encrusted grouper over mashed potatoes are served with fresh-toasted baguettes prepared here daily. You can bring your own cleaned and filleted catch for the chef to prepare. Desserts may include banana pecan delight, white-chocolate mousse, macadamia pie, and key lime cheesecake. ⊠ *MM 48.5, BS,* ☎ *305/743–9018. AE, D, MC, V. Closed Mon. No lunch.*

$-$$ ✕ **Herbie's.** A local favorite for lunch and dinner since the 1940s, Herbie's has three small rooms, including a screened outdoor room, with two counters, where casual American food is served. Specialties include spicy conch chowder with chunks of tomato and crisp conch fritters with homemade horseradish sauce. ⊠ *MM 50.5, BS,* ☎ *305/ 743–6373. No credit cards. Closed 2 weeks each in spring and fall. No lunch Sun.*

$-$$ ✕ **Key Colony Inn.** Run by the same folks who own Little Italy on Long Key, this slightly more upscale eatery features many of the same Italian chicken, steak, pasta, and veal dishes, some at the same price, others for a buck or two more. Food is well prepared, and service is friendly and attentive. For lunch there are well-priced fish and steak entrées ($4.75–$6.95) served with fries, salad, and bread. At dinner you can't miss with the seafood Italiano, a light dish of scallops and shrimp sautéed in garlic butter over a bed of linguine with a hint of marinara sauce. ⊠ *MM 54, OS, 700 W. Ocean Dr., Key Colony Beach,* ☎ *305/743– 0100. AE, MC, V.*

$ ✕ **7 Mile Grill.** The walls of this open-air diner built in 1954 at the ★ Marathon end of Seven Mile Bridge are lined with beer cans, mounted fish, sponges, and signs describing individual menu items. The prompt, friendly service rivals the great food at breakfast, lunch, and dinner. Favorites on the mostly seafood menu include fresh-squeezed orange juice, creamy shrimp bisque, and fresh grouper and dolphin grilled, broiled, or fried. Don't pass up the authentic key lime pie, which won the local paper's "Best in the Keys" award three years in a row. ⊠ *MM 47, BS,* ☎ *305/743–4481. No credit cards. Closed Wed. and at owner's discretion Aug.–Sept.*

$$-$$$$ ⊡ **Faro Blanco Marine Resort.** One of the oldest resorts in the Keys, Faro Blanco has built up a loyal following of repeat guests, thanks to service that's first-rate without being fussy. The property stretches on both sides of the highway, and guest rooms, most with kitchens, are found in cottages; houseboats; three-bedroom, two-bath condominiums; and two lighthouse apartments, one of which sprawls over three floors. A full-service marina and marine repair shop meet boaters' needs, and diving and fishing charters can be arranged. Pets are allowed. ⊠ *MM 48.2, BS and OS, 1996 Overseas Hwy., 33050,* ☎ *305/743–9018 or 800/759–3276,* 𝔽𝕏 *305/743–2918. 125 units. 4 restaurants, pool, docks, boating, bicycles. AE, D, MC, V.*

$$-$$$ ⊡ **Banana Bay Resort & Marina.** Situated among fruit trees and other native and tropical plants—including bananas, of course—this 10-acre resort is ideal for active vacationers. It has the largest freshwater pool in the Keys, a marina with boat ramp, Adirondack-style chairs on a small sandy beach, and a protected area for snorkeling. Arrangements can be made for fishing, sailing, and diving. The crowd is a mix of vacationers, conventioneers, and marina guests. Rooms, decorated in a Caribbean plantation style, have either one king or two double beds and are loaded with amenities. Rates include poolside Continental breakfast daily. Management also runs an adults-only resort in Key West. ⊠ MM 49.5, BS, 4590 Overseas Hwy., 33050, ☎ 305/743–3500 or 800/226–2621, FAX 305/743–2670. 60 units. Pool, 2 tennis courts, exercise room, beach, dock, snorkeling. AE, D, DC, MC, V.

$$–$$$ 🏨 **Coral Lagoon.** Surrounded by lush landscaping on a short, deep-water canal, these charming pastel-color duplex cottages each have a hammock on a private sundeck, a kitchen, and king or twin beds and a sofa bed. Units also have central air, ceiling fans, videocassette players ($1 tape rental), wall safes, and hair dryers, and you can take advantage of complimentary morning coffee, tennis rackets, fishing equipment, dockage, and barbecues. For a fee you can also enjoy admission to a private beach club, charter fishing, and scuba and snorkel trips arranged through the Diving Site, a dive shop that also offers certification. ⊠ MM 53.5, OS, 12399 Overseas Hwy., 33050, ☎ 305/289–0121, FAX 305/289–0195. 18 units. Pool, tennis court, dive shop, dock, library. AE, D, MC, V.

$$ 🏨 **Little Valhalla Resort.** For more than 35 years people have come to the Valhalla Beach Resort Motel (☞ below), an unpretentious Crawl Key lodging with the waterfront location of a posh resort. Those returning will be confused by two new signs—one for Valhalla Beach Motel and one for Little Valhalla Resort—as well as a new fence dividing the property. Brothers Bruce and Chris Schofield, who inherited the property, settled their differences by splitting the business. Chris's half has a very good beach, as well as a dock, picnic tables, barbecue grills, and kayak and canoe rentals, a nice touch since his property borders the state's new park, Curry Hammock, which locals say has one of the Keys' best kayak trails. He offers family-oriented sailing and snorkeling trips to the reefs as well as snorkel-accommodations packages. ⊠ MM 57.5, OS, 56223 Ocean Dr., Crawl Key 33050, ☎ 305/289–0614. 2 rooms, 4 efficiencies. Picnic area, beach, dock, boating. MC, V.

$$ 🏨 **Valhalla Beach Motel.** Bruce Schofield runs this motel, which has a few more units than his brother's next door (☞ above). Rooms have small refrigerators, while efficiencies have kitchens. The property features a small beach, boat ramp, dock, barbecue grills, canoes and rental boats, and Adirondack chairs with umbrellas. Guests seem to have come out the biggest winners in the family dispute. Although there's no visible animosity, both brothers have been trying to outdo each other by upgrading and renovating, bringing new amenities, bed and bath linens, tile floors, and kitchen appliances. Some things haven't changed, like the palm trees rustling in the wind, clean and simple rooms with TVs but no telephones, and peace and quiet. ⊠ MM 57.5, OS, 56243 Ocean Dr., Crawl Key 33050, ☎ 305/289–0616. 4 rooms, 1 suite, 5 efficiencies. Beach, dock, boating. No credit cards.

Outdoor Activities and Sports

BIKING

Some of the best paths in the area include those along Aviation Boulevard on the bay side of Marathon Airport, the four-lane section of the Overseas Highway through Marathon, Sadowski Causeway to Key Colony Beach, Sombrero Beach Road to the public beach, and the roads on Boot Key (across a bridge on 20th Street, OS). There's easy cycling at the south end of Marathon, where a 1-mi off-road path connects to the 2 mi of the Old Seven Mile Bridge that go to Pigeon Key.

Equipment Locker Sport & Cycle (⊠ MM 53, BS, ☎ 305/289–1670) rents cruisers and mountain bikes for adults and children.

BOATING

Captain Pip's (✉ MM 47.5, BS, 1410 Overseas Hwy., 33050, ☎ 305/743–4403) rents 20-ft or larger motor-equipped boats starting at $80 for half a day.

FISHING

A pair of 65-ft party boats, **Marathon Lady** and **Marathon Lady III** (✉ MM 53, OS, at 117th St., 33050, ☎ 305/743–5580) go on half- ($25) and full-day ($42) trips from the Vaca Cut Bridge, north of Marathon. Those who don't want to pay $200–$350 for a half-day charter or share a party boat with 30 or more other anglers are turning to **Sea Dog Charters** (✉ MM 47.5, BS, ☎ 305/743–8255), next to the 7 Mile Grill. Capt. Jim Purcell, a deep-sea specialist for ESPN's *The Outdoorsman,* offers personalized half- and full-day offshore, reef and wreck, tarpon, and backcountry fishing trips as well as combination fishing and snorkeling trips on the 32-ft *Bad Dog* for up to six people. The cost is $59.99 per person for a half day, regardless of whether your group fills the boat, and includes bait, light tackle, licensing, ice, and coolers.

GOLF

Key Colony Beach Par 3 (✉ MM 53.5, OS, 8th St., Key Colony Beach, ☎ 305/289–1533), a 9-hole course near Marathon, charges $7 for 9 holes, $2 per person for club rental, and $1 for a pull cart. The beauty of this course is that there are no tee times and no rush. Play from 7:30 to dusk. A little golf shop meets basic golf needs.

SCUBA DIVING AND SNORKELING

Hall's Diving Center and Career Institute (✉ MM 48.5, BS, 1994 Overseas Hwy., 33050, ☎ 305/743–5929 or 800/331–4255), next to Faro Blanco Resort, runs two trips a day to Looe Key, Sombrero Reef, Delta Shoal, Content Key, Coffins Patch, and the 110-ft wreck *Thunderbolt.*

En Route   To cross the broad expanse of water separating the Middle and Lower keys, you'll travel over the **Seven Mile Bridge,** actually 6.79 mi long. Believed to be the world's longest segmental bridge, it has 39 expansion joints separating its cement sections. Each April runners gather in Marathon for the annual Seven Mile Bridge Run. You can look across at what remains of the **Old Seven Mile Bridge,** an engineering marvel in its day that's now on the National Register of Historic Places. It rested on a record 546 concrete piers. No private cars are allowed on the bridge today, but locals like to ride bikes on it to watch the sunset and to reach Pigeon Key.

THE LOWER KEYS

In truth, the Lower Keys include Key West, but since it's covered in its own section and is as different from the rest of the Lower Keys as peanut butter is from jelly, this section comprises just the limestone keys between MM 37 and MM 9. From Bahia Honda Key south, islands are clustered, smaller, and more numerous, a result of ancient tidal waters flowing between the Florida Straits and the gulf. Here you're more likely to see more birds and mangroves than other tourists, and more refuges, beaches, and campgrounds than museums, restaurants, and hotels.

The islands are made up of two types of limestone, both more dense than the highly permeable Key Largo limestone of the Upper Keys. As a result, freshwater forms pools rather than percolating, forming watering holes that support Key deer, alligators, fish, snakes, Lower Keys rabbits, raccoons, migratory ducks, Key cotton and silver rice rats, pines, saw palmettos, silver palms, grasses, and ferns. (Many of these animals and plants can be seen in the National Key Deer Refuge on Big Pine Key; ☞ *below*).)

Nature was generous with her beauty in the Lower Keys. They're home to both Looe Key National Marine Sanctuary, arguably the most beautiful coral reef tract in the Keys, and Bahia Honda State Park, considered by many one of the best beaches in the world.

Bahia Honda Key

❾ *MM 38–36.*

Bahia Honda translates from Spanish as "deep bay," a good description of local waters. The government owns most of the island, which
★ is devoted to 524-acre **Bahia Honda State Park.** The Silver Palm Trail leads through a dense tropical forest where you can see rare West Indian plants and several species found nowhere else in the Keys. The park also contains the Keys' only natural sandy beach of notable size. Even more unusual is that it extends on both gulf and ocean sides and has deep water close to shore. Plenty of year-round activities are available. The park includes a campground, cabins, a snack bar, marina, and dive shop. You can get a panoramic view of the island from what's left of the railroad—the Bahia Honda Bridge. ⊠ *MM 37, OS, 36850 Overseas Hwy., 33043,* ☎ *305/872–2353.* ☒ *$2 for 1 person, $4 per vehicle for 2–8 people plus 50¢ per person county surcharge; $2 per vehicle an hour before closing.* ☉ *Daily 8–sunset.*

Lodging

$$$ ⊡ **Bahia Honda State Park.** Views from the six bay-front cabin units on stilts are spectacular. Each is completely furnished (no TV or radio); has two bedrooms, full kitchen, and bath; and sleeps six. The park also has 80 popular campsites, suitable for motor homes and tents. Cabins and campsites are very popular, so reserve up to 11 months before your planned visit. ⊠ *MM 37, OS, 36850 Overseas Hwy., 33043,* ☎ *305/872–2353. 3 duplex cabins. Picnic area, beach, boating, fishing. MC, V.*

Outdoor Activities and Sports

Bahia Honda Dive Shop (⊠ MM 37, OS, ☎ 305/872–3210), the concessioner at Bahia Honda State Park, operates offshore-reef snorkel trips and boat rentals. Snorkel trips ($22) run almost three hours (with an hour on the reef) and leave daily at 10 and 2 (also at 1, October–November). Rental craft range from a 20-ft pontoon boat and 22-ft center console fishing-dive boat to kayaks.

Big Pine Key

❿ *MM 32–30.*

Known for its concentration of Key deer, this island is the site of the 2,300-acre **National Key Deer Refuge,** established in 1954 to protect the dwindling population of Key deer, a subspecies of the Virginia white-tailed deer. These deer once ranged throughout the Lower and Middle keys, but hunting, habitat destruction, and a growing human population have caused their numbers to decline to around 250. The best place to see Key deer in the refuge is at the end of Key Deer Boulevard (Route 940), along U.S. 1, and on No Name Key, a sparsely populated island just east of Big Pine Key. Deer may turn up along the road at any time of day—especially in early morning and late afternoon. Admire their beauty, but feeding them is against the law. The **Blue Hole,** a quarry left over from railroad days, is the largest body of freshwater in the Keys. From the observation platform and walking trail, you might see alligators, birds, turtles, Key deer, and other wildlife. There are two well-marked trails: the Jack Watson Nature Trail (⅔ mi), named after Jack Watson, an environmentalist and the refuge's first warden; and the Fred Mannillo Nature Trail, one of the most accessible places to see an unspoiled hardwood hammock and subtropical foliage. The latter has a hard surface for wheelchair access. ⊠ *Headquarters, Big Pine Shopping Center, MM 30.5, BS,* ☎ *305/872–2239.* 🖾 *Free.* ☉ *Daily sunrise–sunset; headquarters weekdays 8–5.*

Dining and Lodging

$ ✕ **No Name Pub.** The Upper Keys has Alabama Jack's and the Caribbean Club. The Lower Keys has this ramshackle American-casual establishment, in existence since 1936, or so the staff's shirts read. As long as anyone can remember, locals have come for the cold beer, excellent pizza, and sometimes questionable companionship. In early 1998 the pub introduced a full menu, featuring pastas, chicken wings, and, of course, pizza. Inside is poorly lighted with rough furnishings, a jukebox, and pool table; outside is a garden area. The pub is hard to find but worth the search if you want to experience the Keys as old-timers say they once were; turn north at the Big Pine Key traffic light, right at the fork, left at the four-way stop, and then over a humpback bridge. It's on the left, before the No Name Bridge. ⊠ *MM 30, BS, N. Watson Blvd.,* ☎ *305/872–9115. MC, V.*

$$$ 🏠 **Casa Grande.** This oceanfront bed-and-breakfast is one of three
★ under separate ownership within a mile of each other, all built on stilts. Run by Kathleen Threlkeld, it has a white-sand beach along a rocky, shallow shoreline. It's markedly Mediterranean, with a massive Spanish door and mainly contemporary furnishings. Spacious guest rooms have color TVs, small refrigerators, air-conditioning, carpeting, and high open-beam ceilings with paddle fans, and there is a screened, second-story atrium facing the sea. Guests cozy up to the sitting-room fireplace and get to know one another on cool nights. ⊠ *MM 33, OS, Long Beach Dr., Box 378, 33043,* ☎ *305/872–2878. 3 rooms. Refrigerators, hot tub, beach, dock, boating, bicycles. No credit cards.*

$$$ 🏠 **Deer Run.** The most casual of the local B&Bs, this lodging is populated by lots of animals: cats, caged tropical birds, and a herd of Key deer, which forage along the beach and lush seafront gardens. Like her fellow innkeepers, longtime Big Pine resident Sue Abbott is caring and informed, well settled and hospitable. Two large oceanfront rooms are furnished with whitewashed wicker and king-size beds. An upstairs unit looks out on the sea through trees and mulched pathways. Guests have use of a living room, a 52-ft veranda cooled by paddle fans, hammocks, a grill, a hot tub on a deck overlooking the ocean, and water toys. Like its neighbors, Deer Run is a great value. Smokers and children are not welcome. ⊠ *MM 33, OS, 1985 Long Beach Dr., Box 431, 33043,* ☎ *305/872–2015,* 🖷 *305/872–2842. 3 rooms. Grill, hot tub, beach, bicycles. No credit cards.*

$$–$$$ 🏠 **The Barnacle.** Tim and Jane Marquis, owners of a dive shop in
★ Louisiana, bought this B&B next to Casa Grande and moved down to run it in 1995. There are two rooms in the main house, both on the second floor; one in a cottage; and another, below the house, that opens to the beach. Each has its own kitchen. Guest rooms are large, and those in the main house adjoin an atrium, where a hot tub sits in a beautiful garden overlooking sea and sky. Furnishings, collected around the world, are colorful and whimsical. The stained-glass windows are very impressive. Full breakfast is included, and paddleboats, kayaks, and snorkel and dive charters and certifications are offered. ⊠ *MM 33, OS,*

1557 Long Beach Dr., 33043, ☎ 305/872–3298. 4 rooms. Kitch-enettes, hot tub, beach, dock, boating, bicycles. D, MC, V.

$$ ⊡ ⚠ **Big Pine Key Fishing Lodge.** The five lodge rooms at this fam-
★ ily-oriented lodge and campground ($24–$31 per site) are one of the
Keys' best buys. They feature tile floors, wicker furniture, louvered
and screened windows, doors that allow sea breezes to blow through,
queen-size beds, a second-bedroom loft, vaulted ceilings, and mini-
kitchens. A skywalk joins them with a pool and deck. Other units
are either spic-and-span mobile homes or efficiencies. Immaculately
clean tile lines the spacious bathhouse for campers. Separate game
and recreation rooms have TVs, a bar, and other amusements, and
there is dockage along a 735-ft canal. A three-day minimum is re-
quired. ✉ *MM 33, OS, Box 430513, 33043, ☎ 305/872–2351,* FAX
*305/872–3868. 16 rooms, 158 campsites. Bar, kitchenettes, pool, Ping-
Pong, shuffleboard, dock, billiards, recreation room, video games.
MC, V.*

Outdoor Activities and Sports

BIKING

A good 10 mi of paved and unpaved roads run from MM 30.3, BS,
along Wilder Road, across the bridge to No Name Key, and along Key
Deer Boulevard into the National Key Deer Refuge. You might see some
Key deer. Stay off the trails that lead into wetlands, where fat tires can
do damage.

In addition to selling and repairing bikes, **Big Pine Bicycle Center** (✉
MM 30, OS, ☎ 305/872–0130) rents old-fashioned single-speed, fat-
tired cruisers for adults ($8 a day or $34 a week) and children (half
price). Helmets are included. Ask owner Marty Baird about his favorite
places to ride.

FISHING

Strike Zone Charters (✉ MM 29.6, BS, 29675 Overseas Hwy., 33043,
☎ 305/872–9863 or 800/654–9560), run by Capt. Larry Threlkeld,
offers fishing charters on air-conditioned boats at $425 for a half day,
$525 for a full day. In addition, sightseeing trips can include time to
fish, as well as bait and tackle.

Little Torch Key

⓫ *MM 28–29.*

Primarily a base for divers headed for Looe Key National Marine
Sanctuary, a few miles away, this key provides accommodations and
diving outfits. The undeveloped backcountry is at your back door, mak-
ing this an ideal location for fishing and kayaking, too. Nearby **Ram-
rod Key,** which also caters to divers bound for Looe Key, derives its
name from a ship that wrecked on nearby reefs in the early 1800s.

Dining and Lodging

$ ✕ **Baby's Smokehouse Grill & Baby's Coffee.** At this rough-and-ready
waterfront eatery, lip-smacking veal, beef, ribs, Long Island duck, and
chicken are grilled, roasted, and smoked until they are fall-off-the-bone
tender. Baby's uses its own grilling sauces and serves tangy house red
and green hot sauces on the side. Lunches come with corn bread or
French bread, dinners with corn bread and a baked sweet potato. Eat
your barbecue alfresco on a patio overlooking the ocean or inside a
warehouse decorated with the fabulous art of Olga Manosalvas, whose
work appears in tony galleries from Key West to the Hamptons. Save
room for Baby's Coffee, whose freshly roasted aroma used to drive Duval
Street passersby wild. Their motto is "If you don't leave full, just ask

for more." There's entertainment on weekends. ⌧ *MM 15, OS, Saddlebunch Keys,* ☏ *305/744–9866 or 800/523–2326. AE, MC, V. Closed Mon.–Tues.*

$$$–$$$$ 🏨 **Little Palm Island.** The lobby sits beside U.S. 1 on Little Torch Key,
★ but the resort dazzles 3 mi offshore on a palm-fringed island at the western edge of the Newfound Harbor Keys. Close by the water, 14 thatch-roof villas on stilts each have two suites with Mexican-tile baths, Jacuzzis, mosquito netting–draped beds, Mexican and Guatemalan wicker and rattan furniture, minibars, and safes. A second-floor suite on a houseboat adds to the mix. The only phone sits in a dolled-up former outhouse, and there's no TV. Instead, indulge in a fountain-fed pool or some terrific snorkeling, diving, and fishing. In the middle of Coupon Bight State Aquatic Preserve, the island is the closest land to Looe Key National Marine Sanctuary. The food draws yachtfolk from all over, who tie up at the marina come dinner time. ⌧ *MM 28.5, OS, 28500 Overseas Hwy., 33042,* ☏ *305/872–2524 or 800/343–8567,* 🖷 *305/872–4843. 30 suites. Restaurant, bar, minibars, in-room safes, pool, sauna, beach, fishing, boating. AE, D, DC, MC, V.*

$–$$ 🏨 **Parmer's Place.** Each holiday the Parmers send out 15,000 Christmas cards to former guests, many of whom return year after year to stay in the pastel-color, rustic, family-style waterfront cottages and rooms spread over 5 landscaped acres. Most rooms have a deck or balcony, all have cable and a full or half kitchen, and none has a telephone. Although there is no beach swimming, docks, a large pool, and concessioner Reflections Kayak Nature Tours (which offers bicycle, Boston Whaler, and kayak rentals in addition to kayak tours) provide plenty of opportunities to enjoy the water. Complimentary Continental breakfast is served outside in a small garden. Guests may dine together or take trays back to their rooms. ⌧ *MM 29, BS, 565 Barry Ave., 33042,* ☏ *305/872–2157,* 🖷 *305/872–2014. 16 rooms, 12 suites, 10 efficiencies, 2 apartments. Kitchenettes, pool, docks, boating, jet skiing, bicycles. AE, D, MC, V.*

Outdoor Activities and Sports

FISHING

The Grouch Charters (⌧ Summerland Key Cove Marina, MM 24.5, OS, Summerland Key, ☏ 305/745–1172 or 305/872–6100), under Capt. Mark André, takes up to six passengers on offshore fishing trips ($350 for a half day, $475 for a full day). He also packages accommodations, fishing, snorkeling, and sightseeing for better deals. The firm's name refers to his original boat, named after his father, whose nickname was Grouch.

SCUBA DIVING AND SNORKELING

Named for the HMS *Looe*, a British warship wrecked in 1744, **Looe Key National Marine Sanctuary** (⌧ MM 27.5, OS, 216 Ann St., Key West 33040, ☏ 305/292–0311), part of the Florida Keys National Marine Sanctuary, contains a 5.3-square-nautical-mi reef. Perhaps the most beautiful and diverse coral community in the region, it has large stands of elk-horn coral on its eastern margin, immense purple sea fans, and abundant populations of sponges and sea urchins. On its seaward side, it has an almost-vertical drop-off to depths of 50–90 ft. Both snorkelers and divers will find the sanctuary a quiet place to observe reef life, except in July, when the annual Underwater Music Festival pays homage to Looe Key's beauty and promotes reef awareness with six hours of music broadcast via underwater speakers. Dive shops and private charters transport hundreds of divers to "hear" the spectacle, which includes Caribbean, classical, jazz, new age, and, of course, Jimmy Buffett.

Blue Dolphin Divers (⌧ Dolphin Marina, MM 28.5, OS, ☎ 305/872–2524, 305/872–2685, or 800/553–0308) runs a 30-ft, single-hulled Island Hopper and offers daily, weekly, and accommodations packages starting at $50 per day. **Looe Key Dive Center** (⌧ MM 27.5, OS, Box 509, Ramrod Key 33042, ☎ 305/872–2215, ext. 2, or 800/942–5397, ext. 2), the closest dive shop to Looe Key, offers two-day and overnight dive packages. It's part of the full-service Looe Key Reef Resort, which, not surprisingly, caters to divers. The dive boat, a 45-ft Corinthian catamaran, is docked within 100 ft of the hotel, whose guests have free use of tanks, weights, and snorkeling equipment. **Strike Zone Charters** (⌧ MM 29.6, BS, 29675 Overseas Hwy., Big Pine Key 33043, ☎ 305/872–9863 or 800/654–9560) offers dive trips to two sites on Looe Key, resort courses, and various certifications. The outfit uses glass-bottom boats, so accompanying nondivers can experience the reef, too.

En Route The huge object that looks like a white whale floating over Cudjoe Key (⌧ MM 23–21) is not a figment of your imagination. It's Fat Albert, a radar balloon that monitors local air and water traffic.

KEY WEST

MM 4–0.

In April 1982 the U.S. Border Patrol threw a roadblock across the Overseas Highway just south of Florida City to catch drug runners and illegal aliens. Traffic backed up for miles as Border Patrol agents searched vehicles and demanded that occupants prove U.S. citizenship. City officials in Key West, outraged at being treated like foreigners by the federal government, staged a mock secession and formed their own "nation," the so-called Conch Republic. They hoisted a flag and distributed mock border passes, visas, and Conch currency. The embarrassed Border Patrol dismantled its roadblock, and now an annual festival recalls the secessionists' victory.

The episode exemplifies Key West's odd station in Florida affairs. Situated 150 mi from Miami and just 90 mi from Havana, this tropical island city has always maintained its strong sense of detachment, even after it was connected to the rest of the United States—by the railroad in 1912 and by the Overseas Highway in 1938.

The U.S. government acquired Key West from Spain in 1821 along with the rest of Florida. The Spanish had named the island Cayo Hueso (Bone Key) after the Native American skeletons they found on its shores. In 1823 Uncle Sam sent Commodore David S. Porter to chase pirates away.

For three decades the primary industry in Key West was "wrecking"— rescuing people and salvaging cargo from ships that foundered on the nearby reefs. According to some reports, when pickings were lean, the wreckers hung out lights to lure ships aground. Their business declined after 1849, when the federal government began building lighthouses.

In 1845 the army started construction of Fort Taylor, which held Key West for the Union during the Civil War. After the war, an influx of Cuban dissidents unhappy with Spain's rule brought the cigar industry here. Fishing, shrimping, and sponge-gathering became important industries, and a pineapple-canning factory opened. Major military installations were established during the Spanish-American War and World War I. Through much of the 19th century and into the second decade of the 20th, Key West was Florida's wealthiest city in per-capita terms.

In 1929 the local economy began to unravel. Modern ships no longer needed to provision in Key West, cigar making moved to Tampa, Hawaii dominated the pineapple industry, and the sponges succumbed to a blight. Then the depression hit, and the military moved out. By 1934 half the population was on relief. The city defaulted on its bond payments, and the Federal Emergency Relief Administration took over the city and county governments.

By promoting Key West as a tourist destination, federal officials attracted 40,000 visitors during the 1934–35 winter season, but when the 1935 Labor Day hurricane struck the Middle Keys, it wiped out the railroad and the tourist trade. For three years, until the Overseas Highway opened, the only way in and out of town was by boat.

An important naval center during World War II and the Korean conflict, the island remains a strategic listening post on the doorstep of Fidel Castro's Cuba. It was during the '60s that the fringes of society began moving here and in the mid-'70s that gay guest houses began opening in rapid succession.

Key West reflects a diverse population: native "Conchs" (white Key Westers, many of whom trace their ancestry to the Bahamas), fresh-water Conchs (longtime residents who migrated from somewhere else years ago), gays (who now make up at least 20% of Key West's citizenry), black Bahamians (descendants of those who worked the railroads and burned charcoal), Hispanics (primarily Cuban immigrants), recent refugees from the urban sprawl of mainland Florida, navy and air force personnel, and an assortment of vagabonds, drifters, and dropouts in search of refuge.

Although the rest of the Keys is more oriented to nature and the outdoors, Key West has more of a city feel. Few open spaces remain, as promoters continue to foster fine restaurants, galleries, shops, and museums to interpret the city's intriguing past. As a tourist destination, Key West has a lot to sell—an average temperature of 79°F, quaint 19th-century architecture, and a laid-back lifestyle. There's also a growing calendar of festivals and artistic and cultural events—including the Conch Republic Celebration in April and a Halloween Fantasy Fest. Few cities of its size—a mere 2 mi by 4 mi—offer the joie de vivre of this one.

Yet as elsewhere when preservation has successfully revived once-tired towns, next have come those unmindful of style eager for a buck. Duval Street is becoming showbiz—an open-air mall of T-shirt shops and tour shills. Mass marketers directing the town's tourism have attracted cruise ships, which dwarf the town's skyline, and Duval Street floods with day-trippers who gawk at the earringed hippies with dogs in their bike baskets and the otherwise oddball lot of locals. You can still find fun, but the best advice is to come sooner rather than later.

Old Town

The heart of Key West, this historic area runs from White Street west to the waterfront. Beginning in 1822, wharves, warehouses, chandleries, ship-repair facilities, and eventually in 1891 the U.S. Customs House sprang up around the deep harbor to accommodate the navy's large ships and other sailing vessels. Wealthy wreckers, merchants, and sea captains built lavish houses near the bustling waterfront. A remarkable number of these fine Victorian and pre-Victorian structures have been restored to their original grandeur and now serve as homes, guest houses, and museums. These, along with the dwellings of famous writers, artists, and politicians who've come to Key West over the past 175 years, are among the area's approximately 3,000 historic structures. Old Town also has the city's finest restaurants and hotels, lively street life, and popular nightspots.

A Good Tour

To cover a lot of sights, take the Old Town Trolley, which lets you get off and reboard a later trolley, or the Conch Tour Train. Old Town is also very manageable on foot, bicycle, or moped, but be warned the tour below covers a lot of ground. You'll want either to pick and choose from it or break it into two days. Or pick up a copy of one of several self-guided tours on the area.

Start on Whitehead Street at the **Hemingway House** ⑫, the author's former home, and then cross the street and climb to the top of the **Lighthouse Museum** ⑬ for a spectacular view. Follow Whitehead north to Angela Street and turn right. At Margaret Street, the **City Cemetery** ⑭ has above-ground vaults and unusual headstone inscriptions. Head north on Margaret to Southard Street, turn left, then right onto Simonton Street. Halfway up the block, Free School Lane is occupied by **Nancy Forrester's Secret Garden** ⑮. After touring this tropical haven, return west on Southard to Duval Street and turn right, where you can view the lovely tiles and woodwork in the **San Carlos Institute** ⑯. Return again to Southard Street, turn right, and follow it through Truman Annex to **Ft. Zachary Taylor State Historic Site** ⑰; after viewing the fort, you can take a dip at the beach.

Head back to Simonton and Eaton streets, where you can admire the antiques in the circa-1860 **Donkey Milk House** ⑱. (A $15 ticket covers admission to four historic houses: Donkey Milk House, Audubon House, Heritage House Museum, and the Duval Street Wreckers Museum.) Then head north on Simonton and take a left on Caroline Street, where you can climb to the widow's walk on top of **Curry Mansion** ⑲. A left on Duval Street puts you in front of the **Duval Street Wreckers Museum** ⑳, Key West's oldest house. Continue west into Truman Annex to see the **Harry S Truman Little White House Museum** ㉑, President Truman's vacation residence. Return east on Caroline and turn left on Whitehead to visit the **Audubon House** ㉒, honoring the artist-naturalist. Follow Whitehead north to Greene Street and turn left to see the salvaged sea treasures of the **Mel Fisher Maritime Heritage Society Museum** ㉓. At Whitehead's north end is the **Key West Aquarium** ㉔.

By late afternoon you should be ready to cool off with a dip or catch a few rays at the beach. After all, this is Florida, and you can't go home without wiggling your toes in the waves. From the aquarium, head east two blocks to the end of Simonton Street, where you'll find the appropriately named **Simonton Street Beach** ㉕. On the Atlantic side of Old Town is **South Beach** ㉖, named for its location at the southern end of Duval Street. If you've brought your pet, stroll a few blocks east to **Dog Beach** ㉗, at the corner of Vernon and Waddell streets. A little farther east is **Higgs Beach** ㉘, on Atlantic Boulevard between White and Reynolds streets. As the sun starts to sink, return to the north end of Old Town and follow the crowds to Mallory Square, behind the aquarium, to watch Key West's nightly sunset spectacle. For dinner, head east on Caroline Street to **Key West Bight** ㉙, where there are numerous restaurants and bars.

Allow two full days to see all the Old Town museums and homes, especially with a little shopping thrown in. For a narrated trip on the tour train or trolley, budget 1½ hours to ride the loop without getting off, an entire day if you plan to get off and on at some of the sights and restaurants.

Sights to See

㉒ Audubon House and Gardens. This three-story dwelling built in the mid-1840s commemorates ornithologist John James Audubon's 1832 visit to Key West. On display are several rooms of period antiques, a children's room, and a large collection of Audubon engravings. Admission includes an audiotape (in English, French, German, and Spanish) for the self-guided tour of the house and tropical gardens, complemented by an informational booklet and signs that identify the rare indigenous plants and trees you'll see. ⊠ *205 Whitehead St.,* ☏ *305/294–2116.* ⌨ *$7.50.* ⊙ *Daily 9:30–5.*

★ **⑭ City Cemetery.** Key West's celebrated burial place covers nearly 20 acres. Among its plots is a bronze statue resembling a ship's mast and the graves of more than two dozen sailors killed in the sinking of the battleship USS *Maine,* recently tidied for the 150th anniversary of the disaster. There are separate plots for Catholics, Jews, and martyrs of Cuba. Interesting headstones abound: DEVOTED FAN OF SINGER JULIO IGLESIAS, GOD WAS GOOD TO ME, and I TOLD YOU I WAS SICK. Although you can walk around the cemetery on your own, the best way to take it in is on a 90-minute tour given by volunteers of the Historic Florida Keys Foundation. Tours leave from the sexton's office. ⊠ *Margaret and Angela Sts.,* ☏ *305/292–6718.* ⌨ *Free, tour donation $5.* ⊙ *Sunrise–6, tours Tues. and Thurs. 9:30.*

⑲ Curry Mansion. This 22-room home built in 1899 for Milton Curry, the son of Florida's first millionaire, is an adaptation of a Parisian town house. It has Key West's only widow's walk open to the public. The owners have restored most of the house and turned it into a winning B&B. Take an unhurried self-guided tour; a brochure describes the home's history and contents. ⊠ *511 Caroline St.,* ☏ *305/294–5349.* ⌨ *$5.* ⊙ *Daily 10–5.*

㉗ Dog Beach. Next to Louie's Backyard, this small beach—the only one in Key West where dogs are allowed—has a shore that's a mix of sand and rocks. ⊠ *Vernon and Waddell Sts.,* ☏ *no phone.* ⌨ *Free.* ⊙ *Daily sunrise–sunset.*

⑱ Donkey Milk House. This classic Key West revival house was built in 1866 by prominent businessman and U.S. marshal Peter "Dynamite" Williams, the hero of the great fire of 1886. Antiques and artifacts fill its two balconied floors. The house, with a veranda off every room, has won several restoration awards. ⊠ *613 Eaton St.,* ☏ *305/296–1866.* ⌨ *$5.* ⊙ *Daily 10–5.*

⑳ Duval Street Wreckers Museum. Built in 1829 and alleged to be the oldest house in South Florida, the museum was originally home to Francis Watlington, a sea captain and wrecker. He was also a Florida state senator but resigned to serve in the Confederate navy during the Civil War. Six rooms are now open, furnished with 18th- and 19th-century antiques and providing exhibits on the wrecking industry of the 1800s. In an upstairs bedroom, an eight-room dollhouse of Conch design is outfitted with tiny early 19th-century furniture. ⊠ *322 Duval St.,* ☏ *305/294–9502.* ⌨ *$3.* ⊙ *Daily 10–4.*

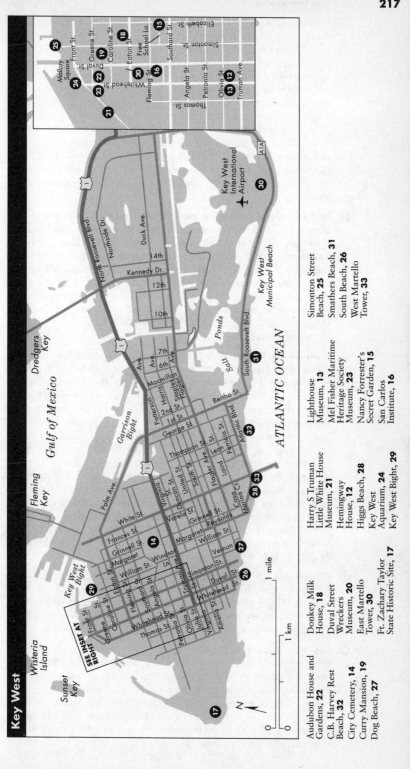

Key West

Audubon House and Gardens, **22**

C.B. Harvey Rest Beach, **32**

City Cemetery, **14**

Curry Mansion, **19**

Dog Beach, **27**

Donkey Milk House, **18**

Duval Street Wreckers Museum, **20**

East Martello Tower, **30**

Ft. Zachary Taylor State Historic Site, **17**

Harry S Truman Little White House Museum, **21**

Hemingway House, **12**

Higgs Beach, **28**

Key West Aquarium, **24**

Key West Bight, **29**

Lighthouse Museum, **13**

Mel Fisher Maritime Heritage Society Museum, **23**

Nancy Forrester's Secret Garden, **15**

San Carlos Institute, **16**

Simonton Street Beach, **25**

Smathers Beach, **31**

South Beach, **26**

West Martello Tower, **33**

⑰ Ft. Zachary Taylor State Historic Site. Built between 1845 and 1866, this fort served as a base for the Union blockade of Confederate shipping during the Civil War (more than 1,500 Confederate vessels were detained in Key West's harbor). Today it's a fort within a fort. A moat suggests how the fort originally looked when it was surrounded by water, and a 30-minute tour is included in the admission price. Because of an artificial reef, snorkeling is excellent here, except when the wind blows south–southwest and muddies the water. Several hundred yards of relatively uncrowded beach and an adjoining picnic area with barbecue grills in a stand of Australian pines are favorites among locals. ⊠ *End of Southard St., through Truman Annex,* ☎ *305/292–6713.* ☞ *$2.50 per person for first 2 people in vehicle plus 50¢ each additional up to $8, $1.50 per pedestrian or bicyclist.* ☉ *Daily 8–sunset, tours noon and 2.*

㉑ Harry S Truman Little White House Museum. On the grounds of **Truman Annex,** a 103-acre former military parade grounds and barracks, the home served as a winter White House for Presidents Truman, Eisenhower, and Kennedy. It has been restored to its post–World War II glory and contains displays of Truman family memorabilia as well as changing exhibits that have ranged from circa-1951 Truman fashion to the Eisenhower Room's presidential photos. Part of the grounds have been converted into a Victorian-style commercial residential development. ⊠ *111 Front St.,* ☎ *305/294–9911.* ☞ *$7.50.* ☉ *Daily 9–5, grounds 8–sunset.*

★ **⑫ Hemingway House.** Hemingway bought this house in 1931 and wrote about 70% of his life's work here, including *For Whom the Bell Tolls.* It is now a museum dedicated to the novelist's life and work. Built in 1851, this two-story Spanish-colonial dwelling was the first house in Key West to have running water and a fireplace. Three months after Hemingway died in 1961, local jeweler Bernice Dickson bought the house and two years later opened it as a museum. Of special interest are the huge bed with a headboard made from a 17th-century Spanish monastery gate, a ceramic cat by Pablo Picasso (a gift to Hemingway from the artist), the hand-blown Venetian glass chandelier in the dining room, and the pool. The museum staff gives guided tours rich with anecdotes about Hemingway and his family and feeds the more than 50 feline habitants, descendants of Hemingway's own 50 cats. Tours begin every 10 minutes and take 25–30 minutes; then you're free to explore on your own. ⊠ *907 Whitehead St.,* ☎ *305/294–1575.* ☞ *$6.50.* ☉ *Daily 9–5.*

㉘ Higgs Beach. This Monroe County park is a popular sunbathing spot. A nearby grove of Australian pines provides shade, and the West Martello Tower provides shelter should a storm suddenly sweep in. ⊠ *Atlantic Blvd. between White and Reynolds Sts.,* ☎ *no phone.* ☞ *Free.* ☉ *Daily 7 AM–11 PM.*

Ⓒ **㉔ Key West Aquarium.** Hundreds of brightly colored tropical fish and other fascinating sea creatures from Key West waters make their home here. A touch tank enables you to handle starfish, sea cucumbers, horseshoe and hermit crabs, even horse and queen conchs—living totems of the Conch Republic. Built in 1934 by the Works Progress Administration as the world's first open-air aquarium, the building has been enclosed for all-weather viewing, though an outdoor area with a small Atlantic shores exhibit, including red mangroves. Guided tours include shark feedings. ⊠ *1 Whitehead St.,* ☎ *305/296–2051.* ☞ *$7.* ☉ *Daily 10–6, tours 11, 1, 3, and 4:30.*

㉙ **Key West Bight.** Also known as Harbor Walk, this site was formerly the Singleton Shrimp Fleet and Ice & Fish House. It is the last funky area of Old Key West. In the area are numerous charter boats, classic old yachts, and the Waterfront Market.

⑬ **Lighthouse Museum.** Behind a spic-and-span white picket fence is this 92-ft lighthouse built in 1847 and an adjacent 1887 clapboard house, where the keeper lived. You can climb 88 steps to the top of the lighthouse for a glimpse of the sizable Fresnel lens, installed at a cost of $1 million in the 1860s; a spectacular view of the island town awaits you as well. On display in the keeper's quarters are vintage photographs, ship models, nautical charts, and lighthouse artifacts from all along the Key reefs. ⊠ *938 Whitehead St.,* ☎ *305/294–0012.* ⊒ *$5.* ☉ *Daily 9:30–5, last admission 4:30.*

㉓ **Mel Fisher Maritime Heritage Society Museum.** Gold and silver bars, coins, jewelry, and other artifacts recovered in 1985 from the Spanish treasure ships *Nuestra Señora de Atocha* and *Santa Margarita* are displayed here. The two galleons foundered in a hurricane in 1622 near the Marquesas Keys, 40 mi west of Key West. In the museum you can lift a gold bar weighing 6.3 troy pounds and see a 77.76-carat natural emerald crystal worth almost $250,000. ⊠ *200 Greene St.,* ☎ *305/ 294–2633.* ⊒ *$6.50.* ☉ *Daily 9:30–5, last video 4:30.*

⑮ **Nancy Forrester's Secret Garden.** Nancy Forrester has devoted more than 25 years to creating a naturalized garden reminiscent of a tropical rain forest. Visitors wind their way under a canopy of rare palms and cycads; along natural trails lined with ferns, bromeliads, and bright gingers and heliconias; and past towering gumbo-limbos strewn with orchids and vines. Many brides and grooms exchange their vows here and then stay in the garden's cottage. An art gallery features botanical prints and environmental art. On rainy days Nancy points out beautiful fungi (except during a thunderstorm), and come February there's a palm festival. ⊠ *1 Free School La.,* ☎ *305/294–0015.* ⊒ *$6.* ☉ *Daily 10–5.*

⑯ **San Carlos Institute.** This Cuban-American heritage center houses a museum with changing exhibits and a research library focusing on the history of Key West and of 19th- and 20th-century Cuban exiles. The institute was founded in 1871 by Cuban immigrants. Cuban patriot Jose Martí delivered many famous speeches from the balcony of the auditorium, and opera star Enrico Caruso sang in the Opera House, which reportedly has the best acoustics of any concert hall in the South. On weekends you can watch the almost hour-long documentary *Nostalgia Cubano,* about Cuba from the 1930s to 1950s. ⊠ *516 Duval St.,* ☎ *305/294–3887.* ⊒ *$3.* ☉ *Tues.–Sun. 11–5.*

㉕ **Simonton Street Beach.** This beach facing the gulf is a great place to watch boat traffic in the harbor. Parking, however, is difficult. ⊠ *North end of Simonton St.,* ☎ *no phone.* ⊒ *Free.* ☉ *Daily 7 AM–11 PM.*

㉖ **South Beach.** On the Atlantic, this stretch of sand, also known as City Beach, is popular with tourists at nearby motels. It has limited parking and a nearby buffet-type restaurant, the South Beach Seafood and Raw Bar. ⊠ *Foot of Duval St.,* ☎ *no phone.* ⊒ *Free.* ☉ *Daily 7 AM– 11 PM.*

New Town

The Overseas Highway splits as it enters Key West, the two forks rejoining to encircle New Town, the area east of White Street to Cow

Key Channel. The southern fork runs along the shore as South Roosevelt Boulevard (Route A1A), past municipal beaches, salt ponds, and Key West International Airport. Along the north shore, North Roosevelt Boulevard (U.S. 1) passes the Key West Welcome Center, shopping centers, chain hotels, and fast-food eateries. Part of New Town was created with dredged fill. The island would have continued growing this way had the Army Corps of Engineers not determined in the early 1970s that it was detrimental to the nearby reef.

A Good Tour

Attractions are few in New Town. The best way to take in the sights is by car or moped. Take South Roosevelt Boulevard from the island's entrance, passing Houseboat Row—a community of unusual houseboats whose residents have included famous authors and artists—before stopping at **East Martello Tower** ㉚, near the airport. Continue past the Riggs Wildlife Refuge salt ponds, and stop at **Smathers Beach** ㉛ for a dip, or continue west onto Atlantic Boulevard to **C. B. Harvey Rest Beach** ㉜. A little farther along, at the end of White Street, is the **West Martello Tower** ㉝.

TIMING

Allow one to two hours for brief stops at each attraction. If your interests lie in art, gardens, or Civil War history, you'll need three or four hours. Throw in time at the beach, and you can make it a half-day affair.

Sights to See

㉜ **C. B. Harvey Rest Beach.** The city's newest beach and park, named after former Key West mayor and commissioner Cornelius Bradford Harvey, has half a dozen picnic areas, dunes, and a wheelchair and bike path. ⊠ *East side of White Street Pier,* ☎ *no phone.* ⊡ *Free.* ⊗ *Daily 7 AM–11 PM.*

★ ㉚ **East Martello Tower.** Housing relics of the U.S.S. *Maine,* the tower also contains a museum operated by the Key West Art and Historical Society. The collection includes Stanley Papio's "junk art" sculptures, Cuban folk artist Mario Sanchez's chiseled and painted wooden carvings of historic Key West street scenes, a Cuban refugee raft, and books by famous writers (including seven Pulitzer Prize winners) who have lived in Key West. Thematic exhibits present a history of the city and the Keys. A circular 48-step staircase in the central tower leads to a platform overlooking the airport and surrounding waters. ⊠ *3501 S. Roosevelt Blvd.,* ☎ *305/296–3913.* ⊡ *$5.* ⊗ *Daily 9:30–5, last admission 4.*

㉛ **Smathers Beach.** This beach features nearly 2 mi of sand. Trucks along the road rent rafts, Windsurfers, and other beach "toys." ⊠ *S. Roosevelt Blvd.,* ☎ *no phone.* ⊡ *Free.* ⊗ *Daily 7 AM–11 PM.*

㉝ **West Martello Tower.** This fort was built in 1861 by slaves and used as a lookout during the Spanish-American War. Within its walls the Key West Garden Club maintains an art gallery and beautiful tropical garden. ⊠ *Atlantic Blvd. and White St.,* ☎ *305/294–3210.* ⊡ *Donation welcome.* ⊗ *Wed.–Sun. 9:30–3:15.*

Dining

American

$-$$ ✕ **Pepe's Cafe and Steak House.** Judges, police officers, carpenters, and anglers rub elbows at breakfast in their habitual seats, at tables or dark pine booths under a jumbo paddle fan. Face the street or dine outdoors under a huge rubber tree if you're put off by the naked-lady art on the back wall. Pepe's was established downtown in 1909 (which makes it the oldest eating house in the Keys) and moved here in 1962. Specials change nightly: barbecued chicken, pork tenderloin, ribs, steak, fresh fish, potato salad, red or black beans, and corn bread on Sunday; meat loaf on Monday; seafood Tuesday and Wednesday; a traditional Thanksgiving every Thursday; prime rib on Saturday; and filet mignon daily. ⊠ *806 Caroline St.,* ☎ *305/294–7192. D, MC, V.*

American/Casual

$–$$ ✕ **Sunset Pier Bar.** When the crowds get too thick on the Mallory Dock at sunset, you can thin your way out 200 ft offshore behind the Ocean Key House. A limited menu of mostly grilled foods includes burgers, chicken wings, crispy conch fritters, potato salad, shrimp, and jumbo Hebrew National hot dogs. Live island music is featured nightly. If you prefer your sunsets with a dash of serenity, look elsewhere. ⊠ *0 Duval St.,* ☎ *305/296–7701. AE, D, DC, MC, V.*

Contemporary

$$$–$$$$ ✕ **Cafe des Artistes.** Dining at this intimate restaurant is so good that
★   guests in T-shirts and shorts don't even blanch at a $100 check for two. It was once part of a hotel building constructed in 1935 by C. E. Alfeld, Al Capone's bookkeeper. The look is studiously unhip with its rough stucco walls, old-fashioned lights, and a knotty-pine ceiling. Haitian paintings and Keys scenes by local artists dress the walls. You dine in two indoor rooms or on a rooftop deck beneath a sapodilla tree. Chef Andrew Berman presents a French interpretation of tropical cuisine, using fresh local seafood and produce and light sauces. The wine list is strong on both French and California labels. ⊠ *1007 Simonton St.,* ☎ *305/294–7100. AE, MC, V. No lunch.*

$$$ ✕ **Louie's Backyard.** Key West paintings and pastels adorn this oceanfront institution, where you dine outside under the mahoe tree. Executive chef Doug Shook shares Louie's limelight with *chef de cuisine* Annette Foley. The changing menu might include roasted rack of Australian lamb with huckleberry port, whipped sweet potatoes, and fried root vegetable strips; grouper with Thai peanut sauce; and stir-fried Asian vegetables. End with Louie's lime tart or the irresistible chocolate terrine Grand Marnier with crème anglaise. ⊠ *700 Waddell Ave.,* ☎ *305/294–1061. AE, DC, MC, V.*

$$–$$$ ✕ **Cafe Marquesa.** This intimate restaurant with attentive service and
★   superb food is a felicitous counterpart to the small Marquesa Hotel. It's a mellow place, with bluesy ballads in the background and an open kitchen viewed through a trompe l'oeil pantry mural. Ten or so entrées are featured nightly, as are all-star regional ingredients: a spicy tequila- and lime-cured salmon tostada with habanero salsa, coconut milk in the Caribbean shrimp chowder with sweet potatoes, and perhaps a mango barbecued pork chop with jícama relish. Some low-fat options are featured. Desserts are quite the contrary: a plum cardamom cake with fresh whipped cream, crème brûlée, and warm apple crisp with caramel sauce. There's also a fine selection of wines and a choice of microbrewery beers. ⊠ *600 Fleming St.,* ☎ *305/292–1244. AE, DC, MC, V. No lunch.*

$–$$ ✕ **Blue Heaven.** The inspired remake of an old blue-on-blue clap-
★   board Greek Revival house with peach-and-yellow trim was once a bordello where Hemingway refereed boxing matches and customers watched cockfights. There's still a rooster graveyard out back, as well as a water tower hauled here in the 1920s. Upstairs is an art gallery (check out the zebra-stripe bikes), and downstairs are affordable fresh eats, in both the house and big leafy yard. There are five nightly specials and a good mix of natural and West Indian foods. Top it off with Banana Heaven (banana bread, bananas flamed with spiced rum, and

vanilla ice cream). Three meals are served six days a week; Sunday there's a to-die-for brunch. Expect a line—everybody knows how good this is. ⊠ *729 Thomas St.,* ☎ *305/296–8666. Reservations not accepted. D, MC, V.*

Cuban

$ ✕ **El Siboney.** This sprawling three-room, family-style restaurant serves traditional Cuban food, including a well-seasoned black-bean soup. Specials include beef stew Monday, pepper steak Tuesday, chicken fricassee Wednesday, chicken and rice Friday, and oxtail stew on Saturday. Always available are roast pork, cassava, paella, and *palomilla* steak. Popular with locals, *sí,* but enough tourists pass through that you'll fit right in even if you have to ask what a "Siboney" is (answer: a Cuban Indian tribe). ⊠ *900 Catherine St.,* ☎ *305/296–4184. No credit cards. Closed 2 wks in June.*

Italian

$–$$ ✕ **Mangia Mangia.** Fresh homemade pasta comes Alfredo, or with mari-
★   nara, meat, or pesto, either in the twinkly brick garden with its specimen palms or in the nicely dressed-up old-house dining room. One of the best restaurants in Key West—and one of its best values—Mangia Mangia is run by Elliot and Naomi Baron, ex–Chicago restaurateurs who found Key West's warmth and laid-back style irresistible. Everything that comes out of the open kitchen is outstanding, especially the pasta, Mississippi mud pie, and made-on-the-premises key lime pie. The wine list, with more than 350 selections, the largest in Monroe County, contains a good selection under $20. ⊠ *900 Southard St.,* ☎ *305/294–2469. AE, MC, V. No lunch.*

Pan-Asian

$$–$$$ ✕ **Dim Sum.** This bright spot in a sophisticated little Oriental kiosk in
★   gardenlike Key Lime Square recently hired a new chef trained in classical French and Oriental cooking. The result is a fusion of the two cultures, in which the presentation is art and the food is out of this world. The menu now features such dishes as teriyaki filet mignon served with a ginger potato tart and duck breast seared, oven roasted, and served atop a pear cabernet sauvignon sauce. Nightly specials range from rack of lamb to more traditional Oriental dishes, such as ahi steak (yellowfin tuna steak grilled to taste and served with a garden seaweed salad and vegetable nori noodles and wasabi soy dressing). The setting is intimate and authentic. There's a good selection of beer and wine. ⊠ *613½ Duval St. [rear],* ☎ *305/294–6230. AE, D, DC, MC, V.*

Seafood

$–$$ **Awful Arthur's Seafood Company.** This casual eatery with outdoor tables, a friendly staff, beer and wine bar, and the motto "Big Mussels, Great Legs, and Fantastic Tails" has the best raw bar in town. The cooked fare—with just about every form of shellfish imaginable—is equally impressive. Lunch and dinner menus feature a few dishes that don't come from the sea: a terrific Portobello sandwich and one steak. Theme nights include Thursday's fried shrimp ($9.95) and Tuesday's all-you-can-eat crab legs ($17.95). ⊠ *628 Duval St.,* ☎ *305/295–0888. AE, D, DC, MC, V.*

$–$$ ✕ **Half Shell Raw Bar.** "Eat It Raw" is the motto, and even off-season the oyster bar keeps shucking. You eat at shellacked picnic tables in an open-air building with life buoys, a mounted dolphin, and old license plates overhead and a view of the deep-sea fishing fleet outside. Although broiled dolphin sandwiches and seafood linguine marinara are also served, the oysters—raw or cooked—are the best bet. ⊠ *Land's End Marina, 231 Margaret St.,* ☎ *305/294–7496. D, MC, V.*

Lodging

Lodging opportunities rival those found in mainland cities. You'll find historic cottages, restored turn-of-the-century Conch houses, and large resorts. Rates are the highest in the Keys, with a few properties as low as $65, but the majority from $100 to $300 a night.

Guest Houses

$$$$
★
Paradise Inn. Renovated cigar makers' cottages and authentically reproduced Bahamian-style houses with sundecks and balconies stand amid a lush tropical garden with a heated pool, lily pond, and whirlpool, light-years from the hubbub of Key West. The only sound disturbing the perfect quiet is the trickling of water from the pool's fountain. Inside, light streams through French doors onto fine earthtone fabrics. Gracious appointments include phones and whirlpools in marble bathrooms, plush robes, polished oak floors, armoires, complimentary fresh breakfast pastries from Louie's Backyard, room safes, and minibars. Suite 205 and the Poinciana Cottage are gilded lilies. One suite is designed for travelers with disabilities. ⊠ *819 Simonton St., 33040,* ☎ *305/293–8007 or 800/888–9648,* FAX *305/293–0807. 3 cottages, 15 suites. Pool, in-room safes, minibars, hot tub, concierge. AE, D, DC, MC, V.*

$$$–$$$$
★
Curry Mansion Inn. Careful dedication to detail by Key West architect Thomas Pope and much care by owners Al and Edith Amsterdam have made the annex rooms exceptionally comfortable, even if not as detailed as the now rarely used rooms in the circa-1899 main house. Each room has a different tropical pastel color scheme; all have wicker furnishings and handmade quilts. Rooms 1 and 8, honeymoon suites, feature canopy beds and balconies. Eight suites are at the restored James House; rooms 306 and 308 face south and have beautiful morning light. Keep in mind that Curry Mansion is a historic attraction, with visitors touring parts of the house during the day. There's complimentary Continental breakfast and happy hour with an open bar and live piano music; guests also enjoy beach privileges at Pier House Beach Club and Casa Marina. A wheelchair lift is available. ⊠ *511–512 Caroline St., 33040,* ☎ *305/294–5349 or 800/253–3466,* FAX *305/294–4093. 28 rooms, 6 suites. Pool. AE, D, DC, MC, V.*

$$$–$$$$
Heron House. With four separate buildings centered on a pool, all slightly different but all Key West–style, Heron House feels like an old town within Old Town. A high coral fence, brilliantly splashed with spotlights at night, surrounds the compound (just a block off Duval Street but quieter by a mile). Neither antiques nor frills is owner Fred Geibelt's thing; superb detailing is. Most units feature a complete wall of exquisitely laid wood (parquet, chevron pattern, herringbone), entries with French doors, and bathrooms of polished granite. Some have floor-to-ceiling panels of mirrored glass and/or an oversize whirlpool. An expanded Continental breakfast and complimentary wine and cheese are included. ⊠ *512 Simonton St., 33040,* ☎ *305/294–9227,* FAX *305/294–5692. 23 rooms. Pool. AE, DC, MC, V.*

$$$–$$$$
Island City House. This guest house is actually three buildings: the vintage-1880s Island City House, with a widow's walk; Arch House, a former carriage house; and a 1970s reconstruction of a cigar factory. Arch House features a dramatic carriage entry that opens into a lush courtyard, and though all its suites front on busy Eaton Street, bedrooms in only numbers 5 and 6 actually face it. Units in Cigar House are largest, those in Island City House the best decorated. Floors are pine, and ceiling fans and antiques abound. Guests share a private tropical garden and are given free Continental breakfasts. Children are welcome—a rarity in Old Town guest houses. ⊠ *411 William St., 33040,*

☎ *305/294–5702 or 800/634–8230,* ⅎ *305/294–1289. 24 suites. Pool, hot tub, bicycles. AE, D, DC, MC, V.*

$$–$$$$ 🖼 **Popular House/Key West Bed & Breakfast.** Unlike the owners of so
★ many prissy hotels that wall the world out, Jody Carlson brings Key West in. Doors stay open all day. Local art—large splashy canvases, a mural in the style of Gauguin—hangs on the walls, and tropical gardens and music set the mood. Jody offers both inexpensive rooms with shared bath (whose rates haven't been raised in 10 years) and luxury rooms, reasoning that budget travelers deserve the same good local style as the rich. Low-end rooms burst with bright yellows and reds; the hand-painted dressers will make you laugh out loud. Spacious third-floor rooms, though, are best (and most expensive), decorated with a paler palette and brilliantly original furniture. The Continental breakfast is lavish. Jody keeps two friendly resident dogs. ⊠ *415 William St., 33040,* ☎ *305/296–7274 or 800/438–6155,* ⅎ *305/293–0306 9 rooms (5 with shared baths). Hot tub, sauna. AE, D, DC, MC, V.*

$$$ 🖼 **Frances Street Bottle Inn.** The ownership changed recently at this simple, pleasant inn, but Dennis Anderson, manager for five years, remained to ensure continuity. Still one of the few moderately priced guest houses in Key West, the two-story Conch house set under huge royal poinciana trees dates from the 1890s. Clean and tidy pastel-color rooms have plain furniture, paddle fans, and air-conditioning. A downstairs bedroom opens to a porch-patio, three upstairs rooms have a balcony, and even the two least-expensive rooms have two exposures. Continental breakfast is included. ⊠ *535 Frances St., 33040,* ☎ *305/ 294–8530 or 800/294–8530. 7 rooms. Hot tub. AE, MC, V.*

Hostel

$ 🖼 **Hostelling International–Key West.** This financial oasis in a sea of
★ expensive hotels gets high marks for location, comfort, friendliness, amenities, and good value. It is two blocks from the beach in Old Town yet costs only $13.67 for members of Hostelling International–American Youth Hostels, $15.25 for nonmembers. During holidays add another 75¢. Dinner and breakfast cost $2 each. When you're not snorkeling ($18.50) or scuba diving at a reduced rate, you can rent bicycles, write letters in the outdoor courtyard, or enjoy a barbecue. There is free transportation to and from the Greyhound station. ⊠ *718 South St., 33040,* ☎ *305/296–5719,* ⅎ *305/296–0672. 86 beds in dorm-style rooms share baths. Bicycles, billiards, recreation room, video games, library, coin laundry. D, MC, V.*

Hotels

$$$$ 🖼 **La Concha Holiday Inn.** This seven-story Art Deco hotel in the heart of downtown is the city's tallest building and a great spot for watching the Fantasy Fest parade. Dating from 1926, it still has its original louvered room doors, light fixtures, and floral trim on the archways. The lobby's polished floor of pink, mauve, and green marble and a conversation pit with comfortable chairs are among the details beloved by La Concha's guests. Large rooms are outfitted with 1920s-era antiques, lace curtains, and big closets. You can enjoy the sunset from the Top, a bar that overlooks the entire island, Atlantic Ocean, and Gulf of Mexico. No-smoking rooms are available. ⊠ *430 Duval St., 33040,* ☎ *305/296–2991, 800/745–2191, or 800/465–4329,* ⅎ *305/ 294–3283. 158 rooms, 2 suites. Restaurant, 3 bars, no-smoking rooms, pool, bicycles. AE, D, DC, MC, V.*

$$$$ 🖼 **Marquesa Hotel.** This coolly elegant, restored 1884 home is Key West's
★ finest lodging. Guests (typically shoeless in Marquesa robes) relax among richly landscaped pools and gardens against a backdrop of brick steps rising to the villalike suites on the property's perimeter. Elegant

rooms contain eclectic antique and reproduction furnishings, dotted Swiss curtains, and botanical-print fabrics. The lobby resembles a Victorian parlor, with antique furniture, Audubon prints, flowers, and wonderful photos of early Key West, including one of Harry Truman in a convertible. Tea is offered poolside. Although the clientele is mostly straight, the hotel is very gay-friendly. ⊠ *600 Fleming St., 33040,* ☎ *305/292–1919 or 800/869–4631,* FAX *305/294–2121. 27 rooms. Restaurant, 2 pools. AE, DC, MC, V.*

$$$$ ⊞ **Marriott's Casa Marina Resort.** Flagler's heirs built 13-acre La Casa Marina in 1921 at the end of the Florida East Coast Railway line. The entire resort revolves around an outdoor patio and lawn facing the ocean. The rich, luxurious lobby has a beamed ceiling, polished Dade County pine floor, artwork, and new island French provincial furniture. Guest rooms are decorated in yellows and tropical limes with color-coordinated Caribbean shades and linens. Among the best rooms are the two-bedroom loft suites with balconies facing the ocean and the lanai rooms on the ground floor of the main building, which have French doors opening onto the lawn. Rooms for nonsmokers are available. ⊠ *1500 Reynolds St., 33040,* ☎ *305/296–3535,* FAX *305/296–4633. 311 rooms, 63 suites. 2 restaurants, bar, no-smoking rooms, 2 pools, massage, sauna, 3 tennis courts, exercise room, health club, boating, jet skiing, fishing, bicycles, children's programs. AE, D, DC, MC, V.*

$$$$ ⊞ **Pier House.** This is Key West's catbird seat—just off the intersec-
★ tion of Duval and Front streets and an easy walk from Mallory Square. Since the 1960s, when David Wolkowsky began restoring and expanding this once-modest lodging, the Pier House has defined Key West's festive ambience. Weathered-gray buildings, including an original Conch house, flank a courtyard of tall coconut palms and hibiscus blossoms. Most rooms are smaller than in newer hotels, except in the Caribbean Spa section, which has hardwood floors, two-poster plantation beds, and some baths that convert to steam rooms or have whirlpools, and in the new Harborview building, whose rooms have private balconies and gulf views. You can gather with locals at the Beach Club's thatch-roof tiki bar. ⊠ *1 Duval St., 33040,* ☎ *305/296–4600 or 800/327–8340,* FAX *305/296–7569. 142 rooms, 14 suites. 3 restaurants, 4 bars, pool, massage, health club, beach. AE, D, DC, MC, V.*

$$$–$$$$ ⊞ **Best Western Key Ambassador Inn.** Every year a third of this com-
★ fortable inn is completely renovated from carpet to ceiling. The latest go-around left the large guest rooms with cheerful Caribbean-style light-color furniture, linens in coordinated tropical colors, and 29-inch color TVs. The grounds—7 acres bordered by salt ponds—are well cared for, and the deck-rimmed pool looks over the Atlantic. There is a par course and a covered picnic area with barbecue grills out back. Each room has a small refrigerator and a screened balcony, and most offer ocean and pool views. The bar serves drinks and light dishes. A complimentary Continental breakfast is included, and a free newspaper is delivered to rooms weekdays. ⊠ *3755 S. Roosevelt Blvd., 33040,* ☎ *305/296–3500 or 800/432–4315,* FAX *305/296–9961. 100 rooms. Picnic area, bar, pool, shuffleboard, coin laundry. AE, D, DC, MC, V.*

$$$–$$$$ ⊞ **Cuban Club Suites.** Originally built as a social club for cigar makers, the "club" was rebuilt as a luxury hotel after a 1983 fire. Eight fully equipped town-house units, 900–1,900 square ft, have either two bedrooms and two baths or one bedroom and 1½ baths. Grouped in two buildings that feel like an exclusive apartment complex, they have king-size four-poster beds, queen-size sofa beds, wing chairs, cathedral ceilings, full kitchens, tile counters and floors, and washers and dryers. Wide balconies overlook the excitement of Duval Street. Guests have pool and beach privileges at the Marriott Reach, and pets are allowed. La Casa de Luces, the club's poor cousin next door, is less

elegant but has many winning characteristics. ⊠ *1108 Duval St. (lobby at 422 Amelia St.), 33040,* ☎ *305/296–0465 or 800/432–4849,* FAX *305/293–7669. 8 suites. AE, MC, V.*

Motels

$$$ 🏨 **Harborside Motel & Marina.** The appeal of this ordinary motel is its affordability and its safe, pleasant location between a quiet street and Garrison Bight (the charter boat harbor), between Old Town and New Town. Units are boxy, clean, and basic, with little patios, ceramic-tile floors, phones, and basic color cable TV. Four stationary houseboats each sleep four. Barbecue grills are available. ⊠ *903 Eisenhower Dr., 33040,* ☎ *305/294–2780,* FAX *305/292–1473. 14 efficiencies. Pool, coin laundry. AE, D, DC, MC, V.*

$$–$$$ 🏨 **Southwinds.** A short walk from Old Town and run by the same friendly folks who operate Harborside Motel & Marina, this pastel 1940s-style motel has mature tropical plantings, all nicely set back from the street a block from the beach. Rooms have basic furnishings. It's as good as you'll find at the price, and though rates have gone up, they drop if demand gets slack. On-premises parking is available, as are wheelchair-accessible accommodations. ⊠ *1321 Simonton St., 33040,* ☎ *305/296–2215. 13 rooms, 5 efficiencies. Pool, coin laundry, free parking. AE, D, DC, MC, V.*

$ 🏨 **Key Lime Village.** This charming little property consisting of 17 cottages (5 large and 12 small) and 12 rooms was built in a fruit grove. Cottages have brick patios surrounded by tropical plants and fruit trees, and wooden chaise lounges surround the pool. The lodging has as much history as it has charm, claiming the distinction of being Key West's first motel and having been the post-jail residence of Dr. Count Von Cosel, who was arrested more than 25 years ago after he was discovered with the body of his beloved Maria Elena, dead seven years. Although the property is just two blocks off Duval Street, it's light-years from the street's hectic pace. Rooms have air-conditioning, paddle fans, and cable, and some cottages have microwaves and refrigerators. Barbecue grills and parking are available. ⊠ *727 Truman Ave., 33040,* ☎ *305/294–6222 or 800/201–6222,* FAX *305/294–4294. 12 rooms (6 share baths), 17 cottages. Pool. AE, D, DC, MC, V.*

Nightlife and the Arts

The Arts

Red Barn Theater (⊠ 319 Duval St., ☎ 305/296–9911), a professional small theater, performs dramas, comedies, and musicals, including new plays. **Tennessee Williams Fine Arts Center** (⊠ Florida Keys Community College, 5901 College Rd., ☎ 305/296–9081, ext. 5), on Stock Island, presents chamber music, dance, jazz concerts, dramatic and musical plays and other performing arts events, November–April. **Waterfront Playhouse** (⊠ Mallory Sq., ☎ 305/294–5015) is a mid-1850s wrecker's warehouse that was converted into a 185-seat, non-Equity community theater presenting comedy and drama November–May.

Nightlife

BARS AND LOUNGES

Capt. Tony's Saloon (⊠ 428 Greene St., ☎ 305/294–1838) is in a building that dates from 1851, when it was first used as a morgue and icehouse; later it was Key West's first telegraph station. From 1933 to 1937 the bar was the original Sloppy Joe's. Hemingway was a regular, and Jimmy Buffett got his start here. Live country and R&B set the scene nowadays, and the house drink, the Pirates' Punch, still wows those brave enough to try it. Pause for a libation at the open-air **Green Parrot Bar** (⊠ 601 Whitehead St., at Southard St., ☎ 305/294–6133). Built in 1890, the bar is said to be Key West's oldest, a sometimes-rowdy saloon where locals outnumber the tourists, especially on weekends when bands play. **Margaritaville Cafe** (⊠ 500 Duval St., ☎ 305/292–1435) is owned by former Key West resident and recording star Jimmy Buffett, who has been known to perform here. The drink of choice is, of course, a margarita. There's live music nightly.

Called "the last little piece of Old Key West," **Schooner Wharf Bar** (⊠ 202 William St., ☎ 305/292–9520) is a laid-back waterside tiki hut where the town's waiters and waitresses hang out. You can hear live music weekends (and sometimes at other times) in the warehouse space next door. **Sloppy Joe's** (⊠ 201 Duval St., ☎ 305/294–5717) is the successor to a famous speakeasy named for its founder, Capt. Joe Russell. Ernest Hemingway liked to gamble in a partitioned club room in back. Decorated with Hemingway memorabilia and marine flags, the bar is popular with tourists and is full and noisy all the time. Live entertainment plays daily, noon–2 AM. The **Top Lounge** (⊠ 430 Duval St., ☎ 305/296–2991) is on the seventh floor of the La Concha Holiday Inn and is one of the best places to view the sunset. (Celebrities, on the ground floor, presents nightly entertainment and serves food.)

DANCE CLUBS

Rebuilt at the same site as the wild and popular gay disco, the Copa, which burned in 1995, **Club Epoch** (⊠ 623 Duval St., ☎ 305/296–8521) caters to a well-mixed crowd that's still wild and eager to party. There are two floors, six bars, a lounge overlooking the dance floor, and a terrace overlooking Duval Street. House dancers set the tone as hip local and celebrity spinmasters groove the tunes. It's open nightly, but dancing is Wednesday–Sunday. In the Pier House, **Havana Docks Lounge** (⊠ 1 Duval St., ☎ 305/296–4600) has live dance music Friday and Saturday nights and a nightly sunset celebration with a band.

Outdoor Activities and Sports

Biking

Key West is a cycling town, but if you aren't accustomed to so many bikes, ride carefully. Paved road surfaces are poor, so it's best to ride a fat-tired Conch cruiser. Some hotels rent bikes to guests; others will refer you to a nearby shop and reserve a bike for you.

Keys Moped & Scooter (⊠ 523 Truman Ave., ☎ 305/294–0399) rents beach cruisers with large baskets, mopeds, and scooters. Rates are the lowest in Key West. Look for the huge American flag on the roof. **Moped Hospital** (⊠ 601 Truman Ave., ☎ 305/296–3344) supplies balloon-tire bikes with yellow safety baskets, as well as mopeds, tandem mopeds, and scooters for adults and children. Helmets are no charge.

Fishing

Though more known for diving, **Captain's Corner** (⊠ 0 Duval St., 33040, ☎ 305/296–8865) also runs fishing charters. As first mate for his mother, Vicki (☞ Guided Tours *in* Florida Keys A to Z, *below*), **Capt. Steven Impallomeni** learned the backcountry. Now he works as a flats-fishing guide, specializing in ultralight and fly-fishing for tarpon, permit, and bonefish. Charters on the *Gallopin' Ghost* leave from Murray's Marina (⊠ MM5, Stock Island, ☎ 305/292–9837). **Key West Bait and Tackle** (⊠ 241 Margaret St., ☎ 305/292–1961) carries live bait, frozen rigged and unrigged bait, and fishing and rigging equipment. It also has the Live Bait Lounge, where you can unwind after fishing.

Golf

Key West Resort Golf Course (⊠ 6450 E. College Rd., ☎ 305/294–

5232) is an 18-hole course on Stock Island. Nonresident fees are $80 for 18 holes (cart included) in season, $60 off-season.

Scuba Diving

Captain's Corner (⊠ 0 Duval St., 33040, ☎ 305/296–8865), a PADI five star–rated shop, provides dive classes in several languages. All captains are licensed dive masters and/or instructors. A 60-ft dive boat, *Sea Eagle,* and the 48-ft *Sea Hawk* depart twice daily. Reservations are accepted for regular reef and wreck diving.

Shopping

Key West contains dozens of characterless T-shirt shops, but some art galleries and curiosity shops have lots worth toting home.

Arts and Crafts

The oldest private art gallery in Key West, **Gingerbread Square Gallery** (⊠ 1207 Duval St., ☎ 305/296–8900) represents mainly Keys artists who have attained national and international prominence. **Haitian Art Co.** (⊠ 600 Frances St., ☎ 305/296–8932), containing 4,000 paintings and spirit flags, claims the largest collection of Haitian art outside Haiti, representing a range of artists working in wood, stone, metal, and papier-mâché. **Lucky Street Gallery** (⊠ 1120 White St., ☎ 305/294–3973) sells high-end contemporary paintings, jewelry, and crafts by internationally recognized Key West–based artists. Exhibits change every two weeks. **Pelican Poop** (⊠ 314 Simonton St., ☎ 305/296–3887) sells Caribbean art in a gorgeous setting around a tropical courtyard garden with a fountain and pool. The owners go to the Caribbean every year to buy direct from the artisans, so prices are attractive. (Hemingway wrote *A Farewell to Arms* while living in the complex's apartment.) **Plantation Pottery** (⊠ 521 Fleming St., ☎ 305/294–3143) is not to be missed for its original, never-commercial pottery. Potters Charles Pearson and Timothy Roeder *are* **Whitehead St. Pottery** (⊠ 1011 Whitehead St., ☎ 305/294–5067), where they display their porcelain stoneware and raku-fired vessels. They also have a photo gallery where they exhibit Polaroid image transfers and black-and-white photos.

Books

Key West's newest bookstore, **Flaming Maggie's** (⊠ 830 Caroline St., ☎ 305/294–3931) specializes in books—and artwork—by or about local authors (Hemingway, Tennessee Williams, Robert Frost, etc.) and for gays and lesbians. It contains a popular coffee bar. **Key West Island Bookstore** (⊠ 513 Fleming St., ☎ 305/294–2904) is the bookstore of the large Key West writers' community. It carries new, used, and rare titles.

Clothes and Fabrics

Since 1964 **Key West Hand Print Fashions and Fabrics** (⊠ 201 Simonton St., ☎ 305/294–9535 or 800/866–0333) has been noted for its vibrant tropical prints, yard goods, and resort wear. It's in the Curry Warehouse, a brick building erected in 1878 to store tobacco. **Tikal Trading Co.** (⊠ 129 Duval St., ☎ 305/296–4463) sells its own line of women's clothing of handwoven Guatemalan cotton and knit tropical prints.

Food and Drink

Fausto's Food Palace (⊠ 522 Fleming St., ☎ 305/296–5663; ⊠ 1105 White St., ☎ 305/294–5221) may be under a roof, but it's a market in the traditional town-square sense. Since 1926 Fausto's has been the spot to catch up on the week's gossip and to chill out in summer—it has the heaviest air-conditioning in town. **Waterfront Market** (⊠ 201 William St., ☎ 305/294–8418 or 305/296–0778) purveys health and gourmet foods, deli items, produce, salads, cold beer, and wine. If you're there, be sure to check out the bulletin board. The owners also operate a fish market, bakery, deli, and juice bar.

Gifts and Souvenirs

Like a parody of Duval Street T-shirt shops, the hole-in-the-wall **Art Attack** (⊠ 606 Duval St., ☎ 305/294–7131) throws in every icon and trinket anyone nostalgic for the days of peace and love might fancy: beads, necklaces, medallions, yin-yang banners, harmony bells, and of course Grateful Dead and psychedelic T-shirts. **Fast Buck Freddie's** (⊠ 500 Duval St., ☎ 305/294–2007) sells imaginative items you'd never dream of, including battery-operated alligators that eat Muenster cheese, banana leaf–shape furniture, fish-shape flatware, and every flamingo item imaginable. In a town with a gazillion T-shirt shops, **Last Flight Out** (⊠ 706A Duval St., ☎ 305/294–8008) stands out for its selection of classic namesake Ts, specialty clothing, and gifts that appeal to aviation types as well as those reaching for the stars. A survivor of Key West's seafaring days, **Perkins & Son Chandlery** (⊠ 901 Fleming St., ☎ 305/294–7635), redolent of pine tar and kerosene, offers one of the largest selections of used marine gear in the Keys, as well as nautical antiques, books, outdoor clothing, and collectibles.

Health and Beauty

Key West Aloe (⊠ 524 Front St., ☎ 305/294–5592 or 800/445–2563) was founded in a garage in 1971; today it produces some 300 perfume, sunscreen, and skin-care products for men and women. You can also visit the factory store (⊠ Greene and Simonton Sts.).

Side Trip

Dry Tortugas National Park

This sanctuary for thousands of birds, 70 mi off the shores of Key West, consists of seven islands. Its main facility is the long-deactivated Ft. Jefferson, where Dr. Samuel Mudd was imprisoned for his alleged role in Lincoln's assassination. For information and a list of authorized charter boats, seaplanes, and water taxis, contact **Everglades National Park** (⊠ 40001 Rte. 9336, Homestead 33034-6733, ☎ 305/242–7700).

A two- to three-hour journey to the park aboard the 100-ft *Yankee Freedom* of the **Yankee Fleet Dry Tortugas National Park Ferry** includes a full breakfast and lunch. A naturalist leads a 45-minute tour, followed by lunch and a free afternoon for swimming, snorkeling (gear included), and exploring. ⊠ *Lands End Marina, 261 Margaret St., Key West 33040,* ☎ *305/294–7009 or 800/634–0939.* ⊠ *$85.* ⊙ *Trips daily 8 AM.*

THE FLORIDA KEYS A TO Z

Arriving and Departing

By Airport Shuttle

One-way shuttle fares from Miami International Airport (MIA) to the Upper Keys range from $45 for the first person ($30 each additional) on **Miami Airport Limo Service** (☎ 305/852–9533) to $78 for the first passenger ($15 each additional) on the **SuperShuttle** (☎ 305/871–2000). To go farther into the Keys, you must book an entire van (up to 11 passengers), which costs $250 to Marathon, $350 to Key West. Super Shuttle requests 24-hour advance notice for transportation back to the airport. **Airporter** (☎ 305/852–3413 or 800/830–3413) operates scheduled van and bus service from MIA's baggage areas to wherever you want to go in Key Largo ($30) and Islamorada ($33). A group discount is given for three or more passengers. Reservations are required.

By Boat

Boaters can travel to and along the Keys either along the Intracoastal Waterway (5-ft draft limitation) through Card, Barnes, and Blackwater sounds and into Florida Bay or along the deeper Atlantic Ocean route through Hawk Channel, a buoyed passage. Refer to NOAA Nautical Chart Number 11451 for Miami to Marathon and Florida Bay, Numbers 11445 and 11441 for Marathon to Dry Tortugas. The Keys are full of marinas that welcome transient visitors, but they don't have enough slips for everyone. Make reservations in advance and ask about channel and dockage depth—many marinas are quite shallow.

For information contact **Coast Guard Group Key West** (✉ Key West 33040, ☎ 305/292–8727 or 305/295–9700 or CG on a cellular), which provides 24-hour monitoring of VHF-FM Channel 16. Safety and weather information is broadcast at 7 AM and 5 PM Eastern Standard Time on VHF-FM Channel 16 and 22A. There are three stations in the Keys: Islamorada (☎ 305/664–4404), Marathon (☎ 305/743–6778), and Key West (☎ 305/292–8856).

Key West Excursions (☎ 941/463–3320 or 800/650–5397) runs ferry service to Key West from Fort Myers Beach and Marco Island on a 92-ft powered catamaran, the *Friendship IV*. The same-day round-trip fare is $95, including Continental breakfast.

By Bus

Greyhound Lines (☎ 800/231–2222) runs a Keys shuttle four times a day between MIA (departing from Concourse E, lower level) and stops throughout the Keys. Fares run from $15 one-way and $30 round-trip for Key Largo to $31 one-way and $60 round-trip for Key West.

By Car

From MIA follow signs to Coral Gables and Key West, which put you on Lejeune Road, then Route 836 west. Take the Florida's Turnpike Extension south (toll road), which ends at Florida City and connects to U.S. 1. Tolls from the airport run approximately $1.25. The alternative from Florida City is Card Sound Road (Route 905A), which has a bridge toll of $1.75. Continue to the only stop sign and turn right on Route 905, which rejoins U.S. 1 31 mi south of Florida City.

Avoid flying into Key West and driving back to Miami; there are substantial drop-off charges for leaving a Key West car in Miami.

By Plane

Service between **Key West International Airport** (✉ S. Roosevelt Blvd., Key West, ☎ 305/296–5439) and Miami, Fort Lauderdale/Hollywood, Naples, Orlando, and Tampa is provided by American Eagle (☎ 800/433–7300), Cape Air (☎ 800/352–0714), Comair/Delta Connection (☎ 800/354–9822), Gulfstream International Airlines (☎ 800/992–8532), and US Airways/US Airways Express (☎ 800/428–4322). **Marathon Airport** (✉ MM 52, BS, Marathon, ☎ 305/743–2155) connects to Miami via American Eagle, to Tampa via US Airways Express.

Getting Around

Chambers of commerce, marinas, and dive shops offer **Teall's Guides,** land and nautical charts that pinpoint popular fishing and diving areas. A complete set can also be purchased for $7.95, postage included, from 111 Saguaro Lane, Marathon 33050, 305/743–3942.

By Bus

The **City of Key West Department of Transportation** (☎ 305/292–8160) operates two bus routes: Mallory Square (counterclockwise around the island) and Old Town (clockwise around the island). The fare is 75¢ (exact change).

By Car

In Key West's Old Town, parking is scarce and costly ($1.50 per hour at Mallory Square). Use a taxi, bicycle, or moped to get around, or walk. Elsewhere in the Keys, a car is crucial. Gas costs more than on the mainland, so fill your tank in Miami and top it off in Florida City.

Most of the Overseas Highway is narrow and crowded (especially weekends). Expect delays behind RVs, trucks, cars towing boats, and rubbernecking tourists.

The best Keys road map, published by the Homestead/Florida City Chamber of Commerce, can be obtained for $2 from the **Tropical Everglades Visitor Center** (⊠ 160 U.S. 1, Florida City 33034, ☎ 305/245–9180 or 800/388–9669).

By Limousine

Island Coaches (⊠ 3134 Northside Dr., ☎ 305/296–480) operates in Key West.

By Taxi

In the Upper Keys (MM 94–74), **Island Taxi** (☎ 305/664–8181) charges $4 for the first 2 mi and $1.50 each additional mi for up to two adults and any accompanying children; extra adults pay $1 per mi. In the Middle Keys, **Cheapo Taxi** (☎ 305/743–7420) rates are $1 for pickup and $1 per mi. Drops beyond MM 61 and MM 40 are $1.50 a mile. **Florida Keys Taxi Dispatch** (☎ 305/296–1800) operates around the clock in Key West. The fare for two or more from the Key West airport to New Town is $5 per person with a cap of $15; to Old Town it's $6 and $20, respectively. Otherwise meters register $1.40 to start, 35¢ for each ⅕ mi, and 35¢ for every 50 seconds of waiting time.

Contacts and Resources

Car Rentals

Avis (☎ 305/743–5428 or 800/831–2847) and **Budget** (☎ 305/743–3998 or 800/527–0700) serve Marathon Airport. Key West's airport has booths for **Alamo** (☎ 305/296–7733 or 800/462–5266), **Avis** (☎ 305/296–8744), **Budget** (☎ 305/294–8868), **Dollar** (☎ 305/296–9921 or 800/800–4000), and **Hertz** (☎ 305/294–1039 or 800/654–3131). **Tropical Rent-A-Car** (⊠ 1300 Duval St., Key West, ☎ 305/294–8136) is based in the city center. **Enterprise Rent-A-Car** (☎ 800/325–8007) has offices in Key Largo, Marathon, and Key West. **Thrifty Car Rental** has an office in Tavernier (⊠ MM 91.8, OS, ☎ 305/852–6088).

Emergencies

Dial **911** for police, fire, or ambulance. If you are a TTD caller, tap the space bar or use a voice announcer to identify yourself. **Keys Hotline** (☎ 800/771–5397) provides information and emergency assistance in six languages. **Florida Marine Patrol** (⊠ MM 48, BS, 2796 Overseas Hwy., Suite 100, State Regional Service Center, Marathon 33050, ☎ 305/289–2320; ☎ 800/342–5367 after 5 PM) maintains a 24-hour telephone service to handle reports of boating emergencies and natural-resource violations. **Coast Guard Group Key West** (☎ 305/295–9700) responds to local marine emergencies and reports of navigation hazards.

HOSPITALS

The following hospitals have 24-hour emergency rooms: **Fishermen's Hospital** (⊠ MM 48.7, OS, Marathon, ☎ 305/743–5533); **Florida Keys**

Hyperbaric Center (✉ MM 54, OS, Suite 101, Marathon, ☎ 305/743–9891), for diving accidents; **Lower Florida Keys Health System** (✉ MM 5, BS, 5900 College Rd., Stock Island, ☎ 305/294–5531); and **Mariners Hospital** (✉ MM 88.5, BS, 50 High Point Rd., Plantation Key, ☎ 305/852–4418).

The Keys have no 24-hour pharmacies. Hospital pharmacists will help with emergencies after regular retail business hours.

Guided Tours

AIR TOURS

Island Aeroplane Tours (✉ 3469 S. Roosevelt Blvd., Key West Airport, Key West 33040, ☎ 305/294–8687) flies up to two passengers in a 1940 Waco, an open-cockpit biplane. Tours range from a quick six- to eight-minute overview of Key West ($50 for two) to a 50-minute look at the offshore reefs ($200 for two).

BIKE TOURS

Key West Nature Bike Tour (✉ Truman Ave. and Simonton St., Key West, ☎ 305/294–1882) explores the natural, noncommercial side of Key West at a leisurely pace, stopping on backstreets and in backyards of private homes to view indigenous plants and trees. The tours run 90–120 minutes and cost $15 with your own bike, $3 more to rent one.

BOAT TOURS

Adventure Charters (✉ 6810 Front St., Key West 33040, ☎ 305/296–0362) operates tours on the 42-ft catamaran *Island Fantasea* for a maximum of 12 passengers. Trips range from a half day into the backcountry to daylong and overnight sojourns. **Coral Reef Park Co.** (✉ John Pennekamp Coral Reef State Park, MM 102.5, OS, Key Largo 33037, ☎ 305/451–1621) runs sailing trips on a 38-ft catamaran as well as glass-bottom boat tours. **Everglades Safari Cruises** (✉ Box 3343, Key Largo 33037, ☎ 305/451–4540) operates daily 60-minute champagne sunset tours year-round on pontoon boats ($20 per person) and a variety of custom tours. Trips leave from Dolphin's Cove (✉ MM 101.9, BS). Bob and Gale Dumouchel have run low-impact ecotours through **Gale Force Charters** (✉ 27960 Porgie Path, Little Torch Key 33042, ☎ 305/745–2868) since 1988. Tours leave from Sugarloaf Marina (✉ MM 17, BS, Sugarloaf Key) and venture into the channels and islands of the Great White Heron National Wildlife Refuge aboard the *Gale Force,* a 24-ft Carolina skiff with a viewing tower. Half-day tours cost $150 for the entire boat, which holds six passengers; full-day excursions cost $250. All tours include snorkel gear, instruction, narration, coolers with ice, walking tours, and beach time. Fishing, snorkel, and kayak tours are also offered.

Key Largo Princess (✉ MM 99.7, OS, 99701 Overseas Hwy., Key Largo 33037, ☎ 305/451–4655) offers two-hour glass-bottom boat trips and sunset cruises on a luxury 70-ft motor yacht with a 280-square-ft glass viewing area, departing from the Holiday Inn docks. M/V *Discovery* (✉ Land's End Marina, 251 Margaret St., Key West 33040, ☎ 305/293–0099) and the 65-ft *Pride of Key West* (✉ 2 Duval St., Key West 33040, ☎ 305/296–6293) are glass-bottom boats. **Strike Zone Charters** (✉ MM 29.6, BS, 29675 Overseas Hwy., Big Pine Key 33043, ☎ 305/872–9863 or 800/654–9560), run by Lower Keys native Capt. Larry Threlkeld, offers glass-bottom boat excursions into the backcountry and to Looe Key. The five-hour Island Excursion ($45) emphasizes nature and Keys history. Besides close encounters with birds, sea life, and vegetation, there's a fish cookout on an island. Snorkel and fishing equipment, food, and drinks are included. This is one of the few nature outings in the Keys with wheelchair access.

Victoria Impallomeni (✉ Murray's Marina, 5710 U.S. 1, Key West 33040, ☎ 305/294–9731 or 888/822–7366), noted wilderness guide and authority on the ecology of Florida Bay, invites nature lovers aboard the *Imp II*, a 22-ft Aquasport, for four-hour half-day ($300) and seven-hour full-day ($450) ecotours. While island-hopping, you visit underwater gardens, natural shoreline, and mangrove habitats. Everything is supplied except the picnic. Tours leave from Murray's Marina (✉ MM 5, Stock Island). *Wolf* (✉ Schooner Wharf, Key West Seaport, end of Greene St., Key West 33040, ☎ 305/296–9653) is Key West's tall ship and the flagship of the Conch Republic. The 74-ft, 44-passenger topsail schooner operates day cruises as well as sunset and starlight cruises with live music.

BUS TOURS

The **Conch Tour Train** (☎ 305/294–5161) is a 90-minute narrated tour of Key West, traveling 14 mi through Old Town and around the island. Board at Mallory Square and Roosevelt Boulevard (just north of the Quality Inn) every half hour (9:30–4:30 from Mallory Square, later at other stops). The cost is $15. **Old Town Trolley** (✉ 6631 Maloney Ave., Key West, ☎ 305/296–6688) operates 12 trackless trolley-style buses, departing from the Mallory Square and Roosevelt Boulevard depots every 30 minutes (9–4:30 from Mallory Square, later at other stops), for 90-minute narrated tours of Key West. The smaller trolleys go places the train won't fit. You may disembark at any of 12 stops and reboard a later trolley. The cost is $16.

CANOE AND KAYAK TOURS

Adventure Charters (✉ 6810 Front St., Key West 33040, ☎ 305/296–0362) offers half-day kayak trips ($35), departing at 9 and 2, and full-day kayak trips ($100), which include snorkeling, fishing, and lunch. The folks at **Florida Bay Outfitters** (✉ MM 104, BS, 104050 Overseas Hwy., Key Largo 33037, ☎ 305/451–3018) know Keys waters well. You can take a one- to seven-day canoe or kayak tour to the Everglades, Lignumvitae or Indian Key, or a night trip to neighboring islands. A well-known nature photographer whose coffee-table book on the Keys is a favored local gift, Bill Keogh of **Lost World Expeditions** (✉ Box 431311, Big Pine Key 33043, ☎ 305/872–8950 or 305/395–0930) leads kayak nature tours through the Lower Keys and Key West, with stops at nearby refuges. **Reflections Kayak Nature Tours** (✉ MM 28.5, OS/BS, Box 430861, Big Pine Key 33043, ☎ 305/872–2896 or 305/872–2157), based at Parmer's Place B&B, on Little Torch Key, operates daily trips into the Great White Heron National Wildlife Refuge and Everglades National Park. Tours last three hours, and $45 covers granola bars, fruit, water, a bird-identification sheet, and the use of waterproof binoculars; snorkeling gear is extra. They also offer six-hour tours ($80) that include lunch and overnight trips into the backcountry.

WALKING TOURS

In addition to publishing several good guides on Key West, the **Historic Florida Keys Foundation** (✉ 510 Greene St., Old City Hall, Key West 33040, ☎ 305/292–6718) conducts tours of the City Cemetery Tuesday and Thursday at 9:30. Sharon Wells of **Island City Strolls** (☎ 305/294–8380 or 305/294–5397) knows plenty about Key West. State historian in Key West for nearly 20 years and owner of a historic preservation consulting firm, she has authored many works, including the magazine-size guide "The Walking and Biking Guide to Historic Key West," which features 10 self-guided tours of the historic district. It's available free at guest houses, hotels, and Key West bookstores. If that whets your appetite, sign on for one of her walking tours, including "Architectural Strolls," "Literary Landmarks," and "The Graveyard Ramble" (which cost $10–$18 for one–two hours), or a personalized excursion ($25 an hour).

"Pelican Path" is a free walking guide to Key West published by the Old Island Restoration Foundation. The tour discusses the history and architecture of 43 structures along 25 blocks of 12 Old Town streets. Pick up a copy at the chamber of commerce. **"Writers' Walk,"** a one-hour guided tour sponsored by the Key West Literary Seminar (☎ 305/293–9291), visits the residences of prominent Key West authors, including Frost, Hemingway, and Tennessee Williams. Tours leave at 10:30, on Saturday from the Heritage House Museum (✉ 410 Caroline St.) and on Sunday from the Hemingway House (✉ 907 Whitehead St.). Tickets ($10) must be purchased in advance at the Heritage House Museum or the Key West Island Bookstore (✉ 513 Fleming St.).

Lodging Reservations

Gay Key West Reservations, Inc. (✉ Box 0657, Key West 33040, ☎ 888/429–5399) books properties that are gay-friendly. **Key West Vacation Rentals** (✉ 525 Simonton St., Key West 33040, ☎ 305/292–7997 or 800/621–9405, FAX 305/294–7501) lists historic cottages, homes, and condominiums for rent. Although it prefers to handle reservations in advance, the **Key West Welcome Center** (✉ 3840 N. Roosevelt Blvd., Key West 33040, ☎ 305/296–4444 or 800/284–4482) gets a lot of walk-in business because of its location on U.S. 1 at the entrance to Key West. **Property Management of Key West, Inc.** (✉ 1213 Truman Ave., Key West 33040, ☎ 305/296–7744) offers lease and rental service for condominiums, town houses, and private homes. **Vacation Key West** (✉ 1019 Flagler Ave., Key West 33040, ☎ 305/295–9500 or 800/595–5397) lists properties throughout Key West.

Publications

The best of the publications covering Key West is *Solares Hill* (✉ 330-B Julia St., Key West 33040, ☎ 305/294–3602). The weekly is witty, controversial, tough on environmental issues and gets the best arts and entertainment advertising. The best weekday source of information on Key West is the *Key West Citizen* (✉ 3420 Northside Dr., Key West 33040, ☎ 305/294–6641), which also publishes a Sunday edition. For the Upper and Middle Keys, turn to the semiweekly *Keynoter,* a Knight-Ridder publication. The *Free Press, Reporter,* and *Upper Keys Independent* cover the same area once a week. The *Miami Herald* publishes a Keys edition with good daily listings of local events. The monthly *Southern Exposure* is a good source for gay and lesbian travelers.

Visitor Information

Florida Keys & Key West Visitors Bureau (✉ 402 Wall St., Key West 33040, ☎ 800/352–5397). **Greater Key West Chamber of Commerce (mainstream)** (✉ 402 Wall St., Key West 33040, ☎ 305/294–2587 or 800/527–8539, FAX 305/294–7806). **Islamorada Chamber of Commerce** (✉ MM 82.5, BS, Box 915, Islamorada 33036, ☎ 305/664–4503 or 800/322–5397). **Key Largo Chamber of Commerce** (✉ MM 106, BS, 106000 Overseas Hwy., Key Largo 33037, ☎ 305/451–1414 or 800/822–1088, FAX 305/451–4726). **Key West Business Guild (gay)** (✉ Box 1208, Key West 33041, ☎ 305/294–4603 or 800/535–7797). **Lower Keys Chamber of Commerce** (✉ MM 31, OS, Box 430511, Big Pine Key 33043, ☎ 305/872–2411 or 800/872–3722, FAX 305/872–0752). **Marathon Chamber of Commerce & Visitor Center** (✉ MM 53.5, BS, 12222 Overseas Hwy., Marathon 33050, ☎ 305/743–5417 or 800/842–9580).

INDEX

Looking for a different kind of vacation?

Fodor's makes it easy with a full line of guidebooks to suit a variety of interests—from sports and adventure to romance to family fun.

At bookstores everywhere.
www.fodors.com

WHEREVER YOU TRAVEL, *H*ELP IS NEVER FAR AWAY.

From planning your trip to

providing travel assistance along

the way, American Express®

Travel Service Offices are

always there to help

you do more.